THE LEADER'S GUIDE *to*
LITTLE LEARNERS, BIG HEARTS

Advancing Empathy & Equity in Early Childhood Education

Christine Mason   Randy Ross   Orinthia Harris   Jillayne Flanders

foreword by Afrika Afeni Mills

Solution Tree | Press

Copyright © 2025 by Solution Tree Press

Materials appearing here are copyrighted. With one exception, all rights are reserved. Readers may reproduce only those pages marked "Reproducible." Otherwise, no part of this book may be reproduced or transmitted in any form or by any means (electronic, photocopying, recording, or otherwise) without prior written permission of the publisher.

555 North Morton Street
Bloomington, IN 47404
800.733.6786 (toll free) / 812.336.7700
FAX: 812.336.7790

email: info@SolutionTree.com
SolutionTree.com

Visit **go.SolutionTree.com/diversityandequity** to download the free reproducibles in this book.

Printed in the United States of America

Library of Congress Cataloging-in-Publication Data

Names: Mason, Christine Y. (Christine Yvonne), 1949- author. | Ross, Randy, author. | Harris, Orinthia, author. | Flanders, Jillayne, author. | Mason, Christine Y. (Christine Yvonne), 1949- Little learners, big hearts.
Title: Advancing empathy and equity in early childhood education : the leader's guide to Little learners, big hearts / Christine Mason, Randy Ross, Orinthia Harris, Jillayne Flanders.
Description: Bloomington, IN : Solution Tree Press, [2025] | Includes bibliographical references and index.
Identifiers: LCCN 2024016241 (print) | LCCN 2024016242 (ebook) | ISBN 9781962188142 (paperback) | ISBN 9781962188159 (ebook)
Subjects: LCSH: Early childhood education--Social aspects. | Anti-racism. | Social justice and education.
Classification: LCC LB1139.5.S64 M368 2025 (print) | LCC LB1139.5.S64 (ebook) | DDC 372.21068/4--dc23/eng/20240913
LC record available at https://lccn.loc.gov/2024016241
LC ebook record available at https://lccn.loc.gov/2024016242

Solution Tree
Jeffrey C. Jones, CEO
Edmund M. Ackerman, President

Solution Tree Press
President and Publisher: Douglas M. Rife
Associate Publishers: Todd Brakke and Kendra Slayton
Editorial Director: Laurel Hecker
Art Director: Rian Anderson
Copy Chief: Jessi Finn
Senior Production Editor: Miranda Addonizio
Copy Editor: Jessi Finn
Proofreader: Sarah Ludwig
Text and Cover Designer: Laura Cox
Acquisitions Editors: Carol Collins and Hilary Goff
Content Development Specialist: Amy Rubenstein
Associate Editors: Sarah Ludwig and Elijah Oates
Editorial Assistant: Madison Chartier

Acknowledgments

How can school leaders foster the positive growth and well-being of all students, including students of different hues, speaking different languages, or raised with traditions carried with their families across vast distances? So many obstacles stand in the way of creating and maintaining school environments that will truly provide the backdrop for success that all students can take with them through the grades, across their years in school, and beyond.

Over years of research and writing, we, the authors, have dedicated ourselves to increasing our understanding of how best to support school leaders and teachers—even as we have seen societal shifts that are frightening. And in spite of setbacks, we have hope. Our hope is with our children—with their enthusiasm, their friendships, their agency, and their loving, compassionate caring for others.

Our hope is also with education and educators, with research, and with the hearts and minds of teachers who have the power to create classroom communities of kindness and caring. So, with this hope, we have endeavored to bring you a guide to practices that can deepen compassion and compassionate action. In acknowledging those who have supported our journey, we begin by thanking all the leaders—the educators—and their communities. Our thanks go to you for your work, your hearts, and your willingness to take up the task of helping to bring about healing for our youngest, their families, and their communities.

We also thank the many who had a huge part in supporting us as we moved forward with this work—the other authors and researchers who we have cited, organizations that are leading the way, and the staff at Solution Tree, especially

Miranda Addonizio, who, as our editor, shepherded our work for many, many months. To Nicole Benquechea, Meghan Wenzel, Hallie Williams, Tyra Prepetit, Amelia Murray, Margaret Bass, Sabrina Chan, Chandni Lai, Alexis Richmond, Whitney Becker, and Leah Bullinger—all research assistants and interns with the Center for Educational Improvement—our heartfelt appreciation for your assistance in conducting background research, as well as framing issues, proofreading, and providing perspective from the vantage point of young professionals.

We thank the many people—academics, parents, early care professionals—who agreed to be interviewed for this book and who shared their excitement for our deep exploration of racial and cultural bias along with the creation of so many positive paths leading us forward. These include Erica Almaguer, Lorelei Ballesteros, Mayra Cajamarca, Kori Hamilton Biagas, Kamilah Drummond-Forrester, Tammy Dunn, Dr. Sheila Gould, Holly Hazard, Dr. Kathy Hirsh-Pasek, Toni Jones, Dr. Ryan Lee-James, Dr. Peggy Martalock, Dr. Ousmane Power-Greene and Melissa Power-Greene, Ivonne Ortega, Dr. Martin Reinhardt, Mia Schultz, Suzanne Stillinger, Alya Stoffer-Koloszyc, and Mrs. H. Vang.

And to Melanie Meren, Dr. Uma Alahari, Julie Bloss, Erica Almaguer, Kristin Jackson, Dr. Heather Walter, and Afrika Afeni Mills, who provided reviews and feedback of early drafts of our material—our gratitude for how you helped us zero in on the needs and concerns of early educators, narrowing our topics and focusing on antiracism through a mindful, compassionate approach.

Chris

To my coauthors, thank you for your perseverance, for the many Zoom calls, for your dialogue and debate, for your deep caring, for your understanding of the power of speaking out against bias and injustice, and for the many words, phrases, paragraphs, and pages that you wrote and rewrote—for sharing your lives and your passion for this work.

As always, thanks as well to my loving and supportive family, and to my church community, including Elder Robert Faison, Rev. Carolyn Boyd, Rev. Kristen McBrayer, and members of Emmaus who helped guide me to understanding White privilege and antiracism as we planned and led workshops for our community. Thanks, too, to Andrew Batcher for organizing the work in Northern Virginia celebrating Martin Luther King Jr. Day and setting up Virginia Listening Tours to respond to threats to disempower educators and block truth telling, as well as to Melanie Johnson and Raquel Ramos of the National Indian Education Association for our travels along the road to Native brilliance and the educational sovereignty of Indigenous peoples.

Randy

Thanks first to my coauthors, especially to Jill, who said to me, "Just write one chapter on bullying for this book about antiracism and early childhood." One chapter? Ha! To Orinthia for inspiring me to go deeper and think harder. To Chris for successfully pulling together all our disparate ideas and writings to make a (hopefully) creative and valuable contribution in these challenging times.

Also, my deep appreciation for all I have learned over the decades from my many mentors and friends—Black, Indigenous, and other people of color who have shared their lives, struggles, and joys with me. And for family: thank you to my long-gone parents—Sidney and Lee Ross—who grounded me in my earliest years in what has been my lifelong path of working for a just society. To my Bengali family, who always lovingly shared your ways, thank you. I am forever grateful to my husband, Ernie Brill, long my partner in challenging racism and anti-Semitism. To my daughters, Shivani and Tara Ganguly, for your support through hard times and for reminders to not work so hard! To my now seven-year-old grandson, Sidney Ganguly, may you—like all Brown, Black, and White children—grow up to live in a safe, joyful, and just world.

Orinthia

I would first like to thank Jesus Christ, whose teachings of love, compassion, and equality have guided me throughout this journey. His example of embracing diversity and fighting against injustice has served as the bedrock of my writings for this book. To my loving husband, Arthur Harris IV, your support and encouragement have been the foundation of my success. Your commitment to fostering inclusivity and belonging in our four young children, Arthur V, Jeremiah, Zaria, and Ezra, is truly commendable. I am blessed to have you by my side. And last but certainly not least, I would like to extend my deepest appreciation and gratitude to my incredible mom, Bishop Toni Jones, who has played an instrumental role in shaping my self-perception and instilling in me a profound love for my Blackness. From not allowing me to perm my hair to encouraging me to play in the sun because darker skin was beautiful, you were teaching "Black girl magic" before the movement even existed. Not only have you dedicated your life to empowering me to recognize the beauty and importance of my Blackness, but your genuine love for all children has maintained your unwavering dedication to the Head Start program for over forty years and counting. Your wealth of experience and extensive knowledge in early childhood education has been an invaluable resource throughout the creation of this book.

Jill

My journey, culminating in this book (for now), began with an interview with Nicole Coakley, an incredibly smart, talented early childhood educator, who had not quite realized her potential. She continues to amaze me, and I will never be able to adequately thank her for bringing me along in her world. Each person in the network of teachers, principals, and colleagues I have met over the course of my career has contributed to making me ask the question, "Is this the best thing for our children?" That question has never stopped circling in my head.

I thank my coauthors, Chris, Orinthia, and Randy, for your prodding and patience and for making me smarter.

Finally, though, my family is my touchstone. They give me space and time and remind me every day what is most important. It is my hope that this work might provide some new ideas, provocative conversations, and deeper understanding of how we all live in this world as we make it a better place for not only my grandchildren, but everyone's grandchildren.

Solution Tree Press would like to thank the following reviewers:

Uma Alahari
Assistant Professor of Early
 Childhood Education
University of Massachusetts Global
Irvine, California

Erica Almaguer
Lecturer in the Child and Adolescent
 Development Department and
 Director of the Associated Students
 Early Childhood Education Center
San Francisco State University
San Francisco, California

Julie Bloss
Retired Principal
Grove Public Schools
Grove, Oklahoma

Doug Gee
Superintendent
Clear Lake Community
 School District
Clear Lake, Iowa

Kristin Jackson
Program Director
Communities in Schools
Wilmington, North Carolina

Erin Kruckenberg
Fifth-Grade Teacher
Jefferson Elementary School
Harvard, Illinois

Pamela Liebenberg
Former Director of Curriculum
 and Instruction
Tuscaloosa County School District
Tuscaloosa, Alabama

Melanie Meren
Fairfax County School Board
 Representative
Hunter Mill District, Fairfax County
 Public Schools
Fairfax, Virginia

Rachel Swearengin
Fifth-Grade Teacher
Manchester Park Elementary
Lenexa, Kansas

Heather L. Walter
Assistant Professor of Early
 Childhood Special Education
George Mason University
Fairfax, Virginia

Visit **go.SolutionTree.com/diversityandequity** to download the free reproducibles in this book.

Table of Contents

Reproducible pages are in italics.

About the Authors xiii

Foreword xix

Introduction: Kind Minds and Big Hearts 1
    Why Leadership to Support Empathy and Equity Is So Important 2
    About Advancing Empathy and Equity, the Book 7

Part 1: Foundations 17

1   Bold Leadership: What's Necessary for Heart Centered, Antiracist Education 19
    Antiracist Leadership in Early Childhood Settings 21
    Legal and Policy Considerations 27
    HEART+ Takeaways 34

2   Historical Threads of Bias: Acknowledgment of What Must Change 35
    Acknowledgment Before Healing 36
    HEART+ Takeaways 43

3   Support for All Students: A Continuum From Multicultural to Antiracist Movements 45
    Privilege and Bias 48
    The Way Toward Change 54
    HEART+ Takeaways 57

4 My Heart to Yours: A Heart Centered Lens 59
Heart Centeredness. 61
Tools and Actions to Address Equity 68
HEART+ Takeaways 70

5 One C to Another: The Five Cs of Heart Centered Learning 71
The Five Cs 72
Heart Centered Learning and Antiracism. 73
A Schoolwide Approach to Heart Centered Learning . . . 78
HEART+ Takeaways 82

6 A Deep Dive: The HEART+ of the Matter 83
H Is for Hope 85
E Is for (Self-)Education. 89
A Is for Acknowledgment 93
HEART+ Takeaways 100

Part 2: Practical Steps Leaders Can Take 101

7 HEART+: A Focus on Action 103
R Is for Resolution. 103
T Is for Teaching 111
+ Is for Local Needs 112
HEART+ Takeaways 117

8 So Many Wrongs to Right: Antibias Education. 119
Bias and Its Impact on Young Children 121
Implicit Bias Reduction in Early Childhood Education . . 128
HEART+ Takeaways 128

9 Circles of Love: School Culture and Restorative Practices 131
A Safe and Supportive School Culture 131
Discipline and Restorative Practices: The Leader's Role . . 138
HEART+ Takeaways 142

10 A Mountain of Courage: Visioning and Action Planning . . 143
Visioning 144
Heart Centered Planning 149
HEART+ Takeaways 161

Part 3: Antiracist Curriculum and Staff Support 163

11 A Light to Shine Together: Professional Development and Supports 165
Professional Development Approaches 166
The Tiered System of Equity Supports 173
Relational Coaching for Equity 182
HEART+ Takeaways 184

12 Curricula for Young Children: The Building Blocks for Equity in Early Childhood 185
State Standards 187
Alternative Early Childhood Curricula 190
Comparison of Curricula From an Antiracist Perspective 201
Curriculum Supplementation for More Inclusive and Representative Learning Experiences 204
HEART+ Takeaways 208

13 A Bar to Be Raised: Equity in Early Childhood Educator Standards 209
Teacher Preparation Programs 210
Standards for Teacher and Early Childcare Provider Preparation 215
HEART+ Takeaways 220

14 Early Childhood Staff Support: Equitable Professional Pathways 221
Roots of Disrespect for Early Childhood Educators 222
Compensation and Culturally Competent Teacher Preparation 224
Solutions for Workforce Support at All Levels 229
HEART+ Takeaways 236

15 A Look at the Future: Leadership to Embrace Change 237
The Potential of Hope 238
Hope Into Action 240
HEART+ Takeaways 242

Epilogue: Toward a More Just and Inclusive World 243
A New Paradigm 244
Reflections on What Matters 247
Well-Being for All 251

Appendix A: Equity Activities for Early Childhood Leaders 253
    Chapter 1 253
    Chapter 2 255
    Chapter 3 256
    Chapter 9 257

Appendix B: Discussion and Challenge Questions for Each Chapter 265
    Chapter 1 Discussion Questions 266
    Chapter 1 Challenge Questions 267
    Chapter 2 Discussion Questions 268
    Chapter 2 Challenge Questions 269
    Chapter 3 Discussion Questions 270
    Chapter 3 Challenge Questions 271
    Chapters 4 and 5 Discussion Questions 272
    Chapters 4 and 5 Challenge Questions 273
    Chapter 6 Discussion Questions 274
    Chapter 6 Challenge Questions 275
    Chapter 7 Discussion Questions 276
    Chapter 7 Challenge Questions 277
    Chapter 8 Discussion Questions 278
    Chapter 8 Challenge Questions 279
    Chapter 9 Discussion Questions 281
    Chapter 9 Challenge Questions 282
    Chapter 10 Discussion Questions 283
    Chapter 10 Challenge Questions 284
    Chapter 11 Discussion Questions 285
    Chapter 11 Challenge Questions 286
    Chapter 12 Discussion Questions 287
    Chapter 12 Challenge Questions 288
    Chapter 13 Discussion Questions 289
    Chapter 13 Challenge Questions 290
    Chapter 14 Discussion Questions 291
    Chapter 14 Challenge Questions 292
    Chapter 15 Discussion Questions 293
    Chapter 15 Challenge Question 294

References and Resources 295

Index 327

About the Authors

Christine Mason, PhD, is the founder and senior scholar of the Center for Educational Improvement (CEI) and an assistant clinical professor of psychology at Yale University. An educational psychologist, researcher, and entrepreneur, Christine served as executive director of CEI from 2009 to 2023, co–principal investigator of the Compassionate School Leadership Academy from 2022 to 2023, and cohost of the *Cultivating Resilience: A Whole Community Approach for Alleviating Trauma in Schools* podcast from 2021 to 2023. She is the lead author of seven books on topics related to mindfulness, student well-being, and school leadership. Her latest release, *Little Learners, Big Hearts: A Teacher's Guide to Nurturing Empathy and Equity in Early Childhood* (2024), is a Solution Tree Press publication, as are two books she coauthored with Michele M. Rivers Murphy and Yvette Jackson: *Mindfulness Practices: Cultivating Heart Centered Communities Where Students Focus and Flourish* (2019) and *Mindful School Communities: The Five Cs of Nurturing Heart Centered Learning* (2020). She also released *Leading With Vitality and Hope: Embracing Equity, Alleviating Trauma, and Healing School Communities* in 2023.

Christine's career has centered on school leadership, uplifting schools, and increasing compassion in schools. She has served as a professor in special education, and was director of research and professional development for several national organizations from 1987 to 2014, as well as interim principal at a private boarding school in Northern India in 2009. Since 2017, she has collaborated with colleagues at Yale University and its Region 1 Mental Health Technology Transfer Center in addressing the mental health and psychological safety of children and youth in schools.

Earlier in her career, Christine chaired early childhood conferences, taught early childhood special education courses, and supervised early childhood preservice teachers and graduate students. Her work in equity was also enhanced by experience as a resource room teacher at Glasgow Middle School in Alexandria, Virginia, which served students from eighty countries; doctoral research in Columbus, Ohio; school-improvement work in Washington, DC, and Columbus and Cleveland, Ohio; leadership of professional learning for a DC-based Transition to Teaching project; and leadership of a U.S. Department of Education early childhood research initiative that served over 80 percent of the charter schools in high-poverty areas of Washington, DC.

To learn more about Christine's work, visit www.edimprovement.org.

Randy Ross, MA, MS, has more than fifty years' experience as a writer, teacher, administrator, coach, and facilitator of dialogue and professional learning. For nearly thirty years, she has worked with community, school, district, and state educational leaders on equity issues in school climate, social-emotional learning, discipline, interracial dialogue, and antibullying policies and practices.

Randy began her career as an early childhood teacher and as a caseworker in a family daycare program, both in Brooklyn, New York. She began her leadership career as interim director of the Connecticut State Head Start Training Center and taught early childhood education courses at several community colleges. Randy went on to teach middle school, serve as a K–5 principal, and work in the Office of Bias Crime and Community Relations under the New Jersey attorney general. While there, she led interracial dialogue activities and initiated New Jersey Cares About Bullying. For the next nine years, she worked at Brown University's New England Equity Assistance Center, where she consulted with leaders of school districts, state departments of education, and the U.S. Department of Education's Region 1 Office for Civil Rights. After retiring from that position, Randy worked as an independent equity consultant with numerous school districts and several state departments of education. She also managed a three-year, $1.5 million grant-funded project on school climate improvement with five middle schools, including extensive coaching with principals and assistant principals, in Wilmington, North Carolina.

Randy has published *The Prudence Crandall Museum: A Teacher's Resource Guide* and many articles online and in educational publications, including articles on bullying and harassment for the Hamilton Fish Institute on School and Community Violence and "Creating Equitable School Climates" for the *State Education Standard* (journal of the National Association of State Boards of Education). After serving on various commissions and nonprofit boards across her long career, Randy retired as cochair of the board of the Social Emotional Learning Alliance for Massachusetts (SEL4MA) and continues as a board member. She also serves as national adviser to the Social Emotional Learning Alliance for the United States (SEL4US), where she co-facilitates the SEL and Equity Community of Practice.

Randy earned her BA and MA in anthropology from the University of California at Berkeley and went on to gain an MS in educational leadership from Bank Street College of Education in New York City.

Orinthia Harris, PhD, has over two decades of extensive experience in both classroom and extracurricular settings. Affectionately known as Dr. OH, she is the founder and executive director of STEMearly LLC, an organization dedicated to reigniting the passion to teach while equipping both educators and students with the essential tools for thriving. Her workshops and training sessions encompass STEM education through a hands-on, experiential approach and an array of diversity, equity, inclusion, and belonging topics. She has presented at numerous national conferences, such as those of the National Association for the Education of Young Children, the National Head Start Association, Smart Start, and the Division for Early Childhood within the Council for Exceptional Children.

Orinthia has also served as a faculty member for STEM and antiracism for CEI since 2014. Within CEI, she has collaborated with institutions such as the State University of New York, the National Indian Education Association, the Michigan Elementary and Middle School Principals Association, the Center for Applied Special Technology, and Yale University. She also has certifications as a CLASS specialist with Teachstone, as an early childhood trainer accredited by the

Maryland State Department of Education, and as a trainer for the Mid-Atlantic Equity Consortium. She was selected as a 2023 Exchange Leader through the Exchange Leadership Initiative, contributing to the initiative's mission of elevating leadership within the early care and education field.

Orinthia has been featured as a recognized authority in early childhood and antiracism education on several podcasts. She has published several articles, such as "Getting Uncomfortable: Antiracism and Mindfulness" and "Six Models for Early Childhood STEAM." Orinthia also has fifteen years' experience teaching grades K–5, including multilingual learners. During that time, she furthered her leadership expertise as a board member for Hope Community Public Charter Schools in Washington, DC, and as acting principal for the summer enrichment program at Howard County Public Schools.

Orinthia's academic journey culminated in the attainment of a doctorate from Notre Dame of Maryland University in May 2020, with a focus on educational leadership for changing populations.

Jillayne Flanders, BA, MEd, and CAGS, is still learning and teaching. Although she is officially retired after thirty-seven years as a public elementary school principal and teacher, Jill continues to advise, mentor, and coach aspiring teachers and administrators and is energized by the commitment of our next generation of educators. It is her greatest goal to ensure that these new educators keep social-emotional learning, antiracism, and relationship building as the fundamental keys in supporting our children in school. She is executive director of CEI, which is in its second year of a federal grant in partnership with Yale University for the Compassionate School Leadership Academy, where Jill serves as co–principal investigator.

Jill previously taught grades 2–4 at Goshen Center School and served as principal at Hadley Elementary School and Plains School, all in Massachusetts. She served as president of the Massachusetts Elementary School Principals Association (MESPA) and as a representative to the National Association of Elementary School Principals (NAESP), its national association. As principal of an early education school community, Jill became a respected advocate for the youngest learners, their families, and teachers, at both the state and national levels. She was honored as the Massachusetts Principal of the Year and National

Distinguished Principal in 2010. In 2011, she was elected to the NAESP board of directors, representing New England and Delaware, for a three-year term. Jill was a contributing author to the NAESP publications *Leading Early Childhood Learning Communities: What Principals Should Know and Be Able to Do* and *Leading After-School Learning Communities: What Principals Should Know and Be Able to Do.*

Jill has also served as an adjunct professor at Westfield State University and has taught and supervised aspiring teachers and administrators at Mount Holyoke College, the University of Massachusetts–Amherst, MESPA, and the Massachusetts School Administrators' Association. She has lectured at Boston University, Springfield College, and Boston College, and contributed to the Saul Zaentz Early Education Initiative at the Harvard Graduate School of Education. Jill continues to consult with the Massachusetts Department of Elementary and Secondary Education's Early Learning Team and Education Personnel Advisory Committee. She has served on the Massachusetts Department of Early Education and Care's Advisory Council from its inception. Jill is an active member of the Social Emotional Learning Alliance for Massachusetts (SEL4MA) and is the current Massachusetts state president of Delta Kappa Gamma, Society of Key Women Educators.

A lifelong resident of Massachusetts, Jill grew up in Scituate, and has resided in Southampton for over forty-five years with her husband. She is the proud mother of three accomplished daughters—an occupational therapy assistant, a second-grade teacher, and an ICU registered nurse—and grandmother to Becca, Noah, Alina, and Elise.

Jill earned her BA, MEd, and CAGS (certificate of advanced graduate study) from the University of Massachusetts–Amherst.

To book Christine Mason, Randy Ross, Orinthia Harris, or Jillayne Flanders for professional development, contact pd@SolutionTree.com.

Foreword

By Afrika Afeni Mills

I grew up in Brooklyn, New York, and my husband and I raised our children in and around Boston, Massachusetts, so I am well acquainted with the cold of winter. There were times when temperatures were so low and the wind so fierce that it didn't seem to matter how warmly we dressed—thick coats, hats, hoods, scarves, mittens, thermals, boots—we still felt the chill down to our bones.

We are living through what feels like a perpetual winter. It seems like each day brings news of increasingly cold hearts, icy words, frigid opinions, glacial policies, polar communities, biting decisions, and the sleet of apathy. We face more heartbreak, more loss, less care, and less goodness, kindness, and compassion. Attributes that we want students to learn—curiosity, humility, vulnerability, and honesty—are more difficult to find and it can be easy to lose hope.

That is exactly why books like *Advancing Empathy and Equity in Early Childhood Education: The Leader's Guide to* Little Learners, Big Hearts are essential. This book builds on the richness of *Little Learners, Big Hearts* by equipping readers with the tools necessary to develop a vision of what it means to be empathetic and equitable and to create and sustain early childhood learning communities that bring that vision into reality.

Well into my teaching career, especially as a teacher developer and instructional coach, I was cautioned that every professional development experience should include takeaways that educators could immediately put into practice in their classrooms. I think that's wrong. Fast application isn't necessarily better. Though a microwave, for example, can heat food fast, it can also cause it to become brittle, dehydrated, and rubbery. Food prepared in a slow cooker, however, tends to be more enjoyable because there is time and opportunity for the creation of new flavor compounds, tenderness, and nutrient retention.

Don't we crave the flavor of truth, the tenderness of compassion, and the nourishment of courage? It takes time for educators to reflect on how we were formed as individuals and practitioners, to explore and grieve the deficit narratives we may hold about people who differ from us, and to interrogate harmful biases and confront our fears about change. We are worth the time it takes to learn to embrace nuance and complexity, build trust, actively listen, courageously lean into discomfort, shift from a fixed mindset to a growth mindset, learn from mistakes, and engage in the process of transformation. In these pages, you will engage with all these experiences.

As you read this book, you will learn about our responsibilities and opportunities as practitioners who embrace empathy and equity, as well as capacity building, competency development, and restorative practices. Through discussion and challenge questions, assessment tools, family engagement supports, and reflective activities, you will learn about hope in a time when we desperately need it, and the importance of education (particularly that of self), acknowledgment, resolution, and teaching.

Because we, as educators, are lifelong learners, we don't have to have everything all figured out. We are always, like students, in the process of becoming, and to that end, we need trusted guides and guidance, models of wholeness, and space to grow. You will find these gifts here.

As I write these words, the United States is celebrating the U.S. women's Olympic gymnastics team winning gold medals. When I look at the team, I am inspired, not only by their excellence, talent, and skill but also by the various hues of their skin: mahogany Simone Biles, caramel Jordan Chiles, almond Suni Lee and Hezly Rivera, and alabaster Jade Carey. We are inspired because they show us the beauty of what's possible.

Winter is passing, and we are at the dawn of a beautiful spring. Something green and strong is reaching up through the soil and bursting through the darkness. In the meantime, let's gather together. Bring your snuggly blankets and hot chocolate with marshmallows. We'll each bring a log to add to the fireplace, and we'll learn how to protect what's budding beneath the soil together. And when we face the wide, curious eyes of our young children, we'll be able to confidently say that when we face the choice to offer rain or drought, we choose rain. When we face the choice to offer nourishment or starvation, we choose nourishment, and when we face the choice to offer sunlight or darkness, we choose light.

INTRODUCTION

Kind Minds and Big Hearts

To learn about race, children need the time, space, and supports to talk about and make sense of what they are seeing and noticing. This requires teachers to embrace the conversation, even if they experience uncertainty or discomfort while doing so.
—Rosemarie Allen, Dorothy L. Shapland, Jen Neitzel, and Iheoma U. Iruka

While we have titled this book *Advancing Empathy and Equity in Early Childhood Education: The Leader's Guide to* Little Learners, Big Hearts, we begin with a practical note—our belief is that leaders need to examine their values and beliefs, search for their own biases, and establish goals for their own development. Therefore, unlike many leader's guides, this book will not simply instruct leaders in how to help teachers and staff implement change. It additionally provides guidance to leaders to help them sift through their own understandings of racism, bias, equity, fairness, and justice, even as it shows them how to enact change in their buildings and with their staff.

This leader's guide is designed for both formal and informal leaders. While we often reference school principals, early childcare directors, and other formal administrators of preK–K, K–3, and the broader scope of elementary schools, we also want to acknowledge the many others who take on formal and informal leadership roles—including teachers, other administrators, and the many researchers, consultants, and agency personnel who are so important to maintaining and advancing promising early childhood practices. As has been acknowledged by so many educational leaders, shared leadership is critical to the field.

As Kristy S. Cooper and colleagues (2016) have pointed out, teacher leaders are critical to influencing their peers, engaging "in actions that lead their colleagues to change their practice" (p. 89). Knowing this, as you read, we urge you to consider both formal and informal leaders, and ways to collaborate to build on the collective efficacy and collective capacity that are so essential for this work (Holcombe et al., 2023).

Why Leadership to Support Empathy and Equity Is So Important

School leaders are charged with so much in the arenas of leadership and management, from handling a myriad of operational details to setting the tone and the climate of the school, including attendance, enrollment, discipline, academic achievement, curriculum, staffing, policies, professional development, evaluation, parental involvement, community involvement, and more. School leaders must balance time addressing their inbox and being visible in their hallways, in classrooms, at meetings, and in conferences, even as we have all cycled through adjusting to the world of new health standards and COVID-induced precautions. With many or all of these areas, disparities in funding and resources have doubled the burden for schools serving students and families who have been marginalized because of their income, race, or ethnicity (Bisram, 2023). Leaders' responsibilities and opportunities for equity connect with all their other obligations because building capacity for equity begins with them.

Responsibilities and Opportunities

Must school leaders assume responsibility for equity? While there are many examples of systemic racism impacting early childhood education, the fact that "early education is the most segregated learning space" in the United States (Hurley, 2024) is often overlooked. In an interview for *Early Learning Nation*, Halley Potter, director of preK–12 education policy at the Century Foundation, explains how systemic economic issues cause this segregation in early childhood programs:

> We have this fractured early education system. We have private programs that charge tuition that is typically unaffordable to lower income families. And then we have many public programs like Head Start which are only open

> to low-income families, or to children who have met certain other criteria for risk factors. So, we're set up for segregation. (as quoted in Hurley, 2024)

And sociologist Casey Stockstill of Dartmouth College, in the same interview, identifies how these systemic economic issues impact many BIPOC families:

> Bringing different funding streams together (called blending and braiding funding) is the first step to increased accessibility for Black, Latino and Indigenous families. That's because we have racial gaps in income and wealth. So, if you have a private program that is expensive and inaccessible to middle-income or lower-income families, that program is going to shut out a disproportionate share of Black, Latino and Indigenous families. There's a hope that programs that do the blending and braiding will also consider racial equity and inclusion, and make their programs welcoming to children and families of color. (as quoted in Hurley, 2024)

As Stockstill and Potter point out, making programs welcoming to children and families of color means recognizing systemic racism (Hurley, 2024). Jason A. Grissom, Anna J. Egalite, and Constance A. Lindsay (2021), in a summary of two decades of research on school principals for the Wallace Foundation, suggest that from an equity perspective:

> Principals can have important impacts on key populations, including low-income students and students and teachers of color. These impacts can occur through direct channels (e.g., by how they manage student disciplinary actions) or through indirect channels (e.g., by working with teachers to implement culturally responsive teaching practices, by hiring greater numbers of teachers of color who are influential for students of color). Principals of color may [also] be high-leverage actors in this regard, as they appear especially likely to have positive impacts on both students of color and teachers of color. (p. xvi)

Early childhood school leaders, program directors, and principals have the responsibility for—and a broad perspective regarding—the students, families, community, and policy considerations that affect their programs daily. They know, or should know, everything that is going on in their programs; from drop-off procedures to food allergies and from building safety to staffing flexibility, the lists can feel endless. The leader's perspective must not only encompass the care and education of their little learners but also support and encourage growth in the expertise of their educators. Successful leaders rely on the relationships they build with the adults in their community. They often have a leadership team that convenes regularly, formally and informally, and is an integral component of a network of observers, practitioners, and family members who are consistently asking, "What is best for this child?" Additionally, they need to be aware of emerging needs and concerns and plan for the next week, month, season, and year.

The leader has the unique opportunity of "super" vision, not the traditional evaluative definition but rather the idea of being able to see (think *vision*) from a super (think *five hundred feet in the air*) perspective. From that overhead position, leaders can notice connections and networks as well as disconnections. They can envision how individual students interact with each other and the adults, and they have the time to observe transition activity, free time, and the more structured environments within classrooms. With this information, school leaders can suggest initiatives, corrections, and innovations that support building a compassionate, equitable experience for the students in their care.

School leadership is the surest way to advance empathy and equity in early childhood school communities—to create the change our schools need. When it comes to increasing equity, advancing promising practices, and furthering antibias or antiracist actions and attitudes, early childhood leaders are working with their staff on implementing new policies, providing professional development, and ensuring that justice and fairness are top priorities. As Kirsten Ivey-Colson and Lynn Turner (2020) assert in an article for *Greater Good Magazine*:

> Anti-racism is a way of life. Like starting any new habit, anti-racism requires a conscious decision to pursue it as a goal and way of being. Intention brings mindful presence and awareness to what we say and what we do.

Leaders have to take into account the attitudes and values of the community and the mandates from the district level. Equity and antibias can be divisive topics where conflicting views are almost inevitable. Common areas of cultural conflict with parents and family members include discipline, gender roles, age-related expectations, sleep, students' responsibilities at home, meals and diet, health and safety, attachment and separation, views on roles of teachers and schools, and significance of play (Derman-Sparks, LeeKeenan, & Nimmo, 2023).

Capacity Building

To lay the groundwork for the process for advancing empathy and equity, leaders need to consider not only how to make a difference but also how to build capacity. As education professors Mollie K. Galloway and Ann M. Ishimaru (2020) state in their case study research on building organizational capacity for equity leadership:

> Building organizational capacity for equity requires enacting leadership as collective activity, with ongoing collaboration across the school community, particularly with minoritized students and families. Findings from the study suggest that such leadership can only be accomplished with shifts in power and educators' understanding that disparate outcomes are a result of structural and institutional conditions. (p. 121)

Galloway and Ishimaru (2020) highlight the power of using high-leverage practices such as visioning, self-reflecting, having equity conversations, hiring for equity, diversifying leadership, and fostering an equitable school climate. They also recommend that school leaders intentionally observe instruction for signs of bias—reminding us that equity and bias and their antidotes are multifaceted and that it is one thing to prepare staff and another to implement equity practices. And they caution that "when professional learning and dialogue routines do not address issues of racism, power asymmetries, and their structural roots, inequities are reinforced" (Galloway & Ishimaru, 2020, p. 121).

As Richard D. Sorenson (2022), professor emeritus at the University of Texas at El Paso, recommends in his book *Equity, Equality, and Empathy: What Principals Can Do for the Well-Being of the Learning Community*, school leaders who are implementing practices to reduce the harm brought on by bias and discrimination also need to consider students' joy, happiness, and positive engagement:

> Well-being is all about positive emotions and moods such as contentment, happiness, pleasure, joyfulness, and satisfaction, as well as the absence of negative emotions such as depression, anxiety, dejection, sadness, despair, and hopelessness. Principals must ask themselves and all members of their learning community if the students are satisfied with their lives, fulfilled in their home and school settings, positively functioning, perceive their lives optimistically and constructively, and have overall good feelings about schooling. (p. 2)

So, as you read *Advancing Empathy and Equity in Early Childhood Education* and think about ways to build capacity, we ask you to proceed with a sense of determination to do the right thing, a spirit of openness to learning, and also a sense of hope.

Although this book revolves around issues and concerns for social justice and equity for our youngest children, like Sorenson (2022), we recommend that leaders undertake our approach in an environment that begins with hope (see chapter 6, page 83) and with proactive attention to compassion as we define it in our signature work on Heart Centered Learning® (HCL; Mason, Rivers Murphy, & Jackson, 2019; see chapters 4 and 5, pages 59 and 71). Embedded within the philosophy of HCL is our comprehensive HEART+ framework (chapter 6), which serves as a guiding compass for nurturing inclusive environments and promoting social justice in early childhood education. At its core are the components of hope, education, acknowledgment, resolution, and teaching, with the + representing how these components can be tailored to fit your local context, acknowledging the unique considerations of each environment.

The journey for leaders always begins with infusing hope into daily interactions with students and families to create a positive and inclusive atmosphere. With hope as a foundation, leaders prioritize ongoing self-education to ensure a continuous evolution of understanding and implementation of antiracist principles. Acknowledging diverse cultures within the educational community fosters inclusivity and appreciation, promoting a sense of belonging and respect among students and staff. In committing to growth, leaders make a resolution to address instances of bias or discrimination, cultivating a culture of accountability and progress within the early childhood setting. Teaching involves integrating practical methods for antiracist teaching into daily interactions with students, thereby promoting understanding and empathy.

As leaders embrace the HEART+ framework and its adaptable components within their local contexts, they pave the way for meaningful change and growth.

In *Advancing Empathy and Equity in Early Childhood Education*, leaders will find guidelines for implementing practical strategies to turn around and enhance their schools and the lives of their staff, students, and families. To build capacity in yourself and others for this to happen, we encourage you to do the following.

- **Start:** Start with yourself. Start somewhere with something you can do. But *start*. We must be far more intentional about our efforts to move away from racism and injustice.

- **Listen and learn:** There are so many wise souls speaking up, writing, and advising us. Be humble, show cultural humility, listen deeply, and continue to learn as you move forward.

- **Believe in goodness and incorporate HEART+ (see chapters 6 and 7, pages 83 and 103):** By incorporating the principles of HEART+ into your leadership, you acknowledge racism and foster cultural competence, inspire hope, cultivate inclusivity, and empower young learners to envision a world free from racism and discrimination.
- **Lead:** Lead by example and remember the words of former U.S. president Barack Obama (2005): "Change is never easy, but always possible."

About Advancing Empathy and Equity, the Book

In *Advancing Empathy and Equity in Early Childhood Education*, we have attempted to address some of the most crucial considerations for school leaders. We do this by citing research, considering policies, providing practical examples and guidelines, and inserting advice from leaders on the ground as well as our own experience and expertise. Our intent is to provide leaders—and aspiring leaders—with sufficient information to start down the road to equity excellence, make considerable progress, and implement sustainable protocols and practices.

In *Little Learners, Big Hearts: A Teacher's Guide to Nurturing Empathy and Equity in Early Childhood*, we introduced a roadmap that supports our HEART+ approach by guiding leaders to acknowledge racism as well as take action both to increase racial understanding and equity and to ensure high-quality teaching (figure I.1, page 8).

As portrayed on this roadmap, a heart centered approach to early equity begins with increasing early childhood staff and leaders' understanding of racism and its impact on young children. The underlying principles for our approach to building empathy and equity are Heart Centered Learning and HEART+. We also ensure that staff and leaders have opportunities to review their own biases and become more conscious of surrounding circumstances, as well as guidance for enhancing school communities.

While our book for teachers and staff includes an overview of family involvement, the role of literacy and literature, and ways to promote curiosity and Heart Centered Learning, this leader's guide explores the related topics of visioning, action planning, professional development, curriculum, and workforce development. We view these as a companion set and encourage leaders to guide their staff by following the recommendations from both books.

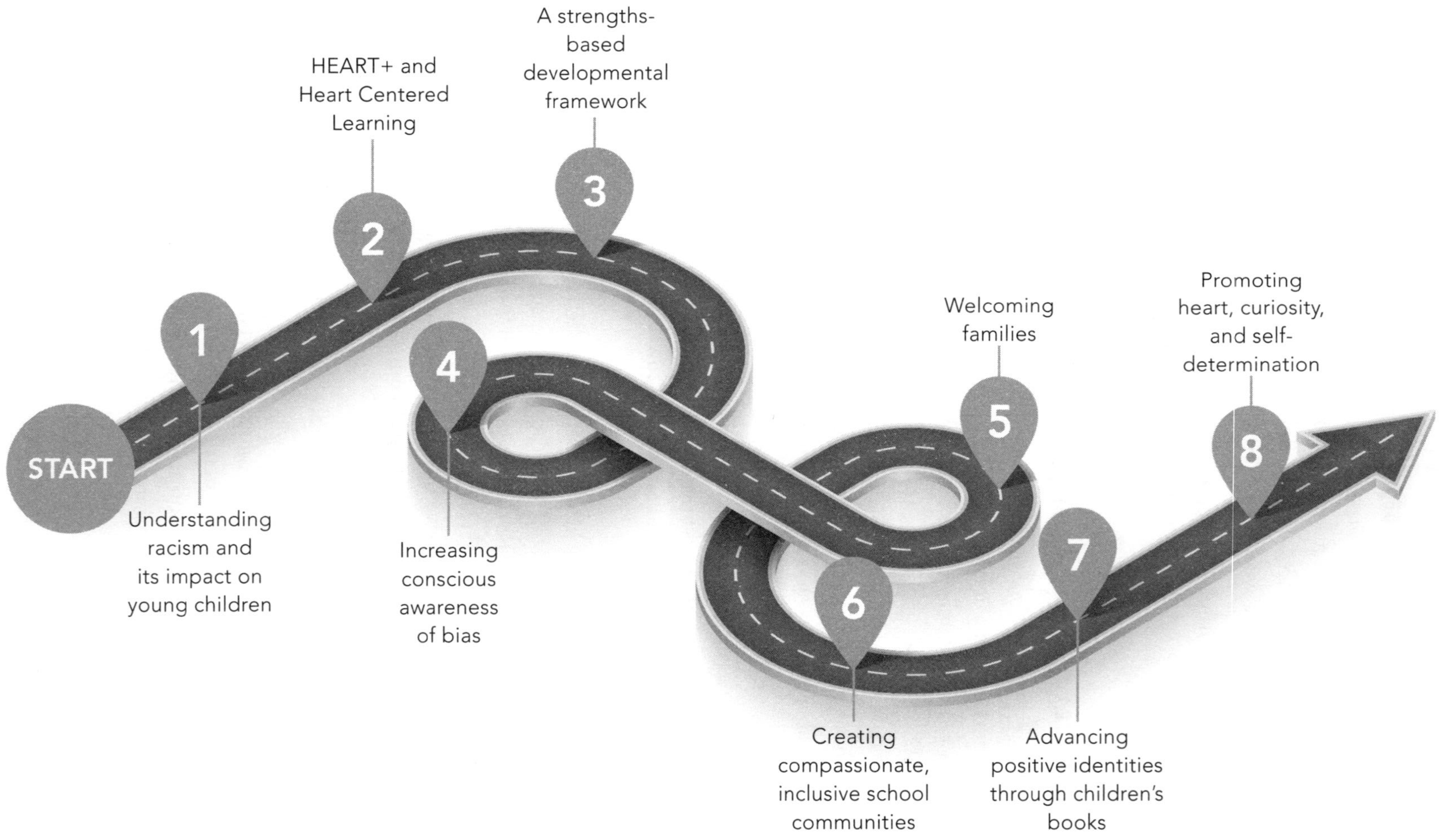

Source: Mason, Ross, Harris, & Flanders, 2024, p. 237.

Figure I.1: A heart centered roadmap to equity in early childhood education.

We have tried to balance considerations for the specific arena of equity and empathy in schools with advice for the process leaders must use. This process includes dialogue, assessments, observations, meetings, individual conferences, professional development, and, moreover, strategies to ensure that school leaders are up to date and knowledgeable about how to lead their staff who may also be involved in significant dialogue and discussion.

Throughout this leader's guide, we do the following.

- Examine the genesis and evolution of racism in early childhood education.
- Define and explain the HCL framework in the context of antiracist early childhood education and the role of early childhood leaders.
- Give school leaders practical tools for examining bias, creating equity, strengthening the caring and skills of educators, and guiding families and communities.
- Envision HCL leadership for the future—a post-pandemic pathway to actively dismantle institutional racism in education.

We share research, practical tips, and reflection questions that you can use on your own or as part of a class or book study group. The book is divided into three parts. Each chapter begins with a principle that summarizes its takeaways for furthering antiracism in early childhood. Table I.1 (page 10) provides a summary.

Within these chapters, we provide opportunities for readers to pause and reflect as well as activities that school leaders can use with their staff and communities as they address racism, bias, and the challenges of building compassionate school communities. We supplement these with additional recommendations for group activities in appendix A (page 253) and with discussion and challenge questions that readers can use individually, in book study groups, or in other professional development sessions in appendix B (page 265). For the leader's guide, we have made the decision to collect these questions at the end of the book to help busy leaders conveniently access them; you can also visit **go.Solution Tree.com/diversityandequity** to access them online.

Before we proceed, we will discuss our word usage within the book, our focus on racism and antiracism in these pages, and you, the reader, as a school leader to help provide a common framework for the ideas we present.

Table I.1: Chapter Summary

	Chapter Title and Key Principle
Introduction	Kind Minds and Big Hearts
Part 1	**Foundations**
Chapter 1	Bold Leadership: What's Necessary for Heart Centered, Antiracist Education **Principle 1:** We can create a better future for young children.
Chapter 2	Historical Threads of Bias: Acknowledgment of What Must Change **Principle 2:** Racism, oppression, and injustice are deep seated; significant and enduring efforts are necessary.
Chapter 3	Support for All Students: A Continuum From Multicultural to Antiracist Movements **Principle 3:** All young children have the right to equitable learning opportunities. It is important to not overlook, negate, or minimize racism.
Chapter 4	My Heart to Yours: A Heart Centered Lens **Principle 4:** Heart centeredness can further much-needed compassion, justice, and equity.
Chapter 5	One C to Another: The Five Cs of Heart Centered Learning **Principle 5:** Consciousness, compassion, confidence, courage, and community are the underpinnings of equity and inclusion.
Chapter 6	A Deep Dive: The HEART+ of the Matter **Principle 6:** Hope, education, acknowledgment, resolution, and teaching can provide an antidote to racism.
Part 2	**Practical Steps Leaders Can Take**
Chapter 7	HEART+: A Focus on Action **Principle 7:** Eradicate racism by speaking up and carrying justice in your heart.
Chapter 8	So Many Wrongs to Right: Antibias Education **Principle 8:** Address implicit and explicit bias through conscious awareness of your own beliefs, taking steps to build a sense of safety and connectedness.
Chapter 9	Circles of Love: School Culture and Restorative Practices **Principle 9:** Listen deeply, build trust, and foster equity.
Chapter 10	A Mountain of Courage: Visioning and Action Planning **Principle 10:** It takes a team to plan for and implement an antiracist school culture.

Part 3	Antiracist Curriculum and Staff Support
Chapter 11	A Light to Shine Together: Professional Development and Supports **Principle 11:** Advance antiracism and cultural competence through professional development, coaching, and differentiated supports.
Chapter 12	Curricula for Young Children: The Building Blocks for Equity in Early Childhood **Principle 12:** Enhance early childhood curricula through culturally relevant pedagogy and intentional efforts to further antiracist practices.
Chapter 13	A Bar to Be Raised: Equity in Early Childhood Educator Standards **Principle 13:** Early education teacher preparation programs must address cultural competence, antibias, and antiracist practices to better support the early childhood care and education workforce.
Chapter 14	Early Childhood Staff Support: Equitable Professional Pathways **Principle 14:** Change is necessary to attract and keep the best workforce—better wages, better training, and higher regard for this essential work.
Chapter 15	A Look at the Future: Leadership to Embrace Change **Principle 15:** Hope + action can lead to transformative change.
Epilogue	Toward a More Just and Inclusive World
Appendix A	Equity Activities for Early Childhood Leaders
Appendix B	Discussion and Challenge Questions for Each Chapter

Word Usage

You will find as you read our book that we use the terms *race* or *racial*, *racism*, *antiracism*, *culture* or *cultural*, and *ethnic*. Sometimes we use them together, sometimes separately, and in other places, we may just write *racism*. We understand that the meanings of these terms are complex, overlapping, and often (although not always) deeply interconnected. When we say *racism*, we generally mean for it to include *lack of cultural competence*. Stylistically, that is wordy and awkward to read. We typically mean racism in its broadest sense, going beyond race to include culture and ethnicity.

Our use of the term *BIPOC* (Black, Indigenous, and people of color) is also a way we try to use inclusive language. We recognize that there is also controversy about the term *BIPOC*, as it implies a hierarchy among all people of color, placing Black and Indigenous people first and mixing everyone else into *POC*.

Orinthia suggests that one historical reason supporting this term is that Black and Indigenous peoples did not come to be part of the American continent by choice. Either they were here already, as with Indigenous tribal peoples, or they were brought here as enslaved peoples. Given that at this time there is no more accurate and inclusive term, we have chosen to use *BIPOC*.

We include definitions of other words used throughout this book in table I.2.

Table I.2: Glossary

Antibias education. "An anti-bias program puts diversity and equity goals at the center of all aspects of its organization and daily life," describing the broad systemic changes that are needed (Derman-Sparks, LeeKeenan, & Nimmo, 2015, p. 11). This approach is rooted in the United Nations Convention on the Rights of the Child (Cohen, 1989), which encompasses the right to freedom from discrimination of all children. Such an approach "includes addressing issues of personal and social identity, social-emotional relationships with people different from oneself, prejudice, discrimination, critical thinking, and taking action for fairness with children" (Derman-Sparks et al., 2015, p. 3). With antibias education, Louise Derman-Sparks, Debbie LeeKeenan, and John Nimmo (2015) describe having the courage to lead, cultivating imagination, engaging in self-reflection and growth, practicing what one preaches, accepting and learning from mistakes, and seeing turbulence as an opportunity for positive change.
Antiracist education. Antiracist education starts with a basic premise: racism is institutional and is prevalent in the broader society and the education system. In antiracist early childhood education, race is not overlooked, negated, or minimized. Rather, it is seen as a core feature, one that guides all antiracist efforts, which acknowledges and addresses the primacy of race in education and social relations (Escayg, 2020).
Cultural bias. As defined by the American Psychological Association, cultural bias (2018) is the tendency to interpret and judge phenomena, in particular when concerning values, beliefs, and other characteristics of the society we belong to. This concept can lead to people creating opinions and making decisions about people before getting to know them.
Cultural competence. Cultural competence is the awareness of how culture shapes an individual's perspectives, ideas, and experiences while recognizing the role privilege and oppression play within that context (Fisher, 2020). Author Ibram X. Kendi explains how we subconsciously have inherited beliefs about culture through a racist lens, which requires awareness and understanding of power and privilege to address and dismantle (Belli, 2020). In this text, we will consistently speak of *cultural competence* as the umbrella term that also implies cultural proficiency—see that definition in this table.

Cultural humility. Recognizing what we don't know about other cultures is cultural humility. Even as we take a multicultural approach, we recognize that learning about other cultures is a lifelong process.

Cultural proficiency. Cultural proficiency includes esteem and learning from differences as a lifelong practice, knowing how to learn about and from individual and organizational culture, interacting effectively in a variety of cultural environments, and advocating for others (Nuri-Robins, Lindsey, Lindsey, & Terrell, 2012).

Microaggressions. Subtle, intentional, and unintentional interactions or behaviors that communicate some sort of bias toward historically marginalized groups, often communicating hostile, derogatory, and harmful messages, are microaggressions (Sue, 2015).

Multicultural education. Multicultural education can take on distinct definitions (Ozturgut, 2011). It can be considered a philosophical concept built on the principle of respecting freedom, justice, equality, and human dignity. One of the most commonly used definitions describes it as an educational reform movement and process with the aim to change the educational structure and open academic achievement to everyone, as equals (Banks, 2001).

Racial inequity. "When two or more racial groups are not standing on approximately equal footing," that is racial inequity (Kendi, 2019, p. 18).

Racism. "Racism is a form of social exclusion, and racial discrimination in all its forms and manifestations is the process by which that exclusion occurs" (Saloojee, 2003). Racial discrimination manifests at the individual, institutional, structural, and systemic levels. It can result from ill will or evil motive; it can be blatant and result from deliberate differential treatment or denial of access; or it can result from apparently neutral policies and practices that, regardless of intent, adversely impact racialized individuals and communities.

Social exclusion. Social exclusion may include a nonrealization, or denial, of certain people's civil, political, and social rights (Walker & Walker, 1997).

Source: Mason et al., 2024, pp. 7–8.

Our Focus on Racism and Antiracism

You may wonder where in this book are discussions of biases other than racism. Aren't all kinds of biases developing in these early years? This is an important question to ask. The history of antibias education shows how different forms of bias have received increasing attention since the 1990s. Many early childhood educators, for example, would now say that young children need to be free to explore their own gender identities, to learn about lesbian and gay families, and to feel support for gender diversity.

We fully endorse early childhood educators addressing these and other forms of bias. At the same time, rather than casting a net wide enough to catch all forms of bias, we have chosen to focus deeply on racism, with its shape-shifting multitude of forms and faces. The question of whether individual or systemic racism is more fundamental than, for example, individual sexism or systemic patriarchy is a worthy question, but it is outside our scope. Without any doubt, racism is fundamental to the problems the United States faces. Most important, racism has a broad but too-often-ignored impact on young children.

In its statement "The Impact of Racism on Child and Adolescent Health," the American Academy of Pediatrics (Trent et al., 2019) writes:

> Although progress has been made toward racial equality and equity, the evidence to support the continued negative impact of racism on health and well-being through implicit and explicit biases, institutional structures, and interpersonal relationships is clear. Failure to address racism will continue to undermine health equity for all children.
>
> Today's children . . . are increasingly diverse. Strategies to address health and developmental issues across the pediatric life span that incorporate ethnicity, culture, and circumstance are critical to achieving a reduction in health disparities.

The American Academy of Pediatrics has put it well. We believe that racial health equity and equity in early care and education are undeniably linked together. Hence, our focus in this book is on dismantling racism in early childhood care and education through antiracist actions and strategies designed and implemented from the practice of mindfulness.

Each chapter in this book includes and ends with some questions to deepen your self-reflection and challenge you to move beyond your present comfort zone (see appendix B, page 265). To start you on that journey, we offer twelve questions to consider that we adapted from the Interaction Institute for Social Change (2019). Not all these questions will feel relevant to everyone. Choose those that feel suited to you now. You may find others appropriate at a later time, or you may want to begin a journal to reflect on your ideas about racism and education as you read this book. These questions may also be useful for discussions with other staff or even family members. Visit **go.SolutionTree.com /diversityandequity** for a reproducible version of these questions to download and share.

1. How do you define your racial and cultural identity? Do you have just one or multiple racial and cultural identities? Why do you choose those?
2. How important to you are your racial and cultural identity or identities? Why?
3. Did you grow up in a family, school, community, or other country where there were many people of different racial and cultural identities? Explain.
4. Did one or both of your parents, caregivers, or other family members (such as grandparents) speak a language other than English? If they did or did not, how has that affected your ideas about families that speak a language other than English at home?
5. Have you ever felt pressured to identify with one racial or cultural group over another? If so, how did you handle that pressure?
6. Do you feel privileged or not privileged in ways other than your racial identity? (Examples include financial status or struggles; sexual orientation; gender identity; religious affiliation, such as Christian, Jewish, Muslim, or no religious preference; and so on.)
7. Do you have close friends who define their racial identity differently than you define yours? If so, how difficult (or not) is it to discuss your racial and cultural backgrounds and other differences?
8. Do you believe that you don't see color when you interact with others whose skin color and features may look different from your own?
9. Has anyone ever said to you, or implied, "You sound (or act) like a White person." If so, how did that feel, and how did you respond, if you did?
10. If you consider yourself BIPOC, how comfortable are you in friendships with White people? What qualities do you need to see in a White person to feel comfortable?
11. Have you ever intervened when someone else acted or spoke in a way you felt was racially or culturally insensitive, hurtful, or even potentially violent? How did you feel if you did or did not intervene?
12. As an early childhood leader, have you worked with racially and ethnically diverse staff? If so, did interracial or interethnic conflicts arise? Again, if so, how did you handle those conflicts?

Regarding You as a School Leader

This is a journey with many different paths and paces. Free speech, civility, and respect are prerequisites for change in a multiracial democracy. Without a commitment to these principles, you may end up creating more fear and negativity. Neither of those will lead to opening your own or others' minds and hearts. We urge you to be compassionate toward others with whom you may disagree. A few deep breaths, or even a short mindfulness activity, may help you move forward in a conversation about challenging racial or cultural topics. As we delve into recommendations for bold leadership within heart centered, antiracist education, it is important to acknowledge that racism is systemic and deep rooted. Therefore, it is essential that we strive toward healing and equity with honest self-reflection and thoughtful engagement.

PART 1

Foundations

CHAPTER 1

Bold Leadership: What's Necessary for Heart Centered, Antiracist Education

> Racism is a heart disease. How we think and how we respond is at the core of racial suffering and racial healing.... The best tool I know to transform our relationship to racial suffering is mindfulness meditation.
>
> —Ruth King

Principle 1: We can create a better future for young children.

Racism is fueled by many factors, including power and fear. Who has the power? Who is afraid and what is the source of fear? Is it the anxiety that one's own children may be victims of racial violence? Or is it the fear that you and your race are losing power? Power wields an enormous influence on our lives. As we say in chapter 3 (page 45), it can dictate societal norms. Justice and equity are not served when norms for young children's development are based solely on the dominant culture's expectations.

Antiracist leaders understand the injustice and the need for a massive undertaking to bring about fairness and ensure the rights for all. It is work that, as Zaretta Hammond (2015) says, involves shifting mindsets, reestablishing trust, being allies to marginalized students and families, and helping students find agency and voice to build their strength and power.

Looking around the United States and the world today, we know that our young children deserve better—that young BIPOC children deserve better. In 1959, the United Nations General Assembly adopted the Declaration of the Rights of the Child, which includes ten general principles (Humanium, n.d.):

1. The right to equality, without distinction on account of race, religion, or national origin
2. The right to special protection for the child's physical, mental, and social development
3. The right to a name and a nationality
4. The right to adequate nutrition, housing, and medical services
5. The right to special education and treatment when a child is physically or mentally handicapped
6. The right to understanding and love by parents and society
7. The right to recreational activities and free education
8. The right to be among the first to receive relief in all circumstances
9. The right to protection against all forms of neglect, cruelty, and exploitation
10. The right to be brought up in a spirit of understanding, tolerance, friendship among peoples, and universal brotherhood

These principles, beginning with equality at number 1 and ending with a spirit of universality at number 10, are central to our heart centered commitment to young children. When we review the history of slavery, genocide, and discrimination, we must ask, "Where were educators? Where were educational leaders during times when people of particular skin hues and facial or body features were treated as less than human?"

People of specific cultures and races have been and too often continue to be dehumanized—treated as less than fully human. We see far too much evidence of ongoing ignorance and dehumanizing actions against BIPOC people (Althoff, 2023; Bisram, 2023; Bryan, 2017; Byman, 2021; Camangian & Cariaga, 2022; Echo-Hawk & Johnson, 2023; Iruka et al., 2022; Jackson, 2019; Kendi, 2016; Perry, 2022; Wilkerson, 2020). Antiracism involves eradicating false beliefs and biases through proactive and demanding activist work. In chapters 6 and 7 (pages 83 and 103), we discuss the HEART+ approach, in which the *A* stands for acknowledging wrongdoing. Leaders, this acknowledgment begins with us. Leading with a compassionate heart, genuine care, and accountability sets a powerful example that will be noticed and emulated by your community. Remember, we cannot abolish what we will not acknowledge, and acknowledging the suffering of others is a crucial first step. This acknowledgment involves listening to the experiences of those affected, validating their pain, and taking responsibility for creating a more just and equitable environment.

Antiracist leadership in early childhood settings means leaders must have a clear message and many other aspects, as we discuss in this chapter. They must also stay abreast of legal and policy considerations related to equity and inclusion for young BIPOC children, including BIPOC children with disabilities.

Antiracist Leadership in Early Childhood Settings

If educators are to be facilitators, what then is the role of the leader? It must include facilitating with confidence as you build a sense of community, belonging, and support. Many education policies and practices do not consider the professional knowledge of teachers and the desire of many to be involved in guiding changes in their schools (Walter, Tuckwiller, Howard, Spencer, & Frey, 2023). When educators are brought into conversations and trained in ways that are individualized to their learning and professional growth needs (differentiation, reflection, and coaching opportunities; see chapter 11, page 165), they can use their voices to advocate for what is best for their students and for themselves. When teachers' voices and choices strengthen education communities and systems, they come together as key partners in the continual educational improvement of the early childhood workforce that can help support positive, meaningful change.

If hundreds or thousands of early childhood leaders work to build a sense of connectedness in their local communities, we may move toward a larger community—an ecosystem—that nurtures empathy and equity. To eradicate racism and increase cultural competence, passionate, indeed transformative, leaders must have courage and a clear message. They must ensure high-quality programs, support each other, collaborate effectively with families, and be reflective. Bold steps are necessary (Sharma, 2017).

A Clear Message

If we are to have equitable and inclusive classrooms, if we are to have schools and early childhood centers that move us beyond racism and toward equal rights and benefits, the message from leaders at all levels should be clear. Racism will not be tolerated; it will be, as Ibram X. Kendi (2016) puts it, stamped out.

Envision stamping out racism. The evidence from efforts in the 1970s, 1980s, and 1990s is clear—simply embracing a celebration of differences is necessary but not adequate.

- Racism is centuries old. It will not be stamped out overnight or even in a few years.
- Focusing on early childhood means laying the foundation for a new generation to identify and defeat racism.
- Adults—educators especially but also families and the community—have the responsibility to guide young children toward inclusion in a compassionate and equitable community where they develop positive identities, support each other, and strive for justice and fairness in all they do.

As we examine what leaders must do, Kendi (2019) again helps us focus:

> Race and racism are power constructs of the modern world. . . . Racism is one of the fastest-spreading and most fatal cancers humanity has ever known. It is hard to find a place where its cancer cells are not dividing and multiplying. (p. 259)

Knowing that, what do we do?

High-Quality Early Childhood Programs

In 2014, the United Nations Educational, Scientific and Cultural Organization (UNESCO) followed up on the Universal Declaration of Human Rights with a 301-page downloadable document, *Teaching Respect for All: Implementation Guide*. That guide has recommendations for policymakers, administrators, and educators within the context of the broader ecosystem, recommending a whole-school approach and recognizing that teachers, students, and administrators are all victims of discrimination. The guide offers strategies for creating non-alienating environments that include mutual respect and advanced teamwork, recognizing and rewarding gains, and developing a shared vision.

For early childhood educators, these basic, broad principles as laid out by UNESCO (2014) and the United Nations (Humanium, n.d.) translate to ensuring access to high-quality early childhood programs (universal preschool). To build the quality of their early childhood programs, leaders will need to focus on the following.

- Help staff become consciously aware of bias.
- Further friendships and support among families of different cultures, races, and ethnicities.
- Implement professional learning to build the capacity of staff to handle the more sensitive situations that might arise.

The World Education Forum (2000) in Dakar, Senegal, affirms:

> All children, young people and adults have the human right to benefit from an education that will meet their basic learning needs in the best and fullest sense of the term, an education that includes learning to know, to do, to live together and to be. It is an education geared to tapping each individual's talents and potential, and developing learners' personalities, so that they can improve their lives and transform their societies. (p. 8)

The challenge, as so clearly laid out in the *Teaching Respect for All: Implementation Guide*, is "how to include those [who have been] excluded and recover or reinvigorate equality for all, without imposing the culture of the dominant groups as the unique norms" (UNESCO, 2014, p. 25).

Leaders Supporting Leaders for Transformational Change

In *Radical Transformational Leadership*, Monica Sharma (2017), a physician and epidemiologist who worked for over twenty years at the United Nations, reminds us of the power that comes from synergy, stating:

> Radical transformation . . . requires us to source the universal values of dignity, fairness, and compassion for strategic design, action, and results. We work in partnerships at home, in society, and in our workplace. Aligning with partners generates synergy. . . . *Being* attuned with like-spirited partners generates resonance. (p. 277)

Where we focus our energies and attention makes a difference. Have you ever become immersed in something only to find that something suddenly popping up all around you? For example, you develop an interest in pickleball or poetry, and suddenly, you notice the new pickleball court or a reading by a local poet. It is almost as if our eyes are opened in new ways by our attention and our focus.

So it is with *synergy*: when we work together toward a common goal, our energies and efforts combine to create greater change than we could achieve on our own. Consider what might happen if the following isolated actions combined.

- Leaders promote more inclusive and representative curricula.
- Educators receive more comprehensive training and support.

- Students receive wraparound services to meet their and their families' needs.
- Schools actively engage families and community members in interracial dialogue groups.

> **Pause and Reflect**
> - Does synergy promote a clear message about antiracism and cultural competence in schools and communities?
> - How could synergy lead to opportunities for teamwork, partnerships, and magnification of initiatives to address racism and promote cultural competence?

Sharma (2017) urges us to "care for each other," fearlessly speak out, and become "mindful implementers," saying that the work is about "wise, ethical, and mindful implementation," and that "every person can lead and generate transformational results within their sphere of influence and accountability" (p. 195). Caring, wise, ethical, and mindful thoughts and actions all contribute to leading with HEART+ and aid the process of healing from the injustice and trauma perpetuated by racism.

Collaboration With Families

As we indicate in chapter 4 of *Little Learners, Big Hearts*, we prefer to use the more inclusive term *families* rather than *parents*. We also emphasize the importance of partnering with and empowering families, rather than simply *engaging* them. Our view is that empowerment involves family-teacher co-creation with equity-focused goals. As Ann Ishimaru, Joe Lott, Ismael Fajardo, and Jessica Salvador (2014) suggest, these goals are driven by families' strengths rather than their deficits.

In *Little Learners, Big Hearts*, we also explain the overall importance of building trust and relationships with families:

> With families, always work on building relationships so that when difficult conversations do happen, they occur in the context of a relationship that you have helped to create—one that is filled with a sense of caring and regard for the other. (Mason et al., 2024, p. 104)

And in reference particularly to BIPOC families, we stress:

> It is critical for White educators to know that because of past hurts (and trauma), trust-building may be a fragile process, requiring first that they acknowledge the past, followed by patience, humility, and compassion. By acknowledging the unique challenges and injustices that BIPOC children and their families may face due to systemic racism, teachers create a cornerstone of trust, building bonds with these families. Such trust is pivotal to creating inclusive and equitable learning environments. (Mason et al., 2024, p. 111)

School leaders set the tone and the standard for interactions with families. Some staff members will naturally be in step with families' needs and lean into collaboration with them. However, school leaders may observe signs that some staff need guidance and support in working with families, especially with families whose race and culture may be different from their own. As Louise Derman-Sparks, Debbie LeeKeenan, and John Nimmo (2015) suggest, there are many ways to partner with families in schools. One way is to openly discuss how they see their children's needs. Here are some possible conversation starters to help teachers and staff get to know more about the children and families they serve:

- Tell me about your child's (temperament, personality, heritage, interests, abilities).
- What are your child's favorite activities?
- Are there experiences your child avoids?
- Describe your child's sleeping schedule.
- Describe your child's eating patterns, favorite foods.
- What languages does your child sign or speak at home? What languages does your child hear or see at home?
- Ask about cultural, spiritual or religious holidays, celebrations, or traditions—What are your practices, and would you be willing to share anything with the class?
- What are your expectations for your child?
- What about your aspirations, hopes, and dreams for your child?
- What do you view as your child's communities?
- Do you have particular concerns about your child, or about school?
- How can I best communicate with you?
- Anything else? (Derman-Sparks et al., 2015, p. 105)

These questions could be used prior to parent conferences to help family members prepare their thoughts. You might also consider questions related to social media (both their children's use of it and whether it is an effective way to communicate with them).

> **Pause and Reflect**
>
> As you engage with families, notice your level of comfort or discomfort.
> - What are strategies you could use to increase your sense of comfort? (See also chapter 4, page 59.)
> - Review Derman-Sparks and colleagues' (2015) list. Which questions do you already use? Which ones might you consider including in your communications with families?

A Reflective Assessment

The National Association of Elementary School Principals (NAESP) has developed a full reflective assessment based on a set of six competency standards for leadership in early childhood education (preK–3; Kauerz, Ballard, Soli, & Hagerman, 2021). Several competencies include self-assessment prompts directly related to the focus of *advancing empathy and equity*. We summarize the competencies and self-assessment prompts most relevant to equity and school climate and include those in appendix A (page 253).

Bold Steps

Consider your leadership, your staff, your interest in transformational change, and your collaborations with families. With an expansive view of leadership, when it comes to antiracism, we are urging you to dream big and take bold steps to bring about equity, with necessary healing, in your community. This will take courage, and many leaders recommend moving with a sense of urgency as well as conviction. Christine and her colleagues Melissa D. Patschke and Kevin Simpson put it this way:

> To reach the goal of fundamental changes in education, educators must start to lead with passion and conviction as they address their most pressing needs, including the need for healing and helping students feel a sense of meaning and purpose. (Mason, Patschke, & Simpson, 2023, p. xx)

Young children will feel a sense of meaning and purpose as they thrive—thriving when the culture promotes student agency and the educators become facilitators. Here are seven key recommendations for those who are or desire to be transformative, heart centered early childhood leaders in the space of antiracism.

1. Ensure that you and your staff are consciously aware of your own biases and prejudices and take steps so that these will not contribute to further racism or prejudice.
2. Develop a common vision with your staff and community for moving into a space of equity, justice, dignity, compassion, and regard for peoples of all colors, backgrounds, and cultures.
3. Use tools (such as curriculum and children's books) that promote excellence and equity.
4. Establish a welcoming culture that contributes to children's and their families' sense of belonging, agency, and well-being.
5. Guard against peer aggression, bullying, and harassment.
6. When you see racism, name it.
7. Continue to advance your knowledge and skills so that you can help grow mindful, compassionate antiracist practices and leadership in your school or center.

We all have biases. Acknowledging your own biases is the first step. Then you can consciously work to address them and promote a more inclusive and supportive environment where all students feel they truly belong.

Legal and Policy Considerations

Educational leaders, from preschool to college, should be knowledgeable about federal and state antidiscrimination laws. These laws form the basis of policies in school districts and in large preschool networks such as Head Start. In the 1960s, Head Start programs helped integrate schools in the Deep South, providing well-paying jobs that insulated civil rights activists from economic and political repercussions imposed by segregationists (Swayne, 2015).

Federal civil rights laws prohibit discrimination based on different categories.

- The Civil Rights Act of 1964 covers race, color, and national origin.
- Title IX of the Education Amendments of 1972 covers sex, sexual orientation, and gender identity. (The final rule under Title IX, effective August 1, 2024, explicitly covers gender identity.)
- Section 504 of the Rehabilitation Act of 1973 covers disabilities.

These laws apply to educational programs or activities that receive federal financial assistance from the U.S. Department of Education (2023). It is important to check your state discrimination laws, since they may add additional categories beyond those covered in federal laws. Leaders must ensure inclusivity for all students, including those with disabilities, and be cognizant of disparities. Both federal and state laws should inform local policies for preK–12 schools.

BIPOC Students With Disabilities and Concerns Regarding Disparities

In reference to students with disabilities, in a UNESCO report on quality inclusion and early childhood, Elena Soukakou, Carmen Dionne, and Olympia Palikara (2024) note students' needs, the benefits of inclusion, and the critical support provided by teachers:

> All children, including those with the most significant disabilities and the highest learning needs, can make significant developmental and learning progress in inclusive settings. . . . Young children who participate and learn together with children presenting with diverse learning profiles can demonstrate greater compassion and empathy and develop a better understanding of diversity and disability as concepts when peer interactions are adequately supported by classroom teachers. (p. 6)

See also *Start With Equity* by Shantel Meek and colleagues (2020), whose fourteen priorities for dismantling racism in early childhood education make frequent mention of inclusion of young children with disabilities.

Learning alongside other students in integrated environments is important both for BIPOC students and for students with disabilities, whether they be BIPOC or White. A premise underlying support for students with identified disabilities in the United States is the value of inclusion. The Division for Early Childhood and the National Association for the Education of Young Children (NAEYC; 2009) articulate this in a joint position statement:

> Early childhood inclusion embodies the values, policies, and practices that support the right of every infant and young child and [their] family, regardless of ability, to participate in a broad range of activities and contexts as full members of families, communities, and society. The desired results of inclusive experiences for children with and without disabilities and their families include a sense of belonging and membership, positive social relationships and friendships, and development and learning to reach their full potential. The defining features of inclusion that can be used to identify

> high quality early childhood programs and services are access, participation, and supports. (p. 2)

Subchapter III (Part C) of the Individuals With Disabilities Education Act (IDEA, 2004) provides guidelines for educational services to infants and toddlers with disabilities. These include provisions for identification of children needing services, distribution of funds to states to assist them in meeting IDEA requirements for maintaining statewide systems of early intervention services for infants and toddlers with disabilities and their families, development of individual family plans, authorization for staff preparation and training, and guidelines regarding equity, disproportionality, and technical assistance resources. Section 303.1(d) authorizes the use of federal IDEA (2004) funds to:

> enhance the capacity of State and local agencies and service providers to identify, evaluate, and meet the needs of all children, including historically underrepresented populations, particularly minority, low-income, inner-city, and rural children, and infants and toddlers in foster care.

The Early Childhood Technical Assistance Center (n.d.) provides detailed state-by-state information on eligibility definitions for infants and toddlers with disabilities. These criteria are included for each state receiving funds under IDEA Part C:

- Definition of developmental delay
- At risk for developments delay policy (if applicable)
- Link to state eligibility policy and additional links to other policies, if available
- Selected categories of diagnosed conditions (e.g., prematurity, low birth weight, very low birth weight, small for gestational age, prenatal exposure to substances, hearing impairment, vision impairment and prenatal exposure to Zika) are included if information is available beyond Part C regulatory language (Early Childhood Technical Assistance Center, n.d.)

These eligibility requirements vary by state. For example, North Carolina provides services to premature infants born at less than twenty-seven weeks and less than 2.2 pounds. California provides services for premature infants born at less than thirty-two weeks and less than 3.3 pounds. Other conditions that most states cover include vision and hearing loss, plus prenatal exposure to substance abuse. The number of eligibility criteria required for services also varies widely. Seventeen U.S. states, territories, or jurisdictions require only one eligibility criterion; twenty-five require two eligibility criteria. The remaining fifteen require between three and six criteria. The way that services are provided also varies from state to state. California and North Carolina have regional service centers across their states. In Massachusetts, a wide range of nonprofit programs provide early intervention services (Early Childhood Technical Assistance Center, n.d.).

Randy recalls a personal experience with early intervention services: her grandson was born premature in the Bay Area of California at twenty-eight weeks and with a low birth weight of just over one pound. Clearly meeting the state's eligibility requirements, he received services from the Golden Gate Regional Center for three years. Most important, his mother did not even need to apply or reach out for services. The center contacted her based on information from the hospital where he had been in the neonatal intensive care unit. A highly skilled early interventionist visited his home twice a week in the beginning and transitioned to once a week as he grew older. When he was two and a half years old and entered a daycare program, the early interventionist started conducting his weekly sessions at that center.

Given the racial and ethnic disparities in receiving services that we describe in this section, contacting families directly rather than waiting for them to apply for services or be referred by a pediatrician would seem to be best practice.

Section 619 of IDEA (2004) also explains services for young children three to five years of age who have special needs, with prescriptions for individual education programs (IEPs) for eligible students. Despite IDEA legislation and regulations that identify features to address equity concerns, multiple disparities in racial and ethnic representation are evident, with Latino/a students the least likely to receive services and American Indian / Alaska Native and White students the most likely to participate in special education programs. These inequities also manifest in classroom placement, with Black and Latino/a students spending more of their school day in self-contained special education classes than in regular classes (which are often the least restrictive environment; Meek et al., 2020). Readers can visit https://sites.ed.gov/idea for further information on IDEA (2004).

Concerns regarding the disparities in services for BIPOC students with disabilities have long been reported. A 2023 report by the Early Childhood Technical Assistance Center and the National Center for Pyramid Model Innovations reveals the following.

- Young BIPOC children are often underrepresented in early intervention and preschool special education programs.
- Even when they do access such services, chronic underfunding often results in inconsistent and inadequate support.

- A significant portion of preschoolers receiving special education services are placed in segregated settings, away from their peers without disabilities.

- When students transition into the K–12 system, racial and ethnic disparities persist. Black students are more likely to be diagnosed under subjective categories, and BIPOC students typically spend less time in general education settings, with more frequent disciplinary action, compared to White students with disabilities.

Indicator E11 from the Early Childhood Technical Assistance Center's and the National Center for Pyramid Model Innovations' (2023) indicators of high-quality inclusion addresses "anti-bias, culturally responsive, sustaining, and identity-affirming practices." According to that standard:

> Providers [should be] aware of the impact of implicit and explicit biases on their teaching. Therefore, they [should] provide learning experiences that are aligned with the child and family's experiences. Providers [should] value and respect all lived experiences. They [should] give children learning opportunities and materials that positively show a variety of cultures and identities instead of applying a color or ability-evasive approach. (Early Childhood Technical Assistance Center & National Center for Pyramid Model Innovations, 2023, p. 8)

And providers are expected to:

1. Show cultural humility when interacting with families. Form and sustain positive and bidirectional relationships where families have specific opportunities to share information about their culture and intersecting identities.
2. Use learning activities and materials that connect to children's experiences, funds of knowledge, home language, and cultural norms beyond token holidays and food.
3. Learn the historical and contemporary impact of systemic barriers.
4. Challenge their bias and assumptions in interpreting behavior and choosing learning materials.
5. Select books, toys, and activities that show the intersecting identities of children and families in non-stereotypical ways. (Early Childhood Technical Assistance Center & National Center for Pyramid Model Innovations, 2023, p. 8)

Note that while IDEA and related legislation provide important safeguards for families and children with serious needs, parents report that their involvement is sometimes fraught with barriers—that sometimes, when they are not asked for their opinions or when their perspectives are ignored, they feel marginalized (MacLeod, Causton, Radel, & Radel, 2017). Moreover, jargon, the complexity of legislative tools such as IDEA, and the maze that parents sometimes go through to get the information they and their children need all stand in the way of effective school-home partnerships (LaRocque, Kleiman, & Darling, 2011). And as Kristin M. Rispoli, Leslie R. Hawley, and Marianne C. Clinton (2018) report in a study of 1,350 Head Start centers, race and culture impact involvement, with White parents reporting greater involvement than Black or Hispanic parents. Centers and websites for individual states, such as Exceptional Lives in California, can provide important tools in enhancing school-home communication (Howard-Karp, 2024).

School, State, and District Policies

School, state, and district policies will also impact the approach that school leaders take to implementing antibias and antiracist practices in their schools. For example, should a teacher (or a student) express explicitly racist or culturally derogatory statements about a student or group of students, the family could bring a complaint, first to the school district and then, if not satisfied, to the Office for Civil Rights (OCR) in their region (see www2.ed.gov/about/offices/list/ocr/aboutocr.html for regional OCR offices). OCR investigates complaints it receives and generally reaches agreement with the school district to address any violations. Antibias curricula and related staff training are often part of those agreements. Randy worked extensively with OCR in Region 1 (New England) and helped several districts implement their agreements through curricular and professional learning initiatives.

Most districts will have an equity policy. As Melanie Meren, a school board member at Fairfax County Public Schools in Virginia, indicates:

> A school division having an equity policy reinforces commitment to equity at the basic level, and a guide for bringing equity into decision making that impacts all facets of early education: curriculum, facilities, schedule, equipment, professional development, family engagement, and more. In Fairfax County Public Schools' efforts to expand early childhood offerings to all, availability of space is being addressed as an equity issue. I urge school leaders to examine how space is being created for equitable early childhood offerings. (M. Meren, personal communication, January 25, 2024)

Meren highlights a critical point about equity, especially racial, cultural, and class equity. Access to high-quality early childhood education for all children, regardless of their family income or background, is itself an equity issue. A 2020 review of international results concluded that these programs are most beneficial for children from lower socioeconomic families (Dietrichson, Kristiansen, & Viinholt, 2020). According to findings in a report of the School Superintendents Association (AASA; Hanover Research, 2022), universal preschool has both long- and short-term benefits.

However, many states have not yet implemented universal preschool programs. "There are three states and the District of Columbia that administer fully universal pre-K programs. Nine additional states have universal eligibility policies—regardless of income or demographic characteristics" (Hanover Research, 2022, p. 10).

Among the six goals for early childhood education in a report from the National Association of State Boards of Education (Hao & Cohen, 2020) are provisions to expand access to high-quality early childhood programs for children birth to five, with equitable access for underserved children and families, and also to "leverage different funding streams and seek innovative solutions to serve the most vulnerable children and make long-term plans to expand access and quality for all children" (p. 16).

Early childhood leaders have a great deal on their plates just managing day-to-day operations; overseeing curriculum; managing health concerns; resolving conflicts among children, staff, and often families; and so on. At the same time, knowledge of legal and policy considerations is critical to seeing the big picture, preventing immediate issues from becoming legal problems, developing future goals, and motivating local and state policymakers to improve conditions for early childhood programs.

Pause and Reflect

- What are your beliefs about race, about bias, and about the role of leaders?
- What are your personal experiences?
- How are your experiences and beliefs impacting your leadership?
- As you have learned more from leaders about antiracism, how have your views and actions shifted?

HEART+ Takeaways

Change is never easy, but we have an obligation to address the lingering injustices around us. If not us, who will? When we work together, we can combine our energy and enact more meaningful change. Everyone has unique perspectives, experiences, and skills to contribute. Leaders, educators, support staff, parents, students, and community members can unite to create a brighter, more equitable future for everyone.

CHAPTER 2

Historical Threads of Bias: Acknowledgment of What Must Change

> The beauty of antiracism is that you don't have to pretend to be free of racism to be an antiracist. Antiracism is the commitment to fight racism wherever you find it, including in yourself. And it's the only way forward.
>
> —Ijeoma Oluo

Principle 2: Racism, oppression, and injustice are deep seated; significant and enduring efforts are necessary.

Neill Alleva (2021), a principal with the Mamaroneck Union Free School District in New York, says the following about equity in schools in an online article for NAESP:

> Minor modifications to the curriculum, new SEL [social-emotional learning] programs, and deeper ties to families aren't enough. School leaders must be willing to take action to disrupt biased, oppressive systems and mindsets that have failed for generations. They owe it to their communities to actively engage in a process that doesn't avoid or ignore racial equality but fosters it.
>
> The active disruption begins with white principals understanding their complicity in serving the privileged and oppressing the marginalized.

Active disruption? Complicity? Are principals and other school leaders ready for the conflict and disagreement that are almost certain when topics that have long been politely ignored are suddenly a key part of the conversations with staff, students, and parents? People have widely varying views about the extent of bias and racism in the United States, as well as about how schools should address them. As Prudence Carter, professor of sociology at Brown University, and Russell Skiba, Mariella Arredondo, and Mica Pollock (2014) suggest:

> Regardless of our attempts to avoid the topic, the issue of race emerges over and over again, permeating our society and conditioning our lives. For Trayvon Martin and Michael Brown [and Eric Garner, Tamir Rice, Alton Sterling, Philando Castile, and many other African American males], the translation of racialized thinking into action yielded deadly consequences. For many other youth in our nation, the consequences of our heritage of presumed racial difference and longstanding segregation play themselves out on a daily basis, through lowered expectations, decreased educational opportunity, and disciplinary overreaction. This is an old problem. . . . The topic of racial disparities understandably remains emotionally charged. As in a family that can never discuss its fundamental secrets, our deeply held and often unconscious beliefs, stereotypes, and biases are too rarely brought to the surface, examined, and finally expunged. (pp. 6, 7)

Before focusing on equity and bias, it's useful to take a step back and consider historical threads. One way of understanding the history of racism and bias is to look at dates and incidents of violence and oppression. Another way is to read and discuss others' observations of significant historical events. In this chapter, we take you on a bit of a journey, highlighting some major issues that have contributed to the current state of affairs in the United States and how leaders can begin to move forward with hope.

Acknowledgment Before Healing

For healing, we need to acknowledge what has happened, to speak the unspeakable truth. This step is necessary, and, although difficult, with mindfulness, we can acknowledge hard truths while simultaneously holding onto hope for a better future, not just in early childhood but in all aspects of society.

Look back over the history of the United States. Consider the disparities that have existed from the time Europeans set foot in North America. Then fast-forward to consider America in the 20th and 21st centuries. Following are some of the factors that contribute to racism and its impact on young children and early childhood education (which we address in the chapters that follow in this book and in *Little Learners, Big Hearts*; Iruka et al., 2022; Roberts & Rizzo, 2021; Shonkoff, Slopen, & Williams, 2021).

- White children tend to be more compliant, making it easier for schools to gravitate toward policies that promote these expectations (see also chapter 5 of *Little Learners, Big Hearts*).
- Black boys in particular are more likely to be suspended or expelled from school.
- Families often live in segregated neighborhoods.
- White people tend to have higher social status and more social power.
- How parents talk (or do not talk) about race influences children's perceptions and attitudes.
- Children of color are underrepresented in children's books.
- Excessive early adversity is associated with socioeconomic status, race, and culture.
- BIPOC children and their families often have reduced access to health care, including reduced access to prenatal health and mental health supports.
- Immigration policies can have adverse effects on children.
- Cultural racism can lead to implicit bias.
- Financial strain is associated with race and culture.
- During the COVID-19 pandemic, BIPOC families tended to have less access to digital networks and technology necessary for virtual education.
- Some U.S. political leaders have promoted bias and discrimination.
- Women and minoritized populations only gained some inherent rights after amendments to the Constitution of the United States.
- Historically, schools in low-income neighborhoods, with a high proportion of BIPOC families, have been underfunded and had fewer resources and fewer high-quality teachers.
- Many families in low-income areas have reduced access to preschools and early care centers.

- From the time of American colonization, slavery and the massacre and treatment of Native Americans formed the foundation for many attitudes and practices that exist in the present.

> **Pause and Reflect**
>
> Review the list of factors contributing to racism in early childhood education. Which ones are of greatest concern to you at this time? Are there others?

Young children and early childhood educators have been plagued with factors creating disparities and reducing their overall sense of safety, security, and well-being. Next, we discuss the observations of antiracist thought leaders who have confronted the historical threads that lead to these hard truths. Then we discuss the role of empathy and how it can offer hope.

Guidance From Those Speaking Aloud Hard Truths

Now, let's examine some leaders in this antiracist work and see how they have acknowledged and spoken aloud some hard truths, while still maintaining belief in the transformative power of this work to enact change. They guide our own leadership in our centers, schools, and institutions.

We begin with Imani Perry. In the chapter "Animated Roulette: Louisville" in her book *South to America: A Journey Below the Mason-Dixon to Understand the Soul of a Nation*, Perry (2022) explains:

> I began this chapter while I was still reeling. A grand jury investigation had been completed regarding the death of Breonna Taylor, a Black woman, an essential hospital worker, who was killed by police officers in Louisville while she was in her bed sleeping. There were months of protests locally. Her image covered national magazines. Our hearts broke for Breonna. In the end, the grand jury charged one of the three officers involved—not for killing Breonna Taylor, but for shooting into the home of her White neighbor. That was called wanton endangerment. There were centuries of such contortions of legal interpretation. Something like justice as a long shot from the outset. (p. 62)

Later, the U.S. Department of Justice opened a civil rights investigation into Taylor's death; however, a mistrial was declared. As of March 11, 2024, the U.S. Department of Justice plans to try a third time to convict one police officer (Nakamura, 2024). Breonna Taylor's tragic story demands our empathy and urges leaders to confront the harsh realities of systemic injustice. In the same work, Perry (2022) emphasizes the necessity of speaking truth even when it's painful, stating:

> It is not enough to set aside a little time or attention here or there to grieve our national sins, then, soft as butter, turn back to proclamation of greatness. Because history is an instruction. And what you neglect to attend to from the past, you will surely ignore in the present. (p. 229)

Only by immersing ourselves in Taylor's perspective, however painful, can we ignite transformative change within our schools. Her memory, if we allow it, can fuel our commitment to dismantle oppressive systems that show up in early childhood education.

Next, let us turn to Ta-Nehisi Coates, a renowned author, journalist, and public intellectual known for his incisive exploration of race, history, and systemic bias in America. Coates, through his powerful writing and analysis, shines a light on historical biases, urging readers to confront uncomfortable truths and grasp the depths of societal racial injustice. In his book *Between the World and Me*, Coates (2015) pens, "I would have you be a conscious citizen of this terrible and beautiful world" (p. 108). He acknowledges the undeniable presence of systemic racism and the oppression faced by marginalized communities while also recognizing the beauty in the hope and determination to create positive change. We want early childhood leaders to embody Coates's (2015) call for conscious citizenship, confronting these harsh realities while striving for a better future.

Let's focus for a moment on the writings of Pulitzer Prize winner Isabel Wilkerson. In *Caste: The Origins of Our Discontents*, Wilkerson (2020) explores the parallels between the caste system in India and the social structure built in the United States:

> In the American caste system, the signal of rank is what we call race, the division of humans on the basis of their appearance. In America, race is the primary tool and the visible decoy, the front man, for caste. (p. 18)

Wilkerson (2020) further explores how this expectation placed on marginalized groups that they endure oppression while the privileged remain unaffected reinforces the need to speak aloud hard truths about systemic injustices. Despite these challenges, she emphasizes the importance of maintaining hope for a better future and striving for transformative change. As Wilkerson aptly puts it in an interview with playwright Lynn Nottage:

> I hope that we are on the cusp of an awakening. There's something about this moment that feels as if it could—it could—be a turning point. But history is always there to remind us that we're on this continuum. Something reaches a breaking point and people recognize it, and then there are efforts to change, and then there's a backlash to that change. Then there's also a very long period of entrenchment, and that builds up to yet another cycle. So where are we in the cycle? How meaningful is this? Where and when might humanity transcend all of this and recognize that we all have more in common than we have been led to believe? Our species depends upon people getting together and recognizing this. (as quoted in Kahn, 2020)

Early childhood educators can draw inspiration from the insightful perspectives of Isabel Wilkerson, Ta-Nehisi Coates, and Imani Perry to inform their practices and advocacy efforts. By acknowledging and speaking aloud hard truths about systemic injustices, while still maintaining hope for a better future, leaders can empower themselves and their communities to work toward equity and justice in early childhood education and beyond.

Systemic racism in the United States is not limited to the saga and ongoing tension, injustice, and inequities that Black and Latino/a Americans experience. The experiences of other groups in the United States, including those of Indigenous peoples, have been equally horrific. Before we turn to the words of Gregory Cajete, we want to share some essential background information (Indian Country Today, 2021).

- There are over 574 recognized tribes in the United States, 225 of which are in Alaska, 103 in California, and 68 in the Southwest (Colorado, Nevada, New Mexico, and Utah).
- According to 2020 U.S. Census Bureau data, the American Indian and Alaska Native population increased from 5.2 million in 2010 to 9.7 million in 2020—an 86 percent increase.

To strengthen our historical context, we draw from the work and visions of Gregory Cajete, a Tewa Indian from Santa Clara Pueblo, an artist, an author of numerous books, and director of Native American studies and associate professor of education at the University of New Mexico. In his book *Look to the Mountain: An Ecology of Indigenous Education*, Cajete (1994) confronts the Western conception of "primitive," contending that it is a product of cultural conditioning rather than an objective truth. He challenges the traditional narrative perpetuated by Western education, arguing that there is no inherent primitiveness in Indigenous knowledge systems.

Cajete (1994) emphasizes the importance of recognizing the richness and complexity of Indigenous cultures and their educational practices, stating, "There is no such thing as primitive in the way Western education has traditionally conditioned people to perceive it" (p. 132). He urges us to acknowledge oppression, including political, economic, and social domination, as well as exploitation and control, and then to work to reclaim the "enormously important heritage" (Cajete, 1994, p. xii) and revitalization of Indigenous ways. Cajete (1994) describes the need for a new kind of educational consciousness that "will allow Indigenous people to make the kinds of contributions to global education that stem from [such] deep ecological orientations" (p. xii).

Building on Cajete's (2020) reflections, Holly Echo-Hawk and Melanie Johnson (2023) provide additional perspective in their chapter "Reclaiming the Brilliance of Native Youth" in one of Christine's books, *Leading With Vitality and Hope: Embracing Equity, Alleviating Trauma, and Healing School Communities* (Mason, Patschke, et al., 2023). As Echo-Hawk and Johnson (2023) report, historians, scientists, and many others have failed to acknowledge the major scientific and cultural contributions of Indigenous people who were early astronomers, established a system of democracy, and influenced the "discoveries" of others. Despite their significant contributions, Indigenous people's scientific achievements have often been overlooked by historians, scientists, and others, a trend identified by Echo-Hawk and Johnson (2023). They state:

> Native brilliance requires support and nurturing, but the American education system has a dismal track record of including Native history in state education content standards, ensuring accuracy in how Native history is taught, and conveying the Native perspective in history. It also lacks partnerships with local tribes and Native organizations to develop collaborations for curriculum development and support for Native students. (Echo-Hawk & Johnson, 2023, p. 67)

To move forward, early childhood leaders should acknowledge the profound influence of Indigenous knowledge on fundamental psychological concepts and educational theories while also confronting the historical injustices perpetuated by the American education system. Despite past failures to recognize the intellectual capacity of Indigenous students and to incorporate Native history and perspectives into curricula, leaders must approach this challenge with both a recognition of some unspeakable truths and a sense of hope. By actively engaging with Indigenous communities, supporting Native brilliance, and promoting inclusive and culturally responsive educational practices, leaders can foster empathy and equity while working toward a brighter future.

Empathy and the Brain

We use the term *empathy* throughout this book, including it in both this book's title and the title of *Little Learners, Big Hearts: A Teacher's Guide to Nurturing Empathy and Equity in Early Childhood*. But what do we mean by *empathy*, what are its limits, and where does it come from in the human brain?

Empathy is complex, with several different aspects, and closely related to compassion (discussed in chapter 5, page 71). Psychologist Paul Ekman (2003) has done fascinating work identifying facial cues to differing emotions, helping us to recognize them. In a remarkable comment, he writes:

> Neither empathy nor compassion is an emotion; they refer to our reactions to another person's emotions. In *cognitive* empathy we recognize what another person is feeling. In *emotional* empathy we actually feel what that person is feeling, and in *compassionate* empathy we want to help the other person deal with his situation and his emotions. We must have cognitive empathy in order to achieve either of the other forms of empathy, but we need not have emotional empathy in order to have compassionate empathy. (Ekman, 2003, p. 180)

In this book (and in *Little Learners, Big Hearts*), we use *empathy* in the broadest sense, including all three types that Ekman (2003) describes.

Where does empathy come from in the developing (and developed) brain? The neuroscience discovery of mirror neurons in the 1990s gives us at least a partial answer. The mirror neuron system involves not just one but multiple areas of the brain (Bonini, Rotunno, Arcuri, & Gallese, 2022). It is composed of neurons that "mirror" another's actions, emotions, language, behaviors, and so on (Rajmohan & Mohandas, 2007). Empathy can be triggered by seeing another person's (or an animal's) distress or even joy, arousing emotions such as fear, worry, or happiness in the observer. Seeing someone cry may lead an observer to feel tears forming. Watching children laughing while at play may evoke our own sense of joy as adults.

Obviously, the mirror neuron system has not been the solution to all our problems, especially not to racism and the lack of cultural competence. There are several reasons for this sad fact. For one, the mirror neuron system does not respond in the same way to people who are different physically or culturally as it does to people who are similar to ourselves (Yuhas, 2013). Additionally, as we discuss in chapter 8 (page 119), the neurological roots of bias begin with nonjudgmental categorization of differences among humans and lead to complex forms of discrimination.

In *Little Learners, Big Hearts*, we discuss the idea of empathy across differences (see chapter 6 in that book). We need to recognize that the mirror neuron system, however much it may lead to empathy, does not in itself lead to a classroom of kind, caring young children. While we are born with this system of mirror neurons with the capacity for empathy, it must be, as Ekman (2003) says, "cultivated" (p. 180). Imagine this metaphor: In their earliest months and years, children's minds are gardens. The seedlings of both weeds and flowers are there, waiting to be cultivated. Which do we nurture with water and nutrients? Answering that very question is one of the aims of this book.

HEART+ Takeaways

In conclusion, our exploration of historical biases underscores the value of acknowledging difficult truths while maintaining hope for a brighter future. Drawing from diverse perspectives and insights, early childhood leaders are equipped to confront systemic injustices and advocate for equity and justice in their practice. As we reflect on overlooked contributions and marginalized voices, we are reminded of the necessity to nurture diverse perspectives and promote inclusive educational practices. Moving forward, it is essential that leaders actively engage with communities, support marginalized voices, and work toward a future where all individuals are valued and respected. By embracing the lessons of our past and fostering inclusive environments, we can create transformative change in early childhood education and beyond.

Many educators have been "race conscious" for decades. However, it's evident that our dosage was not strong enough or focused in ways White people have only recently begun to understand. Too many in America have not fully realized the long-term impact of our ancestors' actions. The inhumanity of these actions—including actual and cultural genocide against Indigenous peoples, enslavement of and ongoing violence toward African peoples, and severe exploitation of Brown immigrants and refugees—lives on as both systemic inequities and intergenerational trauma. Leaders can be positive forces in the right direction by acknowledging those historical threads and their own biases, learning about what can change, and then skillfully enacting that change.

All young children have the right to equitable learning opportunities; however, we are currently falling short of this standard. Racism, bias, injustice, and oppression have impacted generations, robbing them of key resources and opportunities. Acknowledging, understanding, and confronting these hard truths head-on is not easy, but it is the first step in working toward a more just and equitable future. We must learn to celebrate our differences, promote our diverse strengths, and work collectively toward dismantling the systems of oppression.

CHAPTER 3

Support for All Students: A Continuum From Multicultural to Antiracist Movements

> Prejudice is a burden that confuses the past, threatens the future, and renders the present inaccessible.
>
> —Maya Angelou

Principle 3: All young children have the right to equitable learning opportunities. It is important to not overlook, negate, or minimize racism.

Efforts to bring antiracist instruction to students have roots in a historical continuum of movements that includes multicultural education, cultural competence and humility, antibias education, and antiracism. Figure 3.1 (page 46) shows a progression of when educators first used various terms. Note that these are not distinct approaches and that embedded within each of the historical approaches are features from earlier trends. Review table I.2 (page 12) for definitions.

Reviewing some of the related movements in education in the United States, we see that in the mid-20th century, starting as early as the 1960s during the Civil Rights Movement (Banks, 2014), multicultural education became an area of concern, and conscious efforts were made to incorporate a course on multiculturalism into teacher preparation programs. Fast-forward a few dozen years

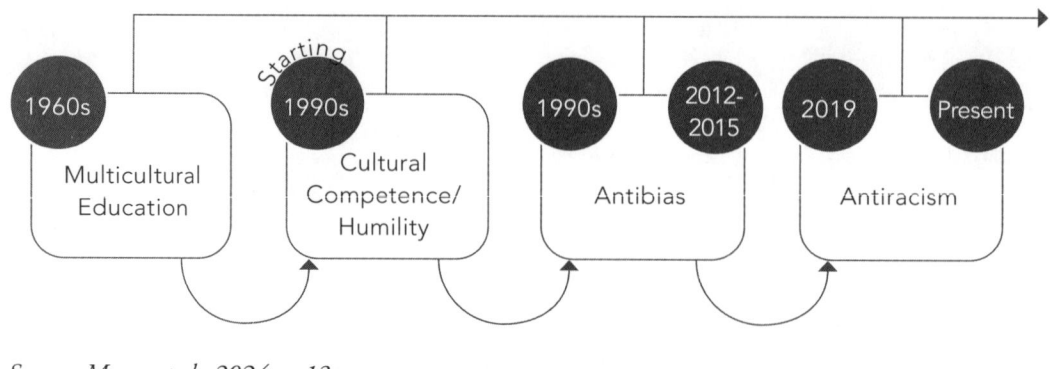

Source: Mason et al., 2024, p. 13.

Figure 3.1: A historical continuum of antiracist frameworks.

to the 1990s, and there was a shift to focus more on cultural competence within multicultural education as educators recognized the importance of learning about the backgrounds and traditions of students coming to the United States from other countries. Asian, African, and Latin American immigration (including refugees) increased dramatically after immigration laws changed in 1965. Many were coming for better economic opportunities and for a better, safer life.

Between 2000 and 2011, Hispanic and Asian populations each grew by 43 percent, the American Indian and Alaska Native population by 18 percent, the Black population by 12 percent, and those identifying as more than one race by 32 percent (Humes, Jones, & Ramirez, 2011). This growth meant that schools were also becoming more diverse (Vittrup, 2016).

In response to this increasing diversity, the No Child Left Behind Act of 2002 acknowledged the achievement gap of BIPOC students and required that achievement data be disaggregated for racial and ethnic subgroups of students. At the same time, some educators began to focus on social justice concerns, moving beyond celebration of differences to a more activist approach to transforming the education of BIPOC students (McDonald & Zeichner, 2009).

Antibias education became a further focus of multicultural education and cultural competence starting in the 1990s. Antibias education is a large umbrella covering not only race and ethnicity but also sex, sexual orientation, gender identity, religion, physical and intellectual challenges, family composition, socioeconomic status, and so on. Some of these are covered under civil rights laws and others are not (Derman-Sparks et al., 2015).

While antibias education originated in the 1990s and continues to be critical, from about 2012 to 2015, educators and many other citizens of all racial backgrounds around the world began to focus more directly on racial and ethnic bias. A series of tragic injustices, such as the horrifying murders of Trayvon Martin in 2012 and George Floyd in 2020, furthered a movement to help people, particularly in the United States, understand our inherent or implicit bias versus overt bias and readily visible racism. These cases gave teachers an opportunity to have meaningful discussions regarding race, equity, and justice. They also reinforced the idea that BIPOC children and adults are unlikely to be treated equally until deeply held perceptions about them are changed.

Then, Ibram X. Kendi (2019) helped refocus the public conversation to antiracism—what an antiracist society might look like and how we can play an active role in building it. BIPOC people and many White people had been defining these issues and fighting against racism for decades, even centuries. Nevertheless, the public conversation had been inconsistent, mostly episodic responses to events in the Civil Rights Movement, urban uprisings, prison injustices, so-called achievement gaps revealed by standardized tests, and so on. A broad-based, widespread, and sustained antiracist movement, with greater White participation, in education, in other fields, and among the general public is expanding. There have also been intense, and in some cases violent, reactions from those who object to the goals of the antiracist movement, seeking to prevent racial progress.

Each of the movements shown in figure 3.1 adds significant value to how we approach equity and cultural competence in classrooms. However, rather than just being part of a progression, each is an important component for creating a sound education that honors the needs of each student and of each educator, with due consideration of race and ethnicity, and antiracist education relies on elements from all the other approaches (see figure 3.2, page 48). Others may see the relationships of multicultural education, cultural competence, antibias, and antiracism differently. For example, William A. Howe and Penelope L. Lisi (2024), in their book *Becoming a Multicultural Educator: Developing Awareness, Gaining Skills, and Taking Action*, focus on multicultural education, while emphasizing the centrality of race and ethnicity within that framework. Different approaches. Same goals.

We realize that some people are privileged and that this privilege has created suffering and barriers to the well-being of others. Elements of all parts of the continuum need to be present to address White privilege and implicit bias—topics that are relevant to antibias and antiracist work in schools, certainly including early childhood education.

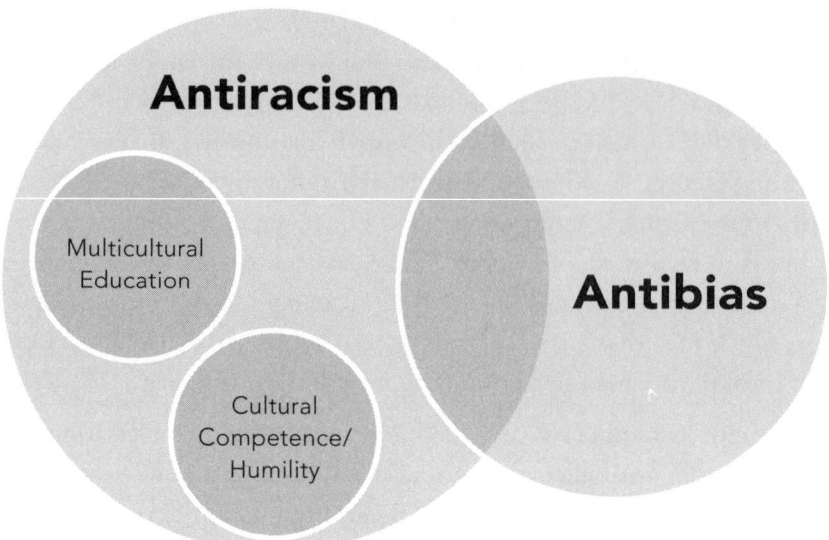

Source: Mason et al., 2024, p. 14.

Figure 3.2: Antiracism education encompasses multicultural, cultural competence, and antibias approaches.

Privilege and Bias

What is *White privilege*? A simple definition would be a system of advantages that accrue to people with White skin, usually without their conscious awareness of how they are being helped. Beverly Daniel Tatum (1999), in her seminal work *Why Are All the Black Kids Sitting Together in the Cafeteria? And Other Conversations About Race*, offers the metaphor of the moving walkway at airports to describe racism. *Active racism*, she says, is walking fast on the moving walkway; *passive racism* is simply being carried along on it, but still going faster than those not on the walkway (Tatum, 1999).

This metaphor equally explains White privilege. Who wouldn't take the walkway if it was available to them? But it isn't available to all. The walkway, originally with a "no entrance" sign, has been around for centuries, with long-term impacts. According to policy researcher Lukas Althoff (2023), "Present-day economic disparities between Black and White Americans are rooted in their ancestral histories, revealing that families enslaved until the Civil War are significantly more disadvantaged than those freed earlier."

The "no entrance" sign and the walkway were designed and built, and have been maintained, by institutions such as slavery; by legalized oppression such as Jim Crow; by residential segregation leading to school segregation (see *Little*

Learners, Big Hearts, page 85); and by embedded conscious and unconscious stereotypes leading groups to be differently valued. If the moving walkway is "for Whites only," as drinking fountains and other public services were just a few decades ago, then not everyone moves ahead on their journey as quickly as those who step on it.

The idea of White privilege should not negate the enormous costs to White people of being born poor with financial and other struggles. Class privilege—including for middle-class, intact Black families—can outweigh the benefits accrued to those in poverty who are White. White privilege is best viewed as systemic, while each of us needs to consider our personal history to see if and to what degree it applies to us.

White Privilege and HEART+

Our HEART+ framework (see chapters 6 and 7, pages 83 and 103) offers a path for those of us who understand we have White privilege to do something positive with it. As you look at the components and consider how to address White privilege, we provide ideas for questions that you may wish to pursue. We recommend you take time to ensure that staff have had experiences in active listening prior to beginning these exercises.

Is it inevitable that White people, and White leaders in particular, have and will always have unearned privileges that have boosted their efforts? *Hope* tells us that the systemic barriers rooted in White privilege can be dismantled, making it possible for the privileges once exclusively available to White people to become accessible to all, creating safer and more secure communities.

First learning about White privilege—if you are White (or very light-skinned and passing as White)—can be a shock and a challenge, especially for White people who have faced many challenges, such as financial barriers. Understanding how class privilege also plays a role does not negate White privilege. It does, however, call for a more nuanced understanding. *Self-education*, particularly for White leaders, is crucial because acknowledging and understanding privilege in the context of oppression is essential. Privilege may engender a blind spot or insensitivity to the struggles and perspectives of BIPOC families and students, leading to a more limited and potentially less empathetic understanding of the diverse realities that exist in the lives of the people the leaders lead. At the same time, understanding one's own lack of privilege (class or otherwise) can become a source of empathy for those struggling against systemic barriers.

Acknowledgment is the tough one. Educating oneself about White privilege through the many available resources is a critical step, but acknowledging its truth in one's own life, for one's own family and community, can be emotionally challenging. It can feel like one's world is turning upside down. "You mean I didn't get here all on my own, without help from society? How dare you say that to me!" This acknowledgment certainly requires stepping out of one's comfort zone (see chapter 11, page 165).

A culture steeped in White privilege is powerful precisely because it is so present and at the same time so very difficult to name or identify. It's the pervasiveness, and sometimes near invisibility, of White privilege that makes it both toxic and hard to dismantle.

For three years in Virginia, Christine sat in monthly Coming to the Table groups that were designed as structured sessions to help adults get in touch with their understanding of race and racism. Participants explored their own awareness of race and bias, using a "talking stick" procedure to have one person speak at a time, without a free-for-all popcorn discussion. This was meant to encourage people to speak openly about their biases and their feelings regarding equity and discrimination. Some members of Chris's group were wrestling with the knowledge that their ancestors had been enslavers, including plantation owners. Over a period of months, members of the group repeatedly discussed the value of openly talking about the shame and personal angst they were feeling as their eyes were being opened to accurate histories of their families' lives.

When it comes to *resolution*, you might ask yourself, "If I can truly acknowledge that White privilege has played a role and continues to do so in my successes, and in those of my family, then what comes next?" Stepping a bit further out of your comfort zone may mean, for example, beginning to talk with other White people about your Whiteness. Since 2020, Jill and Randy have met monthly with three other White leaders of the Social Emotional Learning Alliance for Massachusetts (SEL4MA) in a White accountability group (or WAG). Through their increasingly vulnerable conversations over time, they have delved into racialized experiences and thoughts they had long kept to themselves. Issues of shame and guilt but also hope and joy have brought them closer together and deepened their commitment to antiracism in their social-emotional learning (SEL) and other work, such as in writing *Little Learners, Big Hearts* and this book.

With the HEART+ component of *teaching*, early childhood is the time to lay the foundation of antiracist, culturally aware knowledge, experience, and empathy across differences so that when our little learners are in middle and high school, they are prepared to more fully understand how White privilege operates in their world. Those who protest that we are suggesting early childhood educators discuss White privilege with three- to eight-year-olds are likely looking for ways to shut down, for example, the enlightening approach of windows and mirrors through exploring diverse children's literature (see *Little Learners, Big Hearts*, chapter 7).

We believe our approach is developmentally appropriate, recognizing that many young children's lived experiences raise for them issues of racialized power, a critical aspect of White privilege. As Kerry-Ann Escayg (2019) asserts in her article "'Who's Got the Power?' A Critical Examination of the Anti-Bias Curriculum," young children are beginning to grapple with racialized differences in power. In *Little Learners, Big Hearts*, we share several stories of young children who either assert their racialized power (see the story of Carl and James in chapter 3, pages 81–82) or are disturbed by the power of White people (for example, the police) over Black people (see the story of Iris in chapter 5, page 136). Consciously or not, these young children are learning about the racialized power dynamic in our society.

Holding a grandiose view of oneself or a demeaning view of another—as when White students are given a distorted, limited understanding of BIPOC cultures—leads to actions that perpetuate the damaging delusion that has long existed in the American psyche. This delusion elevates White people above all others, thus continuing the historical impact of White privilege.

Implicit and Explicit Bias

As we say in *Little Learners, Big Hearts*, children aren't born with racialized beliefs. These beliefs are taught and learned by proxy. *Learning by proxy* is the natural process of absorbing ideas and knowledge through exposure to others, which leads to unconscious assimilation. In families that express racism, the underlying tone and racist attitudes toward others can subconsciously influence a child's feelings and attitudes. Racism is transferred in what caregivers say, and don't say, to their children (Weir, 2023). It appears in many guises—at times visible and intentional. Other times, it is subtler and unintentional. Unfortunately, there have been and continue to be pervasive efforts to cover up, ignore, skip over, deny, or dismiss the past, too often led by people in national, state, and local leadership positions.

Research shows that both implicit bias and explicit bias toward other races begin as early as preschool. By the age of three, children in the United States have already begun to associate some racial groups with negative traits, and by age four, they associate Whiteness with wealth and high status (American Psychological Association, 2020). By the time children enter elementary school, they have already been exposed to widespread race-based discrimination (Roberts & Rizzo, 2021). Thus, it is critical that this work begin in early childhood. As 19th century poet Lydia Huntley Sigourney states, "In early childhood you may lay the foundation of poverty or riches, industry or idleness, good or evil, by the habits to which you train your children. Teach them right habits then, and their future life is safe" (Connecticut Women's Hall of Fame, n.d.).

Although most early childhood teachers are caring and compassionate, their implicit or explicit racial bias has been implicated as a driver of racial inequality in education (Dixson & Rousseau, 2005; Warikoo, Sinclair, Fei, & Jacoby-Senghor, 2016). Teachers entrusted with the care of young children are themselves embedded in a society in which racial biases are pervasive and harmful (Nosek et al., 2007).

We cannot examine the pedagogy of antiracist early childhood educators without first acknowledging our own biases. We know that teachers who disregard the impact of their prejudices cannot actively shift biases and dismantle racism. To be effective, teachers must be aware of racism and biases, acknowledge them, and confront them head-on. This is an ongoing process that will need to be repeated over and over and over again.

To guide this process in their schools and centers, early childhood school leaders are responsible for first examining their own biases. We suggest some ways for leaders to go about this personally and individually and also to work with faculty and staff as they make this journey together. It will be uncomfortable. There will be those who are unwilling to engage or cooperate, but nevertheless, this is essential work.

Researchers Amanda Datnow, Mariko Yoshisato, Brandie Macdonald, Jessica Trejos, and Benjamin C. Kennedy (2023) point out:

> Commitments to change involve investing the time, resources, and collective effort necessary to do the ongoing institutional, interpersonal, and introspective work that will—
>
> - Address racism and/or colonial legacies
> - Honor, elevate, and listen to BIPOC voices
> - Confront existing power relations in society
> - Cultivate collective investment and coalition building
> - Foster community engagement
> - Illuminate accountability and truth telling (p. 31)

Datnow and colleagues (2023) also urge educators to "extend collaboration into communities, acknowledging that BIPOC peoples and the practitioners that we engage with are the experts in their lived experiences and in navigating the oppressive systems in which they operate" (p. 35).

We are here to provide suggestions and resources and to inspire school leaders to see that the journey, no matter how uncomfortable, is worth the effort. You can learn about our (the authors') own histories and struggles to understand and deal with racism in our stories in the appendix of *Little Learners, Big Hearts*. We encourage you to read about us and then reflect on your own life.

Racial bias, whether implicit or explicit, is implicated as one driver of racial inequality in education (Dixson & Rousseau, 2005; Warikoo et al., 2016). To uncover and address biases, school leaders should be asking themselves the following questions.

- If many educators in the United States have lower expectations for BIPOC students and lack sufficient respect for their families and cultures, what is the impact on their White-identifying students?
- How does a White educator, whether they be a teacher or an administrator, not project their own privileged biases onto students?
- What can be done?

One critical area that early childhood leaders can begin to examine is differences in their own, and their staff's, expectations for students in their care. As we discuss in chapter 8 (page 119), high numbers of early childhood teachers experience the unconscious, or implicit, bias that leads to lower expectations for BIPOC students. Black educational leaders such as Yvette Jackson (see *Aim High, Achieve More*; Jackson & McDermott, 2012) have addressed the need to have high expectations for all students; yet the message has not been driven home.

What can be done? How can early childhood program leaders address this dangerously negative pattern? What effect does the lack of antiracist instructional practices have on White students and the mindsets they develop that lead to an unexamined sense of White privilege? How can leaders prevent such White teachers from projecting their own privileged biases onto students?

It is imperative for leaders to acknowledge the pervasive issue of racial bias in early childhood education by asking themselves tough questions and actively working to uncover and challenge biases.

Obviously, attitudes must change. In the children's book *Mr. Lincoln's Way* (Polacco, 2001), a Black principal demonstrates his compassionate leadership by giving extra attention to a boy, Eugene, who has used the N-word. Mr. Lincoln recognizes that the young student needs warmth and attention to his passionate interest in birds rather than harsh discipline. A crisis comes when Eugene calls two Mexican immigrant students hurtful names, emulating the hateful bias his father has been spouting. Mr. Lincoln brings him around again by using the image of the wild diversity among the boy's beloved birds.

In *Little Learners, Big Hearts* (chapter 4, pages 124–125), we share the story of Ms. Toni, who patiently and graciously changes a young child's racist attitude gleaned from her parents. Both Mr. Lincoln and Ms. Toni are touching examples of educators who refuse to give up on young children despite the negative racial views they have learned from others. Both the fictional Mr. Lincoln and the real Ms. Toni are Black. If you are a White educator or leader, how would you respond to these students? And even more challenging, how would you respond to the families from whom their children are learning racist views and actions?

Even as we write, we realize that the pain and trauma of those who have been most directly impacted by racism, discrimination, and injustice are very, very deep. As researchers Ali Jawaid, Martin Roszkowski, and Isabelle M. Mansuy (2018) explain, *transgenerational trauma*—the lingering impact of trauma that parents, grandparents, and other ancestors experienced—exists at the cellular level. We are seeking changes in our attitudes, in our ways of being, in our memories, in our present day-to-day lives, and in our visions and plans for our future. And this time, the change must be lasting. We do not need window dressing or the type of change that allows us to "tolerate" our differences. Rather, we seek to embrace and celebrate our differences, knowing that our differences enhance the biodiversity on this planet. If you are like us, you may marvel at the beauty of various skin tones, even as you listen in awe to someone speak another language, or you smile in delight as you taste a foreign food. The complexity of possibilities forms seemingly endless combinations that are ever so enchanting.

The Way Toward Change

Many educators are waking up to the realization that more must be done beyond sincere attempts to implement multicultural curricula and promote cultural awareness. Organizations such as the National Association for the Education of Young Children have established equity-focused positions. NAEYC's (2019) equity statement asserts:

> All children have the right to equitable learning opportunities that help them achieve their full potential as engaged learners and valued members of society. Thus, all early childhood educators have a professional obligation to advance equity. They can do this best when they are effectively supported by the early learning settings in which they work and when they and their wider communities embrace diversity and full inclusion as strengths, uphold fundamental principles of fairness and justice, and work to eliminate structural inequities that limit equitable learning opportunities.

To further illustrate the commitment to equity in early childhood education, ZERO TO THREE (n.d.) also emphasizes the importance of embedding equity, diversity, and inclusion within all aspects of its work; its equity statement declares:

> We recognize that opportunities to grow and flourish are not shared equally by the nation's infants, toddlers, and families due to past and present systemic barriers rooted in racism and limited access to critical resources, such as quality health care services, stable housing, reliable income and employment, and quality child care. Therefore, ZERO TO THREE is committed to helping build a just and inclusive world. We are examining and improving our internal policies, procedures, and culture while humbly committing ourselves to continuous self-reflection and action to address racism.

ZERO TO THREE's stance on antiracist education emphasizes the importance of addressing and dismantling systemic racism from the earliest stages of child development. They believe in the critical role that early childhood professionals play in promoting equity, diversity, and inclusion within their practices and interactions. Like NAEYC, ZERO TO THREE is committed to recognizing and addressing racism, preventing inequitable policies and practices, and fostering environments where every child is valued and supported to thrive.

In this book, we turn to these new statements and standards, aligning with the shared commitment of NAEYC, ZERO TO THREE, and many other early childhood organizations, to combat racism, promote equity, and cultivate nurturing environments for all children to flourish. We have a vision for righting the wrongs of racism and of transforming society, and we believe this transformation must start while children are young—in homes, at childcare centers, and during preK–3 experiences, directed by our school and program leaders. (See Visioning in chapter 10, page 143, and also the additional questions and exercises presented in appendices A and B, pages 253 and 265.)

Some question whether we even need to address our concerns about racial and cultural justice and equity for young children. Yet, as you will see in the chapters that follow, an abundance of evidence underscores the urgency of beginning to address racism during young children's formative years. Your vision, guidance, and action planning as a leader are essential to bringing about these much-needed changes.

The pathway to making an active and conscious effort to dismantle racism and create antiracist early childhood spaces requires elements from multicultural education, cultural competence and humility, and antibias approaches, as well as self-awareness. To disrupt patterns of racism, we need to be able to notice racism within ourselves and our educational programs.

The following are markers you can consider while assessing inequities within early childhood programs. Explore whether these concerns are present in your program.

- Most leadership positions are given to White colleagues, whereas people of color are less likely to be invited to serve on committees and boards, or to take on higher-level duties.
- Teaching staff who are Black or Brown are frequently excluded from outside-of-work activities that White coworkers organize.
- BIPOC teaching staff are not promoted within the organization as frequently as White staff.
- BIPOC students receive more frequent disciplinary actions, resulting in harsher punishment, such as suspension and expulsion. Data from the U.S. Department of Education's Office for Civil Rights (2016) show that Black students represent 16 percent of the population, yet they account for 33 percent of school expulsions. These data hold true for preschool, where it was found that in comparison to White children, Black children are 3.6 times more likely to be suspended (Office for Civil Rights, 2016).
- Classroom materials, including children's books, show predominantly White children and families.
- Students are discouraged from speaking their home language at school.
- Mispronunciation (even after reminders) or mocking of names that are not Euro-American is accepted without challenge.

While school leaders are doing this essential work within their program, they can also be sharing their work with the families and their greater community. School leaders can drive essential changes by planning and implementing informational events for families and the community, providing books and resources to be taken home and shared, and being available for questions, concerns, and probably some pushback. Ultimately, they need to address the question, "What is best for this student?" We believe that in their role as a community leader, the principal or program director must take this opportunity not only to direct equity within their school but also to affect the greater community.

We also need to be realistic: the greatest challenge will probably not be faculty, staff, or even family buy-in—most likely, it will be *time*. Especially among K–3 educators, the most frequent reason for balking at antiracist, culturally competent initiatives or any major change is that they do not have the time, given mandated curricula, contractual obligations, data collection, and every other component of their school day.

HEART+ Takeaways

Bias is not innate—it is learned behavior. When systems around us were designed with racist intentions in mind, their implicit judgments rub off on us and infect our minds, manifesting in our behaviors. In *Little Learners, Big Hearts*, we provide multiple examples of what we can do as educators to add positive experiences for all the students and families we serve. This means that we will have the opportunity to right wrongs, make amends, and help alleviate trauma, including intergenerational trauma faced by students who have experienced racism and discrimination. Many opportunities exist in our day-to-day interactions with students, families, and staff. In the next few chapters, we focus on mindfulness and Heart Centered Learning as proven tools to assist educational leaders in bringing more empathy and equity to the hearts and minds of children and those who serve them.

CHAPTER 4

My Heart to Yours: A Heart Centered Lens

> History has shown us that courage can be contagious, and hope can take on a life of its own.
>
> —Michelle Obama

Principle 4: Heart centeredness can further much-needed compassion, justice, and equity.

School leaders have an obligation, a responsibility, and an ethical mandate to address racism in schools. Yet, the challenges are many. For example, Black preschoolers are less likely to access high-quality early care and education (Barnett, Carolan, & Johns, 2013). Moreover, Black boys are disproportionately affected by expulsions and repeated suspensions (Gilliam, 2010; Gilliam, Maupin, Reyes, Accavitti, & Shic, 2016; Office for Civil Rights, 2016). Early expulsions and suspensions are predictors of various adverse life consequences, possibly due to damaged relationships with schools and teachers and the consequent denial of access to nurturing learning experiences. Unfavorable school attitudes, academic struggles, grade repetition, subsequent suspensions and expulsions, greater risk of dropping out of high school, and increased likelihood of involvement with the juvenile justice system are all pathways to further adversity (Meltzoff & Gilliam, 2024; Zeng, Corr, O'Grady, & Guan, 2019).

Moreover, substantial research confirms that both infants and toddlers, as well as their teachers, show bias and racial preferences (Gilliam et al., 2016). As Nicole Gardner-Neblett and colleagues (2023) report, "Children express bias using race and other cues (e.g., skin color, hair texture, language use) as deciding factors when selecting toys, choosing friends, or predicting the behavior and social values of others" (p. 505). Regarding teacher bias, in a study of 349 preschoolers and 144 teachers, Sarah C. Wymer, Catherine M. Corbin, and Amanda P. Williford (2022) find that race of teacher and child influences a teacher's ratings of disruptive behavior and use of exclusionary disciplinary practices. This is one of several studies indicating that teachers may unconsciously demonstrate bias in the application of disciplinary measures (Gilliam et al., 2016).

In related research, award-winning writer and speaker Ijeoma Oluo (2018) describes a variety of factors contributing to "the disenfranchisement and criminalization of our youth in schools" (p. 126), including the following.

- The racial bias of school administrators and teachers
- Lack of cultural sensitivity to the life circumstances of Black and Brown students
- The pathologizing of Black students
- Zero-tolerance policies
- Increased police presence in schools

Much can be done during a student's early years to counter these influences. As Oluo (2018) explains, the vast majority of teachers are White women with relatively little understanding of the poverty and insecurity facing many BIPOC families. As we discuss in *Little Learners, Big Hearts*, schools with higher numbers of BIPOC students are more likely to have a police presence, with little guarantee that these officers have received adequate antiracist or antibias training (see chapter 8, page 119). In a climate of underlying societal tension and conflict, educators must not only adhere to district protocols and curriculum but also embrace a path of kindness, as suggested by educational psychologist Manya C. Whitaker (2023). Through the incorporation of heart centered considerations, a transformative shift can occur in how school staff and leaders navigate day-to-day encounters, ultimately fostering a sense of well-being for BIPOC students, families, and staff members. In this chapter, we discuss the concept of heart centeredness and how to translate it into actions you can take as a leader.

Heart Centeredness

Adding heart to your school can shift the well-being of staff and students and also contribute to the efficiency and effectiveness of instruction (MacCann et al., 2020). To add heart often begins with deeper observation and attention to factors that one might easily dismiss if they were simply checking off the boxes.

But what does it mean to be heart centered? To answer this question, consider how you feel when you strive to be neutral or analytical, operating from a linear frame versus pausing to consider your emotions. When you add your emotions, you open up to another way of perceiving and acting. This must be done with a balance of heart and head so that one aspect is not overshadowing the other. In yoga, practitioners talk about having a mind-body or heart-head connection—the balance between the two is crucial. With attention on the head *and* heart comes a different awareness of self in time and space.

For leaders in early childhood settings, such as the director of a Head Start program, being heart centered can be exemplified through decision making related to a young child's behavior. Suppose a young child exhibits challenging behavior, and the conventional approach might involve applying strict disciplinary measures or following a linear, rule-based protocol.

A heart centered leader, however, would pause to consider not only the behavior but also the emotional well-being of the young child. They might engage in empathetic listening, understanding potential underlying factors contributing to the behavior. The leader would then collaborate with teachers, parents, and support staff to develop a comprehensive, emotionally supportive plan tailored to the young child's needs.

In this practical example, being heart centered involves recognizing the importance of emotions, empathy, and a holistic understanding of the student's well-being. It goes beyond a purely analytical or rule-based response and fosters an inclusive and compassionate environment within the early childhood program.

Though necessary for all young children, being heart centered is particularly essential for Black and Brown children due to the unique challenges and experiences they may face, including systemic racism, discrimination, and historical inequalities. In essence, being heart centered is a response to the specific needs and experiences of all students, aiming to provide an educational environment that is not only academically enriching but also emotionally supportive and culturally affirming.

Heart centered leadership means that leaders are operating from their hearts—guiding staff, students, and families with a deep sense of compassion. As Ibram X. Kendi and Nic Stone (2023) state in *How to Be a (Young) Antiracist*:

> You do . . . need to move compassionately when it comes to the sufferings and misfortunes of those on the receiving end of racism's varying manifestations. . . . True compassion is feeling with, not feeling for. It's imagining yourself in the position of another and feeling the emotions as though what has happened to the other person is happening to you. And it often requires a level of vulnerability that will leave you feeling exposed and helpless—which is precisely what victims of racism and other bigotries feel All. The. Time. (p. 154)

With a heart centered approach, as Vicki Diane Johnston (2011) says in her book *Heart Wings*:

> Children love to learn. They feel positive interior motivation to self-construction; work in an environment in which they feel safe, confident and interested in the world; and learn in relationship with caring, encouraging, supportive mentors who are leading vital, creative, purposeful lives. It means that children develop in proximity with adults who, while co-creating with the children in a dynamic, interesting space for learning, are sensitive to their emotional state and physical needs. (p. 33)

Now, let's expand that concept to include the adults you work with. Imagine that one of your staff comes to you with a request to take off one day as a mental health day. The rational part of your being could come up with numerous reasons against it: the timing is not good, it would have been nice to have more notice, and there are alternatives that might be easier for you to arrange. However, when you add a kindness element, you might end up with a deeper understanding of your staff's needs and be more likely to be fully supportive, acknowledging to yourself that you and your other staff can shoulder some extra responsibilities to give this staff member needed relief.

Yvette Jackson (2011) describes a principal's mission in adopting guidelines to promote the high achievement and well-being of all students in her book *The Pedagogy of Confidence*:

> The critical player in vitalizing teachers to confidently adopt these practices is a confident and courageous principal. This individual must possess a courage so ferocious that it breaks down the walls of isolation constructed

from the hopelessness induced by repressive policies; courage to support and inspire teachers to advocate for their students; . . . and courage to be a "soul friend" to teachers, students, and parents alike. (pp. 139-140)

To be a *soul friend* is to go beyond rules and regulations to establish a school culture that welcomes and embraces differences.

♡♡ Heart Beaming Exercise

To give you an idea of what heart centeredness feels like, try this heart beaming exercise.

1. Imagine that one of the youngest students at your school is struggling. Perhaps the student is acting out and being disruptive and has already been sent to your office to "calm down" a number of times this year.

2. Read through the following five steps. Then, close your eyes and proceed with the steps.
   a. Put your hands over your heart.
   b. Take a few deep breaths.
   c. Imagine more about the student; what may be happening in the student's life? Continue to visualize what is happening.
   d. Imagine sending love from your heart to the student and the teacher and the classroom. Imagine feeling the love returned.
   e. Continue to breathe deeply and feel the love extending from your heart and coming back to your heart.

3. Reflect.
   a. How do you feel after completing the five steps?
   b. What happened when you added the meditative mindfulness components?

Our personal experience suggests that when we put our hands over our hearts, close our eyes, and breathe deeply, we are connecting the breath with our heart—our source of compassion. With the heart beaming exercise, you have the opportunity to have both a kinesthetic and a visual experience as you see through a heart centered lens (see also *Heart Beaming* [Mason & Banks, n.d.]).

For educators, seeing events through a heart centered lens can add needed perspective. Imagine explaining a troubling event that happened in your school to a neutral party. For example, perhaps one of your new preschoolers who recently immigrated into your country was again crying and screaming for a parent. Or perhaps the problem arose with another student who was acting out and being mean, only this time, your new preschooler was the target of the aggression.

Many of us have comforted many a young child, and we have also handed out consequences for aggressive behaviors. There are some standard steps that typically are effective in providing an immediate consequence. These steps include promptly addressing aggressive behavior to prevent escalation and ensure safety for all involved. They also involve clearly communicating consequences, applying them consistently and fairly, teaching alternatives, and following up with the student to discuss the incident and reinforce positive behaviors. Yet, that effectiveness may be limited. These steps may provide short-term solutions without establishing a much-needed foundation of respect and trust.

Return to the scenario of the preschooler. Put your hands over your heart, close your eyes, take a few deep breaths, and once again imagine that you are sending love to that preschooler, their teacher, and their classroom. Imagine the love also going to the young child who had bullied them. You could even visualize the scenario shifting so that the issues resolve. Stay with your deep breathing and visualization for one to two minutes. Now, open your eyes and consider how your heart may have helped inform your problem solving. Do you notice a shift in your thoughts and feelings? This shift provides some insight into the power of considering what our hearts are telling us.

For each of the scenarios in figure 4.1, consider the differences in perspective that might result from adding elements of mindfulness or compassion to your interpretation of the event. As you look at the Everyday Lens column, consider the multitude of ways you could react or may already be reacting—ways in which compassion may not be central to your response. Then, look at the examples in the Heart Centered Lens column. To understand more about a heart centered approach, you could even pause to use the heart beaming exercise before determining a heart centered response. Such a perspective can be useful for school leaders as well as staff.

In each scenario, a heart centered approach engenders active, compassionate problem solving to arrive at a solution potentially more acceptable to teachers, staff, or families. While none of the scenarios presented in figure 4.1 include a specific reference to a racially related concern or bias, race could be a factor.

Scenario	Everyday Lens	Heart Centered Lens
Teachers and staff are complaining about another day of in-service training.	Options: • Not much can be done. These days are required. • Consider whether all staff need the training. • Talk to district administrators to see if changes might be made or if the situation might improve next year.	What's the underlying cause? Is it the training itself or some ancillary concern? • The training interrupts plans for academic instruction. • Teachers and staff don't find the training helpful. Answers can result in revisions to your approach and greater staff appreciation for the professional development that is offered.
Parents are finding it difficult to meet with staff to resolve discipline concerns.	Options: • Report the difficulty. • Try a virtual meeting. • Consider meeting at another time.	What else can be done? What parental concerns should be considered? Consider trying the following. • Increase text and email communications. • Find more convenient times to meet with parents. • Consider other ways to involve parents. • Ask a social worker to help with a home visit.
Some teachers are reluctant to make accommodations for students receiving special education services.	Options: • Note issues and talk with special education staff to see if they can improve the situation. • Ask the IEP team to meet again and review services.	Problem solve by finding out more about the issues, including whether they are related to the following. • Extra preparation time • Philosophical differences • The need for further guidance about how to implement

Figure 4.1: Heart centered and everyday lenses.

Read the scenarios again, and imagine that staff, families, or students of various ethnic or racial backgrounds are involved.

Heart Centered Learning is about striving for compassion and kindness and allowing the heart to help guide decision making, what we call *heart intelligence*.

The Role of Kindness

Turning around cultural and racial insensitivity, eradicating racial bias and discrimination, and reducing the use of harmful punitive discipline policies that differentially impact BIPOC students will take considerable effort. In the early childhood education arena, the role of school leaders is significant. Leaders have the power to set the climate and tone of the school, reach out to families, ensure that staff get the necessary professional development, and ensure that their school welcomes and supports each student who enters the building (Movahedazarhouligh, Banerjee, & Luckner, 2023).

As significant brain research has demonstrated, the reasons to add kindness to schools and instruction are many.

- First, kindness can help alleviate a tendency for those who have experienced trauma to shift into flight, fight, or freeze mode (Mason et al., 2019; Zelazo & Lyons, 2012). So, kindness may help students be present for instruction, rather than focused on safety—or how to escape danger.

- Second, if a student or family has experienced racism, they are likely to have also experienced a sense of rejection, discrimination, or worse (Smart Richman & Leary, 2009). A kind word, a compassionate conversation, or empathetic listening can shift the dynamic by adding elements of dignity, hope, and respect (see also chapter 6, page 83).

With kindness often comes a sense of warmth and well-being. Consider when someone extended kindness to you. Now check yourself—are you smiling? As international meditation teacher and executive coach Ruth King (2018) indicates:

> Whether we smile inward or outward, the mind and heart respond well to kindness. The power of friendliness has an immediate impact on our body, our mind, and our nervous system. Research tells us that the feel-good neurotransmitters of endorphins, serotonin, and dopamine are all released when we smile. Friendliness and kindness are natural inner resources that can support experiences of freedom from racial distress. (p. 97)

Ultimately, prioritizing kindness in schools is paramount for addressing racial challenges and fostering a nurturing educational space. As a leader, fostering a school culture centered on kindness proves essential for addressing cultural and racial insensitivity, eradicating bias, and reducing harmful discipline policies. Our foundational heart centered approach, combined with acts of kindness, serves as a cornerstone in creating an inclusive and uplifting educational environment.

Kindness gives us a great starting point. Also inspiring is the notion of heart intelligence.

Heart Intelligence

Related to a heart centered lens is the idea of heart intelligence. Joseph A. Mikels, Sam J. Maglio, Andrew E. Reed, and Lee J. Kaplowitz (2011) report that in some instances, adding a feelings component to certain complex decisions results in higher-quality decisions—trusting one's instincts could be a valuable skill. Researchers, including Mikels and colleagues (2011) and Rollin McCraty and Doc Childre (2010), refer to heart-brain coherence and the benefits of mindfulness, yoga, and meditation in increasing the quality of our decisions.

From an antiracist perspective, our heart intelligence will help us make the easy decisions about how and when to extend love, compassion, and support as well as the more difficult decisions about when to have the courage to speak out against bias and racism and how to fight for justice and equity, even when we feel uncomfortable. These are important skills for early childhood leaders. If you are BIPOC, then you likely have many firsthand examples of racism. If you are White, you may recall examples where you saw racism or even played a role in it, however unwittingly. Figure 4.2 (page 68) provides some examples of these polar opposites; can you identify more examples from your own experience?

Leaders, as they expand their heart intelligence, are likely enhancing their emotional intelligence as well (Goleman, 2020). Individuals with high emotional intelligence have a deep awareness of their own and others' emotions and also are able to self-regulate their own emotions. Leaders with high emotional intelligence are also likely to be effective communicators with exceptional abilities to establish and maintain credibility, establish rapport, and handle difficult communications that may include misperceptions and misunderstandings (Zoller, 2015). They are generally more effective leaders.

	Experiences With Racism (Exclusion, discrimination, name calling, harassment, inequity)	**Experiences With Heart Centeredness** (Inclusiveness, kindness, building a sense of compassion and empathy for others)
Seeing it	Movies depict pervasive segregation in schools up until *Brown v. Board of Education*.	Students of various races or from various cultures attend the same school and are educated together.
Hearing it or learning about it in the news	Some political candidates are zealous in calling people names and using racial slurs.	Other political candidates avoid and condemn racial slurs and demonstrate inclusiveness through hiring staff of various races or from various cultures.
Experiencing it firsthand	Someone has been shunned, ignored, or rejected in a community based on their race.	Someone has been welcomed into a new community with hosts who take steps to ensure they are recognized.
Encountering it in your school	BIPOC students are excluded, are more likely to be disciplined, or are bullied.	Staff take active steps to ensure that BIPOC students feel included, monitor discipline referrals to detect possible bias, and teach students about how we are each unique—that some differences (in culture, language, and appearance) are to be celebrated.

Figure 4.2: Experiences with racism and heart centeredness.

Visit ***go.SolutionTree.com/diversityandequity*** *for a free reproducible version of this figure.*

Tools and Actions to Address Equity

To address equity concerns, leaders could turn to a number of tools and approaches. For example, they could provide professional development focused on equity, expand the school library with books addressing racism and equity (see chapter 7 of *Little Learners, Big Hearts*), hold meetings with parents, or even go a step further and empower families to co-lead efforts (see chapter 4 of *Little Learners, Big Hearts*). There is value in each of these.

Teresa A. Byington (2023), early childhood expert and author of *Find the Joyful Leader Within: Banishing Burnout in Early Childhood Education*, shares her approach to fostering continuous self-education and professional development within her team:

> Annually, our team sets individual professional goals centered around diversity, equity, and inclusion. We've united as a team to partake in diverse professional learning experiences. Notably, we successfully completed the Third Option Similarity Training by Miles McPherson, covering crucial topics like identifying blind spots and addressing dishonoring behaviors across six lessons.
>
> We also had team members actively engage in a monthly book club, where they delved into discussions on themes from **Dear Good People** by Dolly Chugh [www.dollychugh.com/newsletter]. Engaging in challenging conversations, our team is dedicated to establishing an emotionally safe environment where every individual can freely express their truth and feel heard. Encouraging self-education, team members share their insights during our regular meetings, fostering an ongoing and healthy dialogue on pertinent topics. (T. Byington, personal communication, January 10, 2024)

In embracing a diverse array of tools and approaches, leaders can effectively navigate and address equity concerns, recognizing the inherent value in each strategy. Yet, if any of these actions is done without the foundational heart centered approach that we recommend, the results are likely to be fragmented. Rather, the overall culture of the school needs to be reviewed with efforts to address racism and center kindness across many dimensions (EAB, 2020).

And as James M. Kouzes and Barry Z. Posner (2023), acclaimed authors who have written extensively about the traits of effective leaders, say, "Genuine acts of caring uplift the spirit and draw people forward" (p. 10). In *The Leadership Challenge Workbook*, Kouzes and Posner (2023) explain five practices of exemplary leadership. Among these is *encourage the heart*. To encourage the heart, they recommend that leaders "recognize contributions by showing appreciation for individual excellence and celebrate the values and victories by creating a spirit of community" (Kouzes & Posner, 2023, p. 99).

The significant change we propose in *Advancing Empathy and Equity in Early Childhood Education* is one that begins with greater understanding of ourselves, our relationships, and our circumstances and moves to compassionate actions to ensure inclusivity, resilience, and well-being. Heart Centered Learning is a necessary complement that will help firmly connect these movements to meaningful interactions in school.

> ### Pause and Reflect
> As you proceed, we urge you to tap into your resilience. Reflect on how you might train your nervous system if you are experiencing cyclical trauma like some of your teachers—BIPOC teachers who may be experiencing racism and bias, some teachers who are underpaid and are working three jobs, and others who are burned-out. How can you bounce back under these conditions? Who can you turn to? What resources do you have to help support others as well as yourself?

HEART+ Takeaways

We all have busy lives, and at times we can lose patience—with a student who is acting out, disrupting class, or bullying others, or even with a colleague who is falling behind. But it is important to pause and consider the situation more holistically. Ask yourself, What's the underlying issue or cause? What is going on at home? Is the student witnessing violence? Neglect? Environmental stress? What else may be happening in your colleague's life? Maybe they are going through a rough divorce or a challenging health episode, or they are taking care of an aging parent. Heart Centered Learning can help you pause and infuse compassion and kindness into your daily routine.

CHAPTER 5

One C to Another: The Five Cs of Heart Centered Learning

Let your face speak what's in your heart. When my kids walk in the room, my face says I'm glad to see them.

—Toni Morrison

Principle 5: Consciousness, compassion, confidence, courage, and community are the underpinnings of equity and inclusion.

Heart Centered Learning is an education approach that focuses less on reaching academic expectations and more on meeting the social-emotional needs of students by providing a framework for infusing five powerful components throughout the school day—the five Cs of (1) consciousness, (2) compassion, (3) confidence, (4) courage, and (5) community (Mason, Rivers Murphy, & Jackson, 2020). As Mason, Rivers Murphy, and Jackson (2020) state, "When teachers and administrators strive for Heart Centered Learning, they place the learners' social-emotional needs at the forefront of their instruction and policies while cultivating a natural safety net within the learning community" (p. 4). This chapter expands on the notion of heart centeredness that we introduced in the previous chapter.

Leading with a heart centered lens, as we explained previously, can add an element of deeper understanding to leader-staff interactions as leaders learn to pause and consider what is happening before they react. Additionally, leaders and staff learn to plan with the heart in mind. For example, when planning a program or activity, a leader would consider the staff and individuals involved and reflect on how recognizing their experiences or relating key elements to their own lives might help create a more inclusive and supportive environment. This approach fosters a sense of pride in their roles and contributions within the organization.

Here is another example: In a community with a high influx of migrants from Latin America, the school leader may invite members of that community to share during the back-to-school night for parents, perhaps music from their countries, and the leader may ask for one or two parents to talk about some aspect of their experience being in that community or in the United States. The leader would then dialogue with the presenter, sharing something about what the countries have in common and perhaps highlighting ways in which parents and families can be involved in the school community during the year.

In this chapter, we address a common thread that early childhood leaders can weave throughout interactions to address racism in its myriad forms, from the overt to the subtle microaggressions that occur in surprisingly diverse ways. With the HCL approach, leaders use each of the five Cs to ultimately achieve compassionate action, build a culture of mindfulness along each stage of the antiracism continuum, and achieve Heart Centered Learning schoolwide.

The Five Cs

Since Christine first developed HCL in 2009, it has evolved as a way to help leaders, teachers, and others in schools center on developing compassion in classrooms throughout the school day. While at any moment, educators can choose to focus on any of the five Cs, there is a hierarchy to follow (figure 5.1).

Although a heart centered approach suggests a need for more compassion, it may also involve a need for greater consciousness or understanding of the views, opinions, and circumstances of those who are involved. (See *Little Learners, Big Hearts* [Mason et al., 2024] and part 2, page 101, of this book.) To get the greatest gains, begin with *consciousness*: awareness and understanding of oneself and one's environment.

Once we are conscious of racism, it is easier to enhance our *compassion* for those who have experienced racism. For school leaders, this means that conscious awareness may include practices to further educators' understanding of racism and discrimination—of past and current injustice. As educators learn, they are then better able to lead.

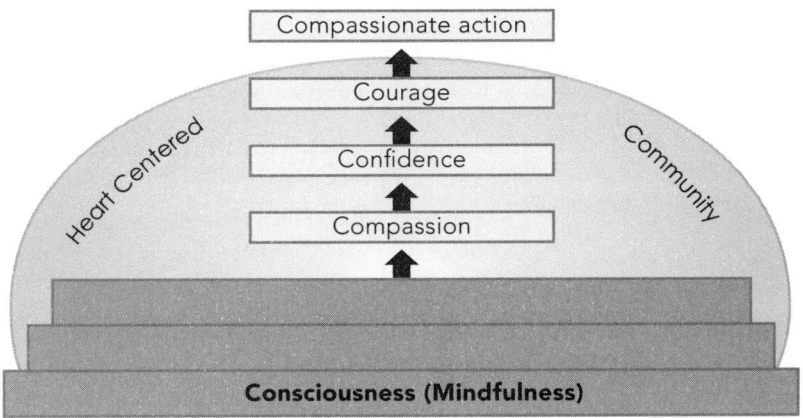

Source: Mason, Rivers Murphy, et al., 2020, p. 16.

Figure 5.1: Five Cs of Heart Centered Learning.

With practice over time, students, staff, and leaders can become more competent in developing and using antiracist, compassionate responses, thereby increasing their *confidence* and *courage*, or their abilities to be antiracist and compassionate under difficult circumstances. For example, we would ideally like to prepare students to stand up for someone who is being harassed or bullied. This may take courage.

With HCL, we suggest that all instruction occur in a heart centered *community* where each student feels a sense of belonging and caring. When administrators put heart centeredness at the core of instruction and of policies and protocols, that consistency can then permeate through the walls of the school to create a larger caring community.

In chapter 4 (page 59), we touched on Yvette Jackson's (2011) idea of soul friends. Let's look at what antiracism might mean for leaders who are soul friends to students, families, and staff for each of the five Cs. As you read through each scenario in figure 5.2 (page 74), imagine how BIPOC students, families, and staff might experience the situation—how their experience might contribute to feelings of inequity and injustice. Imagine as well how you might handle such a situation. As you do this, you can build on the examples we have inserted in the Actions column.

Heart Centered Learning and Antiracism

Let's turn now to how to infuse heart centeredness within a curriculum and community in ways that also address racism and bias for students, families,

Example Situations	The Five Cs	Actions
BIPOC students are opting not to play with dolls of color, and they consistently decline when offered the option.	Consciousness	A leader can conduct professional development sessions, such as exploring the doll test, to gain insights into why students may not be choosing certain dolls. Then, they can provide strategies to encourage celebrating the uniqueness and value of all dolls, thus giving children a sense of love and acceptance not just for themselves but for others.
Members of a marginalized group are targets of hate crimes in your community.	Compassion	Early childhood leaders celebrate various cultures and traditions in highly visible ways, even as they invite families to share their concerns and problem solve with counselors about events in their local community.
Teachers express reluctance to include diverse books in their classroom libraries due to concerns about potential backlash from parents.	Confidence	Early childhood leaders can provide guidance and support to the teachers by offering resources such as recommended book lists. In addition, leaders can send notices home to parents clarifying that the selection of diverse books is a school or center choice. This proactive communication is a first step to help alleviate potential pressure on teachers and emphasize the school's or center's commitment to providing a well-rounded and inclusive learning environment for all students.
Bullying is a problem at school.	Courage	Leaders can emphasize to teachers the importance of actively teaching young children how to be good friends. Encouraging teachers to undergo social-emotional training, utilizing effective tools such as the Collaborative for Academic, Social, and Emotional Learning (CASEL) framework (Jagers, Rivas-Drake, & Borowski, 2018), has demonstrated success in early childhood settings.
You observe a trend among teachers where single mothers of color are experiencing isolation and disrespectful treatment.	Community	School leaders can address the issue by fostering awareness among teachers about the potential bias and stereotyping that may contribute to the isolation and disrespect experienced by single mothers of color. Emphasizing the concept of the "danger of a single story" (Adichie, 2009), leaders can encourage a more comprehensive understanding of each individual's unique circumstances and challenges.

Figure 5.2: Scenarios and actions aligned with the five Cs.

and staff. We do this by beginning with advice from researcher Emma Seppälä (2016), who describes six keys to happiness:

- Live in the moment.
- Tap into your resilience—training your nervous system to help you bounce back from setbacks.
- Manage your energy—learning to remain calm instead of spending time and energy on anxieties and exhausting thoughts and emotions.
- Do nothing—set aside a need to produce and instead engage in fun, idleness, and interesting pursuits.
- Be good—be compassionate—to yourself.
- Show compassion to others. (pp. 11–12)

As you consider how to address racism and bias in your school, we invite you to consider the continuum of opportunities we presented in chapter 3 (figure 3.1, page 46) while you build your inner resilience and foster compassion for yourself and others. Whether considering the multicultural needs of your students, struggling to find the right balance between cultural competence and humility, examining implicit and explicit bias in your school community, or addressing racism head-on, the emphasis on being a leader who is living in a space of vitality will help you be a more mindful, compassionate leader. See also *Leading With Vitality and Hope: Embracing Equity, Alleviating Trauma, and Healing School Communities* (Mason, Patschke, et al., 2023). Let's take up each part of the continuum—multicultural education, cultural competence, antibias, and antiracism—with a focus on heart centered mindfulness.

Heart Centered Mindfulness With Multicultural Education

A heart centered approach for addressing multicultural concerns in your school community begins with a deep curiosity about your own culture. Everyone in the world experiences life through the lens of their own culture, often multiple cultures: values and ways of loving (and ways of hating), educating, and caring for and being a member of a family and community. We cannot learn and truly respect other's culture or cultures without first recognizing, indeed studying, our own. To be a heart centered multicultural educator means going beyond that cultural self-awareness to study the cultures of our students and their families. For leaders, this can involve initiating and supporting cross-grade-level or schoolwide efforts to support cultural awareness.

Heart Centered Mindfulness With Cultural Competence

A heart centered approach to cultural competence begins with self-compassion for what we have not known and still may not know—this is at the core of cultural competence, which is about understanding the cultures of others rather than operating within a paradigm where a dominant culture sets the standards and expectations for learning. Yet, having compassion for our own or other's ignorance does not mean avoiding accountability. Self-blame leads more to anger about, than openness to, human difference. Once we have developed the attitude of cultural humility—or an understanding that learning about cultures is a lifelong process—we can learn how to practice cultural competence with awareness and knowledge of the facts and nuances of cultural variability.

Cultural competence also means being willing to advocate for others while supporting one's own self-advocacy. Moreover, cultural competence for educators implies using culturally responsive teaching methodologies that use "student's customs, characteristics, experience, and perspectives as tools for better classroom instruction" (Will & Najarro, 2022). Teachers and school leaders who are culturally competent do not merely have knowledge; they act on it. Cultural humility and competence include acting as an ally or a partner and never seeing oneself as a "savior" or the one who "needs" to step in and correct a situation when others may be fully capable of doing so. For school leaders, that involves listening to the needs of families, acknowledging their concerns, and asking for their recommendations for what might be done at the school.

Heart Centered Mindfulness With Antibias

In a heart centered approach to antibias, we dig for the courage to name our own biases, whether about gender, sexual orientation, ethnicity, religion, ability, age, occupation, family status, class background, educational level, skin color, physical appearance, body shape or size, citizenship status, or, of course, race. Know that we *all* have some forms of bias (conscious or unconscious), yet we do not have to accept this fact as inevitable or unchangeable. We each absorb social biases without being aware of it. Each of these social biases then privileges some of us over others. When we experience that privilege, we are likely to be unaware, easily accepting it as normal. We must each have the courage to persevere in uncovering any biases that remain (Kendi & Stone, 2023; Nichols, 2022).

School leaders have a responsibility not only to understand their own biases, but to help staff understand their biases, with the courage to examine them in an environment that is safe from *should*s, *ought*s, or ridicule. Once you start to uncover your own biases, it may take several years to undo what you have learned. Shifts in how we see and perceive others often take place over time. What we need is a way to be aware, admit mistakes when they arise, and acknowledge the talents and gifts of others, particularly others who may not have the same skin tone or speak the same language as we do.

Moreover, the journey to understand ourselves and our biases may not be easy. As Washington Collado, former principal and president of the Broward Principals' and Assistant Principals' Association, and colleagues (2021) indicate in their book *Beyond Conversations About Race*, going beyond conversations may involve some tension and discomfort:

> Knowing what discomfort is *not* helps with knowing what discomfort *is*. . . . It starts with a healthy tension. A healthy tension is a push and pull between seemingly opposite opinions, perspectives, concepts, or tasks. . . . Common tensions in conversations about issues of race and racism are logic and objectivity versus gut feelings and subjectivity, candidness versus tactfulness, and realism versus idealism . . . [also,] emotional unease, which typically comes with a healthy tension. There is an edge or disquietude in the air that helps foster disruption. (p. 26)

Collado and his coauthors (2021) explain steps that happen after the tension and discomfort. These include cognitive dissonance—or "holding contradictory beliefs or values simultaneously"—followed by liberation—or perhaps "feeling lighter because you release whatever burdens you" (Collado et al., 2021, p. 27). To assist staff, school leaders can create networks of support when engaging in deep, intense, and authentic work.

Heart Centered Mindfulness Addressing Antiracism

A heart centered approach to antiracism means a willingness to recognize our own implicit racial bias. In the United States, race is among the most sensitive of subjects—for some, *the* most sensitive. Why? Following are some reasons why people might feel sensitive about the presence or possibility of racial bias.

- They feel shame at the United States' history as a nation whose wealth has been built on the labor of enslaved people and underpaid immigrants, stolen Indigenous land, and the suppression of the languages, cultures, and knowledge of Indigenous peoples (Higginbotham, 2020).

- Those in positions of privilege want to believe that all is OK in our great country, that it is good enough, that we have done enough.

- It's common for individuals to attribute their success solely to personal efforts and talents, sometimes overlooking the influence of privileges. Similarly, challenges might be wrongly attributed to perceptions that others receive special consideration or undeserved advantages (Saylor Academy, 2024).

However, implicit bias leads to *microaggressions*—unintended remarks, or acts, rooted in our unconscious racial biases. If we are White, we deeply fear being called *racist*, and this fear may block us from the heart centered awareness and courage needed to bring our unconscious racial bias into our consciousness. School leaders have an obligation to address both antiracism and bias with their staff, even as they help to address microaggressions through school policies that help to remedy the impact of unintended remarks or acts.

A Schoolwide Approach to Heart Centered Learning

What would a holistic, heart informed school or center look like? Mindfulness is, of course, a major part. We will then discuss some promising approaches to consider.

Mindfulness

Mindfulness or, in heart centered terms, conscious awareness of self and others—including our feelings, attitudes, and behaviors—can help guide more compassionate actions. In early childhood centers and schools, principals and other leaders will look for examples of blatant racism, as well as microaggressions and bias—whether it be conscious or unconscious, implicit bias (see chapter 8, page 119).

In *Mindful School Communities*, Mason and colleagues (2020) present examples of how school leaders can further equity in schools, including the following questions that leaders can ask themselves:

- Have I explicitly affirmed and made apparent my belief in the innate potential of all my students for high intellectual performance and personal contribution?
- Have I explicitly inspired, guided, and supported my staff to act on and incorporate into their thinking my expectation that all pedagogy, practices, and opportunities should reflect this belief? (p. 153)

In their chapter on mindful school leadership, Mason and colleagues (2020) go on to ask if leaders have set about:

dismantling practices of disbelief [in the inherent intelligence and strengths of all learners] (including tracking, instructional focus on so-called weaknesses, ignoring strengths and interests, and lack of access to enrichment and personalized learning) that perpetuate marginalizing, low-level instruction that deflates engagement and stymies intellectual development, achievement, and self-determination. (p. 153)

School leaders will also look for opportunities to increase the mindfulness of students and staff. This may occur through formal *mindfulness moments*, or activities such as yoga, breathing exercises, and meditation, all of which lead to greater understanding of self and others. Here are two suggestions.

1. Find time each school day to incorporate mindfulness, meditation, or breathwork. This might include a schoolwide mindfulness exercise that is part of the morning announcements or perhaps a grade-level or team-level exercise that becomes part of the routine that teachers use as students transition back to learning after lunch. For young children, this might involve very simple breaths or perhaps a yoga movement song.

2. Have a mindful moment room or a corner in classrooms where students can go if they feel stressed-out. For young children, this might be a corner that feels warm and cozy with stuffed animals and perhaps beanbag chairs, headsets, and relaxing music.

Use a yoga, meditation, or mindfulness app such as Calm (www.calm.com), Headspace (www.headspace.com), Happify (www.happify.com), or Gaia (www.gaia.com). More recommendations for using apps, books, and other strategies to advance mindfulness in schools are suggested in *Cultivating Happiness, Resilience, and Well-Being Through Meditation, Mindfulness, and Movement: A Guide for Educators* (Mason, Donald, Khalsa, Rivers Murphy, & Brown, 2022).

♡♡ Mindfulness Recommendations

Other recommendations from Mason and colleagues (2020) in *Mindful School Communities* include the following.

- Guide staff and students to "surface their commonalities, recognizing humanity and fostering powerful group affiliations, strong relationships, empathy, and compassion for other cultures" (p. 153).

- Help teachers and students "confidently recognize, appreciate, and build on the value and power of their diverse perspectives and experiences" (p. 153).
- Use a social justice framework to examine social conditions that create suffering for our young children, ensuring the "education builds a practice of freedom . . . rather than a technology of compliance" (p. 160).
- "Find a quiet, peaceful space and meditate daily," "practice intentional breathing," and "make pausing and reflecting (without judgment . . .) a prerequisite to decision making" (p. 162).
- Boost the social intelligence at your school with active listening, thereby building trust, inspiration, empathy, attunement, and teamwork, and developing and influencing others.

Figure 5.3 provides some examples of how leaders can exhibit mindful awareness in a range of settings to create a more inclusive and compassionate environment.

Promising Approaches to Consider

A classroom relying on heart centered, mindful guidelines and activities will find that over a period of a few weeks, the atmosphere of the classroom will shift. As students begin to feel that they are supported and that rules and protocols are fair and kind, we help nurture feelings of safety and trust (see chapter 8, page 119; Mason et al., 2020).

Here are a few examples of promising approaches.

- Jimmy Casas (2017), in his book *Culturize: Every Student. Every Day. Whatever It Takes.*, identifies four key principles.
    a. Expect all staff to be champions for all students.
    b. All staff should expect excellence from each other and their students.
    c. All staff should carry the banner—being a positive light for their school at all times.
    d. Every educator, administrator, and support staff member should be a merchant of hope.
- Casas (2017) goes on to mention a few other keys, including the importance of staff modeling behaviors they want to see repeated, cherishing conversations rather than dwelling on problems, fostering a sense of pride, and ensuring that students have a voice.

Mindful Awareness of Emotions		
The leader is aware that staff are uncomfortable discussing racism and implicit and explicit bias.	**Mindful response:** The leader arranges for opportunities to mentor and coach staff, as well as additional professional development workshops on bias, White privilege, and other such topics.	**Purpose:** It increases staff understanding of their own discomfort regarding bias and racism. Increasing self-awareness is an important step leading to changes in personal behavior and actions that are more supportive of BIPOC students and families.
Mindful Awareness of Sensory Input		
The leader is aware that the school is not a place of comfort for many family members. For example, it has crowded conditions, visual input does not reflect the native countries of many of the families, or food served in the cafeteria does not reflect the culture of many of the students.	**Mindful response:** The leader works with faculty to designate a place and time for family members—perhaps finding a place for an after-school program for families. With faculty and community input, the leader finds images from families' native countries to strategically place throughout the building; the leader works with faculty and the cafeteria food service team to incorporate foods from families' cultures and find ways to include their foods in special events.	**Purpose:** It increases families' sense of comfort and belonging.
Mindful Awareness of Others		
A racial incident has once again rocked the United States, and families are protesting police abuse and discrimination.	**Mindful response:** The leader holds a community meeting—perhaps with other community leaders and family representatives—to discuss the event, to share in grief, and to support changes.	**Purpose:** It increases compassion, goodwill, and the antiracist principle of not remaining silent but rather speaking out against racism and bias.

Figure 5.3: Mindful awareness examples.

- As Sandra Smidt (2020) says in her book *Creating an Anti-Racist Culture in the Early Years*, respect and trust are built through sustained communication; racism itself must be addressed as we help all young children form positive self-identities. Over time, this will involve consciously detecting racism and calling it out when you see it, modeling positive behaviors, and being aware of the critical role that school leaders have in setting the tone and the climate at their schools.

HEART+ Takeaways

When thinking about cultural competence, we must start from a compassionate foundation. Start small—always start with kindness. From there, remember the five Cs and use them to reinforce each other. Gain *consciousness* of oneself and one's environment, enhance your *compassion* for those who have experienced racism, increase your *confidence* in responding compassionately to racist encounters, and develop *courage* to stand up to injustice, all within a heart centered *community* where everyone feels a sense of belonging and well-being. Along the way, mindfulness will be a key tool. It will help you continuously pause, reflect, and learn. As you increase your awareness and understanding, you will increase your empathy and compassion, leading to a more respectful, humble, welcoming, and inclusive environment.

As school leaders implement a mindful, heart centered approach to address racism and bias, here are three keys to remember.

1. Begin with yourself and your mindful awareness of your own implicit and explicit bias (see chapter 8, page 119).

2. It will take time to heal and courage to address racism as it arises. Many have remained silent, perpetuating the harmful impact of racism and discrimination—that cannot continue.

3. To bring a heart centered approach to your school or early childhood center, strive to incorporate breathwork, mindfulness, movement, and meditation at key junctures within your school day. A schoolwide approach will be most successful.

CHAPTER 6

A Deep Dive: The HEART+ of the Matter

there is still time

lift them

—Rupi Kaur

Principle 6: Hope, education, acknowledgment, resolution, and teaching can provide an antidote to racism.

In this chapter, we introduce the HEART+ (hope, education, acknowledgment, resolution, teaching, and local needs) framework, with a focus on hope, education, and acknowledgment. Resolution, teaching, and local needs center on actions that leaders can take and are included in more depth in chapter 7 (page 103). This HEART+ approach to antiracism in early childhood settings begins with verbalizing support, having dialogues, and taking actions that demonstrate commitment to this path of antiracism. This names and affirms hope. In this chapter's epigraph, poet Rupi Kaur (2017) refers to the oppressed in her hopeful call to "lift them" (p. 247). There are many things that we can do to help support others—many small acts of kindness to make a world of difference, particularly for those who have been marginalized or traumatized.

The HEART+ framework is supported by the work of the Center for Educational Improvement with its approach to Heart Centered Learning and mindfulness (chapters 4 and 5, pages 59 and 71), which guides a series of activities to build awareness of self and others, foster compassion, and implement exercises to build skills, confidence, and courage—all within the context of a heart centered community. As shown in figure 6.1, HEART+ and HCL are connected, and HCL is embedded as the core foundation within the framework of HEART+.

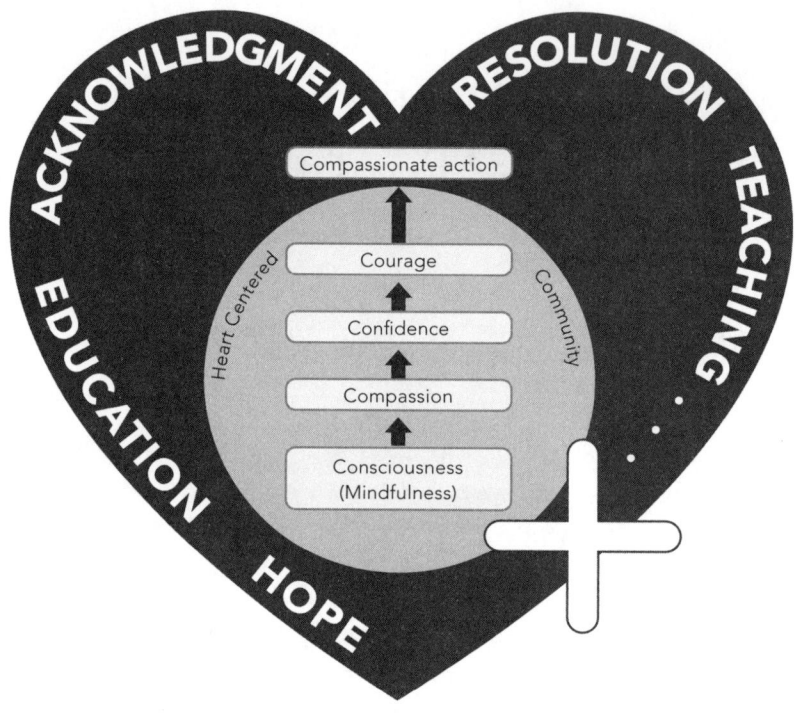

Source: Mason et al., 2024, p. 20.

Figure 6.1: HEART+ and Heart Centered Learning.

Our vision is that each classroom, each school, and each leader will see and acknowledge the almost insurmountable grief of those traumatized through racism, seek a just resolution, and move forward. Furthermore, as leaders, we will demonstrate compassion for everyone and embrace the essential act of forgiveness, enabling ourselves and others to transition from guilt to a path of healing and wholeness.

To guide leaders on a path to more fully supporting equity and inclusion for all people, we developed the acronym HEART+, recommending that leaders consider how to create hope, educate themselves to increase their understanding of bias, acknowledge the detrimental impact of policies and practices reinforcing racism, work toward resolving current and historical imbalances, and lead others so that they, too, grow in their understanding and competence in fully accepting and supporting all people. Figure 6.2 provides a summary.

Hope	To desire with expectation of obtainment or fulfillment; to expect with confidence
(Self-)Education	To focus inward and shoring up our own knowledge
Acknowledgment	To recognize as genuine or valid
Resolution	To resolve; to deal with successfully
Teaching	To help others acquire knowledge or skills
+	To note local conditions that should be considered to move toward healing and wholeness at the local level

Figure 6.2: A summary of HEART+.

We encourage early childhood leaders to adopt a personal mission to delve deeper into these principles for application in their daily interactions with students and families representing diverse cultures. Figure 6.3 (page 86) displays some considerations to guide this work.

The following sections unpack each component of HEART+.

H Is for Hope

Antiracist education is an exercise of hope. This exercise of hope is more than just wishful thinking, which only leads us to passively accept what is. Hope leads us to join the fight to work for a future where there is truly liberty and justice for all. It is the beginning of dismantling systems of oppression, the beginning of freedom and of truth telling. Hope changes our perspective and fills us with possibility and anticipation of how we can work to dismantle racism and systems of oppression in the midst of what seem like horrible and despairing circumstances. Hope gives us a glimpse of how antiracist work is changing early childhood education. It then becomes an invitation to partner with others in working for a better future.

As an early childhood leader, do you actively contribute to cultivating a sense of hope? Consider the following leadership indicators that are present in school communities suffused with hope.

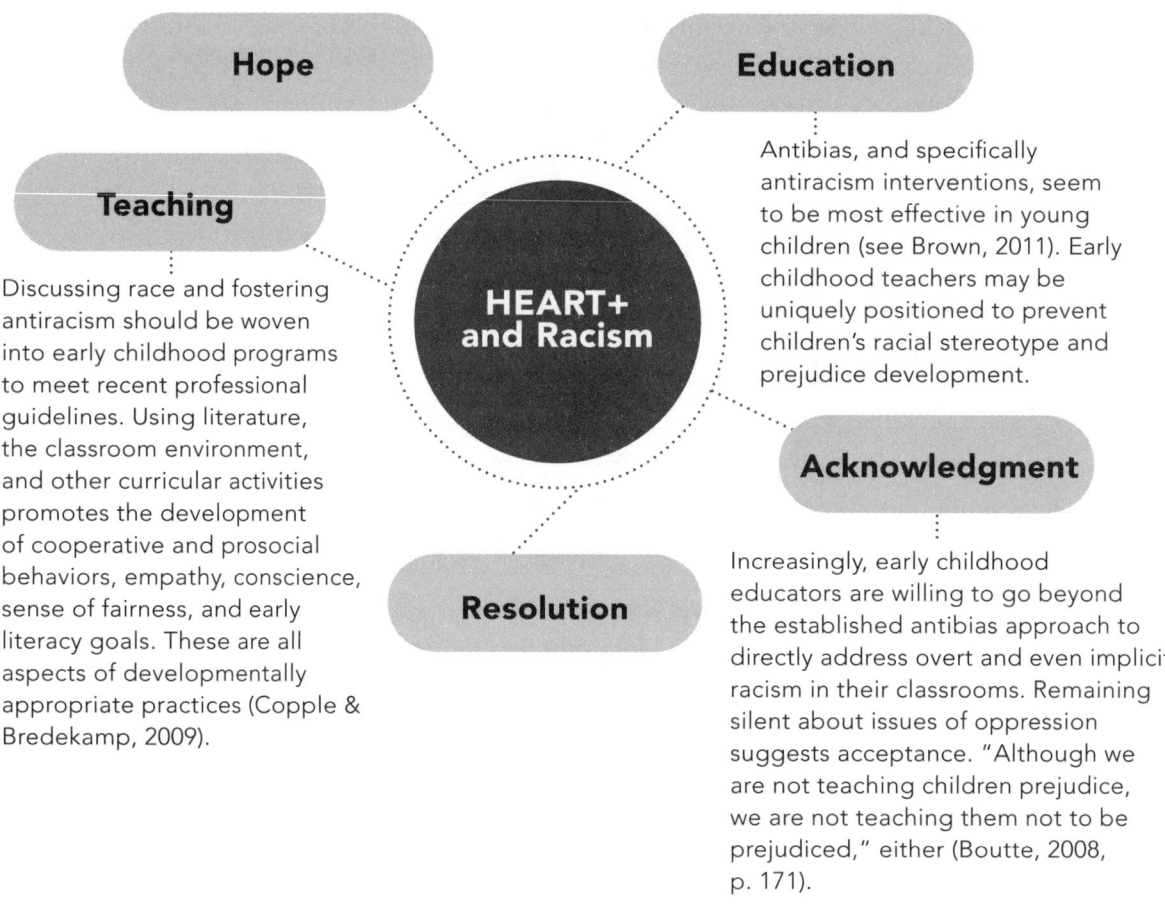

Source: Mason et al., 2024, p. 32.

Figure 6.3: Considerations for exploring HEART+.

- Evidence of a compelling vision for an equitable future that fosters purpose and motivation within individuals and the community
- Inclusive decision-making processes that value diverse perspectives and ensure that everyone feels heard and represented
- Attention to dismantling barriers (cultural and linguistic barriers, accessibility issues, socioeconomic disparities, inadequate professional development, parental engagement obstacles, and so on)
- Staff, families, and students who report feeling safe, loved, and valued

Leaders inspire hope through clearly communicating a compelling vision, recognizing and appreciating team efforts, and empowering individuals to take initiative and contribute to shared goals. Specific activities that may promote hope include the following.

- Regularly share and discuss the center's or school's vision for fostering an inclusive, nurturing, and high-quality learning environment for all young children. Actively seek input from teachers and families to ensure that their perspectives and insights contribute to shaping and refining this shared vision.

- Implement recognition programs to acknowledge and appreciate the dedication and hard work of both teachers and support staff. For example, implement a Spotlight of Success program that entails regular announcements or brief celebrations during staff meetings to highlight individual and collective achievements. These can include accomplishments of both students and staff, fostering a positive and hopeful atmosphere within the center or school.

- Organize events that involve parents, families, and the wider community, fostering a sense of belonging and creating a supportive network. For example, host community gatherings, family fun days, or parent-teacher meetings where everyone can come together to share experiences and build connections.

Leaders who prioritize these actions help the community embrace a strengths-based mindset and antibias actions in the service of hope.

Strengths-Based and Culturally Responsive Leadership

When leaders communicate the importance of the contributions of those they lead as integral parts of the team, it reinforces strengths-based thinking. Strengths-based thinking, as opposed to deficits-based thinking, is a common thread in antiracist practices (MacKee, 2021). Why is this mindset shift so important for instilling hope, and how can leaders make sure both they and those they lead embrace and utilize their strengths? Shifting to a strengths-based mindset is empowering because it centers on what an individual can do to overcome challenges. It is proactive in that it encourages one to see potential rather than dwell on setbacks. When leaders mindfully guide those they lead in reflecting on their strengths, they contribute to building resilience and instilling hope, which is the basis for antiracist environments.

Strengths-based leadership, with its emphasis on recognizing individual strengths, is vital for fostering hope in early childhood by affirming each student's unique abilities and potential. In the context of culturally responsive leadership, aligning strengths-based practices with cultural understanding further ensures that hope is nurtured in a way that respects and values diverse backgrounds. This will help create a positive and inclusive early childhood environment.

Culturally responsive leadership, derived from the concept of culturally responsive pedagogy, involves those leadership philosophies, practices, and policies that create inclusive schooling environments for students and families from ethnically and culturally diverse backgrounds. Common practices include emphasizing high expectations for student achievement; incorporating the history, values, and cultural knowledge of students' home communities in the school curriculum; working to develop a critical consciousness among both students and faculty to challenge inequities in the larger society; and creating organizational structures at the school and district levels that empower students and parents from diverse racial and ethnic communities (Johnson & Fuller, 2014).

Leaders play a key role in fostering a culture of openness and embracing diversity within the educational community. When diversity is framed as a strength, fostered through love, compassion, forgiveness, and hope, staff and students are exposed to various cultural and social groups in a way that begins to dismantle racism and promote empathy and equity in their communities.

Creating a culture of openness instills hope by fostering a sense of belonging and purpose. When teachers feel supported and empowered to embrace diversity, they are more likely to engage in meaningful interactions with colleagues and families (NAEYC, 2019). This not only enhances the quality of education but also cultivates a shared commitment to dismantling systemic biases. Leaders can actively celebrate and showcase the diversity within their educational community, highlighting the strengths that each individual brings. By instilling hope in the potential for positive change, leaders inspire a collective effort toward creating a more inclusive and equitable environment for both staff members and families, fostering a sense of optimism and possibility.

Antibias in the Service of Hope

As we consider the hope in recognizing diversity as a strength, we turn to NAEYC (2020) and its four core goals of antibias education for adults. These goals, which parallel the four core goals for working with young children, are specifically designed to help adults navigate their journey of self-discovery as they work with young children, families, and staff, who sometimes reflect their own experiences and sometimes challenge them. NAEYC recommends that educators meet the following goals:

- **Adult goal 1, identity**—Increase your awareness and understanding of your own individual and social identity in its many facets (such as race, ethnicity, gender, ability, sexual orientation, family structure, and economic class) and your own cultural contexts, both in your childhood and currently.
- **Adult goal 2, diversity**—Examine what you have learned about differences, connections, and what you enjoy or fear across all aspects of human diversity.
- **Adult goal 3, justice**—Identify how you have been advantaged or disadvantaged by the isms (for example, ableism, classism, heterosexism, racism, and sexism) and the stereotypes or prejudices you have absorbed about yourself or others.
- **Adult goal 4, activism**—Explore your ideas, feelings, and experiences of social justice activism. Open up dialogue with colleagues and families about all these goals. Develop the courage and commitment to model for young children that you stand for fairness and to be an activist voice for students. (Derman-Sparks & Edwards, 2020, p. 19)

As leaders embrace these goals and motivate their staff to do the same, they begin to build a sense of hope, a sense of the possibilities for the future.

In the United States, the ideal of liberty and justice for all is an ongoing aspiration that shapes the lives of all Americans. This promise must be collectively and intentionally pursued by those who have the ability to dismantle racism through empowering future generations.

Leaders have the power to make significant positive changes through their ability to inspire and empower their staff and families to see inequity and take an early stand against it. As Ibram X. Kendi (2022) says in his book *How to Raise an Antiracist*, be aware of the "promotion of mistrust" (p. 7), where parents may have warned their children to mistrust another race. A good way to counteract this is to supply parents with information to teach their children about other races or cultures (Weir, 2023).

E Is for (Self-)Education

Engaging in continual self-education is integral for early childhood leaders committed to dismantling racism and fostering empathy and equity in their educational settings. This ongoing learning journey allows leaders to confront and understand their implicit biases, cultivate cultural competence, and implement effective antiracist strategies. As leaders delve into this continual learning journey, a natural progression unfolds, prompting reflection on the challenges and fears associated with addressing racism within the early childhood community.

What challenges or fears do you have about how to address racism within your early childhood community? Three fears that are common to many in this situation are (1) you don't know enough, (2) you may say the wrong thing, and (3) you might not know how to take action (California for the Arts, n.d.). We can overcome fears with knowledge—by talking about them and by becoming more informed.

When you consider the enormity of handling racism in school settings and your own role, what comes to mind? How much do you know about all your staff, your students, their families, their strengths, and their struggles?

Nancy B. Gutiérrez (2021), president and CEO of the NYC Leadership Academy, describes culturally responsive leadership, noting it:

> start[s] with self-reflection. Our personal beliefs and biases—both conscious and unconscious—determine how we see the world, other people, and ourselves: they affect our actions and how the systems we oversee are shaped and function.
>
> To move culturally responsive work beyond yourself, to move toward making systemic change, it's important to then model your beliefs. You can do this by consistently naming equity as a driving force behind your [leadership] actions and decisions.

As you examine what Gutiérrez (2021) says, what comes to mind? What are your personal beliefs and biases? How do you model your beliefs, and where does equity fit in? With these considerations in mind, the book *Finding Your Blind Spots* by author and educator Hedreich Nichols (2022) may be helpful. It's written for K–12 teachers, but its lessons about self-reflecting to acknowledge and mitigate biases can apply to educators of young children as well.

One way to increase your understanding of your own biases around equity is to keep a journal, reflecting on what you observe during the day that has a component of bias or racism. Reflect as well on the good—where you see evidence of cooperation, dignity, regard, and helpful interactions. Reflect on your own role.

Here are three situations that early childhood leaders may experience in which increased self-awareness may be helpful.

1. **Parent complaints about microaggressions:** The early childhood leader receives formal complaints from several parents expressing concerns about microaggressions witnessed or experienced from specific staff members. These complaints have created palpable tension and discomfort within the early childhood center. For instance, a parent may bring forward concerns about a teacher consistently mispronouncing their child's name, which can make the child feel marginalized and unseen. Additionally, they might express discomfort with comments made by staff regarding cultural practices, which can create a sense of alienation and unease for both the child and the parent. These microaggressions, though seemingly small, can have a significant impact on the child's sense of belonging and the parent's confidence in the school environment.

   Why self-awareness is helpful—Heightened self-awareness prompts the leader to introspect on the center's culture, assess their own role in addressing microaggressions, and take proactive steps to foster a more inclusive environment.

2. **Enforcement of antiracist policies:** The leader is responsible for enforcing antiracist policies within the early childhood center, addressing resistance or pushback from staff who may not fully understand the importance of these policies. For example, a leader enforces an antiracist policy that ensures all classroom materials, including books, toys, and learning resources, reflect diversity and inclusion. The leader may face resistance from staff members who are accustomed to using materials that lack representation or perpetuate stereotypes. Addressing this pushback involves educating staff on the significance of diverse representation in early childhood education and explaining how these policies contribute to creating an inclusive and equitable learning environment for all children.

   Why self-awareness is helpful—Increased self-awareness enables the leader to empathize with differing perspectives and facilitate open and constructive conversations that help staff understand the significance of antiracist policies.

3. **Curriculum evaluation for bias:** The leader is reviewing the early childhood curriculum and realizes there may be unintentional biases that perpetuate stereotypes. An example of unintentional bias found in early childhood curriculum could be the overrepresentation of

stories featuring White protagonists or characters from Western cultures, while stories featuring characters from diverse racial or cultural backgrounds are limited or absent. This imbalance may unintentionally reinforce stereotypes and marginalize the experiences of children from non-White or non-Western backgrounds.

Why self-awareness is helpful—Heightened self-awareness prompts the leader to critically examine their own biases and ensures the curriculum review is approached with sensitivity, fostering a commitment to creating a more culturally responsive learning environment.

In the article "Black Boys and Policing: Rethinking the Community Helpers Curriculum," Brian L. Wright (2021), associate professor and program coordinator of early childhood education, and coordinator of the middle school cohort of the African American Male Academy at the University of Memphis in Tennessee, describes in vivid terms the type of education educators need:

> When educators lack the knowledge, skills, and dispositions to infuse the curriculum with readings, activities, and assignments that challenge, nuance, and position and challenge students of color—Black boys in particular—in positive and affirming ways, they (wittingly and perhaps unwittingly) can (re)traumatize these children in disorienting and damaging ways.

Wright (2021) suggests a need to reexamine our curricula—asking who Black boys' community helpers are and who they are not. Black people are five times more likely to be arrested than White people (Srikanth, 2020). Teachers can educate themselves about The Talk that Black parents inevitably have to give their children to prepare them for interactions with police officers (see chapter 4 in *Little Learners, Big Hearts*). Educators also need to acknowledge the differing realities and interactions Black boys and men have with police, the results of which frequently include severe injuries or even death (Edwards, Lee, & Esposito, 2019).

In *Mindful of Race: Transforming Racism From the Inside Out*, mindfulness practitioner Ruth King (2018) writes about racism, saying, "The world's heart is on fire, and race is at its core. Racism is a heart disease" (p. 4). Describing the need for change, she asks:

- How do I work with my thoughts, fears, and beliefs in ways that nurture the dignity of all races?
- How do I comfort my own raging heart in a sea of racial ignorance and violence?

- How do my actions reflect the world I want to live in and leave to future generations?
- How do I advocate for racial justice without causing harm and hate, internally and externally? (King, 2018, p. 9)

In her book, King (2018) also talks about the "messiness" of this work. Learning about racism and how to combat it is not a linear endeavor. The education you experience will be an education of not only your mind but also your heart, and you will need to give yourself time and patience as you learn new ways of interacting with students, staff, and families to honor and promote equity and the cultural strengths of diversity.

As you learn more about antiracism, you may also find that you begin to look at everyday encounters with students and families differently. Your sensitivity will increase.

A Is for Acknowledgment

Recognizing the importance of acknowledging that racism exists even in early childhood environments starts by reflecting on the intersection of your leadership with issues of racism, prejudice, and bias. Racism permeates various aspects of our society, appearing in the news, social media, and politics. Acknowledging racism's presence in early childhood environments can be challenging for leaders due to the discomfort it may evoke and the need to confront systemic issues within their own organizations. Some may fear the potential resistance or pushback that acknowledging racism in early childhood environments could elicit. Acknowledgment will require navigating difficult conversations, challenging ingrained beliefs, and addressing systemic issues within the organization.

In the United States, systemic racism in early childhood settings has manifested in various ways throughout history. During racial segregation, early childhood education was segregated as well, leading to BIPOC students attending inferior schools compared to White students. This continued even after the 1954 *Brown v. Board of Education* decision. Even after desegregation efforts, disparities in funding between schools in predominantly Black and Brown neighborhoods and those in predominantly White neighborhoods persist (Rothstein, 2017). This funding gap directly affects the resources, quality of teachers, and overall educational opportunities in early childhood programs. These inequalities extend to disciplinary practices, with research indicating that Black children, especially boys, face harsher actions, including expulsion, compared to their

White peers, contributing to the school-to-prison pipeline (American Civil Liberties Union [ACLU], n.d.).

Implicit biases among educators can further exacerbate disparities in early childhood settings, influencing interactions and educational experiences for BIPOC students (Chin, Quinn, Dhaliwal, & Lovison, 2020). Acknowledging how these and many other historical and institutional factors, combined with contemporary practices, contribute to systemic racism in early childhood education is essential. This awareness empowers early childhood leaders to foster equitable policies and work toward dismantling barriers that hinder the development and success of all young learners.

Attaining this awareness requires leaders to commit to cultivating mindful self-awareness. This self-reflection must be based on the acknowledgment of the history of racism and its impact on early childhood education. For us, as early childhood leaders, engaging in mindful self-reflection on biases and recognizing how assumptions and privilege impact the environments we lead is a process that requires self-education to ground our acknowledgment in truth. Acknowledgment should lead to a commitment to change a personal bias or behavior toward a particular person or group of people. With mindful awareness, we increase our understanding of and compassion for what people have experienced, including the impact of transgenerational trauma.

As Suzanne Bouffard (2022) writes in an article on equity for *The Learning Professional*, "Discomfort is a common and often necessary part of confronting inequity and redressing it. . . . It can be tempting to revert to defensiveness and dismissiveness instead of listening to understand" (p. 5).

In addition to expressing empathy and sharing personal stories, leaders can create a supportive environment by encouraging open dialogue and providing opportunities for reflection. This may involve implementing equity pauses, or establishing clear guidelines for when to pause conversations to ensure everyone's voice is heard and respected (Bell, 2022). Leaders can guide discussion toward critical self-reflection by posing four questions. These questions encourage staff to consider their own actions and behaviors within the context of equity and inclusion.

1. How might we be contributing to the problem?
2. Where are we making assumptions, engaging in deficit thinking, or blaming others rather than taking a critical eye to our system and our own practices?

3. What forces in our system may be contributing to the inequities we see?

4. How might our current processes, practices, or beliefs be contributing to inequity?

It is important to recognize how systems have developed in ways that perpetuate racism. Moreover, acknowledgment involves understanding how racism has impacted, and continues to impact, leadership in early childhood settings and working to dismantle these systemic biases.

Broken Systems—or Are They?

Even as we understand the trauma of the past and the present, our systems are also set up to promote inequities that impact many of us and those in our communities. Merriam-Webster defines *systemic racism* (n.d.) as "the oppression of a racial group to the advantage of another as perpetuated by inequity within interconnected systems (such as political, economic, and social systems)." Systemic racism goes beyond individual acts of prejudice or discrimination and encompasses institutional and structural barriers that create and maintain racial disparities. Consider the following early childhood system concerns. We further discuss these and related inequities in chapters 13 and 14 (pages 209 and 221).

- **Low pay for early childhood teachers:** Early childhood educators earn one-third of what elementary teachers make (McLean, Austin, Whitebook, & Olson, 2021).

- **Lack of government support for universal prekindergarten:** This can have a disproportionate impact on BIPOC families. Without government support for universal preK, BIPOC families may face limited options and affordability challenges in accessing high-quality preK programs. This can lead to educational inequities, as young children from disadvantaged backgrounds can miss out on crucial early learning experiences (Morrissey, 2020).

- **Costs and fees for credentials and certification (associate's, bachelor's, and other advanced degrees):** The costs and fees associated with obtaining credentials and certifications can be significant. These costs include tuition fees, textbooks, supplies, transportation, and potentially housing expenses. The financial burden imposed by these costs can create barriers that shut out many aspiring BIPOC educators (Lambert, 2024).

- **Lack of consistent standards, similar to those of Head Start and NAEYC, for multicultural, antibias, and antiracism learning:** Both Head Start and NAEYC are initiatives that have emerged in response to the recognition of historical inequalities in educational opportunities and tend to be forerunners when implementing educational standards for multicultural, antibias, and antiracism learning. However, the development of these types of standards often involves input from experts and policymakers, and historically, there has been limited representation from BIPOC communities in these political processes (Thigpen & Reinking, 2021). This lack of representation has led to standards that do not adequately address the unique needs and perspectives of these communities, which perpetuates the historical oppression they have experienced.

How can leaders move beyond these issues to acknowledge what is needed? The following actions are a good place to start.

- Listen seriously to diverse groups and perspectives. Learning about systemic barriers racially marginalized people have faced and how these lead to legitimate anger and grievances can make uncomfortable but necessary conversations possible.
- Instead of judging differences by your own cultural standards, pursue dialogue filled with diverse perspectives.
- Lobby for policies, representatives, and leaders that understand and work to address these systemic barriers.

Leaders can also review the following pledge and see if it can be added for those who are committed to eradicating racism (First Church Stratford, n.d.):

> In pledging against everyday racism and discrimination, I will—
> - Speak up when I hear or see racial injustice
> - Question and identify bias when I see it
> - Be mindful of my own behaviors
> - Promote and appeal to higher principles
> - Set limits on what is said or done around me
> - Seek help and help others to work against racial injustice
> - Remain vigilant and persistent

How Acknowledging Racism Impacts Early Childhood Leadership

We cannot acknowledge that which we do not know. While much has been written about antiracism in the early childhood classroom in the United States, how to create antiracist early childhood spaces remains a highly contested topic. More often than not, early childhood leaders and programs think or teach about race, bias, and equity from two approaches: (1) the colorblind approach that assumes "we are all one" and the color of one's skin makes no difference to our lives and (2) the celebration of differences approach (Doucet & Adair, 2013). These stem from beliefs that, if leaders simply encourage their educators to teach love, kindness, and fairness only, then they do not need to point out or discuss racial bias or inequalities with our young learners. While love, kindness, and fairness can go far, there is more work to be done.

We want to express our acknowledgment to all leaders of early childhood programs for the journey you are on: for your invaluable contributions, your deep commitment to young children, and your caring concern. Recognizing your innate power, we urge you to consider the transformative impact you can have on the early childhood education system. As you contemplate this, one powerful avenue is to begin by fostering a culture of inclusivity within your programs, emphasizing diversity in hiring practices, and ensuring that the teaching staff reflect the varied backgrounds and experiences of the young children they serve. By prioritizing cultural competence training for educators, leaders can create an environment that celebrates differences and dismantles biases and racism.

In addition to creating an inclusive atmosphere, early childhood leaders can advocate for policy changes at both the institutional and systemic levels. This involves actively engaging with local education authorities and policymakers to address funding disparities, promote equal access to quality early childhood education programs, and implement measures that counteract discriminatory practices. By amplifying the voices of marginalized communities and advocating for equitable resource distribution, these leaders contribute to dismantling systemic barriers that perpetuate injustice in early childhood education. In doing so, they not only shape the immediate experiences of the young children in their care but also work toward creating a more just and equitable future for the early childhood education system as a whole.

Don't expect yourself to be perfect, but take heart that it will get easier with practice (National Education Association [NEA] Center for Social Justice,

2020). There are a variety of resources we recommend to guide the work of acknowledging racism and promoting antiracism in the environment in which you lead. Figure 6.4 summarizes the highlights from each of these.

	A Key Idea	Additional Points	Value Added
"10 Principles for Talking About Race in School" (NEA Center for Social Justice, 2020)	Encourage self-expression and give students the right to take a pass and not share.	What barriers to learning might some students be experiencing? How can you address these?	Be aware that race is a social category and power dynamic. Therefore, it is critical to address more than equity—to also focus on justice.
"Addressing Race and Racism Head-On in the Classroom" (Gonser, 2021)	Make sure students see themselves in your classroom (books and posters).	Bring in examples of success from various races across curricula—for example, in science, studying inventors of different races.	Feature stories of resistance and resilience, not just about the injustices.
Stamped: Racism, Antiracism, and You (Reynolds & Kendi, 2020)	A succinct history of Black people in the United States and ways to discredit racist notions. This is a good review for teachers.	This source includes a teacher's guide and ideas for research and book clubs.	This source includes discussion of environmental racism and other resources such as digital platforms.
"10 Resources for Teaching Anti-Racism" (Fingal, 2023)	Developed by the International Society for Technology in Education, this references digital resources and key challenges for teachers in terms of equity and access.	This source provides links to foundations such as the Obama Foundation and the 1619 Project.	This source includes links to sites focused on learning for justice, racism and poverty, history, and culture.

Source: Adapted from Mason et al., 2024.

Figure 6.4: Summary of benefits of antiracism resources.

As we have come to learn, some early childhood centers can have an undercurrent of hatred, discrimination, and racism. Some early childhood leaders become silent perpetrators of racism, not necessarily acting and speaking in ways that support it, but still, perhaps unwittingly, perpetuating it. It's essential to remember that when they make decisions for other people's children without seeking to understand their perspectives, valuing their voices, and acknowledging their challenges, leaders effectively silence those people. Embracing an inclusive approach involves actively listening to and speaking up for the diverse perspectives of both young children and their families, creating an environment where every voice is heard and valued in the decision-making process. Perpetuating racism in the early childhood classroom can occur unintentionally through certain behaviors exhibited by leaders. Here are a few examples.

- Implementing policies that disproportionately affect students from marginalized communities
    - An example of implementing policies that disproportionately affect students from marginalized communities in early childhood education could involve the requirement that families provide their own transportation for their children. In affluent neighborhoods, where families have multiple vehicles or easy access to reliable transportation services, this policy may not pose a significant barrier. However, in lower-income neighborhoods or areas with limited public transportation options, families may struggle to meet this requirement, leading to decreased access to early childhood education services for children from marginalized communities.
    - Similarly, in a Head Start program, a policy mandating that family members attend monthly meetings during work hours could disproportionately impact families with caregivers who have inflexible work schedules or multiple jobs, making it difficult for them to fully participate in their children's education. Such policies inadvertently widen the opportunity gap and perpetuate inequality in access to quality early childhood education.
- Ignoring the problem of teachers committing microaggressions in the classroom and with their students' families
- Disproportionately disciplining BIPOC students
- Not promptly and appropriately addressing racially insensitive incidents

These actions or behaviors may not be overt or intentionally discriminatory but will have a negative impact on the environment. Creating antiracist early childhood environments requires that the often subtler forms of racism be intentionally addressed. If they are not, the unintentional and subtle ways that racism is part of early childhood will continue to have a negative impact on young children, especially those from BIPOC communities.

HEART+ Takeaways

Hope, (self-)education, and acknowledgment are powerful tools to fight racism. When we acknowledge that racism exists and is built into many systems around us, we can allow ourselves to become curious and learn more about how things came to be, and how we can change them moving forward. By turning inward, we can begin the ongoing journey of self-education—confronting and understanding our implicit and explicit biases as well as effective strategies to start to address them. Hope then energizes, motivates, and compels us to act to resolve current and historical injustices and teach and invite others to join in and work together for a more equitable future.

PART 2

Practical Steps Leaders Can Take

CHAPTER 7

HEART+:
A Focus on Action

Our path of healing is active; it is an adventure, an experience. As we heal, we are venturing forward, often into places previously unknown in our minds and hearts.
—Valerie Brown, Marisela Gomez, and Kaira Jewel Lingo

Principle 7: Eradicate racism by speaking up and carrying justice in your heart.

In chapter 6, we provided detail supporting hope, (self-)education, and acknowledgment, the first three elements of HEART+. In this chapter, we turn to examine actions that school leaders and others can take for resolution and teaching regarding equity and justice.

R Is for Resolution

How do we even begin to resolve the pervasive impact of the trauma of racism? And what are the implications for early childhood leaders? Theologian and activist Jim Wallis (2017) suggests:

> We must replace fear with facts when it comes to public discussions about immigrants, refugees, Muslims, racial diversity, and national security. . . . Multiracial truth telling about race as America's original sin is urgently

> needed. . . . We need to clearly affirm diversity as a gift, blessing, and great opportunity. (p. xx)

U.S. representative and political and civil rights activist John Lewis, in *Let Freedom Ring* (Giuliano, 2020), states:

> We have not come to that point where we recognize the dignity and worth of every human being. It is still a struggle. . . . We still have a distance to go before we create one family, one house, the American house.

We can gather from these perspectives that much work remains to be done on an individual and societal basis. However, with a humanitarian focus and fortitude, we can move forward in this journey to dismantle racism in early childhood education. The solutions to racism are many, and they begin with each of us. As we lead, we must be aware that racism exists within the hearts, minds, and actions of many in the United States. Explicit racism is frequently conveyed through bullying behaviors, while unconscious racism may be conveyed in subtler ways. Both forms are damaging and can be found among people of diverse backgrounds throughout our communities.

Here, we discuss the need for action and then provide a protocol for responding to everyday incidents of prejudice, bias, or stereotyping.

The Need for Action

While we often think of resolution in terms of widespread actions for systemic changes, early childhood leaders are frequently faced with situations that require immediate actions contributing to the resolution of racism and lack of cultural competence. For example, bias-related teasing, peer aggression, and bullying among students, and at times among staff, are not uncommon. In chapter 6 of *Little Learners, Big Hearts*, we suggest ways that social-emotional learning can help reduce these negative behaviors. In chapters 6 and 7, you will find children's books that can lead to valuable classroom discussions.

From the perspective of early childhood leaders, what actions support the resolution of bias-related teasing, peer aggression, and bullying among young children? Embracing HEART+ does not mean simply brushing off these behaviors as "normal." Rather than intervening directly, it may mean guiding the classroom educators through several steps. Specifically, leaders can remind them to acknowledge the targeted child's feelings, while also discussing how to build empathy in the child who has teased or aggressively harmed, through words or behavior, another child. Suggestions of specific books with classroom discussion will support the teachers. If the behaviors persist, direct intervention may be called for.

Beyond that, school leaders can review, with the full staff, policies related to teasing, peer aggression, and bullying. Such policies should require that the families of both the target and the aggressor be informed. This is especially important when the behaviors are repeated, but even a single serious episode may call for talking with the families.

Moreover, using a heart centered approach, we recommend considering the root causes behind the aggression, and what can be done to reduce bullying through building a sense of well-being, connection, and support for positive social behaviors, as we help aggressors learn more about and practice self-regulation, or the ability to monitor and modulate emotions, cognition, and behaviors (Berger, 2011). However, for young children, the self-regulation focus is more on helping children understand what they may want (or feel) and then what they can do other than strike out, bully, or be aggressive. (See also self-regulation in reference to Head Start curricula in chapter 12, page 185.)

In her two decades of facilitating trainings with educators on issues of bullying and harassment, Randy was frequently asked about how to address some staff members bullying others. Often there was a racial, ethnic, or sexual dynamic in this adult bullying. In this context, resolution would require reinforcing staff anti-harassment policies and being knowledgeable about employment laws. From a HEART+ perspective, resolution could also mean learning about and directly addressing any racial bias or cultural misunderstandings that may have triggered the negative attitudes and behaviors within the staff.

Microaggressions

Microaggressions are more nuanced than bullying but nonetheless damaging. Assuming that BIPOC families are "less" in some way is damaging. Sometimes a perpetrator of a microaggression is not even aware that the microaggression has occurred. One common example of a microaggression in an early childhood setting is when teachers and staff members mispronounce or consistently misrepresent students' names. This can send a message that their names are difficult, less important, or not worthy of being pronounced correctly. In young children, this can create a sense of otherness and contribute to feelings of alienation or shame.

Orinthia recalls stories told by a friend whose children consistently experience this microaggression and who decided to homeschool them during their early years because of this and other race-related issues. Her name is Christelene Horton, and she is from Saint Vincent and the Grenadines. Her husband, Jah-Sahrrang, is of Korean, Mexican, and Native American descent. They relocated their young family when both received prestigious positions at a major university. They have four children: Jah-Ikaiah, Kaiori, Saichiko, and Jai-Muid. After countless times correcting educators and asking them to correctly pronounce their two older children's names, Horton and her husband decided it was not worth the fight. Horton said it would be better to keep the children at home because "open racism was the norm in school" (C. Horton, personal communication, 2010). As a result, they both homeschooled their children for over ten years. They only enrolled them in public school in 2021, after accepting government positions and relocating to a different state.

Another common example of a microaggression that may occur in leadership is assuming that a teacher whose primary language is not English is less capable or proficient in communication, even if their professional qualifications and skills are strong. This assumption may manifest as overlooking their contributions or underestimating their ability to effectively engage with parents, colleagues, or students, perpetuating stereotypes based on language proficiency rather than recognizing the teacher's unique strengths and qualifications. The solution? Leaders should first prioritize implementing cultural competence training for themselves and their teams to raise awareness about microaggressions and promote understanding of diverse backgrounds. Additionally, fostering open communication and establishing clear policies against discrimination set the foundation for creating an inclusive and respectful environment.

Institutional racism will shift as each of us individually shifts our mindset. The attitudes of those who surround young children—the fear, hatred, and microaggressions that are directed toward them and their families—are impactful. Leaders need to be aware of this and take steps to stop the microaggressions, hate, and fear, even as they seek to provide safe, nurturing environments that will aid with the mind-body-spirit healing many students need.

Resolution starts at the individual level and also includes systemic policies. Early childhood leaders can prioritize creating policies that ensure fair compensation, providing professional development opportunities to nurture diverse leadership, and implementing inclusive hiring practices. Leaders should actively support students by fostering a culturally responsive environment, acknowledging the contributions of BIPOC individuals in curricula, and continuously assessing and adjusting instructional approaches to ensure inclusivity.

Resolution involves concern for the *other*. As Martin Luther King Jr. said, others may have asked, "If I stop to help this man, what will happen to me?" But the Good Samaritan came by and reversed the question: "If I do not stop to help this man, what will happen to him?" (Rose, 2020).

Being consciously aware of inequities, having concern for the other, ending microaggressions, and providing safe, nurturing environments will all build toward resolution, mindset shifts, and movement beyond the status quo. Here are a few things you may be able to do even as we realize that there is a larger societal role.

- When you see or hear something, say something: "We can all learn to speak up in the face of bad behavior. If enough of us do so, we can change the culture to one of courage and action instead of silence and inaction" (Cabral, 2020, p. 39).
- Implement and enforce comprehensive antibullying policies, and provide training for teachers on recognizing and addressing bullying.
- Use resources like *Little Learners, Big Hearts: A Teacher's Guide to Nurturing Empathy and Equity in Early Childhood* with your staff. Resolution in your early childhood environment will also come through fostering open communication, promoting a culture of respect and empathy, and implementing proactive strategies to address conflicts and challenges. By prioritizing these elements, you contribute to a harmonious and inclusive learning environment for both educators and young learners.

Remember, resolution only applies if leaders take action.

Speak Up at School: A Protocol for Responding to Everyday Prejudice, Bias, and Stereotypes

Note: School leaders may also be able to adapt this protocol for professional development with staff.

Imagine the following scenario.

> *You find yourself at a loss for words. A staff member has uttered something insensitive or displayed racial bias, leaving you uneasy or frustrated. You feel the need to address it, but articulating a response is challenging.*
>
> *In an effort to steer clear of sounding authoritative or shaming the person who misspoke, you might find yourself resorting to a forced, strained, or awkward silence. You've observed this behavior before from this staff member and several others.*

How do you, as a leader, prepare to speak up? This protocol includes two main steps; following those, we discuss the notion of calling out versus calling in.

Step 1: Prepare Yourself

Assess your readiness. Consider the following questions.

- "Am I aware of my own strongly held beliefs, political positions, emotional responses, and biases and how they influence what I say and do?"
- "Am I the type of person to speak up against bigotry?"
- "What actions am I taking to create an environment that is safe and welcoming for *all* staff, students, and families?"
- "What actions am I willing to take in creating an environment that is safe and welcoming for everybody in my center or school?"

Be aware of your tone and temperament.

Remember the following.	Refrain from the following.
• Remain calm and thoughtful.	• Shaming
• Don't react with shock.	• Humiliating
• Be firm.	• Using humor
• Be confident.	• Name calling

Assess the risks of speaking up. Some of these may include the following.

- You may be branded too sensitive, too "politically correct," too *something*.
- You may feel the sting of rejection.
- You may fear retaliation by hostile colleagues or families.

So, consider your safety in any moment when you may choose to speak up.

Know the dynamic of change. Consider the following questions.

- "Is now the best time?"
- "Could I handle this in a different way, later, that would be safer?"
- "Is there someone I trust—a colleague, a peer, a mentor—to whom I can speak about this to help me prepare for the next time it happens?"

Try not to let unwarranted fear silence you, but do consider the consequences of speaking up—and weigh them against the consequences of not speaking up.

Step 2: Practice Basic Strategies

There are four basic strategies you can use: (1) interrupt, (2) question, (3) educate, and (4) echo.

Interrupt

Speak up against every biased remark—every time, in the moment, without exception. Think about what you'll say ahead of time so you're prepared to act instantly. Here are phrases you could use.

- "I don't like words like that."
- "That phrase is hurtful."
- "That offends me."
- "I don't find that funny."
- "Using that word does not help others feel safe or accepted here."

These phrases allow you to speak up against bias in a simple, straightforward manner. Sometimes, they may open a dialogue. Other times, they simply allow you to challenge bias and take a vocal stand against it.

Question

Ask simple questions in response to hateful remarks to find out why the speaker made the offensive comment and how you can best address the situation. Here are some examples.

- "Why do you say that?"
- "What do you mean?"
- "Can you tell me more?"
- "What point are you trying to make by saying that?"
- "Did you mean to say something hurtful when you said that?"

Questions place a burden on the person who made the remark. When faced with having to explain a "joke" or support a stereotype, people sometimes find themselves at a loss. Following up with a simple request to find out more information can help the person move toward a deeper understanding of why the remark is offensive. If the speaker falls back on something such as, "C'mon, I was just being funny," then you can use one of your ready interruption responses, such as, "I don't find that funny."

Educate

Explain why a term or phrase is offensive. Encourage the person to choose a different expression. Hate isn't behind all hateful speech. Sometimes ignorance or lack of exposure to a diverse population is at work. Here are some suggested ways to start.

- "Do you know the history of that word?"
- "Using that word does not help others feel safe or accepted here."
- "What message does this send?"

Education happens in schools. So, it's a natural fit to wrap education around moments of bias or stereotyping.

Echo

If someone else speaks up against hate, thank them and reiterate the antibias message. One person's voice is a powerful start. Many voices together create change. Try, "Thanks for speaking up. I agree that word is offensive, and we shouldn't use it."

If several people speak up to reiterate the antibias message and thank the person for speaking up, there will be a positive ripple effect.

Calling Out Versus Calling In

Calling out and *calling in* both have their places when speaking up. "Calling in approaches the situation in a nonconfrontational way that assumes best intent. Calling out is a direct reproach that addresses an intentional pattern and should be used as a last resort" (Nichols, 2022, p. 30). Calling out will likely feel hard and uncomfortable but is necessary in the following situations.

- When we need to let someone know that their words or actions are unacceptable and will not be tolerated
- When we need to interrupt to prevent further harm
- When we need to hit the pause button and break momentum

Here are some suggested phrases to use.

- "I need to push back against that. I disagree. I don't see it that way."
- "That's not our culture here. Those aren't our values."
- "OK, I am having a strong reaction to that, and I need to let you know why."

Calling in provides for multiple perspectives and encourages paradigm shifts. It focuses on reflection, not reaction, and is best for the following situations.

- When there is an opportunity to explore deeper, make meaning together, and find a mutual sense of understanding across differences
- When we are seeking to understand or learn more
- When we want to help imagine different perspectives, possibilities, or outcomes

Here are some suggested phrases for calling in.

- "What sort of impact do you think your [decision, comment, or action] might have?"
- "How do you know it is working?"
- "How did you [decide, determine, or conclude] . . . ?"

T Is for Teaching

As leaders, we have a responsibility to support our teachers in developing antiracist pedagogy and subsequently guide them in teaching approaches that actively contribute to dismantling racism. Antiracist pedagogy is not simply about the incorporation of racial content into courses, curriculum, and discipline. It is also about how one teaches, even in courses where race is not the subject matter. Once we have gained insight and knowledge, acknowledging the injustice that has occurred, and have set about resolving concerns, we then need to support our teachers in a way that begins to dismantle racism. Their daily interactions with students and staff in the building should promote a sense of equity, justice, and fairness for young children. Antiracist teaching goes beyond lesson plans, curriculum, and instruction, although these are also critical components.

Anitra Gallegos, a principal at a middle school in Colorado Springs, Colorado, serving largely Hispanic students with 79 percent free and reduced lunches, explained the importance of early childhood education on the *Cultivating Resilience* podcast, cohosted by Christine:

> As a practitioner and leader of students in the secondary level, I must say that to encourage and inspire our children to be empathetic, resilient, and individuals who operate with an equity lens, this work must begin in elementary. Our children are moving through critical developmental stages that are devoid of these principles and practices. Building principled people

must start as soon as they can interact with each other and content. Waiting too long to engage our students in this work creates gaps in their mental health and social-emotional wellness. And for some, that gap is enough to swallow them and their future! (Mason, Kohler, & Ikler, 2023)

The focus of a leader's role in shaping antiracist early childhood teachers involves providing educators guidance, resources, and support in developing and implementing antiracist pedagogy. Following are ways leaders can actively support antiracist pedagogy among their teachers.

- **Facilitate reflective practices:** Promote reflective practices by creating spaces for teachers to critically examine their own biases, assumptions, and teaching methods, fostering a commitment to ongoing self-awareness.

- **Offer support for difficult conversations:** Provide guidance and resources for navigating challenging conversations about race and equity, fostering an environment where teachers feel supported in addressing these topics with students.

On a daily basis, teachers navigate numerous spontaneous decisions and numerous interactions with their students. In *Little Learners, Big Hearts*, we delve deeply into how teachers' interactions can actively contribute to the creation of antiracist environments. We specifically explore what antiracist teaching entails through the three domains of the Classroom Assessment Scoring System (CLASS) Teaching Through Interactions framework (Teachstone, n.d.b)— (1) emotional support, (2) classroom organization, and (3) instructional support—and provide practical guidance for a teacher's journey toward becoming an antiracist. This comprehensive exploration can serve as a valuable guide, offering educators actionable insights and strategies to incorporate antiracist principles within their daily interactions and thereby foster an inclusive and equitable learning environment.

+ Is for Local Needs

The last part of HEART+ is the +, which we have included as a reminder that whatever you do needs to be adapted to your local environment and to build HEART in a way that considers the local context. In some situations, you may need to focus more on hope; in others, you may want to work on self-education. And as you consider the local context, you may also want to broaden your understanding of the history, trauma, and current strengths and needs of students and families in your local community.

For example, if you are serving a school with a large Cambodian population, you will want to understand the culture of the Cambodian communities, how they are dealing with their historical trauma of genocide and refugee camps, how they have adjusted to being in the United States, and what could help improve their sense of belonging, welcome, and invitation to participate in school activities. If your center, family childcare environment, or preschool includes photographs, cultural symbols, and music from Cambodia, that could be a step in the right direction.

To provide another example, imagine you're the community engagement leader in your early childhood center, and families express concerns about diversity and inclusion. In response, you might organize a community forum to discuss the importance of fostering an inclusive environment for young learners. During the discussion, you address possible concerns from parents about how these topics are approached in early childhood education, ensuring transparency and collaboration in shaping policies that support an antiracist agenda and contribute to a more inclusive community.

Pause and Reflect

- How can the HEART+ approach be tailored to your specific local context?
- How can you deepen your understanding of the history, trauma, and strengths of the students and families in your local community?

Navigating HEART+ in Early Childhood Education: Reflections and Considerations

Sonya McElroy, a birth-to-five specialist in Anne Arundel County, Maryland, explains the importance of HEART+ in an interview with Orinthia.

Hope

Orinthia: How do you infuse hope into your daily interactions with students and families, fostering a positive and inclusive environment?

I prioritize infusing hope by modeling intentional and positive language, particularly when interacting with students and discussing them. I'm committed to shifting language to avoid unintentional negative connotations. This demonstrates a deep understanding of the impact that words can have on perceptions and attitudes.

By choosing to describe children as leaders and clear communicators, you not only highlight their strengths and abilities but also contribute to fostering a positive and empowering environment. This approach not only influences the way students perceive themselves but also shapes the way others perceive and engage with them.

My intentional use of language not only instills hope but also promotes a culture of positivity and empowerment. This mindset has the potential to inspire and uplift students, encouraging them to embrace their strengths and reach their full potential.

Education (Specifically Self-Education)

Orinthia: How do you promote ongoing self-education and professional development among your team to ensure a continuous and evolving understanding of antiracist principles in early childhood education?

Most recently, I have engaged in purposeful professional learning and self-education to ensure a safe and nurturing learning environment for early intervention home visits. This includes employing culturally competent practices to recognize implicit bias that may be communicated through both verbal and nonverbal means. By guiding providers to scrutinize their long-standing values and beliefs, they become better informed about the various ways bias can manifest in interactions with students and families, both positively and negatively.

Specifically, when serving students who identify with a different race, providers should be equipped with the skills, knowledge, and behaviors to intentionally choose communication styles that convey shared values, respect, and acceptance. This proactive approach ensures that interactions foster a positive and inclusive environment for all involved.

Acknowledgment

Orinthia: In what ways do you encourage acknowledgment and celebration of diverse cultures within your educational community, creating an atmosphere of inclusivity?

It is imperative for me that the acknowledgment and celebration of diverse cultures within our educational community are not episodic but rather a way of life. For that reason, I am deeply passionate about fostering student, family, and community voice. By sharing the power dynamic with all stakeholders, I provide everyone with the ability to speak for themselves, fostering shared environments and experiences where individuals can be their authentic selves—the greatest form of celebration, acknowledgment, and value.

Additionally, I recognize it as my responsibility as a leader to ensure that our educational community can see themselves reflected in the leaders and providers across our organization. To achieve this, I have dedicated intentional time to creating a recruitment and hiring process that guarantees a diverse pool of candidates, representing the community we serve, including individuals from different races, genders, ethnicities, religions, and lifestyles. This approach aims to cultivate an inclusive and representative leadership team that resonates with the diversity of our educational community.

Resolution

Orinthia: How do you address and resolve instances of bias or discrimination, promoting a sense of resolution and growth within the early childhood setting?

In our early childhood setting, I address and resolve instances of bias or discrimination by implementing various restorative practices, ensuring that social justice remains a central focus in handling conflicts. Restorative practices involve creating open dialogues around sensitive issues, aiming to gain perspectives and insights into personal values and experiences that inform different belief systems.

Through sitting side by side and engaging in a process of reality interrogation, all stakeholders are provided with a safe and brave space to interrupt the cycle of selecting data to reinforce a belief system steeped in bias. This approach encourages curiosity as a possible catalyst for change. For instance, if someone has had a negative experience with an individual from a particular background, they might develop a fear of all people from that background, influencing their interactions. The person may not be a threat, but past experiences can lead to reactions as if they are being threatened. Interacting in a safe and brave space allows individuals with biases to intentionally interrupt this cycle, introducing new data to initiate a shift in their belief system.

This proactive and restorative approach is deeply ingrained in our culture, not only reducing instances of conflict but also cultivating upstanders within our community. By fostering an environment that encourages dialogue and understanding, we contribute to creating a community that values diversity, empathy, and social justice.

Teaching

Orinthia: Can you share practical methods for integrating antiracist teaching practices into your daily interactions with students, fostering understanding and empathy?

The primary practical method for integrating antiracist teaching practices into our daily interactions with students involves employing an inside-out series of activities. These activities are designed to facilitate a deeper understanding of one's personal values and beliefs, exploring where they originated, how they developed, and in what ways they manifest in interactions with people across various dimensions of difference. This method serves as a powerful tool for providers to assess their cultural knowledge, enabling them to recognize their role in the dominant culture and comprehend the impact on those not in the dominant culture.

These practices, grounded in the inside-out approach, contribute to instilling a value of diversity that is reflected in all processes, procedures, and policies across the educational community. Moreover, this approach ensures that all providers and leaders possess the ability to manage, adapt, and certify culturally competent and responsive practices. By fostering understanding and empathy for all, the inside-out approach becomes an integral part of our educational culture, promoting an environment that is inclusive, respectful, and actively works against racism.

HEART+ Activity: Graffiti Walls

Post six large sheets of poster paper, each including one of the HEART+ components (hope, education, acknowledgment, resolution, teaching, and local needs), on the walls of the room where staff are meeting. Provide each staff member with a large marker and stacks of sticky notes. Staff are invited to circulate around the room and add their thoughts, their questions, or their concerns about HEART+ as it relates to your school and surrounding community. They can add pictures or text.

Give staff about twenty minutes to circulate and write their notes, and then invite them to stand beside the poster that is a priority for them.

At the end of the twenty minutes, staff share out notes from each poster with a discussion of needs and concerns to be addressed in upcoming activities.

Interview reprinted with the permission of Sonya McElroy.

HEART+ Takeaways

Approaching early childhood through a HEART+ lens provides us an opportunity to *see anew* or to *begin again*. As we do this, we are also weavers, weaving threads of race consciousness into our early childhood centers and classrooms, creating a new cloth. When you see bias and injustice around you, speak up! Be kind, but call out microaggressions, prejudice, and stereotypes and how they negatively impact others. Then go a step further and take the time to teach others. Create space for and promote reflection. Invite people to critically examine their own biases, assumptions, and behaviors. Be patient and compassionate, but push others to have difficult conversations and learning experiences. Additionally, take your local context into consideration. Embrace your unique situation—strengths and challenges alike—and work within these parameters. Educational leaders have a unique obligation and opportunity to promote antiracism and advance cultural competence for their local school communities.

CHAPTER 8

So Many Wrongs to Right: Antibias Education

> The more willing you are to step out of your comfort zone, the more comfortable you feel in your life. Situations that used to arouse fear and nausea become easier to relax in. On the other hand, if you stay in your comfort zone all the time, it shrinks.
> —Pema Chödrön

Principle 8: Address implicit and explicit bias through conscious awareness of your own beliefs, taking steps to build a sense of safety and connectedness.

In this chapter, we focus on leading for equity and social justice, particularly on recognizing explicit and implicit biases, with strategies for addressing these with staff and families in the early childhood education context. To understand what we mean by explicit and implicit biases, including how they differ, it is helpful to first sort out some other terms we often hear used, particularly in discussions and writings about racism.

Louise Derman-Sparks, Debbie LeeKeenan, and John Nimmo (2023), in the second edition of *Leading Anti-Bias Early Childhood Programs*, describe the importance of focusing on young children as we pursue a vision for equity:

> Anti-bias education supports children in developing a fuller, truer understanding of themselves and the world, and strengthens their sense of themselves as capable, empowered people. They have a better opportunity to develop curiosity, openness to multiple perspectives, and critical-thinking skills. They can also develop their ability to resist and reject the harm that prejudice, misinformation, and discrimination can do to their sense of competence and efficacy. (p. 12)

Antibias education stands to right so many wrongs, but it will take time. Time, and leaders. Schools need leaders who are adept at transformational leadership—leadership for meaningful change. They need leaders who can balance the ins and outs of sharing leadership, listening and articulating, establishing standards and expectations, forming a compassionate school culture, and advancing the best talents and skills of staff and students. They need leaders who also understand the depths and multiple dimensions of bias and discrimination. They need leaders who are interested in helping young children develop positive self-identities so that no matter their race, ethnicity, skin color, or language, they feel a sense of pride, even as they feel safe and supported.

As we see it, equity is a social justice issue, and antibias education led by dedicated and informed proponents is key to bringing about this justice. We are not alone in that view. For example, Michelle Salazar Pérez (2020), professor of early childhood studies at the University of North Texas, describes the injustice inherent in the construct of race:

> Race has been a way to discriminate, colonize, exoticize, and position individuals and entire communities as the Other. The injustices that have manifested from racialized discourses are countless, from denying people of color basic needs to limiting access to equitable education. Within early childhood, children of color are dominantly positioned as deficit and "lacking," often being measured against a universalized White standard, whether through development, at-risk, or achievement gap measures. (p. 20)

Leadership for social justice will require leaders who can work with others, focus on helping students develop positive identities, and have both a vision for what can be and a realistic understanding of what must be acknowledged.

Early childhood researchers Margaret R. Beneke and Caryn C. Park (2019) explain how, in a curriculum and classroom focused on social justice, teachers help students become comfortable with an array of human differences, including both complex and nuanced differences, which young children are apt to discern. Within this space, teachers also establish a compassionate culture where students feel safe exploring differences and similarities. As they mature, their understanding, their questions, and their need for support and guidance will shift (Banks & Banks, 2010; Beneke & Park, 2019; Kuh, LeeKeenan, Given, & Beneke, 2016). Thus, it is essential to understand the impact of bias on young children as well as how to reduce it in school communities.

> ### *Pause and Reflect*
> Confronting bias is not easy, and it is likely to lead to discomfort. Leaders need to be prepared for this. In these pages, we provide some strategies, such as expressing empathy (see pages 136–137). Leaders could also work on reframing the issue to look at the situation from a different perspective, or they could consider whether the conflict might be *productive*—that is, necessary to move forward and beyond current bias. Consider situations in which you have encountered conflict. Would one of these strategies be useful? If so, which one, and why?

Bias and Its Impact on Young Children

As young children mature, they absorb messages about the construct of race from many sources, including family, teachers, peers, and media. These messages contribute to the gradual development of an internalized racialized identity even as they begin to understand humanity. In essence, each person's racialized identity is both imposed externally and constructed internally (Derman-Sparks & Edwards, 2021).

Catherine Haslam is a researcher at the University of Queensland in Australia investigating the cognitive and social consequences of trauma and disease. Haslam and colleagues describe the importance of positive social identity: it "provides the platform for a sense of psychological connection to other ingroup members in ways that build (or undermine) trust and support; self-esteem; control and agency; and a sense of purpose, direction, and meaning" (Haslam, Haslam, Jetten, Cruwys, & Steffens, 2021, p. 641).

Ethnic identity is another important aspect of developing an awareness of self. According to Patrick Camangian and Stephanie Cariaga (2022):

> Knowledge of self refers to the state-of-mind where students come to know their own personal and cultural identity, history, and place in society. Research on positive ethnic identity development is useful here in that it simultaneously recognizes historically marginalized social groups in a racist, sexist, and homophobic society and explores culturally affirming navigation strategies inside of the existing social system. (p. 908)

Teachers can help students gain a positive sense of self during their early developmental years, including development of language to discuss their identities, and answer their questions in an atmosphere of interest, delight, and accurate information (Derman-Sparks & Edwards, 2021; see also chapter 4 of *Little Learners, Big Hearts*).

As students learn more about themselves and others, teachers may see discomfort or shame, and these feelings might appear in subtle ways. For example, they might manifest as colors used in making or describing a self-portrait. As Louise Derman-Sparks and Julie Olsen Edwards (2021) indicate:

> When children make self-portraits or family drawings, sometimes they choose colors that do not correspond to their actual skin, eye, or hair coloring. It is important to ask the child about these choices. Sometimes they indicate discomfort or shame about the child's actual coloring. It is useful, in a conversational tone, to ask the child to talk to you about the portrait. If the coloring is playful (some children paint themselves with rainbow colors or bright green) and the child seems relaxed, you need not take further action. If the child seems uncomfortable describing the colors in the portrait, it is useful to watch for additional indicators of confusion or self-rejection. If you are concerned, observe the child and make a plan for what you can do to strengthen the child's identity. Check in with other staff about what they have observed and speak with the child's family about what they want their child to know about racial identity and how you can support the child's positive sense of self in the classroom. (p. 39)

As leaders review the various components contributing to positive racial self-identities as well as an antibias or antiracist school community, it is likely they will encounter positive acceptance and willingness to learn but also conflict and disequilibrium. As Debbie LeeKeenan explains:

> I have become more comfortable with conflict and the disequilibrium that is inevitably part of anti-bias work. I try to figure out where people with whom I disagree are coming from. I do not expect quick solutions, and can

sit with the tensions while working towards finding the common ground and third space. (as quoted in Derman-Sparks, 2016, p. 33)

Others write about gaining patience as they work with people who are first hearing about antibias issues and may be reluctant to explore them (Derman-Sparks, 2016). Chapter 2 of *Little Learners, Big Hearts* provides discussion of the role of educators in students' development of positive racial identities and agency (Darling-Hammond & DePaoli, 2020). It is necessary for educators to confront biases for this to happen.

In "Foundations," the first part of this book, we write about bias primarily, and more generally, in the context of our Heart Centered Learning and HEART+ approach. Here we delve more deeply into different types of racial and cultural bias, their roots, and leaders' responsibilities to address them. Before we go further, let's take a moment to define explicit bias and implicit bias and how they differ, consider how to measure bias, and consider the impact of bias on teacher expectations.

Explicit and Implicit Bias: How Do They Differ?

Stereotypes, prejudice, explicit bias, implicit bias, xenophobia—how are these terms different from each other? And how do they help us untangle the roots of racism and cultural incompetence? These terms are interwoven, some being more basic and then leading to others. Neuroscience tells us that the root of bias is the developing brain's need to categorize by noticeable, usually physical, differences (Amodio & Cikara, 2021). This is our human way of making sense of the infinite variety of differences, especially but not only human differences, in the world into which we are born.

After the brain categorizes, it often moves on to generalizing, sorting phenomena into categories that then take on negative or positive values. This then leads to stereotyping. Stereotypes can be positive—most likely for one's in-group, for those who are "like me and like my family or community." They can also be negative—most likely for those defined as being in the out-group, those unlike one's own group, however each is defined.

From stereotype to prejudice is too easy a step. Prejudice develops when one adds the belief that one categorized group's qualities are better or worse than another's (leading to internalized prejudice). Xenophobia, a fear of or discomfort with any group of people from a different culture, religion, or country, is a specific but wide-ranging example of prejudice. Past history and present events show us that political and other leaders can easily manipulate people with xenophobia. Religious intolerance for those with different beliefs is most clearly demonstrated by the anti-Muslim and anti-Semitic attitudes of too many people in the United States. One way to understand this is to look at hate crime statistics.

According to a Brookings Institution report, there was a 32 percent increase in hate crimes against Muslims in and after 2016 (Byman, 2021). Anti-Semitic hate crimes have been on the rise since at least 2013 (Morales Pinales, 2023). FBI statistics show that in 2022, more than half of reported religion-based hate crimes in the United States were anti-Jewish (U.S. Department of Justice, 2023). International conflicts in late 2023 and continuing into 2024 have certainly increased both anti-Muslim and anti-Semitic hate crimes across the United States (Deliso, 2023).

Discrimination occurs when prejudice is expressed through actions, especially when there is a power differential, as there often is between groups distinguished by race, color, gender, religion, national origin or ethnicity, sexual orientation, and so on.

In *Blindspot: Hidden Biases of Good People*, Mahzarin R. Banaji and Anthony G. Greenwald (2013) write:

> Explicit bias is infrequent; implicit bias is pervasive. . . . Early twenty-first century Americans display low levels of explicit (overt) race prejudice in survey studies. This is a well-documented and striking reduction from the overt expressions of prejudice in studies that were done fifty to seventy-five years previously. Even though present-day questionnaire studies show that most Americans now express egalitarian racial attitudes, uses of the IAT [Implicit Association Test, see page 127] have revealed that approximately 75 percent of Americans display implicit (automatic) preference for White relative to Black. (p. 208)

Banaji and Greenwald (2013) go on to say, "Recent survey studies show that only 10 to 15 percent of Americans openly express prejudice against Black Americans" (p. 209). Given the negative racial dynamics evident since the 2016 U.S. presidential election, we might wonder if that percentage is higher than it was when *Blindspot* was published in 2013. We cannot statistically measure such change without repetition of the same surveys, but research on the impact of negative racial speech has shown:

> If politicians increasingly feel at liberty to use *explicitly prejudiced rhetoric* during their campaigns, then the mass public is likely to take cues from such behavior, leading them to express more prejudice themselves. The result would almost certainly be increasingly heightened inter-group tensions which pose a threat to political and social stability in the United States. (Schaffner, 2020, italics added)

Another post–2016 election study showed that people who already held biased beliefs felt emboldened to express them (Müller & Schwarz, 2020). From what we know about how young children "catch social biases" (Skinner, Meltzoff, & Olson, 2017), an increase in "explicitly prejudiced rhetoric" is likely to affect how they—young White children especially—view and act toward children who look different from them and their families.

Rebecca A. Dore, Kelly M. Hoffman, Angeline S. Lillard, and Sophie Trawalter (2014), in research conducted with 159 five-, seven-, and ten-year-olds, found evidence supporting racial bias in children as young as seven and ten years of age. This research looked at ten situations involving perception of pain, such as biting their tongue and hitting their head, and had children compare their own perceived pain to the degree of pain of other children. At age seven, there was a slight racial bias; however, by the time children were ten years old, there was a strong bias.

It is not hard to understand explicit bias through, for example, the frequent use of the N-word as a derogatory term (by people other than Black people themselves, who may defang the term by making it an expression of in-group closeness). Comments such as, "Colored kids are just stupid—why even try to teach them anything?" are not as uncommon as one might hope, particularly in the sacrosanct space of the teachers' lounge or at conferences. Randy heard such comments in the teachers' lounge when she was a middle school teacher in rural northeastern Connecticut from 1985 to 1990 and at an educators' conference in New Jersey, around 1998.

Beliefs that parents do not care about their kids' education are also not uncommon. In 2014, when leading a training in a majority-minority city in western Massachusetts, Randy encountered White teacher participants vigorously objecting to suggestions that working closely with families was a positive way to understand and meet students' needs. "Those parents don't care about their kids' learning" was a common refrain.

In an essay in Mica Pollock's *Everyday Antiracism: Getting Real About Race in School*, John B. Diamond (2008) writes:

> The explanations for racial differences in academic achievement that come up in educators' conversations about student achievement are often linked to taken-for-granted assumptions about racial groups' families and their cultures. . . . When Blacks and Latino/as struggle academically, members of their communities are often thought to be less invested in academic achievement. . . . This presumption makes teachers less likely to consider whether their own instructional practices meet students' educational needs. (p. 254)

Educators' willingness to openly and explicitly share their "real" views about students' racial and cultural backgrounds likely varies over time and from one school community to another. Whether or not racial and cultural bias is explicit, another subtler form of bias is so widespread as to be considered pervasive. This is generally called *implicit bias*.

Definitions for implicit bias vary slightly. Some use the term *unconscious*, while others (like Banaji & Greenwald, 2013) use descriptors such as *covert*, *hidden*, and *automatic*. Bias is understood as a preference for one group over another, which implies a dislike for, or discomfort with, a different group. In *Implicit Bias in Schools: A Practitioner's Guide*, Gina Gullo, Kelly Capatosto, and Cheryl Staats (2019) write:

> By definition, implicit bias refers to stereotypes and attitudes that occur unconsciously and may or may not reflect our actual attitudes. Although unconscious, implicit biases can affect our perceptions, actions, and our decisions across realms ranging from the relatively trivial (e.g., recognizing that "green means go" on a stoplight) to those quite significant (e.g., in a school discipline situation, which student is perceived to be more or less culpable than another). (p. 3)

By *actual attitudes*, the authors seem to mean *conscious attitudes*, clarifying the distinction with *unconscious attitudes*. In this chapter, we use this definition, recognizing that other terms besides *unconscious* may also be useful for understanding implicit bias.

Pause and Reflect

What are some common stereotypes about the group or groups with which you identify? What stereotypes do you hold about other groups?

Measurement of Bias

Measuring unconscious bias is obviously a difficult task even for experienced researchers. To begin to meet this challenge, scientists Mahzarin Banaji, Anthony Greenwald, and Brian Nosek first developed and released the Implicit Association Test (IAT; https://implicit.harvard.edu/implicit/index.jsp) in 1998. The IAT has been modified several times. The "test" is an online experience whereby the participant is offered a set of either-or choices with negative or positive associations that are considered as "preferences." The measurement aspect is the degree of preference a person exhibits by the amount of time they take to complete each set of pairs. The IAT includes a range of subtest topics: race, color, age, gender, sexual orientation, religion, and so on. Two subtests measure the degree of preference toward racially associated hair types (www.projectimplicit.net/perception-institute-collaboration) as well as between objects, specifically weapons and harmless objects (https://implicit.harvard.edu/implicit/selectatest.html).

If you decide to take the IAT yourself to assess your unconscious racial attitudes, we suggest taking several tests, including the two just described.

The Impact of Bias on Teacher Expectations

Research on how implicit bias impacts elementary teachers' academic expectations of their young students, and thereby the racial achievement gap, has been widely conducted. In the Netherlands, with a Turkish and Moroccan population of approximately 10 percent, researchers found that Dutch teachers demonstrated a preference for Dutch children over immigrant children, with a significant correlation between their expectations of each group and academic achievement (van den Bergh, Denessen, Hornstra, Voeten, & Holland, 2010). "The implicit prejudiced attitudes of teachers clearly appear to influence the association between student ethnicity and academic achievement" (van den Bergh et al., 2010, p. 516). Teachers' expectations serve as the link (the *mediator*) between implicit bias and academic achievement. Further, the degree of teachers' implicit bias impacted the size of the achievement gap, which varied noticeably from classroom to classroom, and from teacher to teacher (van den Bergh et al., 2010).

Related research conducted in the United States found that educators, like the general public, hold "slight" pro-White, anti-Black implicit bias, generally shaped by individual factors more than contextual factors. Additionally, researchers identified larger racial disparities in test scores and suspensions in counties with stronger implicit and explicit anti-Black biases among teachers (Chin et al., 2020).

Implicit Bias Reduction in Early Childhood Education

Educators may consider approaching antibias training through a social justice leadership model and its relationship to our HEART+ approach (see chapter 6, page 83). Note that while we strongly advocate for the antibias and equity work we are presenting in this chapter, there are valid questions about whether educators' implicit bias can be significantly reduced over the long term. For example, Sarah D. Sparks (2020) writes:

> Several large-scale analyses of research on implicit-bias training suggest it more often changes short-term knowledge about the vocabulary of diversity than long-term changes in behavior. . . . Anti-bias training can paradoxically lead to more stereotyping, if participants come to think of biases as common and uncontrollable, and can lead white participants to feel threatened without yielding benefits for participants of color.

Sparks (2020) proposes "some better bets for anti-bias strategies" that align with our understanding of research regarding professional development and implementation of successful change strategies within school systems (see figure 8.1).

As an equity-focused professional development facilitator for nearly three decades, Randy has seen the very limited short-term results of "one-and-done" training approaches. Successful, long-term impact requires a range of strategies, many similar to those that Sparks (2020) recommends, to generate a more equitable school climate. As we explain in this section, staff will need leaders' support to succeed, and there are resources that leaders can use, including the tiered system of equity supports (TSES) and whole-school or program approaches (see chapter 11, page 165).

HEART+ Takeaways

Bias impacts young children who absorb negative messages about themselves and others. Neuroscience research shows how the developing brain ingests stereotypes. These messages are not conducive to developing a positive sense of self. Delving deeply into different forms of racial and cultural bias, we find two types: explicit and implicit (or unconscious) bias. One way to measure explicit bias is to examine bias crime statistics, which show an increase in this current period.

Research suggests stand-alone antibias training may not change long-term behavior. For leaders working to make their schools more equitable, studies suggest some alternatives to common pitfalls.

Instead Of:	Try:
Providing antibias training on the school's list of teacher professional development sessions	Integrating training in a comprehensive equity plan that involves teachers and other adults at school in reviewing policy, practices, and structures that can promote bias, not just a stand-alone learning session (See chapter 10, page 143, on action planning.)
Setting goals for antibias training based on the program you adopt	Setting specific goals based on the needs of your school and any problems you have identified to be addressed (See chapter 10 on action planning and visioning.)
Focusing on participants' comfort during difficult conversations about race and bias	Recognizing that individual educators may each have their own racial and cultural experiences while acknowledging that conversations about bias will be uncomfortable and giving participants tools to manage their emotions while accepting feedback (See chapter 9, page 131, for an activity on comfort.)
Giving a detailed checklist of recommendations for participants to use to avoid bias	Emphasizing a few clear strategies for managing bias with examples of what antibias awareness and behavior would look like in practice for different groups within the school (See The Tiered System of Equity Supports in chapter 11, page 173.)
Measuring the success of training by participation, positive reviews, or end-of-training surveys	Connecting training evaluations back to the school's larger data-based equity goals, such as increasing the proportion of students of color referred to advanced courses or shrinking discipline gaps (See chapter 10 on action planning.)

Source: Sparks, 2020. Used with permission.

Figure 8.1: Better bets for antibias strategies.

There are effective strategies that adults, particularly educators, can use to reduce bias of which they are unaware. First, they must learn about their own unconscious bias, including taking several forms of the IAT. For early childhood and other educational leaders, ongoing comprehensive professional learning approaches demonstrate better outcomes than one-shot diversity trainings.

We also recommend the following books for leaders to go deeper into the ideas of this chapter. Some of these may also be useful for early childhood educators' team meetings.

- *Blindspot: Hidden Biases of Good People* (Banaji & Greenwald, 2013)
- *Restorative Leadership: Skills and Processes That Can Support Leaders Model Restorative Day-to-Day Conversations, Meetings, Conflicts, Complaints and Disciplinary Issues* (Hopkins, 2021)
- *Bolstering Student Resilience: Creating a Classroom With Consistency, Connection, and Compassion* (Harlacher & Whitcomb, 2022)
- *Implicit Bias in Schools: A Practitioner's Guide* (Gullo et al., 2019)

CHAPTER 9

Circles of Love: School Culture and Restorative Practices

The only weapons that are useful in this battle

Are the weapons of truth, faith, and compassion.
—Lyla June, Diné Nation (Navajo) musician, poet, anthropologist, educator, community organizer, and public speaker

Principle 9: Listen deeply, build trust, and foster equity.

In chapter 2 of *Little Learners, Big Hearts*, we discuss identity, recognizing the critical role that teachers and schools play in creating psychologically safe learning environments that support positive student identities, student agency, and learning (Darling-Hammond & DePaoli, 2020). In this chapter, we discuss how to build this inclusive, equitable learning and teaching environment, creating a safe, supportive school culture that promotes restorative practices.

A Safe and Supportive School Culture

In *Little Learners, Big Hearts*, we presented a chart of factors that need to be considered to have a safe, supportive school culture. As you review these opportunities in figure 9.1, see if you can zero in on three of the six elements as possible places to begin your journey as a leader and a facilitator.

Family-School Partnerships	Parents, caregivers, and educators work together to keep students fully engaged in learning. Educators value parents and caregivers as children's primary teachers.
Culturally Responsive Practice	Children receive positive, affirming messages woven into the curriculum and pedagogy.
High Expectations of Children	Educators hold and communicate high expectations for all students' learning capacity. Children experience the opposite of the implicit bias that often means low expectations.
Social-Emotional Learning	Students learn how to engage with their teachers and peers, manage emotions, and respond to guidance from educators who understand them.
Developmentally Appropriate Pedagogy and Positive Guidance	Students engage in and know the rules and routines of classroom activities. Educators provide proactive guidance for positive engagement, modeling, and teaching appropriate behavior.
Trauma-Informed Care and Services	Students who have experienced trauma receive services and interventions to help them process and heal their trauma.

Source: Mason et al., 2024, p. 137.

Figure 9.1: Factors impacting a safe, supportive school culture.

To improve equity, professional development and coaching, with tiered supports for equity, are essential. However, leaders must also ensure a school culture and climate that support the needs of BIPOC students and staff. As we say in chapter 5 on antiracist school culture in *Little Learners, Big Hearts*:

> Antiracist school cultures support equity in learning, providing opportunities for students to excel and to feel a sense of belonging. Antiracist schools and centers have a deep understanding of diversity and also staff who have invested time in learning about their own biases and have worked to reduce bias and discrimination. Such cultures are compassionate, culturally

responsive, and affirming. Such cultures embody the principles of HEART+ and incorporate the underpinnings of mindful heart centeredness in each classroom and schoolwide as they strive to build the self-esteem, knowledge, skills, confidence, and talents of each student.

A school with a deep-seated belief in antiracism and concern for students and families of all races will create norms and expectations to address racism. A school that cares deeply about all students and families will acknowledge its antiracist guidelines in its school policies and communications with families. Moreover, its antiracist beliefs will be apparent in discipline protocol, hiring and staffing practices, and curriculum. Each of these factors contributes in innumerable ways to the overall culture or climate of the school. The teachers and educators working within the school are the foundation of its culture. (Mason et al., 2024, pp. 131–132)

Nicole M. Madu (2021) at Southern Connecticut State University translates antiracist theory and recommendations into what can be done in schools and early childcare centers. In her article "Reimagining Early Childhood Classrooms as Sites of Love," she calls out the need to ensure that Black children, and particularly Black boys, experience classrooms as "sites of warmth and affection" (Madu, 2021, p. 5). Acknowledging that Black boys often experience public shaming, she provides concrete examples of how misbehaviors can be handled by redirecting students, privately taking students aside, and showing affection through jokes, friendly banter, and gentle reminders.

In chapter 8 (page 119), we explained in detail how implicit bias maintains inequities in schools. School climate is also connected to implicit bias. Although the relationship between bias reduction and school climate is complex, to simplify it, consider a few ideas.

- Both are about a sense of safety, especially social-emotional safety, for students, staff, and families.
- Both are about how nonacademic considerations strongly affect young children's academic success.
- Both are critical to making fair and effective decisions about behavioral concerns.
- Both are about interpersonal relationships, negative and positive.
- Both require collaboration, team building, and open communication among early childhood staff and with the families of young children from birth to grade 3.

- Both require leadership, since skilled early childhood leaders are essential to improving school climate and critical to carefully opening the Pandora's box of implicit bias, a necessary step to mitigating its contents.

Our definition of an equitable school climate alludes to many of these interconnections: "An equitable school climate supports each student's path to a prosocial identity by being culturally responsive to the patterns and wide range of norms, goals, values, interpersonal relationships, leadership practices, and organizational structures within the school and broader community" (Ross, Brown, & Hamilton Biagas, 2020, p. 17).

Gullo and colleagues (2019) quote Randy's 2013 article on equity and school climate where she writes, "Equity is intrinsic to all aspects of school climate work" (Ross, 2013, p. 39). Gullo and colleagues (2019) then add:

> While the connection to implicit bias through school climate is less explicit, the climate reflects the presence of a culture that either accepts or rejects biased actions. When a school achieves a positive climate where all students are accepted, bias (explicit and implicit) is socially unacceptable. (p. 109)

In addition to our Heart Centered Learning approach, leaders can obtain important resources from the National School Climate Center (NSCC, n.d.), which has developed an assessment and framework that includes items related to (1) interpersonal relationships, (2) social-emotional learning, (3) respect for diversity, (4) teacher-student relationships, (5) leadership and efficacy, and (6) rules and norms.

There are some key similarities in the NSCC (n.d.) and social justice leadership for implicit bias reduction (Gullo & Beachum, 2020) frameworks (figure 9.2).

Equitable school climate improvement is the broader concept, encompassing implicit bias reduction as well as antibullying, SEL, cultural competence, antibias, and so on. Both the school climate improvement process and the implicit bias reduction framework require building collaborative teams. As we all know, this is easier said than done! Differences exist in personalities, values, cultural styles of communication, professional goals—the list of challenges could go on and on. Nevertheless, there are some core practices that can help build effective collaborative teams. Building trust and actively listening are just two of them.

The National School Climate Center Framework Includes Items On:	The Implicit Bias Reduction Framework Includes Items On:
Interpersonal relationships	Relationships
Social-emotional learning	Social-emotional skills and empathic capacity strategies
Respect for diversity	Intergroup contact strategies, including inclusive community, expanded and diverse network, and cultural relevance
Teacher-student relationships	Understanding of individual needs strategies
Leadership and efficacy (including administration and leadership and collective efficacy)	Shared decision-making and collaboration strategies Communication
Rules and norms	Decision-making supports that include restorative conferences

Source: Gullo & Beachum, 2020; NSCC, n.d.

Figure 9.2: Crosswalk between school climate and implicit bias reduction frameworks.

Trust-Building Activities

Leaders can use the following two trust-building activities with school staff.

1. **What Is the Story of Your Name?:** This activity works with pairs, helping people get a bit more comfortable with each other. When you have a multiracial, multiethnic group, if possible, pair people from different backgrounds. The conversations may reveal some family history and cultural or religious backgrounds. If a participant either doesn't know their family story or perhaps doesn't feel comfortable sharing it, they can share a brief story about where they currently live.

2. **Two Truths and a Dream:** This activity is best for small groups of four to five people. Like the game Two Truths and a Lie, each participant shares their two truths about things they have done and then shares a dream of something they have not (yet) done. Keep all statements in the same past tense. Others then try to guess which are the truths and which is the dream.

Here's an example from Randy: "I was a school principal. I worked for UNICEF. I visited Vietnam." (Can you guess which are Randy's two truths and which is her dream?)

Active Listening Activity

The Greater Good Science Center at the University of California at Berkeley offers a wide range of activities, including this one for active listening:

> This exercise helps you express active interest in what the other person has to say and make them feel heard—a way to foster empathy and connection. This technique is especially well-suited for difficult conversations . . . and for expressing support. It may also help facilitate constructive conversations across political, cultural, or other differences; however, studies have found that, when there's a power imbalance between people of different groups, it's important for the person with less social power to give their perspective while the person with more social power listens and tries to take their perspective. (Greater Good in Action, n.d.)

The following active listening guidelines are drawn from the Greater Good Science Center (Greater Good in Action, n.d.) website but adapted for the kinds of conversations we believe interracial, cross-cultural teams would be having when working together on a project, such as reducing implicit bias. That focus will certainly raise communication challenges. The activity requires at least ten minutes. Depending on the group and issues being discussed, you could use up to twenty minutes.

To do the activity, find a quiet place where you will be able to talk with no interruptions. If you are working on a specific project or goal together, that may be the focus of your conversation. It could also be something more general but relevant to your relationship or that of the full team. One example might be the need to improve communication within your team. The following active listening practices are essential for problem solving. They are not listed in any specific order, and you may not need or want to use all of them in a conversation. The included examples are designed to improve active listening with a partner, but they also can apply to group conversations. Each of these suggestions can be enhanced by practicing mindful breathing, which calms the active mind and supports paying close attention. Remember that active listening helps us learn deeply and simultaneously shows respect for the speaker.

- **Paraphrase** what you hear the other person saying or describing. This is a way of checking for understanding and shows that you are paying close attention to what the other person has been saying.

- **Ask questions** to encourage the other person to share more about their thoughts and feelings. Avoid jumping to conclusions. In interracial and cross-cultural conversations, this is especially important since we tend to draw conclusions out of our own experience and perspective.

- **Express empathy** with the thoughts and feelings the other person expresses. Do not argue or disagree. Use phrases like, "I can see why you feel that way" or "I can feel your frustration." If you do not feel empathy, do not fake it. That will not build trust, a key goal of active listening. In either case, you can simply nod and say, "Mm-hmm," for example, to show that you are actively listening to the other person. Other reassuring responses could include, "I hear you," "Go on," and so on.

- **Use body language** that shows you are carefully listening. Avoid facial expressions and other forms of body language that indicate disconnection. Show that you are giving full attention to what is being said. *Agreement is not required, but attention is.*

- **Avoid making or expressing judgments**, since your goal is to understand what the other person is saying and feeling. We previously suggested that the focus might be on team communication. Judgments—or, even worse, blame—take the focus off the problem and put it onto individuals, even if those individuals are contributing to communication issues.

- **Avoid giving advice**, since active listening is a step toward mutual problem solving. Advice (accepting or rejecting) then becomes the focus of the conversation.

- **Take turns** so that both of you have an opportunity to express what you are thinking, your perspective, and how you are feeling.

- You can **end by together summarizing** areas of agreement but also areas where you have different perspectives.

Discipline and Restorative Practices: The Leader's Role

The relationship between bias and school climate will certainly be impacted by disciplinary practices within your school—in a reciprocal way. Bias has long been part of disciplinary practices as students from BIPOC cultures have been called out more frequently for not following the norms and expectations of many classrooms (Gilreath, 2023).

As we discuss in *Little Learners, Big Hearts*, as well as in chapter 8 (on leadership to address bias and promote cultural competence; page 119) and in chapter 10 (on action planning; page 143), disparate disciplinary practices impact Black children, and boys in particular (Bryan, 2017; Gilliam et al., 2016). The "preschool-to-prison pipeline," as this is called (Al-Shamma et al., 2021), has detrimental long-term effects. We know that implicit bias is at least partly a root cause (Goff, Jackson, Di Leone, Culotta, & DiTomasso, 2014), and therefore, addressing implicit bias is essential.

Restorative practices offer concrete strategies to reduce this disproportionality (Trout, 2021). Restorative practices focus on repairing harm and fostering accountability within the school community. They emphasize relationships, empathy, and dialogue as central components of discipline and conflict resolution. Instead of punitive measures that isolate and shame individuals, restorative practices seek to involve all parties affected by an incident in a constructive dialogue aimed at understanding the impact of behavior, repairing harm, and rebuilding trust. This may involve techniques such as circle discussions, mediation, or restorative conferences where students, teachers, and sometimes even parents come together to address issues and find solutions collaboratively. Staff members need preparation to effectively use restorative practices both with young children and among themselves.

Staff Preparation for Restorative Practices

For restorative practices to be implemented effectively, many within the school community—not only teachers but ancillary staff, teaching assistants, and families—will need to be involved. Preparing school staff to use restorative practices will necessitate a series of action steps with professional development, modeling, guidance, and changes in policy and protocol within a school.

Sean Darling-Hammond (2023), writing in *Principal Magazine*, describes the double focus of restorative practices:

1. **Community-building practices**—Such practices are designed to foster an interconnected school community and a healthy school climate; a good

example is community-building circles that help students and staff deepen interpersonal relationships.
2. **Repair practices**—These practices attempt to bring together all stakeholders to resolve issues and take productive steps in the future and include conflict-responsive dialogues, mediation, and harm-repair circles.

Darling-Hammond (2023) makes clear that providing professional learning will not in itself be sufficient for staff to use restorative practices effectively: "School leaders must spread awareness, secure staff buy-in, ensure that all students have access, and sustain implementation of such practices." Changing long-held, highly punitive behavior management policies and practices such as "zero tolerance" is not easy. Sometimes, schools have zero tolerance written into formal policies, and other times, administrators and teachers simply believe it is the best approach. It may be an ingrained aspect of the school culture. Changing the practices that rest on such ingrained views is much more difficult than changing policies, although that may be where you have to begin.

How might early childhood educators justify using punitive discipline with very young children?

Randy's Story of a Head Start Visit

In the early 1980s, Randy was asked to visit a local Head Start program in a church basement, about a mile from where she lived in Northeast Connecticut. The church sat on the edge of an idyllic, green commons, next to an old, renovated inn that was thought to have sheltered runaway enslaved people more than a hundred years earlier. The town's population was then largely White, working-class, poor families. When Randy was given a tour around the basement daycare program, she saw several children, perhaps four or five years old, kneeling on the cold concrete floor. When she asked the head teacher about it, the response was that this "would teach them a lesson they wouldn't forget." Carefully challenging this discipline method, Randy asked whether there might be other ways to approach what they considered "misbehavior." The response has stayed with Randy all these decades: "That is our culture here in New England. Life is hard, very hard, here, and we know it is best for our kids to learn that early in life." Rather than showing empathy, the motto was "toughen them up." While Randy was very uncomfortable with this response, she did not challenge the teacher at that moment but included it in her report about the visit. She has long felt that while she avoided a confrontation, she failed to protect the children.

> **Pause and Reflect**
> - What do you think (and feel) about the explanation "it's our culture" for punitive practices?
> - If you came across the perspective that the Head Start teacher from Randy's experience expressed, how would you respond?
> - Would you see this as an opportunity to introduce restorative practices? If so, what obstacles would you encounter and how might you address them?

Restorative Practices With Young Children

While the steps for implementing restorative practices vary slightly depending on the age level of the students and the specific program being used, here are a few of the typical steps.

1. Acknowledge the harm or hurt that has been done and the role of each of the players. Often this may involve two people who are in conflict.
2. Hear from each of those involved—learn about their opinions about what happened.
3. Problem solve to come up with a solution that might rectify the situation. This might involve an apology or an action, perhaps something as simple as returning a favorite toy or coming up with a way to take turns sharing toys.
4. Implement the solution.
5. Check back to see how those who are involved feel about the solution—is it working? Or is something else needed?

The idea is to keep the tensions low, not to do anything to exacerbate the situation or heighten the distress of any parties, and to use this as an occasion to learn and practice important social skills.

There are multiple benefits of restorative practices (Bedinger & Curtis, 2020).

- They promote a sense of belonging and connectedness within the school community, fostering a positive school climate where students feel valued and supported.
- By focusing on understanding and addressing the root causes of behavior, rather than merely meting out punishment, restorative practices help prevent future conflicts and misbehavior.

- These practices encourage empathy, communication, and conflict-resolution skills among students, equipping them with valuable life skills that extend beyond the classroom.
- Restorative approaches can reduce rates of suspension, expulsion, and other disciplinary actions, contributing to improved academic outcomes and overall well-being for students.

In chapter 5 (pages 150–151) of *Little Learners, Big Hearts*, we share the views of Vermont early childhood leaders Lisa Bedinger and Stacie Curtis (2020) about the value of restorative practices. They point out that these practices are valuable not just for reducing discipline problems, especially racial disproportionality in suspensions and expulsions, but also for fostering a feeling of community in preschool settings (Bedinger & Curtis, 2020).

In *The Restorative Practices Handbook: For Teachers, Disciplinarians and Administrators*, Bob Costello, Joshua Wachtel, and Ted Wachtel (2019) underscore the community-building goals of restorative practices:

> Simply put, to be "restorative" means to believe that decisions are best made and conflicts are best resolved by those most directly involved in them. The restorative practices movement seeks to develop good relationships and restore a sense of community in an increasingly disconnected world. (p. 7)

This framework does not just spring up out of nowhere. For restorative practices to be effective, there must be leadership to find the financial resources for training, leadership to persuade staff and families of its potential, leadership to change long-embedded practices that emphasize punishment over learning, and finally leadership to sustain a difficult change process. To begin, leaders can prepare staff members for engaging with restorative practices. (See appendix A, page 253, for a scenario to illustrate what restorative practices can look like in conflicts between families.)

Restorative Practices With Staff

Restorative practices can be useful not just with students but with conflicts between and among adults—staff and families. Belinda Hopkins (2021), in her mini-book *Restorative Leadership*, describes how leaders can model restorative practices in conversations, meetings, conflict resolution, complaints, and disciplinary issues. After all, adults in early childhood education and other school settings have conflicts they frequently do not know how to resolve and need leaders to help them do so.

Sometimes there are cross-racial or ethnic conflicts among staff, as one longtime Head Start teacher explained in an interview for *Little Learners, Big Hearts*. Ms. Smith (not her real name by her request) explained that the major staff conflict in her current program was between Black and Latina staff, with derogatory gossip fueling the conflict. The White administrator knew this was occurring but did not intervene. The negative impact on the school climate was significant in this teacher's view. Restorative approaches to a gossip-fueled staff conflict would potentially help defuse such a dynamic.

Hopkins (2021) outlines five core beliefs of restorative leadership. She writes that restorative practitioners believe the following:

1. Everyone has their own unique perspective on a situation or event and needs an opportunity to express this and feel heard.
2. What people think at any given moment influences how they feel at that moment, and these feelings inform how they behave.
3. Our actions and deeds impact those around us. It can be helpful to reflect on the wider ripple effects of any given action or incident.
4. When our needs are met, we can function at our best, [understanding] that all our actions are strategies we have chosen to meet our needs at the time.
5. It is those who are affected by an issue or problem who are the people best placed to find ways forward—in collaboration with each other. (Hopkins, 2021, pp. 8-10)

HEART+ Takeaways

This chapter highlights the importance of having an inclusive, equitable school climate that promotes restorative practices. Through safe and supportive spaces, educators can create a climate where students from all backgrounds feel valued and supported. Moreover, the integration of restorative practices can help limit biases and disproportionate disciplinary actions that may adversely affect marginalized students.

Additionally, equitable learning environments and initiatives can promote diversity and inclusivity within classrooms. School leaders play a pivotal role in both modeling restorative approaches and promoting inclusive practices. Through actions like these, educators can build trust within schools and promote a culture of belonging and respect.

CHAPTER 10

A Mountain of Courage: Visioning and Action Planning

> I describe my work in part as haunting the past. I'm trying to train my attention on those who were disregarded in the past as a way of shaping our ethics for the present and the future. So, it's sort of like trying to catch ahold of freedom, dreams that have existed over the course of generations, train my gaze and shine a light on them.
>
> —Imani Perry

Principle 10: It takes a team to plan for and implement an antiracist school culture.

The challenge we put before leaders reading this book is, "What can you do? How can you bring us closer to a vision of justice, a world with more compassion, and communities that seem to really care about their young children? And with our care for young children, what then would shift for our education systems? What might we eliminate? What would we expand?" In this chapter, we provide some concrete ways school leaders can take action to effect change within and beyond their school communities. These include visioning and heart centered planning.

Visioning

Tomorrow is another day. If we could wipe the slate clean, and envision a new country, one perhaps less flawed, with greater equity and well-being for all, what would it be like? If we could envision a new world, what would we want? If we could redact a few dozen world events, what would we strike from our list of worldly conquests and diasporas, and what might we propose in their place?

In his book *Native Minds Rising: Exploring Transformative Indigenous Education*, Gregory Cajete (2020) reminds us:

> The potential of teaching for vision and engaging students in the creative process of visioning is literally revolutionary in its implications for contemporary education. . . . It would be a culturally based methodology.
>
> To "Indigenize" contemporary Western education would require a global transformation of proportions we have never seen. . . . We move mountains by first moving ourselves, and the way we educate makes all the difference in the world. (pp. 180, 182)

While Cajete is describing a vision to Indigenize education, his words are relevant to many of the visions for startling, impactful change. He is prescribing a process of beginning with our own internal processes, and our hopes and dreams for ourselves. Where there has been darkness or despair, apathy, neglect, or abuse, major—not minor—changes are essential. The vision for increasing empathy and equity isn't limited to one grade, one age, or one school, but rather is for widescale systems change.

Let's start with a vision for what would be: Could you imagine a world without hate, without genocide, slavery, caste systems, or injustice? Could you envision significant healing around the globe?

> **Pause and Reflect**
> Close your eyes. Take a couple of breaths. What visions come to mind?

The Coalition for the Future of Education (2022), an initiative of the Center for Educational Improvement, developed a vision that speaks to seeing clearly what could be:

> We envision a world that leans in with heart and compassion for self, others, and our environment, where people and institutions are dedicated to expanding conscious acts of caring, building resiliency, and advancing learning, equity, and justice.
>
> We envision safe and equitable schools with education that serves as the foundation for our humanity; it is flexible and empowering. There is room for adventure, students drive their own learning, learning and self-understanding are celebrated, and communities support their individual and collective self-care, and well-being.

Note that the vision of the coalition is for advancing equity, creating an empowering environment that serves as the foundation for our humanity, and celebrating learning and self-understanding—certainly in line with the HEART+ tenets of hope, (self-)education, acknowledgment, resolution, and teaching with the added consideration of local needs and concerns. In this section on visioning, we remind ourselves that while changing the world is not something we can accomplish overnight, we can make a difference in our own communities. We discuss the sort of leaders we will need. And we continue with ways that visioning can contribute to safe and supportive school cultures and climates.

We Are Not Trying to Change the World—Yet

Before reading further, let's pause for a moment. We really aren't suggesting that our readers set out to make substantial, long-lasting changes to impact billions of people around the globe. Yet. However, it was wonderful to spend a few moments considering what the world might be like. So, for now let's focus on one corner of the world: young children and education. Let's be more specific and consider, particularly, BIPOC students. From a world of options, we have fine-tuned our radar, zeroing in on BIPOC infants, toddlers, preschoolers, and students as they enter their first years of schooling. These young children, their families, and our school staff are an area where we have a deep commitment—a commitment without distractions, without the obstacles that will pull us away from our mission.

With a mission to improve the lives of these young children and their families, with a focus on students, what might you do? Here are three things that immediately come to mind.

1. Get to know them better to understand more about their interests, their joys, their sorrows, and their needs.

2. Consider how to help build their sense of well-being and their trust that we can help make their communities better, a trust that we will listen and provide support.

3. Consider, with them, their priorities.

And as we continue to focus on students, we would consider how they feel about themselves, their identities. How do they feel about their families, their communities, and their groups? As Katheryn A. Ocampo, George P. Knight, and Martha E. Bernal (1997) explain, we would start to look at their social identities—so we would expand our awareness beyond an understanding of the individual student to their groups. We would look at what is working well and where things need to change. While the reflection and subsequent actions of isolated educators won't change the world, they can change the world for students, their families, and staff.

In *Leading With Vitality and Hope*, Mason and colleagues (2023) describe visioning as an inner and outer journey, one where we ask leaders to be clear about their own visions as they lead visioning with others. So, the question for leaders is how we get from A to B, knowing that A today is flawed. What can we contribute to make the world just a little bit better for so many?

Let's be clear: we can start with our own visions, but for change to occur, we cannot close our eyes and wish away the pain and sorrow or pretend they don't exist. We must acknowledge the realities: the current status and our past, including the differences between dominant cultures and those of people who have been marginalized.

Leaders Who Facilitate

Visioning will take leadership—leaders who, as Louise Derman-Sparks and colleagues (2023) have suggested, are facilitators. When it comes to bias, discrimination, equity, and the creation of a better space for many, leadership involves so much more than goals, strategic plans, and formulas. It certainly involves time and money; however, it truly takes leaders who have their ear to the ground, who have a superb sense of timing, and who know when to stay silent, when to press on, who to involve, and how to support their teams.

As Susan MacDonald (2016), author of *Inspiring Early Childhood Leadership: Eight Strategies to Ignite Passion and Transform Program Quality*, writes:

> Leaders need to watch for the following indicators that their school environment is becoming toxic.

- Gossip
- Staff complaints, criticism, or distrust of leadership
- Staff use of negative language to describe children or their parents
- Negative subgroups within the staff
- Lack of focus on the positive things happening in the program (p. 33)

And as she goes on to state:

> Positive interactions can change the flow of negativity. Shifting conversations from the downward spiral of negativity takes practice, but with persistence, positive dialogue can successfully act as a reset button to the damaging impact of negative conversations. (MacDonald, 2016, p. 37)

Whether they are dealing with negativity or finding strategies to shift conversations, leaders will need courage to believe in human potential and accept and learn from mistakes, as the road to implementation is often bumpy and will often require some shifts in thinking and action along the way (Derman-Sparks et al., 2023).

And as Mason, Patschke, and Simpson (2023) say, it will take *vitality*, which may involve doing what we can to strengthen the well-being of leaders, students, and staff as they vision together. The best facilitation will come from clear thinking. After the COVID-19 pandemic, we asked, "What is required right now?" which led to nine steps for visioning.

1. Begin with a sense of urgency, focusing on what is most crucial.
2. Acknowledge stress and trauma to build self-care and vitality.
3. Do something to help students, staff, and families heal.
4. Remember and embrace equity and justice.
5. Increase your conscious understanding of yourself and others.
6. Turn to others; leadership takes teamwork.
7. Share in visioning.
8. Implement for success and sustainability.
9. Lead with heart and hope; your vision and your plans will evolve over time.

Review the nine steps and consider what actions you might take. Figure 10.1 (page 148) provides some examples.

Steps for Leading to Implement a Vision	Notes on What You Can Do
1. Begin with a sense of urgency, focusing on what is most crucial.	When changes in disciplinary practices are needed, start by conducting a brief review for equity and fairness; revise the most egregious practices, such as eliminating out-of-school suspensions and expulsions, and substituting these with opportunities to build empathy and understanding.
2. Acknowledge stress and trauma to build self-care and vitality.	Leaders can further self-care by modeling good self-care, offering yoga or meditation classes, and including mindful moments throughout the school day.
3. Do something to help students, staff, and families heal.	Ideas may include a wellness fair, celebrations that further a sense of positivity and joy, or acknowledgment of grief and trauma as they impact your community.
4. Remember and embrace equity and justice.	Look for ways to further equity and justice with your BIPOC staff as well as families and students.
5. Increase your conscious understanding of yourself and others.	Take time for reflective meditation, helping students understand their emotions and further self-awareness.
6. Turn to others; leadership takes teamwork.	Share leadership and involve the community, staff, and students in visioning, making sure it is an inclusive process with BIPOC involvement in a variety of roles—including leadership roles.
7. Share in visioning.	Provide time for a series of visioning meetings, with leaders of diverse backgrounds sharing in the planning, implementation, and rollout of your vision.
8. Implement for success and sustainability.	Consider expectations and criteria for success as well as how to build capacity and ways for ongoing involvement and progress monitoring.
9. Lead with heart and hope; your vision and your plans will evolve over time.	As you implement your vision, expect that, as circumstances change, your vision may change as well. Visioning is a dynamic process.

Figure 10.1: Template for steps to implement a vision.

*Visit **go.SolutionTree.com/diversityandequity** for a free reproducible version of this figure.*

To make the truly significant changes that are needed, we must find a way to go beyond pockets of greatness to overcome obstacles and arrive at sustainable change.

A Vision for an Antiracist School Culture and Climate

What obstacles could emerge as you continue your visioning? Could they be related to historical trauma—the trauma of slavery, of forced relocation, of poverty, or of broken promises? Could they be related to recent trauma? Or perhaps they may be related to bias. Some of the issues will undoubtedly be related to systemic issues: underrepresentation, cruelty, a simple lack of caring, and looking the other way. Sometimes these obstacles are related to a lack of resources, funding, staffing, or even preparation of staff and their readiness to address the extant challenges. Here we discuss aspects of a safe and supportive school culture, how to improve school climate while reducing implicit bias, and a meditating activity that will help leaders lay the groundwork for these goals.

Heart Centered Planning

The steps we recommend for leaders as they develop a school dedicated to antiracism have many implications for the immediate and broader school community—for teachers, students, and staff, and also families, neighborhoods, and local businesses. We are advocating for an antiracist, heart centered approach, where, as changes are made, a sense of community also evolves.

In planning to expand your approach to antiracism in your school, there is much you, as a school leader, could do to increase your possibilities for success. Following a few simple steps should help you gain clarity and support your journey to antiracism. Building on the visioning we discuss in the previous section, the process is similar to what Christine has written about in her books *Visioning Onward* and *Leading With Vitality and Hope* (Mason, Liabenow, & Patschke, 2020; Mason, Patschke, et al., 2023).

1. Draft your own possible vision for an antiracist school community. As you do this, refer to the information in chapter 6 of this book (page 83) and in chapter 1 of *Little Learners, Big Hearts* about HEART+. Are you considering hope, self-education, acknowledgment, resolution, and teaching, plus local conditions?

2. Hold a small, informal meeting with trusted supporters so they can share meaningful input or ideas that may contribute to success. To identify potential supporters, consider individuals within your school

community who have diverse perspectives and connections and appear willing to consider innovations, and even to challenge your and others' current thinking. After identifying these individuals, you could extend personalized meeting invitations to them. Through this, such meetings can harness collective wisdom and promote meaningful change.

3. **Consider if there is a need for healing.** Shawn Ginwright (2018), professor of education in the Africana Studies Department at San Francisco State University, coined the term "healing-centered" engagement:

> The classroom is the place where problems are solved among students. In a circle, with community agreements in place, support, trust and authenticity build community rather than create an exclusionary and punitive environment in the school disciplinarian's office. When challenging behaviors arise in classrooms, the school psychologist, the nurse, or the guidance counselor [is] called to offer support through a trauma-informed lens, supported with healing-centered strategies for well-being.
>
> Imagine educators with strong enough relationships with each other that systems are in place for adults to take a break when needed, that teachers eat together, take walks together and meet not just to talk about students and work but to regularly celebrate each other. Imagine a school where parents are moving freely through the building to observe, learn, help and support the children and the educators working with them.
>
> A healing-centered school offers the training that educators, students and parents need to build those relationships, develop the tools and skills needed to work together and create mutual systems of support. (Adams, 2020)

With healing-centered engagement, there is a significant focus on building and enhancing relationships. If healing is needed, how can you build community as you help bring about healing? Justin Hendrickson's description of his southeast Seattle school in the book *Race Resilience* demonstrates how the journey you are embarking on may involve struggle:

> South Shore is richly diverse in every way—economically, religiously, linguistically, and ethnically. It is a school with challenging needs. . . . We are now a cohesive preK–8 organization; we are one school. This is the foundation of a healthy school environment. . . . Today, we struggle and problem-solve together. The climate of our school is now more cordial.

> We honor and learn from our differences, which make us feel stronger. We gave ourselves time to reflect and think about the changes we needed to make for ourselves first. We have a racial equity team to help us develop skills to be an antibiased, antiracist team.
>
> We've laughed a lot and cried together. . . . Our racial equity team continues to keep us focused on being more knowledgeable about being a racially and culturally responsive staff and our social-emotional learning team keeps a check on our social-emotional needs. (Romero, Warner, & Hendrickson, 2022, pp. 41, 43)

If you are to put healing and relationship building at the center of your efforts, then you will need to not only envision the future but, as we discuss in chapter 9 (page 131), take a hard and realistic look at your current school culture and climate. With future planning in mind, here are a few questions to consider.

- Are there racial or ethnic conflicts within the staff that have not been addressed?
- Do any staff members feel (justifiably or not) that others have targeted them?
- Does there seem to be jealousy about compensation or other status issues?
- Do some staff members feel that leaders show favoritism, possibly based on race, ethnicity, past relationships, status, and so on?
- What efforts, if any, has leadership taken to address staff member concerns about such divisions?

In implementing Heart Centered Learning in support of antiracism, school leaders are often faced with difficult decisions, even as they may be enthusiastic and eager to make significant changes. Some of these decisions involve what to do and what not to do. Other equally important decisions are related to timing.

Some communities will be quite open to the antiracist recommendations that are included in this book, and the timing may be rather straightforward. In other communities, as this chapter explains, leaders may need to proceed more cautiously, building internal support in the community—among staff and with some of your parent leaders or district administrators—before implementing a full-fledged heart centered plan. Overall, effective leadership and support can empower antiracist movements within school cultures. When inclusive visions can guide schools, true healing-centered engagement can occur.

As you review and implement the three phases we describe in the following sections, do so with healing and community building in mind. This might mean working with different configurations of stakeholders in small groups as well as through large visible events to help inspire staff and to keep the dialogue going. The three phases involve (1) consciously preparing the ground, (2) meditating for courage, and (3) acting on your plan with courage.

Phase 1: Consciously Preparing the Ground

If we want the ideas we pursue to take root, leaders will be wise to prepare staff and to consider how to nurture the ideas that emerge from visioning. If we as school leaders are culturally responsive and leaning into being antiracist, we will be sensitive to how our actions and words are perceived by others, tuning into their emotional reactions. We'll also be sensitive to how we are *feeling* about the interactions we've had. Whether we feel relieved that we had a great discussion, or we feel discomfort or remorse, each of these feelings can help inform our decision making:

> Philosophers, researchers, therapists, and others have described the importance of adding heart to our decisions. . . . They found that adding a feelings component to certain sorts of complex decisions results in higher-quality decisions. . . . While we strongly endorse heart centeredness, this is different than acting solely from an emotional space without considering consequences or the wisdom that comes from analysis and intellectual understanding. (Mason, Rivers Murphy, et al., 2020, pp. 28–29)

We encourage you to start planning with the small group of supporters you identified, and then sometime fairly soon, after your planning begins, expand the group, ensuring that there is representation across all stakeholder types—including race, gender, and community segments. Greater buy-in and staff and community commitment will occur if, during the initial stages of visioning, leaders extend invitations to stakeholders who demonstrate dedication to equity and inclusivity, or open invitations to members of the community who are simply eager to contribute. In this way, diverse perspectives and voices can be included in the planning process.

As your team begins to plan for change, consider the current state of your school culture as well as what is happening in your district, in your state, and nationally. This means embracing a level of consciousness about your goals. School staff must also be ready to work together to prioritize an antiracist climate.

As Russell M. Linden (2002) indicates, "Collaboration is about co-labor, about joint effort and ownership. The end result isn't mine or yours, it's ours" (p. 6).

Conscious preparation for school climate improvement strengthens opportunities for meaningful family engagement. As with staff, there may be racial and cultural challenges to this engagement. Families and their home cultures are integral to the culture and climate of all schools, but especially within early childhood care and education.

Some culturally competent, antiracist guidelines for your school climate improvement team include the following.

- Be sure all voices are at the table: staff, volunteers, and families.
- Meet at times that work for as many team members as possible.
- So that everyone is comfortable speaking from the heart, develop group norms that recognize and address racial, linguistic, and cultural power imbalances.
- Include a team-building activity, a social-emotional check-in, or both in every meeting. Do not just assume all members of the team understand how to work together or are feeling calm and ready for the work. Effective collaboration takes time and focused effort, especially in diverse groups.

When planning to improve school culture and climate to enhance cultural sensitivity, leaders and their teams will need to do the following.

- Develop goal statements.
- Define needs.
- Assess current status.
- Establish criteria for future success.
- Identify strategies for implementation.

Figure 10.2 (page 154) offers an example of the first part of an action plan to eliminate suspensions and expulsions in a preschool.

To prepare the ground for the antiracist school improvement, it will help to use an assessment to measure the culture of your school. The following list includes examples of compassionate, culturally responsive assessments.

- The Center for Educational Improvement's School-Compassionate Culture Analytical Tool for Educators (S-CCATE; https://s-ccate.org)

Goal statement (including subgoals)	Goal: Eliminate student suspensions and expulsions. Subgoals: 1. Identify educators' reasons for using suspensions and expulsions. 2. Identify racial and gender disparities in suspensions and expulsions. 3. Identify causes of suspensions and expulsions.
Definition of need (based on assessment)	Discipline data and classroom observations show the following. • Suspensions in our early childhood three- to five-year-old classrooms are being used due to limited skills in positive classroom management for effectively addressing individual students' social, emotional, and behavioral needs. • Black children, especially Black boys, are suspended at a significantly greater rate than White children in our three- to five-year-old classrooms.
Measure of current status (using assessment data)	Four percent of our three- to five-year-old children have been suspended over the past twelve months, and 1.5 percent have been expelled. Racial and gender disaggregation of our suspension data for three- to five-year-old children shows Black children are three times more likely than White children to be suspended, and eight out of ten suspended boys are Black boys, double their ratio in the school's population.
Measure of future success (using assessment data)	• Zero suspensions and expulsions • Improved, culturally responsive classroom management skills • Improved skills in supporting all students' social, emotional, and behavioral needs with attention to cultural differences in those needs
Strategies	Training for staff on: • Culturally responsive classroom management • Teaching culturally responsive social-emotional skills • Implicit racial and gender biases leading to inappropriate judgments about Black children's behavior • Working with mental health professionals and with families to address children's behavioral needs • Monitoring disaggregated behavioral data to identify trends (no change, reduced suspensions and expulsions, increased suspensions and expulsions)

Figure 10.2: Compassionate school action plan for improving school culture and climate (part 1)—Goals and strategies.

Visit **go.SolutionTree.com/diversityandequity** *for a free reproducible version of this figure.*

- Teachstone's (n.d.a, n.d.b) CLASS (https://teachstone.com/improve; see chapter 7, page 103)
- The NAEYC Class Observation Tool (https://bit.ly/3r7iyEX)
- The Environment Rating Scales Institute (ERSI) Environment Rating Scales (for infant-toddler, early childhood, and family daycare programs; www.ersi.info/scales.html)
- Harvard University's IAT (https://implicit.harvard.edu; see chapter 8, page 119)
- Focus groups with staff, family, and community members to identify both strengths and concerns

When selecting culturally responsive assessments, consider the following questions (Regional Educational Laboratory Program, n.d.).

- In what ways does the assessment make reference to culture?
- How does the assessment allow students to draw from their cultural fluencies?
- How does the assessment support students in bridging their social and cultural identities with their academic identities?

Here are examples of the questions from S-CCATE. Staff respond on a scale of 1 to 4, 4 being high, to questions about the environment, teachers, and administrators, the community, and students (Center for Educational Improvement, 2018):

- Rituals are used in classrooms and the school to contribute to a positive school culture (e.g., celebrations, morning meetings, school spirit, mentoring).
- Teachers and administrators further participation and a sense of belonging (e.g., connectedness to the larger school community) for all students.
- Teachers and administrators demonstrate fairness, equity, and justice in their relationships with students.
- Students show empathy for others.

The assessment phase will likely reveal uncomfortable information. For example, you may learn that staff believe administrators should be doing more to promote equity and compassion, or the aggregate data from BIPOC staff may suggest that they are less enthusiastic about the school's approach to discipline. However, conscious self-reflection and collaboration can help reduce defensiveness and further productive dialogue. Spending time meditating, journaling, or even mindfully reviewing—without judgment or defensiveness—what is happening and how students, families, and staff are feeling about your school can be helpful. It is particularly helpful if you do not rush to find a solution, but rather first sit in reflection to try to understand more about your circumstances.

When considering the desires and wishes as well as the well-being of staff and students, think of the potential value of using self-assessments and interviews. Heather L. Walter, an early childhood professor at George Mason University, and Hallie B. Fox, an educational consultant studying school climate, used these approaches to examine teacher well-being during the COVID-19 pandemic. They found that empathetic school leadership, work with teams, and access to additional resources were all instrumental in increasing teachers' sense of well-being. Such a framework could be a useful component in preparing to develop meaningful action plans (Walter & Fox, 2021).

To successfully improve the antiracist climate of our classroom or school, even as we assess the school climate and culture, we must each individually develop our own self-reflective, culturally conscious practices. As a team, we must remain open to learning about others' life experiences and their perceptions of our classroom or school.

Phase 2: Meditating for Courage

The action plan example we offer is very detailed, but it is one thing to put words into a plan and another to act on it; this is where resistance arises: "You want me to look at myself? You want me to change what I am doing? Are you telling me that the way I have always run my classroom can be improved? How dare you!" Responding to resistance and defensiveness calls for patience and courage.

Courage means taking conscious action, recognizing fear and anxiety. The call to courage may mean standing up for what you believe in, even if you feel anxious about the consequences. It arises from a place of deep moral commitment within oneself. It may also mean joining with others to mutually inspire each other's courage. However, you are likely to find that you will need both moral and intellectual courage:

> moral courage—standing up and acting when injustices occur, human rights are violated, or someone is treated unfairly—[and] intellectual courage—challenging old assumptions and acting to make changes based on new learnings, understandings, and insights gleaned from experience and educational research. (Mason, Rivers Murphy, et al., 2020, p. 100)

As James Baldwin (1962) says, "Not everything that is faced can be changed, but nothing can be changed until it is faced." As you contemplate how to take action for significant change, we invite you to find time to meditate on the courage you will need and the courage you have! The suggested meditations can be used by individuals or by your planning team.

Now is the time for us to take some deep breaths—to center ourselves with a meditation on courage. Sit either on the floor or in a chair with your feet firmly on the ground, your spine straight, and your eyes closed, gaze lowered. You can record the following ahead of time (at a slow to moderate pace) or have someone read it to you as you follow along.

- *Take a few deep breaths, slowly inhaling and exhaling.*
- *Imagine that you are on a path, walking alone and enjoying being outdoors.*
- *All is going well—you can hear birds singing, smell the sweet fragrance of flowers, and feel a gentle breeze. (Pause.)*
- *Continue to breathe slowly and deeply. Enjoy your walk. (Pause.)*
- *You turn a corner, and the path becomes steeper. (Pause.)*
- *You gaze upward and decide that although the path is steep, you want to keep going forward.*
- *You continue to climb, and although the path narrows, you are making good progress. (Pause.)*
- *Continue to breathe deeply. (Pause.)*
- *As you look ahead, you see where a fallen tree blocks the path.*
- *You approach and realize that, yes, you will be able to climb over it. (Pause.)*
- *With a little extra effort, you are able to climb over the tree. You congratulate yourself.*
- *You are almost to the top. As you round another corner, you are surprised to see that the path ahead is changing; you will need to head down a hill and over a small stream before continuing to climb upward. (Pause.)*
- *You look at your options—to turn around or go forward—remembering that if you reach the top, the way down on the other side will be easier. (Pause.)*
- *So, taking a few deep breaths, you head down the hill. (Pause.)*

- *When you reach the stream, you have two options: to walk across a makeshift tree bridge that is a few feet above the stream, or to walk several yards to a group of boulders and climb over the boulders.*
- *You make a decision, glad that you are wearing sneakers, and proceed across, being careful with each step you take. (Pause.)*
- *Whew, you have made it to the other side.*
- *You glance back, glad that you successfully crossed the stream.*
- *A few more feet, and you are at the top of the hill. As you reach the top, you are out of breath. It was not an easy climb. Yet, the view is spectacular. (Pause.)*
- *You take a few deep breaths and, remembering your journey, open your eyes.*

Like your mountain climb, some actions we take will require courage. It may be the courage to keep going, to make tough decisions, or to persevere. Whatever the case, you will realize you have courage, and that courage is available to you and will help you as you proceed.

Please note this meditation is one example, and there are many others for meditating on courage—both guided visualizations and other examples of strengthening your resolve and providing a neural pathway to better decisions. However, Christine has used meditations such as the preceding one many, many times throughout her career, sometimes inserting an idea like, "As you round the corner, appearing before you is a word or action to guide you," relying on a meditative sense of discovery to help prepare her for action.

Phase 3: Acting on Your Plan With Courage

Once you have bolstered your preparedness for planning, please return again to part 1 of your action plan: goals and strategies (figure 10.2, page 154). Then proceed with your team to develop part 2 (figure 10.3), which provides details regarding steps, timelines, and responsibilities. This example outlines a plan for subgoal 3 from our plan to eliminate suspensions and expulsions.

Once you have developed an action plan for a subgoal, the next step is implementation. As you implement, work with your community to monitor programs and adjust as needed.

As you proceed, also look for opportunities to celebrate the work within your community; this is hard work, and it takes time. "It takes time to build a heart centered school community, through infusing and weaving consciousness,

Instructions: Use a copy of this form for each subgoal from part 1 of the action plan.

Goal: Eliminate student suspensions and expulsions.			
Goal and Tasks What needs to be done for the goal (or subgoal) to be achieved?	Timeline How long will it take to accomplish this task?	Responsibility Who are the people responsible for this task?	Resources Needed What funds, training, external support, and so on are needed?
Subgoal 3: Identify causes of suspensions and expulsions—consider educator attitudes (conscious and unconscious) potentially leading to recommendations for suspensions and expulsions.			
Task 3.1: Training on— a. Impact of suspensions and expulsions on young children's mental health, traumatic experience, and future K–12 education (for example, increased likelihood of dropping out and so on) b. Meaning of implicit bias, including research showing its impact of suspensions and expulsions of Black children and other children of color	Two months after acceptance of action plan	Leadership team	Funds for hiring trainer or using organizational resources such as technical assistance center (for example, Head Start Technical Assistance Center)
Task 3.2: Having staff members take IAT and reflect individually and collectively on personal results	Three months after acceptance of action plan	Individual staff member responsibility	Time to take IAT
Task 3.3: Classroom observations by video with follow-up conversation	Three months after acceptance of action plan	Impartial external observer who records classrooms	Funds maybe needed to hire video observer consultant
Task 3.4: Exploration of restorative practices as alternatives to discipline	Four months after acceptance of action plan	Leadership team	Funds maybe needed for restorative practices training for staff

Figure 10.3: Compassionate school action plan for improving school culture and climate (part 2)—Timelines and responsibilities.

Visit go.SolutionTree.com/diversityandequity for a free reproducible version of this figure.

compassion, confidence, and courage into the classroom, school, and beyond so that every community member feels its sustaining effect" (Mason, Rivers Murphy, et al., 2020, p. 125).

Remember the words of the great and courageous activist and congressman John Lewis (2018):

> Do not get lost in a sea of despair. Be hopeful, be optimistic. Our struggle is not the struggle of a day, a week, a month, or a year, it is the struggle of a lifetime. Never, ever be afraid to make some noise and get in good trouble, necessary trouble.

This work of antiracism and cultural competence development is hard, often emotionally painful and discouraging. The wins seem few and far between. The challenges, especially the systemic challenges, certainly can feel overwhelming. Opening our school climate to be culturally inclusive and racially equitable is a daily task. We know we need to look back and see our missteps: Did we take on too much, too soon? Did we have the resources needed in our planning? Did we get the support we expected, or at least hoped for? If not, how do we address our concerns when working on our next goal?

Considering the action plan example discussed in phase 1 and implemented in phase 3, there may be several opportunities to celebrate. *Even with all those challenges and questions, we must stop and make the time to celebrate the small victories—maybe even some big ones!*

Celebrations can build an antiracist, culturally responsive community in many ways. In 2018, a group of South San Francisco, California, fifth graders learned about how in 1960, six-year-old Ruby Bridges courageously defied jeering White crowds while walking to her newly integrated school. Using the antiracist SEL skill of advocacy, these students gathered locally and statewide, virtually and in person, to share their ideas for a day to recognize Bridges's bravery. In 2021, the California legislature passed a resolution making every November 14 Ruby Bridges Walk to School Day. There is now an initiative to make this day a national school event. The *Pacifica Tribune* of Pacifica, California, describes the event in 2022:

> On Monday morning, Raina Davis-Turner and Georgina Byrch walked from the Pacifica Fire Station on Edgemar to Ocean Shore School in Pacifica, carrying a handwritten poster that read, "RUBY WALKED FOR JUSTICE & EQUALITY FOR ALL." The second graders were marching in a large crowd

of parents and students who had gathered to celebrate Ruby Bridges Walk to School Day.

"Ruby Bridges was a Black girl who went to an all-white school," said Raina.

"And she also was the only student in her class," said Georgina.

"And when she was walking there, policemen had to go with her," added Raina. (Seager, 2022)

Shivani Ganguly (Randy's daughter), mother of a kindergartner who learned about Ruby Bridges that day, described the impact on herself and her son:

> I was really thrilled that Ocean Shore believes in teaching about racism even to the youngest kids. My son's teacher read the class a book about Ruby Bridges and answered lots of their questions. It helped me begin to talk with him at home about racism. My son is brown-skinned and may face racism in the future. I want him to know how to stand up against it, for himself and for others. (S. Ganguly, personal communication, November 16, 2022)

Celebrations are indispensable in building racially and culturally inclusive communities and warm, positive school climates. When staff members have worked together with intentionality and commitment toward important goals, celebrating milestones builds commitment, confidence, courage, and community.

HEART+ Takeaways

A collective, equitable vision can guide actions in a healthy school environment as school leaders instill hope in their community to support students, families, and staff. Leaders can also foster empathy and understanding within classrooms through encouraging culturally sound practices and involving others in goal setting and action planning. Using a heart centered approach to planning, leaders can tackle difficult problems with a mindful awareness of needs and concerns. Although successful implementation is never assured, such shared leadership and planning can contribute to community support—a vital component of creating a backdrop for equity, student well-being, and empathy and compassion for self and others.

PART 3

Antiracist Curriculum and Staff Support

CHAPTER 11

A Light to Shine Together: Professional Development and Supports

We do not heal in isolation. Connecting with others is how we develop compassion for others and for ourselves.

—Desmond Tutu

Principle 11: Advance antiracism and cultural competence through professional development, coaching, and differentiated supports.

As we learn more about the roots of bias, we urge our readers to consider, once again, what they can do. What should we do as we strive to implement an antiracist, culturally competent agenda in our schools?

We know that not everything will go smoothly as we strive to overcome bias and create an antiracist environment that will more fully support all students and families. Sometimes conflicts and disagreements will arise. Some educators may think we are coddling students who are not living up to whatever expectations, especially behavioral ones, that they have. Other educators may struggle to move away from White-centric developmental norms or be hesitant to move toward a more student-centered approach with greater agency afforded to individual students.

We suggest that early childhood leaders can take staff through the visioning process we share in chapter 10 (page 143). Following a visioning process, action planning (see chapter 10) is important: turning the shared vision into action.

As you consider the recommendations in this chapter, we caution readers to view our recommendations as a package. We discuss professional development, the tiered system of equity supports (TSES), *and* relational coaching. It is not professional development, TSES, *or* relational coaching as stand-alone activities. To truly differentiate professional development to meet the needs of individual staff, schools must adopt all components. To obtain the much-needed changes and move forward, staff participation in a professional development session alone will not suffice. Tools are needed to help individual staff members and teams problem solve as they explore how to implement the recommendations to reduce racism and bias and bring about greater equity. And additional supports are sometimes necessary to demonstrate new practices in classrooms and to mentor and coach teachers to increase the efficacy of the new practices.

Professional Development Approaches

Alana Harte (2022), a former teacher and equity consultant, provides six sound strategies for equity development in an article for Edutopia. She begins by recognizing a problem that often exists in schools as they begin their equity work:

> During a training I recently attended, I noticed a concerning trend: Equity-minded faculty listened with rapt attention, asked questions, and reflected in groups on the insight they gained. For them, it was an exciting opportunity to learn more about improving their craft and honoring student identity. Faculty who were not equity minded were silent, their disinterest palpable, doodling on sticky notes and waiting for time to pass. For them, it was yet another obligatory and uninspiring meeting. (Harte, 2022)

As you review the six strategies that Harte (2022) recommends for professional development, consider which might be priorities for you to use at your school and why.

1. **Differentiation and vertical alignment:** Be up-front with the basics in order to establish a shared language among all staff members. This foundation will be useful as topics get more sensitive and complicated. From here, staff members might receive more personalized learning depending on what they teach, what they're interested in pursuing, and what their role in the community is. Leaders can emphasize the ongoing nature of equity learning and its potential for personal growth.

2. **Inclusivity:** Harte (2022) compares the mindset needed for equity work to that of educators who consider reading a foundational skill for all content areas. All staff members are part of the equity journey, supporting and leading this work in various ways.

3. **Open discussions:** Leaders can emphasize that learning about equity is a journey. No one will uncover and dispel their implicit biases in a single session. The key is having conversations in which staff members are encouraged to participate with a protocol that prioritizes honesty while supporting emotional safety.

4. **Opportunities for reflection:** The goal for equity-focused professional development should be to give staff members a chance to look at the ways they think about and engage with others. Participants may feel discomfort and even the need to defend themselves, but a safe environment for the conversations will also help ensure that these revelations are meaningful and effect change rather than cause shame.

5. **Connection to a bigger strategic plan:** Just as students need to know what they're learning, staff members need clear objectives to work toward with equity work. Professional development can't be a one-off. Some goals that Harte (2022) suggests include "dismantling ability groups, modifying grading policies, incorporating restorative practices, posting images with people from underrepresented groups, improving interaction with all students, creating a culture of belonging, and improving student outcomes overall." Connected to this is the need for accountability measures.

6. **Prioritization:** School staff members are no strangers to new initiatives. But if school leaders make clear that time should be spent on equity, that will become a schoolwide focus. Leaders can integrate an equity focus in their classroom observations and evaluations as well as build it into existing meetings. Rather than being an agenda item, it should be a lens through which to view all efforts.

Gina Gullo and Floyd Beachum (2020) propose a model they call the *social justice leadership for implicit bias reduction framework*, which we first touched on in chapter 9 (page 131). Gullo (2021) further refines this framework, listing the following considerations.

- **Decision-making supports:** Shared decision making, restorative conferences, and collaboration
- **Intergroup contact:** Inclusive community, expanded and diverse network, and empathic capacity
- **Information building:** Understanding of individual needs, community supports, and communication
- **Mindfulness:** Social-emotional skills, cultural relevance, and mindful conversations

While implicit bias reduction is their stated goal, the four sets of practical strategies in three domains (relationships, flexibility, and morality) also constitute a compelling approach to attaining an equitable school climate.

Let's focus on a few of these strategies as we consider the role of the school leader as a facilitator—a facilitator who will be consciously aware of the differing needs of staff, students, and families. In related work, Gullo and Beachum (2020) describe the following.

- **Using a structured six-step *decision-making process* to guide shared decision making, especially at "vulnerable decision points":** That process begins with "(1) defining the problem, (2) defining objectives and issues, (3) developing alternatives, (4) estimating consequences of decision choices, (5) making trade-offs and selecting and, finally, (6) implementing and monitoring the decision" (Gullo & Beachum, 2020, p. 8).
- **Implementing *restorative practices* that include having conferences with the parties who are in conflict and facilitating meetings to review options, perhaps involving peer mediation:** While used more frequently at upper-elementary and secondary school levels, simplified versions of this approach can be used with young children (see *Little Learners, Big Hearts*, chapter 5, pages 149–151, for more about using restorative practices with young children). Additionally, the process can be useful in working with staff and families. See chapter 9 in this book (page 131) for more about restorative practices with adults.
- ***Fostering relationships* to enhance empathy, relatability, and the school and community climate:** These can be enhanced through intentional efforts to acknowledge needs and concerns and intentional efforts to build a sense of inclusion and empathy in the community.

- **Turning to *culturally responsive* positive behavioral interventions and supports (CR-PBIS):** These should include a process for acknowledging the role of student and family culture in considering interventions to address behavior and discipline concerns.

- **Expanding *intergroup interactions* between individuals of different subgroups within the school community:** Use protocols to honor differences and demonstrate administrative supports for different subgroups within your community.

- **Reducing stress and increasing conscious awareness of the needs and options through *mindfulness techniques*:** We discuss these further on page 78. Engage in mindful consideration of specific circumstances with a compassionate understanding of the options that might be most productive and helpful in alleviating concerns of specific individuals or groups within your community.

In their book *Implicit Bias in Schools: A Practitioner's Guide*, Gullo and colleagues (2019) recommend both individual and institutional activities (tied to the strategies in the implicit bias reduction framework) to reduce implicit bias. Following are many of their recommendations (from chapters 5 and 6, pages 79–93 and 97–115, of their text) for effective activities, including several examples we believe align with the Heart Centered Learning and HEART+ approach.

1. **Hope:** Create opportunities for self-empowerment by connecting with others who feel similarly. Use your existing assets, including your position as a leader, to influence and motivate others.

2. **Education:** Seek additional education and experiences outside your comfort zone. Perhaps join a committee or volunteer group that enables you to meet and engage with people who have diverse identities, viewpoints, and experiences.

3. **Acknowledgment:** Decorate your personal space, screen saver, hallways, and so on with counter-stereotypical exemplars. Use books—for children, staff, and families—with role models (and not just Martin Luther King Jr. and Rosa Parks). Consider including an "equity heat map" (see *Evident Equity* [Mascareñaz, 2022]).

4. **Resolution:** Engage in reflection and institutionalize stress-relief activities. Recruit a diverse staff and create diverse working groups, such as a school climate team. Reduce in-the-moment decisions that are more susceptible to implicit bias.

5. **Teaching:** Educate beyond the classroom through speaking and writing, working with families and others in the community to bring up the impacts of both implicit and explicit bias.

6. **+:** Foster intergroup contact with diverse individuals and groups in your community, possibly engaging them in your school as volunteer mentors, readers, and storytellers. Older folks may just need to be asked and are often very willing to come to classrooms, especially those of young children.

Decision-Making Supports

One area needing further explanation in Gullo and Beachum's (2020) implicit bias reduction framework is disciplinary decision-making supports. We highlight this area because it is fraught with the dangers of implicit bias in decision making, leading to disproportionality that negatively impacts Black and Brown children (boys especially) in discipline (Beachum & Gullo, 2020; Carter et al., 2014), academic achievement (Peterson, Rubie-Davies, Osborne, & Sibley, 2016), special education (Iruka et al., 2023), and social-emotional learning (Caven, 2020; Simmons, 2019). These impacts can be seen in early childhood as well as in later grades, from elementary to secondary levels.

Decision-making supports can be structured and shared. Structured decision-making supports often use a flowchart, supported by detailed explanations of each step in the decision-making process, as previously explained. Shared decision making (either instead of structured decision making or in addition to it) proposes that flexibility and supportive interpersonal relationships (as with students and their families) are often needed to adjust the process and results of a structured approach. A "restorative meeting" (Hopkins, 2021) is an example of combining structured and shared decision making.

Jason E. Harlacher and Sara A. Whitcomb (2022), in *Bolstering Student Resilience: Creating a Classroom With Consistency, Connection, and Compassion*, offer a model, with numerous specific resources, that blends structured and shared decision making. With this approach, teachers use strategies such as explicit teaching, reteaching, prompting, and self-monitoring to help students better understand expectations and receive more systematic feedback to strengthen engagement, understanding, and learning. While Harlacher and Whitcomb (2022) do not address implicit bias directly, coauthor Sara Whitcomb explains the relevance for early childhood educators:

The model we propose supports classroom teachers as they work to develop systems and practices encouraging inclusion, differentiation, and empathic responses to student social and emotional needs and learning. In our book, we focus on classroom support strategies to foster healthy relationships and approaches for responding to various challenging behaviors with compassion and curiosity, while increasing predictability and decreasing ambiguity in the environment.

Our problem-solving approach (structured decision making) identifies patterns of student behaviors and communication between educators and students to understand such patterns (shared decision making). This shared decision making would be especially valuable with younger children because it supports them developing at an early age self-awareness about their own behavior and social awareness of how their behavior affects others. Since behavioral expectations from families and communities may differ widely from each other and from classroom expectations, an approach like this helps both the teacher and the child identify potential cultural differences and work through them, nurturing connection and compassion. (S. Whitcomb, personal communication, January 19, 2024)

A Scenario

Keeping in mind the six decision-making steps outlined previously (page 168), consider this scenario.

Two school staff members have had a long-standing conflict over how best to work with Usama, an immigrant student who, with his mother, is a refugee from Iraq. The family has experienced significant trauma: the father was killed in the Iraq War, and mother and child escaped to Jordan and then came to the United States through a refugee resettlement program. The student, now in second grade, speaks little English and alternates between withdrawal and angry outbursts. The classroom teacher believes that the student needs discipline for the disruptive outbursts to adapt to the community's language and culture, make friends with other students, and essentially "become American." The multilingual teacher works daily with Usama to support his English acquisition and believes that, because of his significant trauma, building trust with him is a necessary first step before he can meet the classroom teacher's academic and behavioral expectations. The disagreement has escalated to an argument with accusatory language in the teachers' lounge. (Note: This scenario is based on Randy's work in 2009 with a school where a similar situation occurred. The U.S. Department of Education's Office for Civil Rights in Boston requested her help.)

How could a leader use decision-making supports to resolve the conflict and ensure that the teachers provide what Usama needs?

- **Defining the problem:** Two teachers have very different approaches to teaching a young student. The classroom teacher believes having the student quickly assimilate and implementing school behavioral rules without exception is the best route, while the multilingual teacher advocates for a slower, less pressured approach, prioritizing building trusting relationships with the student and his mother. This disagreement has escalated emotionally to the detriment of the student, the individual teachers, and overall staff morale as the conflict has become public.

- **Defining objectives and issues:** The main objective is to resolve the teachers' disagreement so both of them can cooperate in the best interests of the student. An additional objective is to improve communication between the two teachers so they are able to resolve their disagreements professionally and amicably.

- **Developing alternatives:** The assistant principal could ask the principal to discipline both teachers for unprofessional behavior, putting notes in their files about the incident. As an alternative, the assistant principal could suggest a restorative meeting that would include himself, the school counselor, and the two teachers. Belinda Hopkins (2021), in her mini-book *Restorative Leadership*, suggests two initial questions: "What were you thinking?" and "What were you feeling inside?" (p. 26). In this situation, a leader might ask, "What happened in the teachers' lounge? How was your relationship in the past, before having to work together with Usama? Who has been harmed by this relationship, and by the incident? How have they been impacted? What do you need so you can move forward together to best support the child?" Hopkins (2021) writes, "The answers encourage empathy, leave room for the person to acknowledge that they themselves have been affected" (p. 29). This is the basis for making decisions moving forward.

- **Estimating consequences of decision choices:** It is necessary for both stakeholders to recognize that their conflict is not in the best interests of the student. They consider the following—meet with Usama's mother to learn more about the child and his past experiences, his behavior at home, and so on; discuss what they learned from the mother and how it may or may not change their approaches; use email or occasional meetings to provide information on Usama's progress; and meet with the school counselor or the assistant principal if they reach an impasse in their collaborative relationship. At a future time, they may meet to assess to what degree these choices are working and whether any other practices are necessary. An additional restorative meeting can be another option.

> ### *Pause and Reflect*
> - Ask several colleagues to do a role play using the preceding scenario about Usama and the restorative meeting. Consider how you might answer the questions.
> - Do you think implicit bias might play a role in either teacher's actions? What are your thoughts about the next steps?

The Tiered System of Equity Supports

Before or during the visioning process, learning about bias and reflecting on it personally, alone and in small groups, is a powerful way to support each other through a challenging exploration. Consider adopting—and modifying as needed—our plan for a tiered system of equity supports.

As educators, we are all familiar with the multitiered system of supports (MTSS) model. We know it is used in a variety of contexts at all grade levels: behavioral interventions, academic supports, SEL and mental health, and so on. We propose that the MTSS approach is also helpful in scaffolding professional development on bias, recognizing that it is a challenging area for adults to learn about and to internalize, and thereby make real, long-term changes in their behaviors.

As part of an overall equity strategy for a school or center, we propose a TSES model. Activities that address discomfort in discussing bias as well as seeing the origins of one's implicit bias are linked to TSES. While professional learning experiences are crucial, challenging situations that call for both structured and shared decision making often arise. One example is implementing restorative meetings among adults to improve collaboration. Another approach is to understand that implicit bias is more likely to occur at "vulnerable decision points." In such situations, using mindfulness practices can prevent hasty decisions that may involve unconscious bias.

In the TSES model graphic in figure 11.1, we propose a series of scaffolded activities.

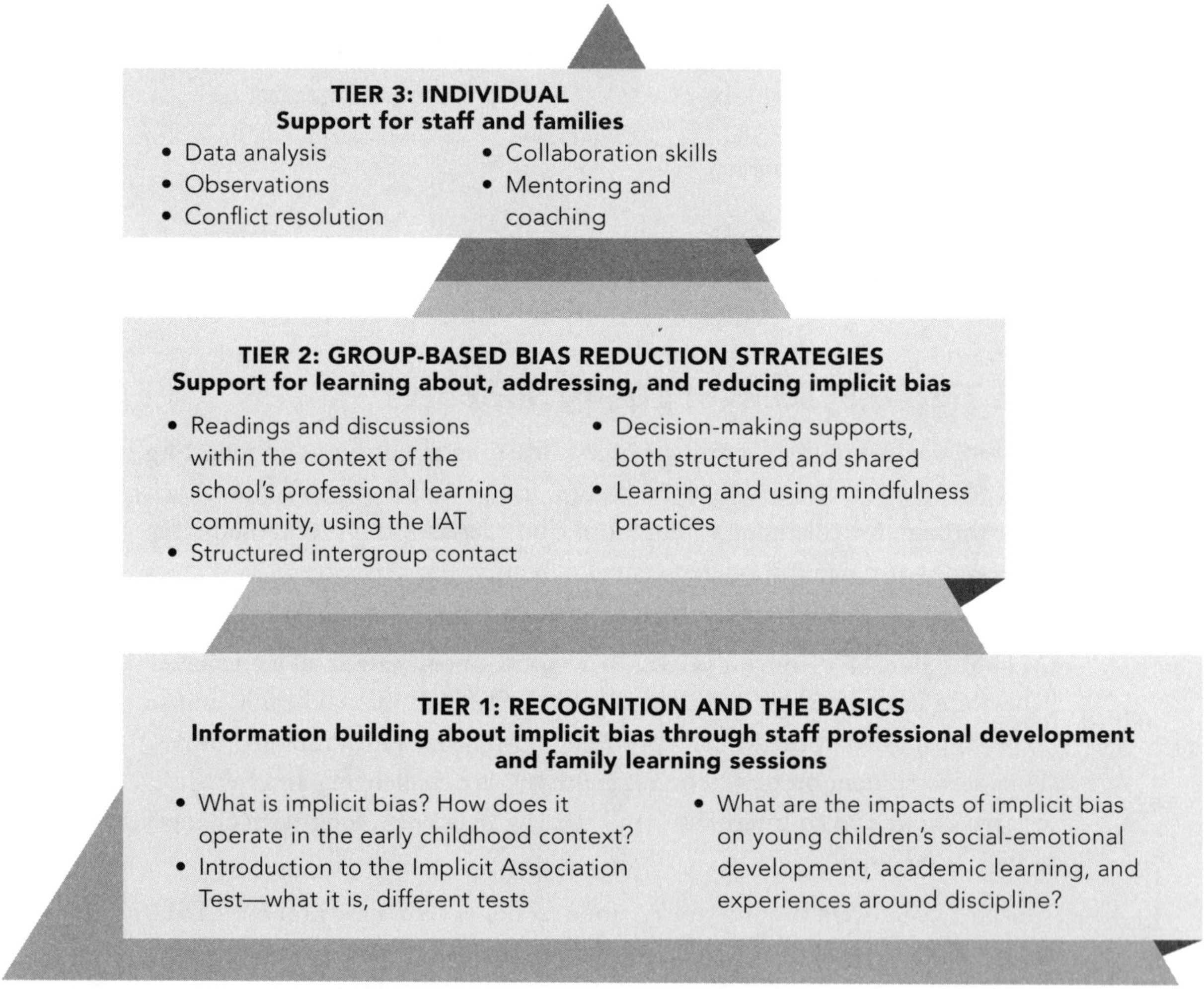

TIER 3: INDIVIDUAL
Support for staff and families
- Data analysis
- Observations
- Conflict resolution
- Collaboration skills
- Mentoring and coaching

TIER 2: GROUP-BASED BIAS REDUCTION STRATEGIES
Support for learning about, addressing, and reducing implicit bias
- Readings and discussions within the context of the school's professional learning community, using the IAT
- Structured intergroup contact
- Decision-making supports, both structured and shared
- Learning and using mindfulness practices

TIER 1: RECOGNITION AND THE BASICS
Information building about implicit bias through staff professional development and family learning sessions
- What is implicit bias? How does it operate in the early childhood context?
- Introduction to the Implicit Association Test—what it is, different tests
- What are the impacts of implicit bias on young children's social-emotional development, academic learning, and experiences around discipline?

Figure 11.1: Tiered system of equity supports in early childhood education—Strategies for building knowledge and skills with staff and families.

The three tiers are as follows.

- **Tier 1: Universal supports**—Promote awareness and information building as goals.

- **Tier 2: Group supports**—This tier is a little different from the familiar MTSS model. It is proposed not for staff who need extra support, but rather for all staff, in small groups, to deepen and personalize the information offered at Tier 1. For families, Tier 2 support would be an option offered through, for example, family nights, rather than a requirement as it is for staff.

- **Tier 3: Individual supports**—This tier offers a set of interventions when a staff member (or multiple staff members) continues to demonstrate implicit bias in areas such as discipline referrals and academic results. This support must be based on data and could be determined, for example, through doubly disaggregating data by teacher, race or ethnicity, and gender of students. Indicators could include consistently sending Black students to the director or principal but rarely sending White students.

Another source of data is conversations with families. For example, if BIPOC families express discomfort with a particular teacher or request that their children be placed with another teacher, leaders can keep track of such reports. Such data may offer signs of implicit bias but in themselves would not be conclusive. Classroom observations, followed by conversations, with mentoring or coaching, would be necessary.

In sum, be comprehensive in your approach to working with staff when multiple data sources (not just a single incident) show a need for improvement in equitable outcomes and interactions. Be patient but also willing to make difficult staffing decisions.

Tier 1: Concentric Circles for Earliest Messages

We suggest using this activity with staff *after* people have used the IAT (see chapter 8, page 119). It may give them more insight into their experience with the IAT.

The purpose of the concentric circles activity is to provide an opportunity for participants to explore stereotypes, often unconscious ones, in a way that reduces defensiveness. This activity can be used with groups of as many as one hundred staff members and as few as ten. For big groups, a large space is necessary, such as a gymnasium or cafeteria. With a smaller number of participants, a classroom (with furniture pushed aside to create an open space) could be sufficient. We suggest using this activity at Tier 1, but it could also be effective at Tier 2, after participants have learned basic information about bias. The protocol to use is as follows. The facilitator should use these directions to lead the concentric circles activity.

1. Ask participants to form two circles with equal numbers of people, an inner circle and an outer circle, with participants facing each other so each person has a partner. If numbers permit, have about six to ten people in each circle. If there is an odd number of people, an extra facilitator can join a circle. If no extra facilitator is available, ask for a volunteer to step out but to still consider the questions asked in step 6 and to join the discussion after the activity.

2. Instruct participants, "During this exercise, you will have the opportunity to respond to several questions, talking solely with your partner. The person listening should only give feedback with body language, eye contact, and simple paralanguage expressions like *aha*." You may explain the practice of active listening.

3. Tell participants, "After one of you responds for one minute, I will call the time and say, 'Switch.' It is then the other person's time to respond, without interruption or discussion. When each pair has responded to the question, I'll say, 'Rotate,' and ask the outer circle to move one person to the right, forming new pairs for the next question."

4. Start with an "easy" question so participants get used to doing the exercise, practicing active listening, and moving to a new partner. The first question could be, "What is one of your favorite holidays and why?" Or you might ask something more directly related to your program, school, or community. Be sure you aren't asking a yes-or-no question.

5. Ask participants in the concentric circles, "What are your earliest memories about . . . ?" You can use as many of the following groups as you have time for, but be sure to include the ones with asterisks: Native American,* Black,* Latino/a,* Asian,* White,* Muslim, or Jewish people. If there are specific immigrant groups in your community, such as Haitians or Ukrainians, naming and asking about those groups could add attention to local concerns.

6. Ask participants to move out of their circles into whatever space is conducive to a discussion. With a large number of participants, if possible, form smaller groups so the discussion engages all or most of them. Use these discussion questions.

    - What were some of your earliest messages about which groups? Were you aware you were holding these messages? Have they become stereotypes? Do you think they may have affected anything you said or did in the past?
    - When you were asked about your earliest memories of the group with which you identify, what was your response?
    - If you are White, when White people were mentioned, what was your response? What does it mean to identify as White given that Whiteness is seen as the norm in our society?
    - What is a stereotype? How do we learn them? How do we teach or transmit them to others? How are they harmful? What are some long-term effects of stereotypes?

To close the activity, offer participants a quiet moment, with a few slow breaths. Ask them to consider how they felt when they started the activity and how they are feeling now, after the discussion. Accept all possibilities, such as "I feel more anxious," "I am curious," "I learned about myself and others," and so on. If it helps the discussion, share your own experience of the activity.

In *Little Learners, Big Hearts*, we discuss the role implicit bias plays in a range of racial and cultural inequities among young children and some strategies for addressing school-community tensions rooted in such biases. These sections may be useful particularly for Tier 1 of TSES and follow-up after the concentric circles activity. See table 11.1 (page 178) for suggestions on where to find various topics related to bias in our teacher's guide.

Tier 2: Movement Beyond My Comfort Zone

Pema Chödrön (2019), in her book *Welcoming the Unwelcome*, adapts famed psychologist Lev Vygotsky's (1978) zone of proximal development model to discuss how we, as adults, can move beyond our comfort zone without immediately feeling an excessive, even paralyzing or panic-inducing sense of risk (see figure 11.2, page 179). This activity could be used as a complement for a collaborative team that is reading one of the challenging children's books we discuss in chapter 7 of *Little Learners, Big Hearts*; watching a film or documentary about Black, Latino/a, Asian, or Indigenous history and culture; or reading a challenging short story, novel, or poem about race and culture.

Table 11.1: Additional Resources for Discussing Implicit Bias

Area of Implicit Bias Impact	Brief Summary	Chapters in *Little Learners, Big Hearts*
Discipline	Research has confirmed that implicit bias is a major cause of educators' disproportionate disciplinary decisions in early childhood, especially for Black boys, significantly resulting in the preschool-to-prison pipeline. Restorative practices offer a critical alternative.	Chapter 3, pages 90–92; chapter 5, pages 148–151 (restorative practices)
Academics	Implicit bias leads to low academic expectations of many BIPOC children. Attention to multilingual and multicultural learners' needs requires educators to be aware of their own implicit bias about these differences.	Chapter 3, pages 88–91; chapter 4, pages 113–115; chapter 7, pages 184–189
Original SEL versus transformative SEL	Educators unaware of their implicit bias may use SEL as a form of social control. The revised approach to SEL, called transformative SEL (or t-SEL), avoids this potential concern when teaching social-emotional competencies.	Chapter 5, page 149; chapter 6, page 171
Bias-related teasing, peer aggression, and bullying	Implicit bias reinforces the power imbalance that is central to these behaviors.	Chapter 6, pages 158–159, 161, 166
Family relationships	Implicit bias undercuts family empowerment when staff focus on deficits, failing to see the strengths diverse families pass on to their children and to the school community.	Chapter 4, pages 108–110
Community tensions around race and culture	Interracial and intercultural conflicts, including microaggressions, are often hidden by implicit bias (or exposed by explicit bias) in a school community and need to be addressed with caution and sensitivity but also directness.	Chapter 1, pages 42–43; chapter 3, pages 81–82; chapter 4, pages 104–105, 119–120; chapter 6, pages 155–176

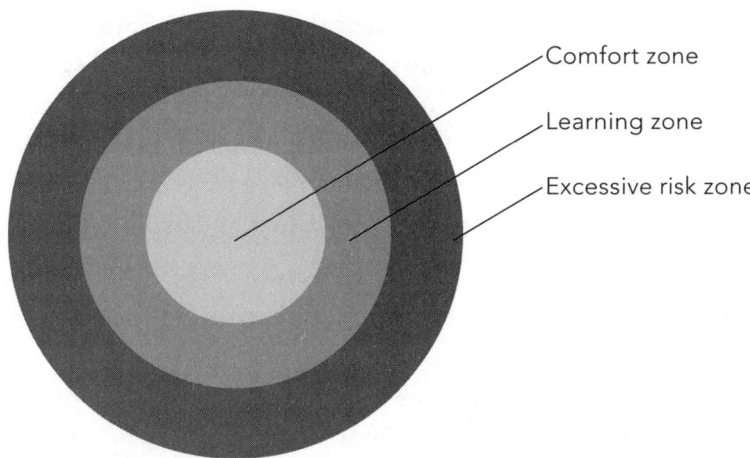

Source: From Welcoming the Unwelcome: Wholehearted Living in a Brokenhearted World *by Pema Chödrön. Copyright © 2019 by the Pema Chödrön Foundation. Reprinted by arrangement with The Permissions Company, LLC on behalf of Shambhala Publications, Inc., Boulder, Colorado, shambhala.com.*

Figure 11.2: Movement beyond my comfort zone.

This mindfulness activity should take place in small groups to facilitate deeper conversation during the debrief discussion. The protocol is as follows.

1. **Explanation of three zones:** If possible, all participants should have their own copy of the graphic in figure 11.2. If not, then the graphic could be projected onto a screen that all can see. As the facilitator, read the following background information, very slowly, to orient participants:

   > The comfort zone is what we're most attracted to. It's where we prefer to hang out.... The learning zone is where we stretch beyond our comfort.... The outermost circle in this model is called the "excessive risk" zone. This area is usually too challenging to nurture growth.... If you force yourself to be in this outer zone, you'll be too traumatized to learn anything.... But if you spend as much time as you can hanging out in your learning zone, eventually you'll be ready for some of these greater challenges. Everyone's three zones are very personal to them. (Chödrön, 2019, pp. 59–60)

2. **Mindful breathing:** Ask participants to close their eyes, if they are comfortable doing so, and slowly begin breathing in and out. Out breaths should be slower than in breaths, perhaps breathing in on a count of three and out on a count of six.

3. **Comfort zone:** As they continue their slow, measured breathing, ask participants to imagine a physical place where they feel safe and comfortable, perhaps but not necessarily with other people or maybe with a pet. Guide them with a few suggestions, such as lying in bed, sitting on a swing, relaxing in a pool or lake, and so on. Allow two to three minutes for participants to settle into and explore their comfort zone.

4. **Movement out of comfort zone:** Ask participants to imagine physically moving out of their comfort zone and into a more challenging place, perhaps a store or a room where they see people who look different from themselves or whose language or dialect is different from their own. This could be a memory of such a situation or an imaginary scene they create. It could, for example, involve an interaction with a colleague or a family whose race, culture, language, or even political viewpoint is different from their own.

   Ask participants to notice any sensations of tightness in their body, changes in their breathing, or random but rapid thoughts going through their mind. Ask them to sit with those feelings and thoughts and to explore them with curiosity. What is causing their discomfort, or even fear? How strong is that discomfort? Does it feel more like fear? What are they feeling on a scale of 1 to 10, with 1 being low level and 10 being high level? If their level of discomfort is around 5 or maybe 6, they are likely still in the learning zone. If it's higher, they may be moving into the excessive risk zone. If this is the case, ask participants to modify the scene or story they have created, not to move back into their comfort zone but to remain in their learning zone.

5. **Next steps:** Ask participants to stay in their learning zone while identifying some learning goals. Offer suggestions that they explore ways to expand their intergroup contact, watch films about Black history, or read several challenging children's books (see *Little Learners, Big Hearts*, chapter 7), but make it clear these are just suggestions. Have them discuss these activities with a friend or colleague.

6. **Discussion:** Ask participants to move into a space for discussion. If numbers are greater than ten to twelve, create small groups for this debrief discussion. Here are some question prompts you might use: "What was the scenario you created in your mind for your comfort zone? What was the scenario you created to challenge yourself in the

learning zone? How did you feel? Slightly or very uncomfortable? Actually fearful? How did you manage the fear, if you did? Did you move back into the learning zone or even the comfort zone? What goal or goals did you come up with for next steps? What can you do today, tomorrow, or in the future to keep challenging yourself while exploring your learning zone?"

The comfort zone activity can be repeated in groups over the course of the school year. You might also suggest that participants go back to it in pairs or small groups of colleagues, perhaps at a time of curriculum or event planning, or even on their own.

Tier 3: Targeted Interventions for Skeptical Staff

It is important to recognize that many educators may not be interested in or willing to do the self-reflection needed to explore their own implicit bias. They may consider this a private or political matter and feel it is not the school leader's right to challenge them or probe their views. How you respond is critical, especially in this time of political polarization. Approaching the conversation through a pre-existing relationship is best, as it may allow for a more open dialogue.

Whatever the leader's relationship with the challenging educator has been, discussing data (including but not solely observations) is a practical place to begin. Unless you can show through data and direct observation that a staff member's bias is negatively impacting colleagues, families, students, or all three, you may have to reconsider your concerns or wait out the educator's presence.

One principal Randy coached for three years was frustrated with several staff members who made clear they were not interested in supporting the equity initiatives she was leading. This principal's approach was to continue strengthening these initiatives in her school. As the overall equity focus developed across curricula, discipline, and relationships with families, these tenured staff members transferred to other schools in the large district.

On the other hand, you may find that with time and support, some of these staff members will change on their own. Surprises do happen! For more on individual interventions with more skeptical staff members, see chapter 9 (page 131), where we discuss restorative practices with staff members, and the next section on relational coaching for equity.

Relational Coaching for Equity

Earlier in this chapter, we presented a tiered model of professional learning about implicit bias and strategies to reduce it. We discussed approaches for Tier 1 and Tier 2 and some for Tier 3. Here we offer an additional approach for working with staff members, or potentially family members, who are uncomfortable with, even unwilling to do, the self-reflection necessary to change behavior that is rooted in bias, explicit or implicit. We discuss how relational coaching can be a Tier 3 approach, although it is certainly not limited to that level.

Coaching in education usually means instructional coaching. While instruction, including curriculum, is central to learning, our view in this leader's guide and in *Little Learners, Big Hearts* is that antiracist, culturally competent social-emotional learning is carried out through relationships within the early childhood education community—among young children, between adults and young children, and among adults, including staff, program leaders, and families.

By using the term *relational coaching*, we are emphasizing that whatever the content being discussed in a coaching context, it is first and foremost based on nurturing positive relationships between the coach and coachees. This is true of good instructional coaching (Lang-Raad, 2018; Turner, 2023) as well as coaching around issues as complex and emotionally challenging as implicit bias.

A major responsibility of early childhood leaders is coaching staff to enable them to promote equity, specifically antiracist and cultural equity, in their classrooms and with families. This is often thought of simply as *supervision*, but coaching is a different approach. Coaching can be an important follow-up to professional development because a coach can assist educators in applying what they have learned in professional development sessions or through articles and books (such as *Little Learners, Big Hearts*!). According to Bob and Megan Tschannen-Moran (2010) in their book *Evocative Coaching: Transforming Schools One Conversation at a Time*, "Coaching facilitates learning that sticks" (p. 3). They go on to say:

> Coaching becomes evocative when the coach's concern for consciousness generates increased self-awareness, self-knowledge, and self-monitoring on the part of the teacher. This lays the groundwork for all experiential learning. Mindfulness, defined as the nonjudgmental awareness of what is happening in the present moment, represents both the consciousness that makes conversations evocative as well as the consciousness generated by such conversations. There is no way to foster learning and growth apart from mindfulness. (Tschannen-Moran & Tschannen-Moran, 2010, p. 12)

In chapter 5 (page 71), we discuss our five Cs—(1) consciousness, (2) compassion, (3) confidence, (4) courage, and (5) community. The evocative or relational coaching approach clearly rests not just on consciousness and mindfulness, as explained here, but on the other four elements as well.

Elena Aguilar, author of numerous books on coaching, focuses very specifically on racial and cultural equity dynamics in schools and in her coaching process. In her book *Onward*, Aguilar (2018) describes a Black principal she calls Richard who is struggling to build trust with the White female teachers in his school. He learns that "they're afraid of my blackness, and then I'm expected to take care of *their* emotions" (Aguilar, 2018, p. 114). He says this in response to a teacher expressing her discomfort, even fear, when she is around him, perceiving what she believes to be his anger. The principal describes his own caution, saying, "I barely talk above a whisper when I'm with them!" (Aguilar, 2018, p. 114). Aguilar (2018) goes on to write, "I've worked with numerous African American women leaders who were told they were too loud or too angry and that they 'intimidated' their staffs" (p. 114). She underscores the need for "self-reflection and building cultural competence in ourselves and in others" (Aguilar, 2018, p. 114).

Randy recalls a similar experience when she was co-leading a training with her Black colleagues and mentors in a diverse but also quite wealthy school district in Camden County, New Jersey.

> *Larry (name changed), our unit leader, was demonstrating ways in which racial images are so embedded in our culture that we barely notice them. He held up empty boxes of rice with its picture of Uncle Ben and of pancake mix with a picture of Aunt Jemima. One teacher in the circle became very agitated. When Larry asked her to describe what she was feeling, she blurted out that his anger was "frightening" her. Larry was visibly shocked. As the one White trainer in the team, having seen that Larry was animated but certainly not angry, I stepped in to point out that White people too easily feel threatened when a Black person, especially a Black man, is in charge, and especially when he is challenging racism. I asked the teacher to reflect on why she had reacted in that way. She was both embarrassed and resistant.*

Consider these two incidents and what they might mean in a coaching situation. If you are a BIPOC leader, most likely you have encountered such racially charged dynamics in coaching White educators on your staff. If you are a White leader and a White staff member expresses such unfounded fear, perhaps of a child's family member, then you have a responsibility to address the stereotypes behind the reaction. Relational coaching offers the possibility that if enough trust has been built, the staff member may be open to the deep reflection required to address their unconscious biases.

Aguilar (2018) also strongly supports the value of mindfulness to help us as leaders through challenging situations, suggesting that practicing mindfulness is like "hitting an internal pause button on the drama of life" (p. 127). She goes on to say, "Mindfulness connects us more directly to the present moment. Our perceptions are often distorted by bias, habits, fears, or wishful thinking" (Aguilar, 2018, p. 128).

> ### *Pause and Reflect*
> 1. Have you ever experienced, either as a leader or in another role, others being afraid or very uncomfortable around you because of their racial stereotypes and lack of cultural understanding?
> 2. Have you ever witnessed such a dynamic? If so, how did you feel and what did you do?
> 3. How could you apply the five Cs as a leader to address situations such as those described previously, with Richard as the principal and Larry as a trainer?
> 4. How might mindfulness help you coach a staff member who expresses emotions similar to those of the White educators in the two scenarios of Richard and Larry?
> 5. Can you remember a recent interaction with staff where you could have pushed the pause button to possibly get different results than what occurred? Explain.

HEART+ Takeaways

Leaders can develop equity, a positive school culture, and increased sensitivity to the needs of BIPOC students and their families through professional development that considers the various needs of staff and builds in plans for differentiation, inclusivity, open discussions, reflection, and strategic alignment with an eye toward equity and inclusion as priorities. Professional development is more effective when it is paired with other supports, such as relational coaching, a tiered system of equity supports, and strategies to help staff stretch beyond their comfort zones in order to further develop self-awareness.

CHAPTER 12

Curricula for Young Children: The Building Blocks for Equity in Early Childhood

> I leave you love. I leave you hope. I leave you the challenge of developing confidence in one another. I leave you a thirst for education. I leave you respect for the uses of power. I leave you faith. I leave you racial dignity. I leave you a desire to live harmoniously with your fellow men. I leave you finally a responsibility to our young people.
>
> —Mary McLeod Bethune

Principle 12: Enhance early childhood curricula through culturally relevant pedagogy and intentional efforts to further antiracist practices.

All education concerns itself with raising students who are confident, capable, and ready to take up the mantle of working for a better world. However, the traditional approach to schooling, which gives all students the same treatment irrespective of the teachings of their home cultures or beliefs, can unintentionally favor the learning styles and practices of some students at the expense of others. Moreover, some curricula may lean heavily toward an academic (reading and writing) orientation at the expense of other factors supporting the development of young children (Krogh & Morehouse, 2020). From our heart centered perspective, we encourage schools to find curricula that are supportive of student engagement, interests, cultural identity, and agency (see also chapter 8 in *Little Learners, Big Hearts*). As we say in that chapter:

> Early childhood educators stand at an almost perfect spot for promoting learning as young children naturally are explorers. Infants and toddlers gradually expand their understanding of self and others as they learn more about the world or worlds in which they live. They do a lot of this through movement—moving from space to space, and through poking and prodding, grasping, feeling textures, and using objects (stacking, throwing, dropping, and smashing together). They learn what feels good, what sounds they like, and what is unpleasant. And for many young children, this learning happens without much adult intervention, although we may ignite this learning along the way through adding toys and objects to the environment—giving them new adventures—as we also give them adequate time to explore, to play, and to discover. (Mason et al., 2024, pp. 204–205)

Each state has early childhood standards to assist educators and leaders in planning and evaluating curricula, and these can be helpful in evaluating whichever early childhood program your school chooses to use. In this chapter, we consider these standards in our review and comparison of seven alternative early childhood curricula, looking at state standards and developing antiracist recommendations. The alternative curricula we explore in this chapter offer valuable benefits for all students, providing more inclusive and culturally aware learning experiences.

- We examine language, vocabulary, images, inclusiveness, relationship to instructional exercises, learning centers, classroom organization, amount of structure, recommendations for young children with disabilities, and approaches to help students who are developing at their own pace.
- Included in this chapter are examples from Head Start, HighScope, Montessori, Core Knowledge, Reggio Emilia, Expeditionary Learning, and Curiosity Corner.
- This chapter also includes guidelines for antiracist, antibias, and multicultural approaches when using these curricula. These guidelines and ideas can be useful for both early childhood leaders and staff.

We have tried to provide details that might help both experienced and inexperienced school administrators. Knowing that school administrators often leave many curriculum, instruction, and even classroom organization and management decisions to early childhood staff, we have also designed the chapter to be informative for school staff who may be making curricular and instructional recommendations to administrators. We recommend that school leaders share insights from this chapter with school staff who may be responsible for or interested in identifying curricula to support a compassionate, antiracist approach to learning.

State Standards

Each state or province has standards for early childhood education. Moreover, internationally, many countries have standards and expectations for early childhood. In the United States, Massachusetts is considered a leader in progressive education, having released new focus indicators in 2022. These represent high-leverage practices for supporting students' academic and social-emotional needs and promoting an antiracist, culturally responsive school environment. The Massachusetts Department of Elementary and Secondary Education (2022b) provides four guiding principles for teachers and administrators.

1. Prioritize the **social-emotional well-being** of students and educators as the foundation for effective teaching and learning.

2. Promote **culturally responsive, antiracist teaching and leading practices** that directly aim to disrupt patterns of inequities and systems of oppression against Black, Latino/a, Asian, Indigenous, and multiracial communities.

3. Provide all students with the supports they need to access **grade-level instruction**.

4. Engage students and families in learning through **meaningful partnerships**.

Within the Massachusetts framework are guidelines for administrators and teachers across areas related to curriculum, instruction, learning environment, collaboration with families, management of human resources, reflection, professional collaboration, and continuous learning (see figure 12.1, page 188).

The Massachusetts standards address a variety of key practices for teachers. For example, they highlight the importance of cultural relevance, recommending that teachers do the following.

Overview

The focus indicators highlight high-priority practices for antiracist and culturally responsive teaching and leading. Because teachers and administrators depend on one another to be effective in meeting the needs of every student, the focus indicators for teachers and administrators are complementary.

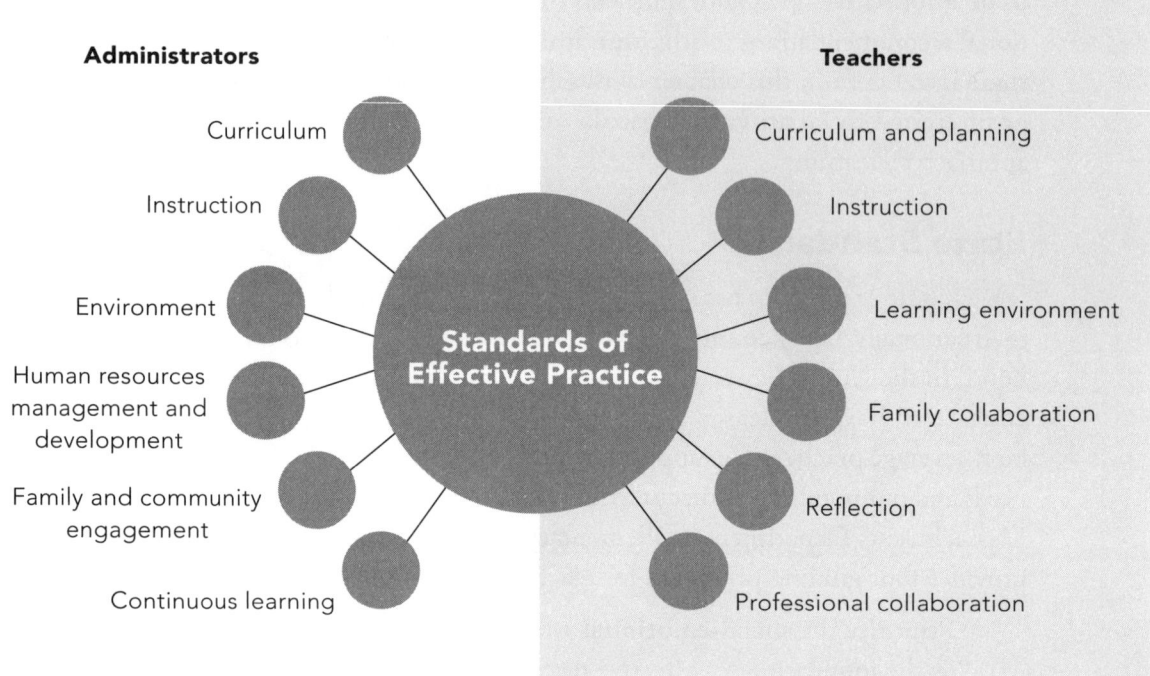

Source: Massachusetts Department of Elementary and Secondary Education, 2022a. Used with permission.

Figure 12.1: Massachusetts indicators for antiracist and culturally responsive teaching.

- Build on and draw from knowledge of their students' identities, skills, developmental levels, cultures, languages, and communities to inform curriculum and planning.

- Skillfully implement curricular materials using evidence-based, inclusive, and culturally responsive instructional methods and activities.

- Use appropriate inclusive practices to make grade-level content accessible and culturally relevant to all students and support individual differences in all students' learning needs, abilities, interests, and levels of readiness.

- Encourage students to think critically, ask questions, and analyze sources, perspectives, and biases in order to deepen learning and make connections between the content and real-world problems.

- Leverage families' cultural and linguistic knowledge and expertise to support student learning.

The Massachusetts Department of Elementary and Secondary Education (2019, 2022b) has standards for preschool and kindergarten curriculum and learning, infants and toddlers, SEL, preK STEM, and dual languages available on its website. It also has a separate website devoted to early learning (www.mass.gov/orgs/department-of-early-education-and-care). That website expands on such concepts as the importance of playful learning, cultural responsiveness to families, inclusiveness, and talks about racism with families and children.

The Early Childhood Program Standards for three- and four-year-olds (Massachusetts Department of Education, 2003) are part of the Massachusetts curriculum framework. The Massachusetts Department of Elementary and Secondary Education also adopted SEL and play standards in 2015 and updated them in 2022. These include expectations tied to the CASEL and NAEYC standards for areas such as awareness of emotions, self-management (impulse control), relationships, empathy, problem solving, and decision making. While these standards do not address racism, antiracism, or antibias, they do reference cultural considerations (Massachusetts Department of Education, 2003; Massachusetts Department of Elementary and Secondary Education, 2015, 2022b).

- By the end of preschool, students will demonstrate interest in or curiosity about others' families, languages, and cultures.
- By the end of kindergarten, students will demonstrate awareness and appreciation of themselves as part of a family, culture, language, community, or group.

These standards indicate that educators are required to treat all students and adults fairly and equitably, including meeting the following expectations (Massachusetts Department of Elementary and Secondary Education, 2015).

- Staff treat students and adults with equal respect, regardless of gender, race, age, language, religion, culture, or family composition.
- Staff provide all students, including those who have disabilities or whose first language is not English, with equal opportunities to take part in all activities.
- Photographs and posters reflect a multicultural and antibias perspective.
- Students appear comfortable, relaxed, happy, and involved in play and other activities.

- Staff assist students in dealing with emotions such as anger, sadness, and frustration by comforting them, identifying their feelings, and helping students use words to solve their problems.
- Staff foster prosocial behaviors among students, including cooperating, helping, taking turns, and talking to solve problems.

The standards also use a phrase repeatedly, perhaps some twenty times within fifty pages: "Each child may require differing levels of support based on ability, learning style, culture, family, and experience to progress developmentally" (Massachusetts Department of Elementary and Secondary Education, 2015, p. 7). All in all, the Massachusetts standards should be helpful for early childhood leaders as they consider curriculum options and as they go about the process of implementing curricula in their schools and centers. Such progressive standards prioritize social-emotional well-being, culturally responsive teaching, and equitable access to grade-level instruction. Furthermore, they highlight the importance of using inclusive and culturally relevant curriculum so that students can feel valued and supported.

> ### Pause and Reflect
> Examine your state standards.
> - How do they compare to the information we have provided for Massachusetts?
> - How do they address antiracism, antibias, cultural competence, and multicultural representation?

Alternative Early Childhood Curricula

State standards can be met through state early childhood curricula, but alternative curricula are available. How are racism, antibias, antiracism, and multicultural competence addressed in these early childhood curricula? How do these curricula relate to state standards? Let's start with an overview of some of the most common curricula.

In the following sections, we provide general background information on the development, goals, and approaches taken of seven widely used curricula. We also highlight key features that speak to the concerns of this book. Please note that promoting equity and justice is not just about following principles of antiracism, antibias, cultural competence, and multicultural representation; it also must involve features related to the overall quality of the program, including age appropriateness, inclusivity, attention to social-emotional concerns and students' well-being, and structured positive interactions in the classroom.

Note that several of the curricula we present were specifically developed to address issues related to poverty, equity, and the well-being of young children who might particularly benefit from preschool experiences. The curricula have several concerns in common, including language development, social interaction, and advancement of early learning. Several of them are aligned to the Head Start Early Learning Outcomes Framework (ELOF; Head Start Early Childhood Learning and Knowledge Center, n.d.).

- HighScope mostly aligns with ELOF. With HighScope, active learning and scaffolding include teaching practices that support young children's learning and development in the majority of ELOF sub-domains.

- Core Knowledge minimally aligns with ELOF. It includes some teaching ideas and cross-curricular connections that briefly describe learning activities that support young children's development as described in each of the ELOF domains.

- Curiosity Corner shows moderate evidence of aligning with ELOF. This includes its theme guide, which has a strong focus on oral language and vocabulary development and assessment, built-in scaffolds and prompts to help students thoroughly learn procedures and cooperative learning structures, and integration of social-emotional skills and strategies.

Head Start

Perhaps the most widely used of the early childhood programs we review is the Head Start curriculum.

- Head Start began as an eight-week pilot to help break the cycle of poverty, providing low-income preschool children (ages three to five) with a comprehensive program to meet their social, emotional, health, nutritional, and educational needs.

- After it demonstrated success in promoting school readiness in young children from low-income families, Congress authorized to expand it

- to full-day and full-year services in 1998, and in 2007 reauthorized it, with bipartisan support and designation of Early Head Start to support expecting families and children ages birth to age three.

- A key tenet of the program is being culturally responsive to the communities it serves, and the program strengthens parental involvement through regular visits to the children's homes, opportunities for parents to volunteer in the program, and special activities. The program also connects young children and families to other services and resources in their communities. And it provides a career path for community members, with about 25 percent of staff members being previous Head Start parents (Office of Head Start, 2022).

The Office of Head Start awards grants to local public and private nonprofit agencies in every U.S. state and territory, in migrant worker camps, and in tribal communities. Although all grantees must meet certain requirements and performance standards, they have the flexibility to choose different program models to meet the needs and resources of their communities.

The Head Start program serves more than one million children and their families each year in urban, suburban, and rural areas in all fifty states, the District of Columbia, Puerto Rico, and U.S. territories, including American Indian and Alaska Native and migrant and seasonal communities (Office of Head Start, 2022).

Head Start focuses on promoting school readiness and addressing young children's social, emotional, health, nutritional, and educational needs. Cognitive self-regulation skills (Joseph & Alvarez, 2022), or executive functioning, are crucial to school readiness. Maintaining focus, persisting toward a goal, solving a problem, and demonstrating flexible thought and behavior are all examples of executive functions.

Following are suggested Head Start teaching practices for emotional and behavioral regulation (Head Start Early Childhood Learning and Knowledge Center, 2019). Feeling safe and supported is important for all young children.

- Infants and toddlers:
    - Soothe with voice and touch.
    - Name emotions so young children can recognize and eventually use those words.

- Support self-regulation by keeping safe and appropriate toys and other materials within reach, providing more than one of particular favorite toys, and ensuring enough space for active play.
- Ensure equitable access to appropriate learning experiences.
- Recognize emotional cues and respond effectively.

• Preschool students:
- Involve young children in creating simple rules using positive language.
- Teach appropriate behavior using positive guidance strategies.
- Encourage young children to process strong feelings by acting them out or representing them visually (provide props and art supplies).
- To help young children practice how to process their feelings, use role play. For example—

"Oh dear," says Ms. James. "I know you want to paint today, Oliver, but all the easels are taken. I can't let you push Omar out of your way because you might hurt him. Let's practice what you could say to Omar instead of pushing him. I'll pretend to be Omar, and you can tell me what you want." (Head Start Early Childhood Learning and Knowledge Center, 2019)

HighScope

HighScope (n.d.a) was developed in 1962 by David Weikart and colleagues as a response to the persistent failures of high school students from the poorest neighborhoods of Ypsilanti, Michigan. First piloted as part of the Perry Preschool Project in a study of high-quality early education's impact on 123 Black children with risk factors of failing in school, it has been widely researched. Today, there are HighScope institutes in Canada, Mexico, the Netherlands, Chile, Ireland, Portugal, South Africa, China, the United Kingdom, Peru, South Korea, and Indonesia.

In a HighScope preschool program, teachers create an active and engaging learning environment that encourages young children to explore and interact with peers and teachers. It supports young children as they make decisions, build academic skills, develop socially and emotionally, and become part of their classroom community (HighScope, n.d.b).

Key elements of HighScope include the following.

- **Active learning is imperative:** HighScope encourages young children to gain knowledge through their natural play and interactions.
- **Teachers are partners:** They work alongside young children and promote learning. Teachers share control, scaffold young children's play, use encouragement instead of praise, and take a problem-solving approach to support young children resolving conflicts.
- **Independence is encouraged:** The classroom's arrangement promotes independence and encourages children to act on their intentions.
- **There is a consistent daily routine:** The curriculum balances a variety of experiences and learning opportunities. Young children engage in individual and social play, participate in small- and large-group activities, assist with cleanup, socialize during meals, develop self-care skills, and exercise their muscles. The foremost part of the routine is the plan-do-review sequence, where young children make decisions about what they will do, carry out their ideas, and reflect on their activities with adults and peers.

Montessori

Maria Montessori, an Italian educator, physician, and scientist, initially developed the Montessori approach (www.montessori.org) in 1907 for a childcare center in San Lorenzo, a poorer, inner-city district of Rome, to address the needs of some of the area's most disadvantaged and previously unschooled children. She also developed her methods with children whose disabilities were deemed too significant for traditional schools. There are between 12,400 and 15,800 Montessori schools in 148 countries (Murray, Aboulela, Sajid, Emafo, & Debs, 2023).

Young children's curiosity and desire to learn form the basis for the Montessori curriculum, making the active participation of the educator key in creating antiracist and antibias learning experiences. Teachers focus on building trusting relationships. They support young children as they develop peer relationships, help students develop self-discipline and self-control, and allow students to resolve disagreements, only getting involved when truly necessary. Teachers demonstrate acceptable behavior and use disputes as learning opportunities to clearly show what is allowed and how to handle problematic behavior (Aljabreen, 2020). Classrooms are multi-aged so that older peers can model behavior and step into a leadership role. There is also a focus on practical skills; materials include breakable objects so that young children understand real consequences rather than those imposed by a teacher. Young children can also choose to clean, prepare food, or practice lacing and tying shoelaces.

Montessori teachers complete rigorous and specific training to learn techniques and prepare to guide young children in their learning, including ways of interacting with young children to help them feel as respected and motivated as possible. "The teacher's goal is to help and encourage the children, allowing them to develop confidence and inner discipline so that there is less and less need to intervene as the child develops" (Edwards, 2002, p. 8). Teachers also learn the ways that Montessori materials begin to introduce concepts in mathematics, reading and writing, and fine motor skills through young children's independent work.

The Montessori curriculum develops around children's learning styles, interests, and skills, and pacing is dependent on students' mastery. Students have opportunities for individual, small-group, and large-group interaction. Montessori helps young children develop independence and social skills, but a student who needs constant direction may be overwhelmed by the self-directed nature of this approach. However, in a well-run Montessori classroom, either the primary teacher or another adult will aid any students who struggle with self-direction to facilitate as much independence and productivity as possible.

Despite the public perception of Montessori preschools as not racially or socioeconomically diverse, many advocates are fighting to change this and diversify the programs.

According to an article published in the *Journal of Negro Education*, "Over 25% of public Montessori students are Black" (Lillard, Taggart, Yonas, & Seale, 2021, p. 2). So, the diversity of Montessori classrooms is clearly increasing. In this same article, the authors examine Montessori as a culturally responsive pedagogy in areas such as developing the whole child, fostering positive relationships, and ensuring that instruction is appropriate for each child's individual development. Says Angela K. Murray, director of the Center for Montessori Research:

> Not only does Montessori align well with culturally responsive pedagogy but it also tends to align with many Indigenous cultures around the world. An article based on a case study in Hawaii was published in the *Journal of American Indian Education* about Montessori and its overlap with Indigenous culture [Schonleber, 2011]. As the lead editor of the chapter on Montessori in Africa in *The Bloomsbury Handbook of Montessori Education* [Murray et al., 2023], I found that the ideology of Montessori schools seemed to

resonate with many communities that they reached. Montessori's emphasis on connecting with nature, forming trusting relationships, and a sense of spirituality and the self appears parallel to many Indigenous ideas. (A. Murray, personal communication, November 7, 2022)

Core Knowledge

Core Knowledge asserts that educational excellence and equity require a coherent, cumulative, knowledge-based curriculum. The program, developed by the Core Knowledge Foundation, an independent nonprofit organization, was founded in 1986 by E. D. Hirsch. The Core Knowledge Foundation identifies and distills the core shared concepts that it believes all students should learn in U.S. schools. The intent of the curriculum is to help students develop strong knowledge foundations grade by grade from preschool to grade 8.

The Core Knowledge curriculum developers believe that "knowledge builds on knowledge" and that equal access to knowledge is integral to education (Core Knowledge Foundation, 2023). It aims to create coherent and cumulative learning experiences, and it includes antiracist and multicultural approaches that feature practice activities, multicultural exposure and interaction, and immersion through specific texts.

Core Knowledge has three main attributes (Core Knowledge Foundation, 2023).

1. **Content specific:** The Core Knowledge Sequence clearly specifies essential knowledge in language arts, history, geography, mathematics, science, and the fine arts. It is not a list of facts, events, and dates to be memorized, but a content guide to foster steady academic growth and progress.

2. **Cumulative:** The Core Knowledge Sequence provides a clear outline of knowledge, language, and skills that build cumulatively from grade to grade. This helps ensure that students are ready to learn and that teachers can confidently predict students' knowledge and skills and build on them.

3. **Coherent:** The Core Knowledge Sequence ensures a coherent approach to building knowledge within and across grade levels, with cross-curricular connections.

Reggio Emilia

The Reggio Emilia curriculum (Reggio Children, n.d.) was created in Italy after World War II (in 1945) by Loris Malaguzzi (1993) in close partnership with Renzo Bonazzi, the then mayor of Reggio Emilia, and the local community. Normed on preschool, it focuses on the community and free inquiry. Today, there are 1,200 individual members of the North American Reggio Emilia Alliance, including educators and advocates (Hobson, 2020).

In this curriculum, school is seen as an environment for young children to explore and produce culture and knowledge. "Children construct their knowledge and values from interactions with, and actions on, the physical and social world" (Firlik, 1996, p. 217).

This student-centered curriculum focuses on the students in their environment. It aims to create a sense of belonging within the school community and to strengthen students' sense of identity, including their racial or ethnic identities. By incorporating Reggio Emilia instruction, the idea of "typical" students is reassessed: all students become full participants, learning how to be familiar and comfortable with diversity, and identify ways to accommodate differences.

In this curriculum, students and teachers are seen as "capable, resourceful, powerful protagonists of their own experience" (Wien, 2008, p. 6). Students are free to move, explore, touch, and discover the world around them in an engaging, creative, and supportive environment. Teachers encourage students to freely express their ideas with their native languages. Reggio Emilia supports artistic expression in a wide range of mediums, and teachers and students collaborate to make decisions together about what to explore and discuss.

Reggio Emilia emphasizes the principles of community, responsibility, and respect, and argues that instruction should be self-guided, custom, flexible, and based on students' interests. There isn't a tight or prescribed sequence or timing, so in-depth learning is possible (Aljabreen, 2020). A core component of the Reggio Emilia curriculum is the concept of an in-depth project that allows open-ended and long-term collaboration.

The Reggio Emilia perspective shifts the focus of the classroom away from the teacher and onto the students. It views students as capable, self-reliant, intelligent, curious, and creative (Edwards, Gandini, & Forman, 1998; Project Zero & Reggio Children, 2001). Eight core tenets guide this philosophy: (1) the environment as the third teacher, (2) one hundred languages of children, (3) long-term projects, (4) teacher-researcher, (5) image of the child, (6) negotiated learning, (7) documentation, and (8) social relations.

The very nature of the Reggio Emilia approach honors the rich cultures, traditions, and familial experiences students bring with them to the classroom. This approach is not limited to a focus on learning outcomes, academic gains, and the notion that all students need to exit each grade with a common knowledge base. Building early childhood programming and curriculum on this approach, through an antiracist lens, can help teachers dismantle systems of oppression and barriers that prevent BIPOC students from receiving quality early childcare.

Adopting the Reggio philosophy means committing to the ongoing examination of our environment so that students see representations of themselves within the intelligent materials in the classroom. This approach treats the classroom as the third teacher (Edwards et al., 1998; Ontario Ministry of Education, 2012), encouraging teachers to take a great deal of care in the creation and setup of the environment of the classroom and the materials that they introduce.

Beyond the classroom, documentation practices used with the Reggio Emilia approach can improve interactions with families as well. Documentation, the seventh tenet of the Reggio philosophy, promotes communication, collaboration, and reflection among students, teachers, and families (Dahlberg, 2012; Forman & Fyfe, 2012; Rinaldi, 2012; Schroeder-Yu, 2008; Thornton & Brunton, 2015). It allows teachers to "present and represent the experiences, thoughts and ideas of the students and to showcase their learning processes" (Fernández Santín & Feliu Torruella, 2017, p. 53).

When approached through an antiracist lens, Reggio Emilia views the experiences of families of different races, religions, and nationalities from a strengths-based approach. This means difference is viewed as something that enriches the community and society. Teachers honor families and build respectful partnerships with them. Reggio-inspired educators respect the role that parents and families play in student learning and development and intentionally create opportunities for family involvement in the classroom.

The Reggio Emilia philosophy also emphasizes the importance of community beyond the classroom. Because this philosophy is community supported, localized, and activity based, it affords us the opportunity for authentic engagement in true antiracist activism. Solutions often come from the communities that are most impacted by the inequities created by systemic racism. Building on educational approaches like Reggio Emilia and innovating through an antiracist lens can give even our youngest citizens the tools to engage in dismantling the systemic racism that impacts the structure of our society.

Expeditionary Learning

Expeditionary Learning Education (2016) was created in 1991 by a partnership between the Harvard Graduate School of Education and Outward Bound. It emphasizes teamwork, courage, compassion, and active learning, with the mission "to create classrooms where teachers can fulfill their highest aspirations, and students achieve more than they think possible, becoming active contributors to building a better world" (Expeditionary Learning Education, 2016, p. 9).

The curriculum focuses on self-discovery, asserting that emotion, challenge, and appropriate support lead to the best learning outcomes. Students must use perseverance, imagination, and self-discipline, and teachers focus on helping students overcome their fears and discover they can achieve much more than they think they can. In Expeditionary Learning, everyone is responsible for their own learning and participates in both individual and group activities. Additionally, students are encouraged to only compete with themselves and to hold themselves to high academic standards. Introspection and reflection are important and allow students to explore their thoughts, make novel connections, and create new ideas.

With Expeditionary Learning, empathy is valued, and everyone's ideas are respected, building a community of mutual trust and curiosity. Expeditionary Learning proponents believe that diversity and inclusion increase richness of ideas, creativity, problem-solving capacity, and respect for others. Students learn about and appreciate their different histories, talents, communities, and cultures. Heterogeneity is encouraged within schools and learning groups. Service and compassion are also emphasized, and the curriculum prepares students to learn from and be of service to others (Expeditionary Learning Education, n.d.a).

Expeditionary Learning focuses on three dimensions of student achievement (Expeditionary Learning Education, 2016).

1. **Mastery of knowledge and skills:** Students demonstrate deeper understanding of core concepts; transfer knowledge and skills to novel, meaningful tasks; think critically; and communicate their ideas clearly.

2. **Positive character:** Students develop mindset attributes to set them up for success throughout life (such as initiative, responsibility, perseverance, and collaboration), become ethical citizens (such as empathy, integrity, respect, and compassion), and apply their learning to improve communities.

3. **High-quality work:** Students demonstrate higher-order thinking, consider multiple perspectives, demonstrate transfer of understanding across contexts, and create authentic work that is meaningful to the community beyond the classroom.

Learning expeditions (Expeditionary Learning Education, n.d.b) are the signature curricular structure. They are long-term, in-depth studies that include real-world connections to inspire students toward higher levels of academic achievement. Learning expeditions involve doing original research, thinking critically, solving problems, and building character and academic skills.

For example, in this lesson (learning expedition) designed for second graders, students build their literacy and citizenship skills (Expeditionary Learning Education, n.d.c). First, they engage in a series of focused read-alouds to explore the guiding question, "What is school, and why are schools important?" Then they read a text and learn about schools around the world, some challenges communities face in sending students to school, and how they solve these challenges. Then the class divides into small groups to research the similarities and differences between their own school and three schools from the text, and each group creates an informational book.

The students consider the following guiding questions and big ideas.

- **What is school, and why are schools important?** A school is a place designed for students to build knowledge and skills, foster character and relationships, and create high-quality work.

- **Why is it hard for some children to go to school in their communities?** Things like weather and location can make it difficult for children to go to school.

- **How do communities solve those problems so their children can go to school?** Communities think of solutions to make sure students have a place to go to school.

- **How are schools around the world different? How are they similar?** Despite similarities and differences, they are all places designed for learning.

In this lesson, students work to become effective learners and ethical people by developing the mindsets and skills for success in college, career, and life, as well as how to treat others well.

Curiosity Corner

Curiosity Corner (Success for All Foundation, n.d.) is used in Head Start centers, preschool classes in elementary schools, childcare centers, and early childhood education centers, mostly in high-poverty neighborhoods. More than three hundred sites in twenty-nine states are currently implementing Curiosity Corner. Two sets of eighteen themed units form the basis of the program (Head Start Early Childhood Learning and Knowledge Center, 2019). Each day, teachers present young children with learning experiences through a series of daily activities (What Works Clearinghouse, 2009). According to the Head Start Early Childhood Learning and Knowledge Center (2019) criteria, the strongest evidence for this curriculum presents itself in the professional development and curriculum materials category. The curriculum provides good training and support for teachers and includes an effective and systematic set of materials (Head Start Early Childhood Learning and Knowledge Center, 2019).

Curiosity Corner uses developmentally appropriate and age-appropriate activities that target nine developmental domains. It presents young children with a wide array of literacy-enhancing experiences to promote their language development so they will be better prepared for kindergarten. Young children explore new concepts with partners and small groups, motivating and supporting each other to learn. *Plan and play* gives young children the opportunity to use imaginary play to explore new concepts.

The Curiosity Corner program focuses on oral and vocabulary development. Subjects like mathematics, science, art, and music are also explored. Built-in scaffolding and prompts help young children learn routines and cooperative learning structures (Success for All Foundation, n.d.). This helps students thoroughly learn procedures and ensures many opportunities for student interaction and partner work, integration of SEL skills and strategies, and online data tools and analysis, including videos from Sesame Workshop, to enhance instruction.

Comparison of Curricula From an Antiracist Perspective

For this review, we examine two very different curricula: Montessori and Core Knowledge. Montessori, which focuses on a whole-child education, fosters confidence and independence, which are prerequisites for an antiracist education. Core Knowledge is known for its results—increases in academic outcomes at little cost of implementation (Marcus, Cobb, & Shoenberg, 2000). When these curricula are augmented by programs designed to incorporate an active antiracist practice, they could potentially become powerful tools to teach young children the skills they need to recognize, confront, and dismantle bias.

Strategies that allow for expression and autonomy, like the nonhierarchical structure of the classroom and the practice of following students in their learning, as well as allowing students to move freely, can result in reduced use of exclusionary discipline and disproportionate responses for students of color. Montessori teachers' preparation to confront their biases may also help improve teachers' perceptions of the abilities of their students of color, beginning the long process of correcting a cultural deficit mindset and biased expectations for students of differing races (McCaffrey, 2017).

Teacher self-examination could be a point of connection between antiracist education and Montessori practice. It is crucial for teachers to examine their own beliefs, racism, and prejudices (Castagno, 2014; Henze, Lucas, & Scott, 1998; hooks, 2003; Matias & Mackey, 2016). The Montessori approach includes the spiritual preparation of adults to rid them of bias and prejudice. Antiracist education strategies are also beginning to be integrated into Montessori teacher training to help teachers in this journey of self-examination, and major Montessori organizations are making efforts to further diversity, equity, and inclusion (Canzoneri-Golden & King, 2020). Part of these might include acknowledging how existing and selected curricula, knowledge, and content have been, and continue to be, influenced by systems of power and oppression (Henze et al., 1998).

Rosemary Henze, Tamara Lucas, and Beverly Scott (1998), in their review of Montessori programs, share guidelines for conducting effective conversations about race, power, and privilege in educational settings and beyond.

- Create shared definitions of racism, power, and privilege.
- Acknowledge how differing identities intersect with our perceptions and understandings of those issues.
- Explain how some people have more power and privilege based on systemic factors following lines of race, class, and gender.
- Legitimize the feelings of frustration and anger that those with less power and privilege may experience.
- Develop strategies for participants to engage in further discussion of these topics.
- Include a cool-down period for reflection, closure, and resolution.

As alternative approaches like Montessori and the Core Knowledge curriculum have entered the mainstream, they have also proven to be inequitable in the outcomes they offer young children of different backgrounds. In fact, negative outcomes such as disproportionate disciplinary responses, a stubborn opportunity gap wherein students of color experience lower rates of achievement due to social and economic factors outside their control, and lower academic scores for children of color have persisted at many public Montessori schools (Canzoneri-Golden & King, 2020).

Without an active anti-oppressive element embedded within the curriculum, even alternative approaches struggle to overcome the basic Eurocentrism and tenets of White superiority that exist in mainstream American culture.

- Although Montessori has served disadvantaged populations well, especially in its genesis as a program for Rome's poorest urban children, it historically espoused a belief that it was supranational and superseded the typical prejudices of particular nations, and therefore did not require an active anti-oppressive practice (Rambusch, 1962, 2007). However, both of the major Montessori organizations in the United States now have diversity, equity, and inclusion initiatives as well as opportunities for antibias and antiracism training for teachers (American Montessori Society, n.d.a; Association Montessori Internationale, 2022). This shows a more up-to-date understanding of these issues and a push toward remedying the historical injustices within the practice.

- Core Knowledge chooses to focus on what founder E. D. Hirsch believes to be a canon of cultural knowledge, but this canon persistently favors Eurocentric narratives at the expense of voices of color (Nunke, 2019). While this curriculum does include a more thorough narrative, it is often in the form of multicultural education, which perpetuates the marginalization of other cultures by treating their expression as something unusual and foreign.

- The Core Knowledge curriculum also tends toward a colorblind approach, which creates a curriculum that centers on White and Eurocentric values and referents. Core Knowledge's curriculum in particular fails to address the "political nature of knowledge and schooling," and ignores the fact that constructing knowledge inherently is a political process, as professor of educational policy Kristen L. Buras (1999) states in her critique of E. D. Hirsch's work.

Despite claiming to teach universal skills and knowledge to create engaged and informed members of society, the Core Knowledge model ignores the vast cultural knowledge of people of color.

- Montessori has a reputation for being found in more exclusive private schools, so it can seem like a program that does not "see color," but there is rising awareness of antibias and justice issues. The Montessori method also lends itself to valuing all students for their differences in thought and experience and celebrating uniqueness and individual voice (Banks & Maixner, 2016). Given those two points and the fact that topics of learning are not decided by the teacher but driven by student interest, it is no longer true that Montessori defaults to a colorblind approach. However, some systemic issues remain. In some Montessori schools, greater efforts are needed to further teacher understanding of bias and racism.

Curriculum Supplementation for More Inclusive and Representative Learning Experiences

Programs such as Montessori, Core Knowledge, and the others we discuss can augment their curricula with antiracist aspects and critical consciousness to create a more well-rounded curriculum. Culturally relevant pedagogy, which is sometimes called *culturally responsive pedagogy* (Mensah, 2021), and antibias and antiracism training are good examples (Canzoneri-Golden & King, 2020). Each aims to incorporate a more diverse and inclusive style of education that acknowledges and integrates the historical and social contexts of a wider range of ethnicities.

Culturally Relevant Pedagogy

Culturally relevant pedagogy aims to counter the cultural deficit mindset that teachers may hold about students' home cultures and advances a new way of looking at cultural differences that emphasizes their diverse strengths and values. It also centers the community as a vehicle for learning so that the skills students learn at home are considered as valuable as the academic skills they learn in the classroom. This approach often integrates content that is relevant to students' cultural backgrounds.

For example, in a lesson focused on teaching longitude and latitude, elementary students plotted various points on a map following the path of runaway enslaved persons from the south of Ohio north to Canada to freedom (Canzoneri-Golden

& King, 2020). In addition to teaching map-reading skills and reinforcing geography knowledge, this lesson centered the academic and cognitive skills around relevant narratives and a celebration of cultural strength.

One organization that supports culturally relevant pedagogy for early childhood educators is the National Center on Early Childhood Development, Teaching, and Learning (NCECDTL), established in 2015, which is funded by the Office of Head Start and the Office of Child Care within the Administration for Children and Families, U.S. Department of Health and Human Services. NCECDTL identifies, develops, and promotes the implementation of evidence-based culturally and linguistically responsive practices that lead to positive child outcomes and support strong professional development systems across early childhood programs for ages birth through five. One example of this is *A Culturally Responsive Approach to Implementing a Curriculum* (NCECDTL, 2021). This resource provides support to education staff from all program settings in the implementation of curriculum that is responsive to children's and families' cultures. Specifically, this resource presents information about various cultures and how they contribute to beliefs, values, and teaching practices.

Antibias and Antiracism Training

Antibias and antiracism training, which also emphasizes awareness and inclusion of a student's home culture, goes a step beyond culturally relevant pedagogy. It incorporates critical consciousness and direct analysis of the ways that power and race intersect in a society. When these skills are nurtured, students are able to recognize and name different forms of bias. Antibias and antiracism training begins teaching students concrete terms for bias at a young age in the belief that being able to name and talk about bias will equip students with the skills necessary to confront it in their lives.

For example, with an antibias and antiracist approach, students learn that there is no physiological or genetic basis for race. Instead, it is a social and historical construct that has impacted the treatment of different groups for hundreds of years (Pollock, 2008). Promoting this awareness in young children is the first step to teaching them to dismantle bias and inequity.

Table 12.1 (page 206) summarizes the similarities and differences between culturally relevant pedagogy and antibias and antiracism training.

Table 12.1: Similarities and Differences Between Culturally Relevant Pedagogy and Antibias and Antiracism Training

Supplemental Curriculum	Key Points	Example
Culturally Relevant Pedagogy	• Counters negative mindsets • Offers a strengths-based lens for looking at cultural differences • Centers the community as a vehicle for learning • Integrates curriculum content that is relevant to students' cultural backgrounds	Elementary students plot the paths of runaway enslaved persons (Canzoneri-Golden & King, 2020); learning focuses include map reading, geography, academic and cognitive skills, and celebration of cultural strength.
Antibias and Antiracism Training	• Also emphasizes awareness and inclusion of students' home cultures • Incorporates how power and race intersect in a society • Helps students recognize and name forms of bias using concrete terms • Equips students with the skills necessary to confront bias in their lives	Students learn that race is a social and historical construct (Pollock, 2008); learning focuses include this awareness as a first step to dismantling bias and inequity.

Culturally relevant pedagogy and antibias and antiracism training provide big-picture strategies for addressing the deficits in alternative curricula. It is critical that educators learn to acknowledge and convey the effects that racism has had on the treatment of various groups in society. This includes recognition of the following.

- There is no neutral selection of curriculum content.
- When educators select content without an active anti-oppressive mindset, one group's culture is often lifted up as a standard, negatively impacting others.

- Educators can make informed choices about what material they present to their classrooms and provide students with narratives of many diverse groups.

Both approaches offer some practical strategies for crafting an antiracist curriculum. These include the following.

- **Teach accurate words and information about racial identities as early as possible** so that students begin to understand how to speak about differences as well as recognize the shared humanity between themselves and their classmates of different races (Derman-Sparks & Edwards, 2020).
  - To this end, students should be encouraged to explore the similarities and differences between their features. One activity could include providing students with life-size cutouts of themselves as well as mirrors, crayons, and paints in all shades and talking about how, although eyes, hair, and skin can look different for different races, they function the same for all people, regardless of color (Derman-Sparks & Edwards, 2020). This activity also provides a valuable opportunity to notice indicators of self-rejection or internalized bias, which should be addressed and interrupted as quickly as possible.
- **Make racial diversity visible in the learning environment** by ensuring that people of many different racial and ethnic identities are represented in learning materials, including families of mixed heritage and biracial families. Educational content should include narratives about people of color that relate to not just their cultural trauma (for example, only using stories with antislavery and civil rights activist Black characters) but all their walks of life (Derman-Sparks & Edwards, 2020).
- **Help students learn the narratives of colonization from multiple perspectives in age-appropriate ways** so that they are able to understand social problems from points of view other than their own and do not perpetuate status quo beliefs about race and racism. Young children are especially attuned to fairness, which makes them well prepared for learning about the history of inequitable treatment and sensitive to pursuing more equitable relations for different groups (National Council of Teachers of English, 2016).

- **Encourage dramatic play as a space in which students explore their environment, their bodies, and their places in the world**, especially as a means to develop empathy through negotiation of multiple perspectives or roles. This can include providing multimodal resources for play, such as an array of visual, spoken, gestural, written, and other modes of communication. This ensures that equitable context is available for students of different social groups and cultures (National Council of Teachers of English, 2016).

HEART+ Takeaways

The methods discussed in this chapter, and many more like them, can help remedy the inequities of student outcomes seen in alternative curricula. This is critical for increasing students' sense of self and feeling of belonging—both critical components of Heart Centered Learning. Programs that counter a colorblind or multicultural approach by teaching a comprehensive awareness of the treatment of different groups throughout history and embracing the values and wisdom that different cultures have to offer can be valuable extensions of curricula that do not embed an anti-oppressive mindset into their material. By incorporating culturally relevant pedagogy and antibias and antiracist principles, we can raise students who are confident in their own cultures, understanding of the cultures of others, and ready to confront bias in the world. Intentional efforts to advance antiracist practices can lead to enhanced early childhood curricula.

CHAPTER 13

A Bar to Be Raised: Equity in Early Childhood Educator Standards

Anti-racist emphasis in teacher preparation is important so teacher candidates understand how racism impacts schooling and see how they can be part of changing those systems and beliefs.
—Julie Feldman-Abe

Principle 13: Early education teacher preparation programs must address cultural competence, antibias, and antiracist practices to better support the early childhood care and education workforce.

To move forward with cultural competence and racial equity, and create classrooms that address bias and racism, higher standards in college-level programs for preparing early childhood educators must be a priority. Improving educator preparation, in whatever form it takes, is one path to ensuring that learning environments are meeting the needs of all learners, including young children who are BIPOC, immigrants, and multilingual.

In this chapter, we discuss how teaching about cultural competence promotes retention of early childhood educators. We also explore teacher and program standards in this preparation.

Teacher Preparation Programs

Leaders can advance antiracist teacher preparation in three ways: by (1) engaging in their own self-study and self-reflection through both informal and formal coursework, (2) promoting changes to teacher and educator preparation programs, and (3) finding resources and time for staff to gain the needed skills and expertise as part of in-service professional learning programs.

For many years, preservice and in-service programs have correctly included expectations that participants will learn about developmental milestones, curricula, instruction, classroom organization, and assessment of learner outcomes. Given today's pressing concerns about equity and justice, more is called for—teachers and early childhood caregivers must learn how to integrate cultural competence and antiracism into each of those expected areas of knowledge. They must also learn how to address the barriers to these changes, both internal to themselves and external within their schools and communities, by embracing race-visible teacher education and self-reflection.

Cultural Competence and Antiracism in Teacher Education

As many people in our society have become more aware of the need to address racism, teacher preparation programs, schools, and childcare centers have begun to take a hard look at the skills and knowledge requirements for educators. Here are just two examples of education course descriptions from four-year and two-year early childhood education programs:

> Education 205: Equity in Educational Settings—An overview of current issues and research related to race, class, culture, language, and other social factors in schools across the United States. . . . The course introduces culturally relevant pedagogy and analyzes teaching practices in order to equip students with effective models to teach all children and partner with all families. (Framingham State University, n.d.)

> Child Development 017: Teaching Children in a Diverse Society—Development of social identities in diverse societies including theoretical and practical implications of oppression and privilege affecting young children, families, programs, classrooms, teaching, education and schooling. Exploration of various classroom strategies emphasizing culturally and linguistically appropriate anti-bias approaches supporting children in becoming competent members of a diverse society. Self-examination and reflection of one's

> own issues and understanding of educational principles in integrating social identity, stereotypes and bias, social and educational access, media, schooling, better informed teaching practices and/or program development. (Pasadena City College, n.d.)

Universities are now offering new options, many of them online and some of them as special webinars. For example, Pennsylvania State University, as part of its Better Kid Care online program, offers a free on-demand course called "Antiracism: Self-Awareness and Communication." This two-hour course introduces antiracism and two components for culturally responsive teaching. Students who complete the course do the following (Penn State Extension, n.d.):

- Discover that race is not biologically determined and that racism is a human construct.
- Make use of data collected from a self-assessment to determine placement within the phases of adult antibias development.
- Plan ways to embed self-awareness and culturally responsive communication, two of the eight competencies for culturally responsive teaching, into everyday practices.

Such courses and online options are important beyond the need to educate prospective teachers about antiracism and cultural competence. These experiences are also important for the early childhood profession more broadly. Research by Cara M. Djonko-Moore (2020) demonstrates:

> Early childhood teachers with high motivation to remain in the profession had significantly more undergraduate coursework focused on diversity, felt their teacher education programs better prepared them for teaching culturally and linguistically diverse children, and did an effective job working with children from diverse backgrounds.

This makes sense: when teachers have a deeper understanding of the students and families they are serving, they are more likely to feel confident in their role and enjoy their work.

Cultural competence is enhanced in teacher and childcare worker preparation through gaining knowledge and materials reflecting diversity, equity, culture, and the achievements of people of various races and ethnicities. Ideally, learners will also do the following.

- Study social justice issues.
- Experience working directly with students from diverse cultures.

- Come to understand more about their own biases, including how these biases may impact the students and families in their classrooms.

Organizations concerned with teacher education are speaking out about the importance of cultural responsiveness. The National Association of Early Childhood Teacher Educators' (NAECTE, n.d.) position statement encourages new teachers to "respect and attend to children's culture, values, and language as inseparable from their learning and development, considering the many influences from their community as well as family to develop a culturally responsive curriculum" (p. 1). And in its response to the murders of George Floyd and other Black and Brown people, the NAECTE (n.d.) says:

> We recognize our duty to inspire future early childhood teachers to open their hearts and minds and take up anti-racist and anti-bias education, becoming advocates of justice. . . . We must employ efforts to uplift cultural assets and recognize and value funds of knowledge as opposed to the current deficit narratives we continue to encounter. (pp. 1–2)

As Maria Rosario T. de Guzman, Tonia R. Durden, Sarah A. Taylor, Jackie M. Guzman, and Kathy L. Potthoff (2016) indicate, developing cultural competence involves the following.

- Increasing self-awareness
- Developing social skills and behaviors around diversity
- Gaining the ability to advocate for others
- Going beyond tolerance, which implies that one is simply willing to overlook differences
- Recognizing and respecting diversity through words and actions in all contexts

Displaying the cultural competence behaviors of active listening, empathy, and effective engagement can help us create a welcoming environment and establish appreciation of similarities and differences among cultures (de Guzman et al., 2016).

Considerations for cultural competence, antiracism, and antibias have also been informed by the need for culturally relevant and sustainable pedagogy (Ladson-Billings, 2014), including providing for community- and student-driven learning from a strengths-based perspective. The implications for teacher and early childhood care provider preparation are extensive. Classroom interactions begin with racially and culturally aware teachers (see chapter 3, page 45). As John Michael Holland (2012) concludes in his review of Head Start literacy, cultural understanding is vital for developing meaningful relationships with parents and families as well as for supporting student engagement.

One important way to close the cultural competence gap is to find and hire teacher candidates and early childhood practitioners who have graduated from associate's, bachelor's, and master's programs with a focus on diversity. As we discuss in chapter 14 (page 221), the degree levels can, unintentionally, reinforce inequities in the early childhood workforce.

Randy spoke with two teacher educators who are great embodiments of culturally competent teacher education programs. Peggy Martalock is coordinator of Greenfield Community College's early childhood teacher preparation program. Her students are mostly young White women from rural western Massachusetts, who are often the first in their families to attend college. Martalock integrates social justice concerns throughout the courses, knowing that the ideas and values of racial, class, and cultural equity will help her students understand not just their own lives but those of the children they will soon, or already, care for. Despite innumerable challenges, she seeks to create and sustain pathways leading to further study and better compensation. Martalock says:

> I want my students both to gain the knowledge they need to meet basic requirements of a certificate or an associate's degree for work in settings with diverse children and families, and also to see themselves as professionals who can go on to a four-year college. (P. Martalock, personal communication, November 29, 2022)

Erica Almaguer, a graduate of San Francisco State University, is both a lecturer in the university's Child and Adolescent Development Department and director of Associated Students' Early Childhood Education Center. She describes herself as a Latina woman of color dedicated to the needs of children and families in her community. She freely admits, "As we all do, I come with my own experiences and biases from my background" (E. Almaguer, personal communication, November 21, 2022). Almaguer leans deeply into the challenging conversations she knows her mostly young White female students need to reflect on:

> Sometimes international and White students feel very uncomfortable with topics like Black Lives Matter. They may, for example, have a family member in law enforcement, but they need to understand that BLM started because of police brutality against BIPOC. It helps them better

understand the communities they are likely to work in. Children grow up in a community context and these topics are relevant. (E. Almaguer, personal communication, November 21, 2022)

Race-Visible Teacher Education and Self-Reflection

A major facet of antiracism is to name racism when it appears. This is part of what Elyse Hambacher, professor at the University of New Hampshire, and Katherine Ginn (2021) describe as race-visible teacher education, which includes a "humanizing pedagogy" where teacher educators "turn their gaze inward and away from reductive, dehumanizing stories, engaging instead in critical self-reflection about their own beliefs and how those are rooted in various forms of systematic oppression" (p. 338).

Alana Butler, Cathryn Teasley, and Concepción Sánchez-Blanco (2019) suggest that in early childhood settings, educators need to embrace critical alternatives to colorblindness and help young children identify injustice, even as these educators work to achieve "an anti-oppressive, antibias learning environment for all our children" (p. 56).

The recommendations for the development of antiracist cultural competence in teacher and early childcare provider preparation are aligned with the five Cs we introduced in chapter 5 (page 71).

1. **Consciousness:** Self-reflection about one's own racial and cultural experience is the starting place for developing cultural competence. With conscious self-reflection, one can more smoothly incorporate new knowledge and new experience.

2. **Compassion:** Although cultural competence follows reflection and knowledge, these are not enough. They must deepen into caring and compassion for oneself as a learner, for the young children in one's care, and for the children's families and communities.

3. **Confidence:** Working hard to get through the challenges of early childhood teacher preparation, on top of daily work and family responsibilities, increases confidence in oneself and in one's mentors, coaches, and instructors.

4. **Courage:** To persevere through the challenges and barriers at each level of professional development takes personal courage. It also takes courage to advocate, with others or alone, for antiracist and culturally

competent practices in an environment that may not welcome such efforts.

5. **Community:** Early childhood collaborative teams include colleagues, coaches and mentors, administrators, and policymakers. Along with families, support from all these groups is essential to effectively preparing early childhood teachers of all racial and cultural backgrounds.

By addressing internal barriers, early childhood teachers and caregivers individually become aware of their own biases, carefully observing their reactions to and interactions with others who are different from themselves. In *Little Learners, Big Hearts*, we offer numerous opportunities for such self-reflection, including an understanding of implicit bias. This self-reflection is not just for teachers and caregivers. It is just as important, if not more so, for leaders so you can guide your staff and your academic programs to effectively promote antiracism and cultural competence in classrooms and schools. In chapter 3 (page 45), we discuss this as being one of early childhood leaders' responsibilities. In chapter 11 (page 165), we delve more deeply into how leaders can meet this responsibility through diversified professional development strategies.

How can recommendations from professors such as Gloria Ladson-Billings (2014), Elyse Hambacher and Katherine Ginn (2021), and Alana Butler and colleagues (2019) be integrated into teacher and early childcare provider preparation programs? The road is demanding. It begins with learning about and reflecting on such research studies and recommendations, followed by creating courses, such as those we have cited, that address these issues. Ultimately, however, state licensure standards must evolve to reflect what we are learning.

Standards for Teacher and Early Childcare Provider Preparation

State licensure standards are the essential guide to programs for professional preparation. Across the United States, these standards lack consistency and are often contradictory. Regulation of childcare programs varies state by state and program by program. As we write this, numerous states are revising their K–12 education standards to be more in line with their currently conservative political leadership. This will likely impact some states' early learning standards. Teachers and early childcare providers can stay abreast of changes in these standards by visiting the websites of and becoming members of associations such as NAEYC. Other websites that have useful information on changes to standards include the websites of Harvard University's Center on the Developing Child (https://developingchild.harvard.edu) and the National Institute for Early Education Research (https://nieer.org). The following sections discuss the Unifying Framework and competencies for early childhood educators as well as accreditation, licensing, and funding of early childhood centers.

The Unifying Framework for the Early Childhood Profession and Professional Standards and Competencies for Early Childhood Educators

Developed through the collaboration of fifteen national organizations, the Unifying Framework addresses the need for coherence across preparation programs as well as implementation in community and school settings. It includes recommendations for three distinct and practical designations.

1. Early Childhood Educator I (a certificate requiring at least 120 hours of coursework)
2. Early Childhood Educator II (a certificate requiring an associate's degree)
3. Early Childhood Educator III (a certificate requiring a bachelor's or master's degree)

Although these professionals work together as part of a teaching team, each designation has a distinct scope of practice, level of professional preparation, and level of mastery of the Professional Standards and Competencies for Early Childhood Educators (Power to the Profession, 2020).

The framework is based on a series of agreed-on principles. Here are two that reflect the concepts we discuss in this chapter (Power to the Profession, 2020).

1. Early childhood educators who have recognized early childhood degrees and credentials support each and every child, birth through age eight, across all settings.
2. Early childhood educators of all professional designations (Early Childhood Educator I, II, and III) are valued, respected, and well compensated for the influential roles they play.

Cultural competence is infused through the six Professional Standards and Competencies for Early Childhood Educators. For example, standard 1 (child development and learning in context; NAEYC, 2020) states that early childhood educators must do the following:

> Know that young children are developing multiple social identities that include race, language, culture, class, and gender, among others. Educators recognize the benefits to children of growing up as bilingual/multilingual individuals and the importance of supporting the development of children's home languages.
>
> Understand that all children and families are widely impacted by society's persistent structural inequities related to race, language, gender, social and economic class, immigration status, and other characteristics, which can have long-term effects on children's learning and development. (p. 12)

Both the Unifying Framework and the Professional Standards and Competencies for Early Childhood Educators are documents that lay the groundwork and offer a map for the future of culturally competent, antiracist early childhood teacher preparation. That ground is not flat, nor is it easy to traverse. There are mountains to climb and rivers to cross for all of us—those who are preparing to be or already are culturally competent early childhood teachers and caregivers and those who design and provide that preparation. School leaders will find that as they stay abreast of changes in educator preparation programs, they are better positioned to hire staff with skill sets that support antiracism.

Accreditation, Licensing, and Funding of Centers

In addition to standards for teacher preparation and certification, there are also standards for the early childhood education programs themselves. To successfully implement cultural relevance and antiracism, changes are also necessary in the standards and expectations for these programs. In its report *Delivering on the Promise of Effective Early Childhood Education* (James & Iruka, 2018), the National Black Child Development Institute offers a succinct set of core elements of affirming, inclusive early childhood settings. It notes that there are significant racial gaps in preK program quality: "Studies show that, when compared to White and Latino children, Black children are least likely to be enrolled in high-quality, early childhood education programs" (James & Iruka, 2018, p. 14).

Accreditation and licensing are two much-needed vehicles for maintaining minimum standards and expectations for early childcare centers, preschools, and other early childhood education programs. According to the U.S. Census Bureau, in 2014, there were almost 10.4 million slots in licensed childcare programs, equating to approximately 197 licensed slots per 1,000 children ages birth to twelve (National Association for Regulatory Administration, 2014). Child Care Aware of America (2022), in partnership with national stakeholders, developed a childcare-licensing database in 2017. According to its data, there were 93,124 licensed centers in 2022 in the forty-one states where it collected data (Child Care Aware of America, 2022). More information on standards for early childhood centers is available in annual reports in the Caring for Our Children collection of standards (National Resource Center for Health and Safety in Child Care and Early Education, n.d.; https://nrckids.org/CFOC).

Accreditation requires early and school-age programs to meet standards that exceed minimum state requirements. Twenty-five states rely on a statewide quality rating and improvement system, and twenty-one of these states include accreditation in this system. In our review of these accreditation agencies, we found just a few supporting the shift toward antibias and antiracism in their standards. Given the number of existing accreditation agencies, bringing about significant change toward a culturally responsive perspective will be a formidable task. Here are some organizations we discovered that provide accreditation that includes attention to equity.

- NAEYC's Early Learning Program (https://bit.ly/3rZo90e)
- The National Association for Family Child Care for infant and toddler, preschool, and school-age programs (https://nafcc.org/accreditation)
- The American Montessori Society for Montessori programs, birth through high school (https://bit.ly/3QyaY0w)
- The National Early Childhood Program for infant and toddler, preschool, and school-age programs (https://necpa.net/page/accreditationprocess)

School leaders can stay up to date regarding certification requirements by going to these websites or becoming members of organizations such as these. Individual U.S. states also have standards for early learning programs that include cultural competence. The following list features three examples.

1. **New Jersey Preschool Teaching and Learning Standards:** These include suggestions for inclusion of characteristics, values, and practices of diverse cultural groups and deepened knowledge of diversity and multiculturalism, such as making books available in a variety of languages, featuring artwork that reflects a diverse spectrum of races and cultures, and including dolls of different ethnicities and

races as well as props, musical instruments, and foods from various cultures (New Jersey State Department of Education, 2014).

2. **North Carolina Foundations for Early Learning and Development:** Social connection strategies for infants and toddlers recommend that centers provide materials and activities that show other cultures and people from a variety of backgrounds in positive ways to help young children see and experience the diversity of human experience (diversity should include all types—gender, race, ethnicity, sexual orientation, and so on; North Carolina Foundations Task Force, 2013).

3. **Washington Early Childhood Education and Assistance Program Standards:** These include standards for creating educational communities of antibias practices that support dimensions of human difference, addressing personal and social identity and social-emotional relationships with people of diverse backgrounds and identities, confronting prejudice and discrimination, and championing critical thinking and taking action for fairness (Washington State Department of Children, Youth and Families, 2023).

It will be no surprise to early childhood educational leaders that the COVID-19 pandemic caused not only severe disruptions in childcare but the closing of many programs. According to a report:

> Nationally, 63 percent of child care centers and 27 percent of family child care (FCC) homes were closed in Spring 2020. Yet, some programs remained open to care for children. Among programs that were open, enrollment decreased significantly due to public health measures (e.g., reduced capacity for social distancing) or parents' concerns about contracting COVID-19 at CCEE [child care and early education] programs. Program closures, coupled with drops in enrollment and attendance, made it difficult for CCEE programs to generate enough revenue to cover their operating expenses, and some providers decided to permanently close their programs. Providers who temporarily closed continued facing challenges to re-open. (Lin & McDoniel, 2023, p. 2)

In general, low-income families were particularly hard-hit by program closures. Ying-Chun Lin and Meghan McDoniel's (2023) report indicated that, more specifically, "program closure rates tended to be greater in communities with a higher proportion of individuals who identify as Hispanic, suggesting that Hispanic families might be more likely to experience program closures than White families" (p. 4).

Both federal and state funding helped shore up those programs that remained open in the face of declining revenues, resulting in lower enrollment. Increasing fees were a particular burden on lower-income families. The state and federal funds that were provided during the pandemic are no longer available as we complete this leader's guide, as the window for the American Rescue Plan childcare stabilization grants has ended (Popli, 2023). Efforts to avoid what is being called the "childcare funding cliff" vary from state to state. Sustained, adequate funding from the federal government is not likely in the present political climate. In the next chapter, we discuss the power of organizing at a state level to gain the desperately needed funding, either directly to centers or as subsidies to families.

HEART+ Takeaways

All students, including our youngest, deserve an education with highly qualified teachers and staff. Intentional efforts to advance equitable practices are necessary to grow the early childhood workforce, promote greater equity and inclusion for staff as well as students, and enhance both classroom learning and our students' well-being.

CHAPTER 14

Early Childhood Staff Support: Equitable Professional Pathways

If there is happiness at age three, it will last until you reach eighty.
—Lisa See

Principle 14: Change is necessary to attract and keep the best workforce—better wages, better training, and higher regard for this essential work.

Caregivers and educators from diverse racial, cultural, and socioeconomic backgrounds provide nurturing supports to young children from birth to age eight in a variety of settings. Individuals' life experiences, as well as their education, may support or hinder their cultural competence. Those whose life experiences naturally support cultural competence are also more likely to be in lower-paying positions, such as home or family daycare provider and classroom aide:

> Although the early educator workforce is racially and linguistically diverse, that diversity is not distributed equitably across positions within the field. Women of color are overrepresented in the lowest-paying jobs, underrepresented in leadership roles, and frequently paid unequal wages for equal work. Intentionally disrupting racial and ethnic stratification requires implementation of mechanisms that facilitate racial justice. (McLean et al., 2021, p. 30)

Moreover, historical racism, sexism, low compensation, disjointed teacher preparation, and limited cultural competence, including in the needs of dual-language learners, are acutely entangled:

> Childcare, domestic work has been associated with Black women. And dare we say that Black women in American society are often viewed negatively and disrespected and are likely at the bottom of the hierarchy in our country. And so, the result of these opinions and these perspectives is that the childcare field has been and still is rife with racialized and gendered discrimination and exploitation and these issues are tied directly to Black women. They originated with Black women, but they also affect all women. And that's really important to know. Certainly, the field looks very different than it did in the 1600s—who's taking care of who, and there are a wide range of women in the field now. But the framing, and that context, is really important to know. (Lloyd, 2022)

This disrespect, even denigration, has clearly led to low compensation and barriers to professional development.

- The early care and education workforce receives extremely low compensation compared to other educator roles (Coffey, 2022).
- Lack of public investment and low wages result from little to no respect for those who care for and educate young children (Milli, 2022).

In this chapter, we specifically address the challenge of how pay inequities (including but not exclusively based on race) impact early childhood teachers' current and future access to credentials, state licensure, and certification. The following sections discuss the issues of lack of respect for early childhood educators, compensation, cultural competence in multiple career pathways, and linguistic diversity. Finally, we summarize some solutions, including widely recommended policies.

Roots of Disrespect for Early Childhood Educators

The lack of respect for early childhood educators and caregivers has roots in the racist and sexist history of the United States. As we underscore throughout this book, it is impossible to understand the task of creating and furthering culturally competent, antiracist early childhood care and education without examining these historical threads, including the history of the workforce in this field. Quoting Maurice Sykes, a longtime leader in the early childhood field, Sarah Carr (2021) highlights the racial roots of the limited public investment in early care and education:

> It also stems from a longstanding degradation of child care and domestic work in the United States that is both gendered and racialized. . . . Enslaved people commonly worked as wet nurses "who were to serve and feed masters' children at the neglect of their own, many of whom starved to death." . . . "I think the field has to realize that in spite of everything it thinks about itself, it is still regarded as a servant class."

Chrishana M. Lloyd, Julianna Carlson, Hannah Barnett, Sara Shaw, and Deja Logan (2021) explore this perspective in illuminating detail in Child Trends' *Mary Pauper: A Historical Exploration of Early Care and Education Compensation, Policy, and Solutions*. The authors specifically tie the current challenges of fair compensation and accessible educational opportunities not only to the history but also to the racial and cultural diversity of the current early childhood care and education workforce:

> Poor compensation of the early care and education (ECE) workforce has deep historical roots. Domestic work, including child care, has long been undervalued, in large part because of notions about race and women. This devaluing of people who are (and have been) minoritized, people of color, and women has been codified into local, state, and federal policies over centuries, showing up in racist and sexist policies in the funding and structure of the ECE system. One of the key ways in which the primarily female ECE workforce is affected is inadequate compensation. (Lloyd et al., 2021, p. 1)

The historical context of early childhood care and education highlights how systemic challenges can perpetuate racial and gender biases. As stated by Lloyd and colleagues, this deep-seated undervaluation of childcare clearly hails from historical inequities. Thus, there is an urgent need for acknowledgment of this history and for significant systemic change. More specifically, such change should dismantle disparities and provide equitable opportunities for early childhood education workers.

Compensation and Culturally Competent Teacher Preparation

Early educator compensation is abysmally low across various roles within the overall workforce. The 2023 median hourly wages for early childhood care and education providers are shown in figure 14.1.

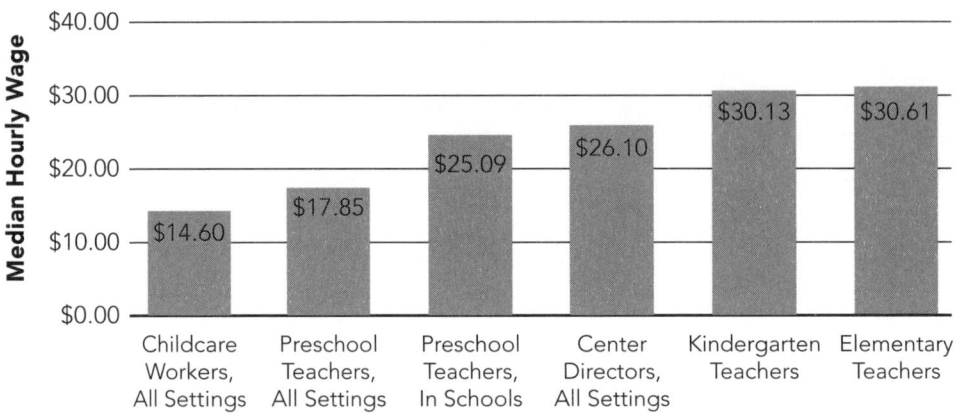

Source: U.S. Bureau of Labor Statistics, n.d.

Figure 14.1: Median hourly wages by childcare occupation.

In 2019, childcare workers in all settings earned an hourly wage one-third of that of elementary teachers (McLean et al., 2021). This presents a serious barrier to increasing the educational level of those in the childcare field to a bachelor's degree since education costs would be prohibitive for many. Yet, when considered through a racial and ethnic lens, the disparities in this picture are even sharper, showing the continuity of the racist history.

- Teachers "working full-time exclusively with infants and toddlers are paid up to $8,375 less per year than those who work with preschool-age children," and Black women "are more likely than their peers to work with infants and toddlers" (McLean et al., 2021, p. 40).

- Black educators in early childhood settings are, on average, paid seventy-eight cents less hourly than White early childhood educators; additionally:

    The pay gap is more than doubled for Black educators who work with preschool-age children ($1.71 less per hour compared with their White peers) compared with the pay gap for Black educators who work with infants and toddlers ($0.77 less per hour compared with their White peers). (McLean et al., 2021, p. 40)

Simply stated, there is a vicious cycle here: the more education, generally the higher the level of compensation. Yet without increased education, compensation is likely to remain inadequate both to pay for further study and to support a family. And this cycle is "disproportionately felt by women of color" (Power to the Profession, 2020, p. 8). Policy changes from above—combined with pressure from below—are desperately needed.

Here is what two early childhood educators say about how low pay impacts their staff and programs:

> While I commend the $15/hour ordinance, it's still not enough to live in LA County. It would mean the world to the industry to make an ECE degree free. We know this field isn't going to be a lucrative one, so taking on student debt to continuously be in debt is driving folks away from our industry. This model continues to oppress women and women of color in particular.
>
> —ECE program executive director, Santa Monica, California (NAEYC, 2021, p. 6)
>
> Early childhood education is seen as a luxury, not as a necessity, and as such, it is increasingly difficult to get administrators to agree to allow these programs to continue. We could retain full-time staff with more funding, and replace equipment that is outdated. We would be able to pour funds into culturally appropriate materials and provide training to our employees.
>
> —Early childhood educator, Fremont County, Wyoming (NAEYC, 2021, p. 48)

In the joint NAEYC and Education Trust (2019) report *Increasing Qualifications, Centering Equity*, early childhood educators of color describe their concerns about rising academic requirements: "I don't want to have to be told that unless I get this [degree], then my career is over after I've done all this, you know?" (p. 5). But at the same time, they understand the value of it: "We pretty much just focused on [children's] development, what they need, how we need to approach them; . . . the respect that we have to have for all backgrounds in regards to where they come from" (NAEYC & Education Trust, 2019, p. 6).

We echo the concerns of these educators, recognizing the need to increase the depth of guidance given to early childhood educators around antiracism. Historical disregard for cultural differences among children and their families calls for increased emphasis on cultural competence, especially (but not solely) for White early childhood educators and caregivers.

We know from extensive research that students tend to do better in school when they are taught by someone who looks like them—from the same racial, ethnic, or linguistic background (Workman, 2019). As of 2019, 44 percent of children aged birth to five in the United States identified as "non-White." The early childhood workforce closely mirrors those demographics, with nearly 40 percent of early childhood educators identifying as "non-White." In comparison, only 18 percent of the K–12 teaching workforce identifies as "non-White." The number of children who speak a language other than English at home is increasing. Racial, ethnic, and linguistic diversity is a vital strength in the early childhood education field. However, childcare workers need enhanced compensation and expanded opportunities for further education in early childhood education. These changes will bring about an equal playing field with K–12 teachers. The following sections focus on career pathways and linguistic diversity.

Cultural Competence Through Multiple Career Pathways

Cultural diversity within early childhood education settings is an invaluable strength. However, to fully leverage such diversity, workers should receive enhanced compensation and better educational opportunities. To this end, career pathways appear to be especially promising, as they can provide flexible and inclusive opportunities for professional development to diverse sets of educators. Furthermore, these pathways can help address the problems of low pay among early childhood educators by providing educators with opportunities for credentialing in flexible schedules.

Career pathways provide career advancement through a progression of training and credentials that reflect progressively higher competencies and are tied to roles or job titles. They offer flexible education and training opportunities for a variety of learners, such as immigrants, dual-language learners, and individuals with disabilities. A key feature of career pathways is stackable credentials, which are a sequence of credentials that build on prior knowledge and competencies that can build an individual's portfolio of qualifications and help them move along a career pathway. Stackable credentials give the early childhood education workforce educational flexibility by letting them move from shorter-term certificate programs to longer-term degree programs (Lloyd et al., 2021). See table 14.1.

Cultural Competence and Linguistic Diversity

In 2022, approximately one-third of all children birth to age five in the United States were multilanguage learners. In some states, the percentage is

Table 14.1: Early Childhood Education Career Pathways

Career Pathway	What, Where, and How Long	Alignment With Further Education	Potential Job Role	Cultural Competence
Childcare Certificate	Introductory courses at community college; one year; in class or online, includes a practicum	Credits usually count toward an associate's degree.	Assistant teacher	Depends on specific community college early childhood education courses, but if the program is NAEYC accredited, inclusion of cultural competence is required
Child Development Associate Credential	Mostly in their workplaces (for example, home or family daycare); infant-toddler or preschool center-based programs; portfolio and child development associate competencies examination requirements Flexible time to complete, but requiring a minimum of 120 hours of coursework and 420 hours of classroom experience; can be online, depending on the child development associate program	If taking basic introductory two- or four-year college courses, some credits (approximately six credits) may transfer to a two-year college early childhood program; students in a career and technical high school can earn a child development associate credential in their junior and senior years.	Center-based assistant or head or lead teacher; family daycare owner or teacher	Integrated with child development associate competencies; a child development associate option for bilingual specialization; the assessment can be in the educator's language of daily work Competency examples: Functional Areas—"9.2: A non-biased environment is provided . . . 9.4: Candidate helps children experience sympathy/empathy and respect for others" (Council for Professional Recognition, 2023)
Associate's Degree	Introductory courses for 60 credits; two years for full-time or longer for part-time—in class or online; includes a practicum	States require early childhood education course credits to align with four-year college requirements in early childhood education.	Center-based head or lead teacher; family daycare owner or teacher	Depends on the specific community college early childhood education courses and state licensure requirements, but if the program is NAEYC accredited, inclusion of cultural competence is required

continued ▶

Career Pathway	What, Where, and How Long	Alignment With Further Education	Potential Job Role	Cultural Competence
Bachelor's Degree	Either the full 120 credits (including general education credits) or acceptance of 60 credits from an associate's degree at a community college; additional practicum hours beyond an associate's degree	States require alignment of community college early childhood education credits.	Head or lead teacher or program director	Depends on the specific college early childhood education courses and state licensure requirements, but if the program is NAEYC accredited, inclusion of cultural competence is necessary
Master's Degree	Requirements vary.	It leads to a PhD or EdD.	Program director or college instructor	Likely addressed, but may not be required (or even permitted) in some states, depending on their political environment
Registered Apprenticeship Programs (Through the U.S. Department of Labor)	Mostly job based; can earn credits for work experience with a coach; some coursework required, and credits may transfer to a child development associate credential	It may lead to a child development associate credential or associate's degree.	Assistant or lead teacher	Not required, but may be included depending on the courses taken and the coach's approach
Professional Development Workshops or Conferences	Usually on-site but may be at a professional conference, such as that of a state association for education of young children or NAEYC	Not applicable	Expanding knowledge in their current position and supporting a move to the next level of responsibility	Staff needs; program director's decisions; technical assistance providers' suggestions

significantly greater: California, 59 percent; Texas, 49 percent; New Jersey, 47 percent; New Mexico, 44 percent; and Nevada, 43 percent (Migration Policy Institute, n.d.). While Spanish is the primary language of multilingual learners in the United States, many other languages are spoken in young children's homes: Arabic, Russian, Cantonese, Vietnamese, Mandarin, Tagalog, Urdu, Hindi, and Haitian Creole. The list goes on and on (Giang & Park, 2022).

Clearly, we need many more early childhood teachers knowledgeable about how young multilanguage learners are capable of both learning English and maintaining fluency in their home language. Respect for this process is an example of linguistic cultural competence, which emphasizes young children's assets rather than focusing on perceived deficits. Multilingualism is an asset for students of any age, especially for young children, whose brains are developing so rapidly. Research has shown the following.

- Bilingualism enhances some aspects of executive functioning, including better focus (Kamenetz, 2016).
- Bilingual children as young as three can take the perspective of another person, an aspect of cognitive empathy that is usually not observed until later (Astington & Edward, 2010; Kamenetz, 2016).
- Another example of linguistic cultural competence is *translanguaging*, when a person, child or adult, mixes two languages in a communication: "¡Felicidades! You worked so hard on that colorful picture, Alicia!" (Castro, 2020).

In sum, educators in early childhood education spaces who are themselves multilingual can help young learners gain more language and culture skills. Such skills can enhance children's cognitive development, empathy, and overall executive functioning. Thus, the need for multilingual educators, along with better compensation and education, is especially great.

Solutions for Workforce Support at All Levels

At all levels, we should train, support, and prepare childcare workers and educators to understand and address equity, diversity, cultural competence, antibias, and antiracism. Solutions must span the individual, program, and systems levels. Overall, we need to increase wages, make training and education affordable and accessible, expand recruitment and apprenticeships, and provide more support for trainees from diverse backgrounds. NAEYC and the Education Trust (2019) provide recommendations for each level: individual level, program level, and systems level. We acknowledge the emerging challenge of private-equity interest in childcare, which leads to the last solution we want to highlight: organize!

Individual Level: Affordable and Accessible Higher Education

The Child Care Services Association (2022a, 2022b) offers two programs that support individual early childhood educators in gaining access to higher education.

1. **T.E.A.C.H. Early Childhood (www.teachecnationalcenter.org/teach-early-childhood):** This initiative, active in nearly half of the United States, "is a national, evidence-based strategy that creates access to higher education for teachers, directors and family child care providers working with young children in out-of-home settings" (Child Care Services Association, 2022b). T.E.A.C.H. provides comprehensive scholarships to enable early educators to take coursework leading to credentials and degrees. T.E.A.C.H. components include
(1) comprehensive scholarship, (2) college education,
(3) compensation, (4) commitment, and (5) counselor.

2. **Child Care WAGE$ (www.teachecnationalcenter.org/child-care-wages):** This initiative "provides education-based salary supplements to teachers, directors and family child care providers working with young children in regulated early care and education settings to increase workforce retention, education and compensation" (Child Care Services Association, 2022a).

Program Level: Qualified Staff

NAEYC and the Education Trust (2019) recommend several strategies for workforce support at the program level, including registered apprenticeships. This earn-while-you-learn strategy treats "employment as a central asset to degree attainment rather than a barrier" (Garcia & Sklar, 2022, p. 52). Registered apprenticeships bring on-the-job learning together with coursework and mentoring, leading to a credential, an associate's degree, or even a bachelor's degree. However:

> Early childhood centers . . . are typically small, independently run organizations. To implement a Registered Apprenticeship, responsibility for managing administrative processes and paperwork, supporting each

> apprentice and mentor, and securing funding for the program would likely be borne almost entirely by the director of the center. (Workman, 2019, p. 8)

This is potentially a heavy lift for program leaders.

Grow-your-own programs, another recommendation, "are an increasingly popular strategy for recruiting and preparing racially and linguistically diverse teachers already living in the communities they would serve" (Garcia & Sklar, 2022, p. 52). For example, "Chicago's need to expand public pre-K and identify culturally competent, bilingual teachers to serve young English learners" led to recruitment of local paraeducators who work with a mentor, take classes leading to licensure, receive a small salary for living expenses, and secure reduced tuition (Garcia & Sklar, 2022, p. 52).

NAEYC and the Education Trust (2019) also recommend professional learning and coaching.

- Professional development and coaching increase overall job satisfaction, lower levels of anxiety, and offer opportunities for higher salaries and career advancement. Professional development for home-based or family childcare providers is particularly important given their greater barriers to attending degree programs. "Hispanic and non-Hispanic Black home-based teachers and caregivers participated in more PD than their non-Hispanic White counterparts" (Warner-Richter, Paschall, Tout, & Lowe, 2020, p. 3).

- Teachstone's (n.d.b) focus on high-quality teacher-student interactions utilizes the results of the CLASS observation system "to create tailored professional development and coaching opportunities that help teachers improve their teaching practices" (Teachstone, n.d.a). This data-driven approach is critical for creating an equitable classroom and school climate. Teachstone's (n.d.b) CLASS observation system, its professional development approach, and its coaching model recognize the need for and incorporate principles of equity, diversity, and inclusion. (See also chapter 1, pages 46 and 48–49, of *Little Learners, Big Hearts*.)

Systems Level: Feasible Pursuit of Higher Education

At the systems level, NAEYC and the Education Trust (2019) focus on lessening the time educators will need to obtain early childhood teaching and advanced degrees.

- **The T.E.A.C.H. initiative:** This program "helps states leverage the financial resources necessary to provide access to higher education and support for the early care and education (ECE) workforce, and it creates new and diverse teachers and program leaders" (Child Care Services Association, 2022b). With its focus on building the capacity of both higher education and individuals, T.E.A.C.H. helps educators achieve their goals.

- **Community college baccalaureates:** By eliminating transfer gaps and making higher education more financially accessible, these are now available in twenty-five states (as of 2022). Community college baccalaureate programs may be "an entry point for promoting greater access to bachelor's degrees for students of color" (Garcia & Sklar, 2022, p. 51).

- **Higher education consortia and collaboratives:** Members of these consortia promote solutions to four key barriers early childhood teachers face. These barriers include (1) lack of alignment in transferring from community to four-year colleges, (2) insufficient guidance and support for academic success, (3) course schedules lacking the flexibility that working teachers need, and (4) unpaid student internships (Garcia & Sklar, 2022).

Also critical to the systemic level is a set of policies, applicable both nationally and within individual states, promoting needed changes in the early childhood education arena. In this chapter and elsewhere in this book, we have addressed most of the ten policy recommendations proposed by the Hunt Institute, Educational Alliance, the Manny Cantor Center, the Century Foundation, and the Education Trust (2022) in an issue brief called "Strong Foundations: Promoting Diverse and Inclusive Preschool Settings." While these broad policy recommendations provide something of a roadmap, they do not consistently emphasize the need for a shift toward antiracism and cultural competence as intrinsic to each one. Nevertheless, many of the proposed policies could be implemented with that explicit focus, as we have explained particularly in this chapter. We have added, as needed, a more explicit focus on equity in describing eight of the policy recommendations (with the original policy statement in bold; Hunt Institute et al., 2022).

- **Support increased and innovative funding** through advocacy for greater investment to support low-income and BIPOC families and programs.

- **Promote mixed-delivery systems** enabling families to choose diverse cultural and linguistic settings appropriate for their and their children's needs.

- **Promote equitable recruitment within the early childhood workforce** that reflects the racial and ethnic diversity of the students and their families.

- **Develop comprehensive training and professional development** for all educators that includes self-reflection, as well as content and strategies that support students from diverse racial and cultural communities.

- **Address the compensation needs of the early childhood workforce**, recognizing the current racial and program inequities.

- **Revise early learning standards** to ensure curriculum, quality, and developmental benchmarks reflect cultural and racial diversity in the programs.

- **Increase the research base** with explicit attention, for example, to how teachers' and leaders' unconscious biases may impact curricular and disciplinary choices, the latter potentially leading to the preschool-to-prison pipeline.

- **Require transparent and disaggregated data** to gain a deeper understanding of economic, racial, and ethnic variations in, for example, enrollment, financial resources, school readiness, and so on.

Private Equity: An Emerging Challenge

A new challenge to the field of early childhood education has begun to emerge. Private-equity firms are seeing the childcare "industry" as a source of potential profits. Since the 1970s, there have been numerous corporate-owned child-care chains. In the early 2000s, private equity began to show an interest. "Four of the top five for-profit child-care chains . . . are controlled by private-equity funds" (Harris, 2024). Sarah Carr (2024), writing in the Hechinger Report, describes the phenomenon: "Investor-backed chains now manage an estimated one in 10 child care centers in the country." So why might this be a problem specifically for early childhood educators?

> Though private-equity-backed child-care providers can—and often do—offer good services to families, their business model can also prove ruinous. In other sectors, private-equity groups have been notorious for extracting

exorbitant fees from businesses they've acquired in leveraged buyouts; when they've had a chance to raise wages for workers or pay down their private-equity debts, they've regularly opted for the latter. (Harris, 2024)

States can put "guardrails" into their childcare regulations to limit, for example, tuition hikes and profit margins. Vermont, Massachusetts, and New Jersey have either proposed or passed regulations such as these (Carr, 2024). Informing legislators about issues related to private equity, especially when they are considering an influx of much-needed early childhood funding, will require significant advocacy and organization.

Last, but Not Least: Advocacy and Organizing!

The North Carolina Early Education Coalition (n.d.a) makes this unequivocal: "Child care teachers are essential. They are the workers behind the workforce. . . . Families rely on our early education system in order to keep working, and our state's economy does, too."

Elected officials may want to represent their constituents' best interests, but very few have real-life experiences that help them understand the issues facing the early childhood workforce. They need the input of those who possess both the expertise and experience in childcare to make the best decisions with the greatest impact.

Additionally, advocacy efforts extend beyond interacting with policymakers. To amplify your message and build greater public support, you can help by educating the public about the essential role that early childhood educators play in supporting young children's healthy development, working families, and your state's economy. This education can be as simple as having conversations with family, friends, or colleagues; raising awareness on social media; or using local media and events in your community to highlight key issues (North Carolina Early Education Coalition, n.d.a).

There are numerous examples of advocacy that are bringing results, even if not the ultimate solutions. The Wisconsin Early Childhood Action Needed (WECAN), formed in 2020, is:

> a grassroots group that connects parents, ECE and child care professionals, other business owners, and community members. [WECAN hosts] trainings to build educators' confidence as advocates. . . . During the state budget process, [they] helped WECAN members create messages on how child care impacted each section of the budget. When they had the opportunity to

speak, they did so with confidence. In short, [WECAN is] empowering early educators across Wisconsin to get involved in the policymaking process and witness how their stories are important and can make a difference. (Hendrickson, 2022)

In North Carolina, the Worthy Wages Campaign is designed to "help raise awareness and tell policymakers that early educators deserve worthy wages for their worthy work" (North Carolina Early Education Coalition, n.d.b). Further:

> Despite their essential role, child care teachers remain woefully underpaid and undervalued for the critically important work they do. These teachers, overwhelmingly women and primarily women of color, have remained in the classroom this whole time earning low wages and risking their own health to care for the children of working families. (North Carolina Early Education Coalition, n.d.b)

The Worthy Wages Campaign Toolkit (North Carolina Early Education Coalition, n.d.a) could be useful for early childhood leaders in other states and localities looking to organize among themselves and with their staff, families, and policymakers. It contains easily modifiable sections, including key advocacy issues, talking points, resources and data, templates for contacting policymakers, and social media strategies.

In Massachusetts, Strategies for Children (n.d.b) promotes:

> pursuing a common agenda—The Early Childhood Agenda—for all in the field, while building a more robust, statewide advocacy infrastructure. Key roles are—
> - Advocate
> - Research, analyze, distill information
> - Convene, build community and relationships
> - Communicate and share information

A critical component of Strategies for Children's (n.d.a) approach is the *9:30 call*, held daily on Zoom, Monday through Thursday, 9:30 to 10:00 a.m. There are also options for participation in the evenings and in Spanish. Speakers include legislators, researchers, local organizers, and collaborating nonprofit leaders. Approximately 75 percent of "callers" are from center-based administration. Others include family childcare and before- and after-school providers.

Commonalities in these three organizing efforts, and many other similar advocacy groups, include support for educators and caregivers (including those in home daycare), data and resources, policy goals, and collaborative relationships. Amy O'Leary, executive director of Strategies for Children, sums up the need for leadership and action:

> So, you have local state and federal officials. Our delegation in Washington, DC, is supportive of this issue. So, we need to remember that they support this; to thank them and encourage them to fight the fight in Washington, DC. And if you're at the state level, sharing your story, we have a blog on early education where we want to lift up the voices of families and educators to tell the story and what are the solutions that work. We also know that people can talk to their early educators, ask them questions, get information about how much their salary is, get mad about how low it is, and then think about what those policy solutions are. But as you said about the relationship; building relationships with people, I think that the pandemic has taught us that we value this and that people need other people to solve these problems. (Croke, 2021)

HEART+ Takeaways

The early childhood education arena is wrestling with disparities in compensation, career advancement, and cultural competence. Many efforts on multiple levels (local, state, and national) are needed to promote accessible educational opportunities, fair wages, and more. Grassroots movements, general policy advocacy, and community engagement can help raise societal awareness and support for antiracist movements.

CHAPTER 15

A Look at the Future: Leadership to Embrace Change

> If you inspire change in another by acting in alignment with your values and integrity, the people you change will become a new vehicle of inspiration for others. This will increase positive change, rippling out far into the future. If you want to live in a kind world, then change the world with kindness.
>
> —Duncan Autrey

Principle 15: Hope + action can lead to transformative change.

Looking into the eyes of your youngest students, what would you want for their future? Consider an infant only a few months old, a toddler, and a child preparing for their first day of school. Children are so innocent, so precious, and so vulnerable.

As early childhood leaders, we have opportunities and options—opportunities to make a difference and options to be trailblazers, to take bold steps into a better world rather than wait for someone else to lead.

As you consider your youngest learners, what would you want not only for their future, but also for their present? Perhaps a sense of joy, happiness, and well-being. Perhaps a sense that they are OK, safe and secure, and resilient—that they can overcome the obstacles they will surely face.

Even as we imagine this future, we are caught with the realization that our students are not starting on equal footing. Risks, adversities, and setbacks are more likely for some than for others. It is a hard truth.

However, as educators have repeatedly discovered, we can make a difference. In this chapter, we focus on hope and how it can translate to concrete action for a better future.

The Potential of Hope

Let's spend a moment lining up the odds. We know it takes knowledge and wisdom, as well as caring and compassion, to bring about greater empathy and equity. But how do we achieve the knowledge and wisdom we need? The NYC Leadership Academy (2020), describing six critical dispositions for school leaders who want to bring about more equity, calls for leaders who:

1. Reflect on their personal assumptions, beliefs, and behaviors
2. Model personal beliefs grounded in equity, even as they may personally feel anxiety, fear, or anger; encourage vulnerability and risk taking while acting as role models for equity and setting aside fear and anxiety for the greater good
3. Purposefully build the capacity of others to identify and disrupt inequities
4. Communicate high expectations for all students and respectfully partner with families, practicing cultural competence
5. Confront and strive to alter institutional bias and deficit-based approaches for minoritized populations' knowledge and wisdom
6. Lead shared visioning and action planning to create a better future

With this model, leaders gravitate toward our HEART+ principles, with time for reflection, strengthening of their beliefs and knowledge, and action. Part of this plan requires living and breathing hope, daily. Consider a vision without limitations, the sky as the limit. We need to change to permeate the air we breathe, even as it impacts the ground beneath our feet and, as John O'Donohue (2008) would say, the *space between us*.

On a similar note, professor emeritus Richard Sorenson (2022) recommends that leaders model, coach, and teach hopefulness, saying, "Hope and optimism boost quality, engagement, productivity, peace of mind, and overall well-being.

Creating an atmosphere of interest, eagerness, excitement, and optimism about schooling is a hallmark of hopeful leadership" (p. 8).

In *The School Leaders Our Children Deserve: Seven Keys to Equity, Social Justice, and School Reform*, George Theoharis (2009) describes the sources of resistance to equitable change that educational leaders face. The first of these he calls "resistance from within the school site" (Theoharis, 2009, p. 88). We have discussed in depth how individuals, whether staff or families, may resist antiracist, culturally competent change. As an example of this resistance, he quotes a principal who says:

> At least once a month, White parents came to my office and said "I'm not racist, but I'm worried about what's happening in my child's classroom. I don't want to blame it on the African American and Latino kids." Without exception, the parent would then blame whatever the issue was on an African American or Latino kid. (Theoharis, 2009, p. 95)

Theoharis (2009) goes on to identify a second source of resistance, or barrier, to change: "resistance from the district level" (p. 88). Early childhood programs may be independent of school districts or embedded within them. Even for independent programs, such as private preschools or home care situations, the district's expectations for certain levels of academic preparation, social-emotional maturity, and acculturation to Eurocentric values or behaviors are ever-present for leaders. Managing these expectations while dealing with a bureaucracy and maintaining one's reputation as an effective early childhood educator, and while truly meeting young children's developmental needs, is certainly a balancing act worthy of a circus performer (or an early childhood leader!).

The third area of resistance, according to Theoharis (2009), is "resistance from the institutional level" (p. 88), which includes a lack of financial and time resources, harmful state and federal regulations, and principal preparation that lacks realistic guidance for becoming a social justice leader.

Facing resistance, where do we start? Let's look at what Teresa Byington, professor at the University of Nevada, said about the importance of hope, the starting point for HEART+, in an interview with Orinthia:

> We infuse hope by giving students and families something to look forward to that will have a positive outcome in the future. One way that we promote positive and inclusive environments is by focusing on children's social and emotional development.

> We teach early childhood educators how to guide children in solving problems and developing self-regulation skills. Teachers help the preschoolers in their classrooms learn how to recognize and manage their emotions. Children learn how to be a good friend, cooperate, and have empathy for others. These actions create a positive and inclusive classroom climate.
>
> Children gain skills that will help them have greater success in school and life. This instills hope for a brighter future. (T. Byington, personal communication, January 10, 2024)

Moreover, as the inspirational James Baldwin said in an interview in Istanbul in 1970:

> Hope is invented every day. And so, I'll say this really quickly. . . . There's reason to think that we are on the precipice of change, but there's no guarantee. But wherever human beings are, we at least have a chance because we're not only disasters; we're also miracles. (as recalled by Princeton University professor Eddie Glaude; Abdelfatah & Arablouei, 2020)

We start with hope, but there is more to the story.

Hope Into Action

OK, so we believe in hope. However, we also believe in action—in what individuals and groups can do. Throughout this book, we have highlighted many actions that leaders can take to make our hope an actual reality. The core of successful hope-based actions is a focus on leadership centering the whole-child approach.

Here is a prime example of the powerful impact of hope + action. Six primary recommendations for improving the lives of Native American children in the United States through a whole-child approach emerged from a series of virtual listening sessions with over five hundred participants that the National Indian Education Association (NIEA, 2024) conducted with the Center for Educational Improvement in 2023. These include recommendations for turning to promising educational practices, claiming "educational sovereignty," establishing state and regional initiatives, expanding compassionate healing practices, and finding more resources, funding, research, and policy changes in support of Native students (NIEA, 2024).

Melanie Johnson, director of the Whole Child Initiative, explains that NIEA offers culturally responsive education and trauma training for educators and staff, and since the COVID-19 pandemic, has offered virtual home learning educational materials and online resources (M. Johnson, personal communication, October 14, 2022). Even as NIEA collaborates with others on building alliances, conducting research, and changing policies, it has reached over forty thousand Native students through the Whole Child Initiative. NIEA (2024) also provides training to professionals about the effects of historical trauma that pervade tribal communities. NIEA educates to make a difference, even as it works with others on hope, (self-)education, acknowledgment, resolution, and teaching.

The same focus on the whole child is clear in Bernida Thompson, Bodunrin O. Banwo, and Rasheki Kuykendall-Walker's (2020) chapter in the book *African-Centered Education: Theory and Practice*:

> When we begin our day at Roots [their school], we are thinking about the whole child. We strategize about how we can holistically give African children an educational experience that is filled with an atmosphere and climate steeped in authentic African centeredness. We start this process with ceremonies and rituals. Our ancestors define our school; they surround our children on our walls; they are spoken about with reverence; and they are honored in the morning ceremony.
>
> Each morning, the entire village (school) starts with a Circle of Love ceremony. . . . Village members play drums, sing songs, chant, and recite words and battle cries selected to orient our students into their day and our community. (p. 52)

In the same book, Rona Frederick (2020) describes certain heart centered values:

> Treat all children as intelligent human beings and be present. By present Baba Trure [the teacher] means looking at the child, looking at body language, building strong relationships, and being attuned to who the child is.
>
> Mama Amma teaches with love, care, high expectations, and a great understanding of the spirit of each child. . . . Mama Amma takes them on adventures to Africa through storytelling. They learn the parts of their body through movement. They sing songs in several languages. These children learn to read, write, and most important to love themselves and others. (p. 38)

To make a critical difference, the most significant leadership is transformative—that is, leadership that starts from the inside out. In transformative leadership, a leader actively creates the conditions to help people in the organization undergo transformative learning. "Transformative leadership includes taking actions to create something new, bigger, and better. With transformational leadership the focus is on motivation and preparing people for change—so transformational leadership sets the stage for transformative change" (Owen & Mason, in press).

As Renee Owen and Christine Mason (in press) say in the upcoming book *Becoming a Transformative Leader From the Inside Out: The Nested Leadership Model for Educators*:

> To become a transformative leader takes time and a great sense of timing. Making the right moves involves reading the context, finding support, and knowing when to challenge staff and students.
>
> All transformative work is done with heart—having compassion for staff and students and being both patient and strategic with the amount of change people can tolerate. Therefore, the transformative leader has an awareness that one move may be better for your immediate community, while recognizing that in a few years you may need to promote additional changes.

Owen and Mason (in press) continue with these words of caution:

> As educational leaders, particularly leaders who are held accountable by the public, it is critical that you know about the values and attitudes of your local and state communities. The work as transformative change agents must occur with that awareness; otherwise, particularly in the climate in the United States today, you are at risk.

It is a divisive time. So even as we have hope and seek resolution and healing, we also urge leaders to act as they can, to band together, and to make the difference they can—one student, one teacher, one staff, one school, and one community at a time. Our collective will and action are critical.

HEART+ Takeaways

Leaders can help create a better future for young children by beginning with the present, supporting a climate of hope, and helping students and staff through optimism and concrete actions that demonstrate expectations for equity and fairness. Together, we can make a critical difference.

EPILOGUE

Toward a More Just and Inclusive World

> As long as poverty, injustice, and gross inequality persist in our world, none of us can truly rest.
>
> —Nelson Mandela

Leaders will find that much work remains. As Nelson Mandela acknowledges in the preceding quote, the road to freedom and equity is long. Even as we advance, other forces seem to be at play. Yet, education has an important role in advancing a vision and creating a better future for *all* children and *all* people. Early childhood leaders must be willing to move ahead of the conventional approaches, guiding their teams toward new directions that prioritize empathy and equity.

Throughout this book, we have chosen to emphasize our vision for the future, believing that *hope* comes with self-*education*, *acknowledging* racism, actively collaborating for *resolution*, and *teaching* our students (HEART+) through a Heart Centered Learning lens. We have described how our heart centered five Cs model—consciousness, compassion, confidence, courage, and community—lays the foundation for educators to bring about real, positive change.

Leaders in early childhood education need to pioneer initiatives that foster empathy, ensuring that educators and caregivers are attuned to the emotional well-being of children. Additionally, they should lead efforts to create an inclusive environment where each child feels a sense of belonging, regardless of their background. Programs that counter the colorblind approach and go beyond multiculturalism by teaching the history of group treatment and embracing diverse cultural values can enhance curricula that lack an anti-oppressive focus.

Leaders—all of us—lose out when bigotry and racism prevail, when hatred is repeated, and when injustice scores another win. There is an accumulating grief that accompanies these losses. And as this grief accumulates, it increases the work we have before us. It is one thing to heal a cold, another to heal a pandemic—a centuries-long pandemic of ignorance, violence, discrimination, and coldheartedness.

For healing to occur, leaders in early childhood need to begin with our youngest learners—babies, toddlers, and young children. Let's discuss how leaders can transition into a new paradigm, acknowledging the inevitability of change and our personal commitment to driving it forward.

A New Paradigm

The paradigm shift needed in educational leadership begins with a commitment to an education system grounded in hope. *Leading with hope* is not about wishful thinking without any certainty of fulfillment. Leading with true hope is founded on expectation, trust, and confidence.

Leaders should expect that every interaction among teachers, students, and families transpires with a recognition of the dignity and worth of every human being. Leaders should trust and validate the stories of those who have been marginalized and seek to right the wrongs of the past, even at the expense of their own privilege. This is compassion in action, and compassion is the doorway to justice.

Acting out of compassion toward those who are victims of things that are wrong often helps us understand why things are wrong and how we might be able to make them right (Wallis, 2014). Lastly, leaders should have confidence in the words of representative John Lewis: "Nothing can stop the power of a committed and determined people to make a difference in our society. Why? Because human beings are the most dynamic link to the divine on this plane" (Washington Post Staff, 2013).

It's all too easy to wonder whether the changes we describe in this book are really possible. This question can haunt us when the social and political climate of our day seems to be waxing worse with no discernible end in sight. If we are not careful, we can become discouraged and depleted of hope. When hope leaves, apathy will then threaten to set in, making us callous, bitter, and hardened. It is therefore imperative that we never lose hope in the truth that change will come.

Heart centered teaching and learning is happening, and HEART+ is being implemented as racism is acknowledged and teaching incorporates antiracist parameters, certainly in many more places than we know about.

Leaders, by now, you are likely to have gotten our points. Basically, we are saying this.

- **Start:** Start with yourself. Start somewhere with something you can do. But *start*. We must be far more intentional about our efforts to move away from racism and injustice.
- **Listen and learn:** There are so many wise souls speaking up, writing, and advising us. Be humble, show cultural humility, listen deeply, and continue to learn as you move forward.
- **Believe in goodness and incorporate HEART+:** As early childhood leaders on an antiracist journey, we can believe in goodness by fostering environments rooted in empathy, kindness, and respect for all. By incorporating the principles of HEART+ into our leadership, as we acknowledge racism and foster cultural competence, we inspire hope, cultivate inclusivity, and empower young learners to envision a world free from racism and discrimination.
- **Lead:** Lead by example and remember, "Change is never easy, but always possible" (Obama, 2005).

In *Little Learners, Big Hearts*, we identify a roadmap for educators in early childhood communities to follow to nurture empathy, bring about greater equity, and reduce racism and discrimination. We include that roadmap again in the introduction to this text (page 8). Leaders can guide staff, students, and their families on a journey that enriches their understanding of the eight key components. Leaders can also give them practical experiences to promote conscious awareness of explicit and implicit bias, deeper understanding, and compassion, and support them to resolve to advance the well-being of BIPOC students.

We suggest that you look again at the roadmap and consider your own knowledge and understanding using a five-point Likert scale, with 5 being high (proficient) and 1 being low (in need of improvement), in figure E.1. Then, turn to your staff, students, and families and rate your perception of their degree of knowledge and understanding. (Note: *Little Learners, Big Hearts* includes separate chapters on each of these factors.)

Look at your ratings. What are your strengths and areas of greatest need? Are these the same for your school community? Where might you begin to advance greater equity?

Component	Assessment of Self	Assessment of School Community	Notes
1. Understanding racism and its impact on young children	1 2 3 4 5	1 2 3 4 5	
2. HEART+ and Heart Centered Learning	1 2 3 4 5	1 2 3 4 5	
3. A strengths-based developmental framework	1 2 3 4 5	1 2 3 4 5	
4. Increasing conscious awareness of bias	1 2 3 4 5	1 2 3 4 5	
5. Welcoming families	1 2 3 4 5	1 2 3 4 5	
6. Creating compassionate, inclusive school communities	1 2 3 4 5	1 2 3 4 5	
7. Advancing positive identities through children's books	1 2 3 4 5	1 2 3 4 5	
8. Promoting heart, curiosity, and self-determination	1 2 3 4 5	1 2 3 4 5	

Figure E.1: Self- and community assessment of equity roadmap components.

*Visit **go.SolutionTree.com/diversityandequity** for a free reproducible version of this figure.*

In this book, we include additional parameters for school leaders (see figure E.2). Once again, rate yourself and your school community.

Once again, look at your ratings. What are your strengths and areas of greatest need? Are these the same for your school community? Where might you begin to advance greater equity?

Component	Assessment of Self	Assessment of School Community	Notes
1. Furthering antiracism principles	1 2 3 4 5	1 2 3 4 5	
2. Curricula supporting empathy and equity	1 2 3 4 5	1 2 3 4 5	
3. Team planning and goal setting	1 2 3 4 5	1 2 3 4 5	
4. Enhancing the early childhood workforce	1 2 3 4 5	1 2 3 4 5	
5. Leadership for change	1 2 3 4 5	1 2 3 4 5	

Figure E.2: Self- and community assessment for leaders.

*Visit **go.SolutionTree.com/diversityandequity** for a free reproducible version of this figure.*

Now look at your combined ratings in figures E.1 and E.2. What conclusions do you reach? Where might you want to put your efforts? Are there others in your school community who might help you complete this review as you begin planning for your next steps?

Reflections on What Matters

We, the authors, have included our personal reflections and next steps here in the hope that they will inspire your own self-work.

Chris says:

> The year 2023 was a year full of tragedies—murders, floods, hate crimes, ongoing wars, and the reemergence of old conflicts. While our two books (both *Little Learners, Big Hearts* and *Advancing Empathy* and *Equity in Early Childhood Education*) center equity, antiracism, and a reduction in prejudice, with a focus on early childhood centers and schools, many of the principles are applicable to far-ranging situations in communities around the world.
>
> Whether your community is a school or a civic center, a local park, or a world trade organization, the principles of welcoming families, advancing positive identities, and leading with heart can promote harmony, goodwill, and resolution of conflict. They also can enhance workforce preparation, equity in pay, and further individual agency. We encourage school leaders

to realize the value of taking the principles beyond school walls into their daily lives and helping others understand how these principles apply in work, business, education, and play. We can strengthen the "goodness" of our inner core by living by these guidelines.

And as you do this, focus on bringing joy to others, connecting in meaningful ways, and as I say in *Little Learners, Big Hearts*, "Be gentle." Around the globe, people are living in crisis, as a multitude of problems continuously unfolds. So, as you set about doing your part to make the world a better place, be gentle—with yourself and others. Be gentle, realizing that change takes time. Be gentle even as your patience wears thin. Stand firm, voice your concerns, and be gentle—with compassion for yourself and others.

Chris's next step:

Cultivating Happiness in Schools is one of the latest initiatives of the Center for Educational Improvement. We are seeking ways to support more mindfulness, yoga, and meditation in schools. Related to this work, I am headed to Nepal (yes, this was on my bucket list!) to share ideas at an international yoga festival and with local schools there. I am committed to continuing to advance empathy, equity, compassion, and, yes, happiness in schools—and to encouraging others across their lives to continue on paths to bringing healing and wholeness to their lives and their families, friends, and communities.

Jill says:

Compassionate, effective leadership is built on a foundation of relationships. It takes time. It takes patience and kindness. It takes listening without judgment. Intertwining a kindness curriculum based on empathy and equity should be clearly expressed and reinforced within each relationship.

Our HEART+ and mindfulness components serve to illustrate what we mean by a kindness curriculum, and we hope that you have found each facet of our guide helpful in supporting your work as a leader. Educators can enhance student brain development, and we have neuroscience proof that practicing these skills can change the brain.

But the first step is building relationships—with the students in your care, the adults who parent the children, and the educators who are within your school community. Not only do we prioritize building relationships, but we absolutely endorse a focus on emotional intelligence and social-emotional learning skills being practiced and reinforced for adults and children in your care. The work of Abraham Maslow's hierarchy of needs in 1943 suggests people are motivated to fulfill basic needs of security and safety before they can reach self-actualization and should be elevated before Benjamin Bloom's (1956) proposed hierarchy of developing educational objectives. Yes, Maslow before Bloom, as early educators see on a daily basis in their programs.

Jill's next step:

Do something!

We have offered a wide repertoire of activities, discussion topics, personal reflection prompts, and resources for you. We acknowledge this will be uncomfortable work at times. But doing nothing is not an option. Your students and families look to your leadership for guidance, and early childhood is not too soon to begin the work of antiracism and antibias awareness.

I have found using the wonderful array of current children's literature is one way to open the conversation. Students and their families should see themselves reflected in the books, posters, and activities you provide in your program. Read aloud, share your libraries, open discussions, and take that first step.

This is a way to do something!

This is essential and important work built on relationships, nurtured with HEART+ and mindfulness, and always offering hope that our children and grandchildren will grow into a loving, equitable world.

Orinthia says:

As an early childhood leader striving for a more just and inclusive world, I recognize the importance of challenging my own assumptions. I ask myself, "What assumption am I making that I am not aware of that gives me what I see?" Taking a reflective stance, especially considering the dire circumstances we often witness in education, we can draw a different frame around the circumstances we face. This process demands humility as a leader, acknowledging that we may hold unconscious assumptions that influence our perspective. When we do not take on this posture of humility, we are likely to suppress the voices of the very people we need to make the changes we seek. This lack of humility can inadvertently perpetuate existing disparities and hinder the collaborative efforts needed to achieve meaningful and sustainable transformation.

Nelson Mandela said, "True leadership demands the humility to sincerely listen, the courage to embrace diverse voices, and the commitment to foster meaningful transformation through collective collaboration." I commit to this posture of humility in my leadership role, acknowledging the richness that diversity brings to our collective journey, and actively working together with my team to create lasting and meaningful transformation.

Orinthia's next step:

My plan for continued growth in leadership and early care education is to daily take a HEART+ inventory. I created the HEART+ (hope, education, acknowledgment, resolution, teaching, and local needs) acronym to guide myself and other early childhood educators through the process of self-development and systemic change. My plan will always begin with hope. The paradigm shift needed in educational leadership begins with a commitment to an education system grounded in hope. Leading with hope is not about wishful thinking without any certainty of its fulfillment. Leading with true hope is founded on expectation, trust, and confidence. Leaders should expect that every interaction between teachers, students, and families transpires with a recognition of the dignity and worth of every human being. I aspire to be an early childhood leader who is committed and determined to lead with hope.

Randy says:

Researching and writing for more than two years both *Little Learners, Big Hearts* and *Advancing Empathy and Equity in Early Childhood Education* has been a challenge and a joy. While I have had a lifelong commitment to understanding and challenging racism and cultural bias, I have not had until now the opportunity to dive deeply into the research on topics such as implicit bias, and specifically, how implicit bias develops in early childhood. Learning, and then writing, about this area has changed my understanding of the most effective ways to root out bias, especially implicit bias. Having been an educator for over fifty years, I look back and see the multitude of ways that I misunderstood or simply did not effectively address bias among staff, families, and students themselves. I wish I could go back and act with the self-awareness I am still developing. But, I know I did my best with what I understood at the time. With deepened self-awareness and self-compassion, each of us can move forward. Writing these books has given me the joyful opportunity to do better, to make up for my own errors by offering compassionate clarity to you, our readers. Over time, and with mindful reflection on my own past, I have deepened my compassion for those who are caught in the dangerous delusions of racism and cultural bias.

Randy's next step:

I commit myself to deepen my practice of "compassionate antiracism," learning from others who have walked this path. I continue to read and reflect on the words of Black writers and other writers of color, many of whom we have mentioned in these two books. White writers are also working to understand the complex changes in our society and in our wider world. We are living in an extremely dangerous time—socially, politically, and environmentally. Can we bring together all peoples, especially young people of all backgrounds, to work in harmony and share power for the survival of our democracy and of our planet, with all of her inhabitants? These are my deepest concerns as I am about to enter my ninth decade of life.

Our individual messages, as related here and throughout this book, are to promote kindness, empathy, antiracism, and cultural acceptance; to build bridges; and to lead with compassion. Compassion is often the doorway to justice. Major social reform movements, like the Civil Rights Movement and the Anti-Apartheid Movement, centered on compassion and the belief in the dignity of every person. Remember, each time we stand up for our ideals or act to right an injustice, we, according to Robert F. Kennedy (1966), send forth "a tiny ripple of hope, and crossing each other from a million different centers of energy and daring those ripples build a current which can sweep down the mightiest walls of oppression and resistance."

Well-Being for All

Hope, healing, compassion, and love—these are central to creating a sense of harmony and well-being. Yet, so often, so many factors get in the way—factors like history, conflict, hatred, and the cumulative impact of traumatic events; factors such as White privilege, power, and fear.

As so many leaders in the fields of education, early childhood education, and antiracist and antibias have stated, to heal, we must acknowledge realities and we must address bias and discrimination. We really can't move forward until we consciously set out to uplift others. However, as United Nations secretary-general António Guterres says, "We have to transcend our differences to transform our future. When we achieve human rights and human dignity for all people—they will build a peaceful, sustainable and just world" (United Nations, 2017).

We invite you to join us as we intentionally set about adding more conscious understanding, compassion, and courage to our corner of the world. In chapter 10 (page 143), we explain that we are not setting out to change the entire world—yet. However, we have a vision, and we see "our corner of the world" as a place that is more than a pocket of excellence; rather, it's a network of caring professionals intending to use the power of our knowledge, commitment, research, and expanding capacity to stand with and by our youngest. We intend to be standing with and by them so that their early years are a time of joy and excitement, giving them a firm foundation to live in a world filled with endless possibilities, nurturing their curiosity, and laying the groundwork for their future—a future of promise, peace, and prosperity for each and every young child.

APPENDIX A

Equity Activities for Early Childhood Leaders

Chapter 1

A Reflective Assessment

Divide your staff into teams of three or four people. Each team is assigned one of the National Association of Elementary School Principals equity standards and given one to two weeks to review the standards and consider an internal audit of its standard. When you meet again in one to two weeks, each team shares its findings, including evidence and recommendations.

NAESP has developed a full reflective assessment based on a set of six competency standards for leadership in early childhood education (preK–3; Kauerz et al., 2021). Competency 4 is to "ensure equitable opportunities" (Kauerz et al., 2021), and several other competencies include self-assessment items directly related to the focus of *advancing empathy and equity*. We summarize the competencies and strategies most relevant to equity and school climate in the following list.

- **Competency 1: Child development and how it affects instruction and interactions**—Items cover leaders' willingness to learn about issues related to stress and trauma, focus on school culture and climate and building community among all stakeholders, connect with students' cultural backgrounds to support their self-efficacy, and prioritize professional development to foster positive student behavior.

- **Competency 2: Family and community partnerships**—Items cover leaders' awareness of varied student and family needs, the school's communication plan and its capacity to partner with and provide support to families, and the presence of a process and staff to liaise with and support families.
- **Competency 4: Equitable opportunities**—
    - *Strategy 1: Culturally competent self-awareness*—Items cover leaders' willingness to self-examine related to race and privilege, dynamically create an equity action plan, and talk with community members to understand diverse perspectives.
    - *Strategy 2: School climate*—Items cover leaders' work on relationships that contribute to an open and equitable climate and professional development to support teachers in creating inclusive classrooms that affirm differences.
    - *Strategy 3: Identification of disparities*—Items cover leaders' work to conduct an equity audit; their focus on data for suspensions, expulsions, attendance, and inclusion of students with varied needs; and the school's development of a dynamic process for monitoring progress and pushing for improvement.
    - *Strategy 4: Resources for equitable opportunities*—Items cover leaders' awareness of inequities and how they manifest in various aspects of school and their creation of pathways for gathering input on school practices from traditionally marginalized families.

Users are asked to rate their adherence to each item (highly inaccurate, inaccurate, accurate, or highly accurate) and then provide written evidence. The full assessment is available from NAESP (Kauerz et al., 2021).

Family Involvement

Heather Walter, a professor of early childhood special education, explains an assignment she has often given to preservice students in early childhood education:

> One thing that is challenging for early interventionists (especially ones new to the field) is going into homes that are "not like theirs," and they often do this alone without adequate mentorship as they are not in classroom-based placements. This, I believe, is a big barrier to success and where bias often collides as values, cultures, and experiences of the educator have not

been adequately reflected on—therefore, they go into homes assuming—which creates trust barriers.

Therefore, an assignment I used to do is to have preservice teachers (in any field placement but especially home visiting) walk around the neighborhood, really be mindful of what is around and what they see, and reflect on that experience as *only* a starting point to then reflecting on how this differs from their own environment and how it is similar—and how they think they should enter a person's home in *any* environment to partner with families in practices for their children. (H. Walter, personal communication, May 24, 2024)

If you are teaching a university course, this may be a good assignment to ask graduate or undergraduate students to complete sometime during the first six to eight weeks of a semester. If you are reading this either independently or as part of a book study, there are two possible modifications: (1) complete this with a neighborhood where you would like to gain a better understanding of families, or (2) complete this as a meditation and then identify the similarities and differences.

After completing one form of this exercise, find time and a space to dialogue with others and compare experiences and conclusions, including implications for your collaboration with families.

Chapter 2

Book Study Activity

Consider the books and authors we mention in this chapter (Imani Perry, Ta-Nehisi Coates, Isabel Wilkerson, Gregory Cajete, and others). Much could be gained by reading a text, whether it be nonfiction, fiction, or historical fiction, that includes a racism theme. Discuss the possibility of devoting four to six weeks to reading and discussing one of the books mentioned. Some of the questions that you might address in the book study include the following.

- What were major themes in the book?
- Was there anything in particular that stood out, made you stop and reflect, or gave you pause?
- Did the book impact your ideas about racism or discrimination? If so, how?

- As a result of reading this book, are you likely to change anything about how you interact with people of other races or cultures?

See also the challenge questions for chapter 2 in appendix B (page 265).

Chapter 3

Understanding Bias Activity

This activity, I Am . . . I Am Not . . . for bias recognition, was created by Orinthia for her work in early childhood science, technology, engineering, and mathematics (STEM).

- **Objective:** The goal of this activity is to promote self-awareness and challenge biases among staff members or students by reflecting on personal identities and dispelling stereotypes.
- **Materials needed:**
  - Stop sign cutouts for each participant (with words "I am not" on one side and "I am" on the other)
  - Writing materials (such as markers or pens)
  - Popsicle sticks or other small thin sticks about a foot long and glue or tape for attaching
  - An alternative is to provide each participant an index card and have them draw the stop sign and words "I am not" on one side and words "I am" on the other; young children may enjoy the stop sign cutouts most and adults may find the index cards easiest to use
- **Instructions:**
  - Begin by explaining the purpose of the activity—to explore personal identities and challenge biases.
  - Emphasize the importance of self-reflecting and understanding the impact of biases on our perceptions.
  - Ask participants to record a stereotype or misconception they often encounter on the "I am not" side.
  - Ask participants to record one aspect of their identity on the flip side of the sign.

- Encourage honesty and vulnerability, emphasizing that the goal is self-reflection and understanding.
- Divide participants into small groups.
- Have participants, in their groups, share their "I am . . ." and "I am not . . ." statements.
- Facilitate discussions by asking questions such as, "How do these stereotypes impact individuals? In what ways might biases affect our interactions with others? How can we challenge and overcome biases in the workplace?"

Coming to the Table Activity

Visit the Coming to the Table website (https://comingtothetable.org) and review the suggested steps and processes. Coming to the Table's Linked Descendants working group offers actions that descendants of enslaver families can take (BitterSweet Editors, 2022). As you review the guidelines, consider whether any of the recommendations will be useful in your school or community. The danger of staying in the comfort zone is that leaders, especially those in early childhood education, may fail to grasp the significance of self-awareness. Insensitivity toward people begins with a lack of awareness of self.

Chapter 9

Level Playing Field Activity

Before you begin, try to fulfill the following requirements.

- Schedule at least sixty to ninety minutes for the activity, including discussion.
- Find a large, clear indoor or outdoor space to accommodate the number of participants.
- Recruit a multiracial group of participants, in which at least 15–20 percent of the participants are BIPOC. (Note: You may need to find ways to repeat this several times over a period of several months so that the non-BIPOC participants each have an opportunity to participate.)
- If possible, there should be at least two facilitators, one BIPOC and one White.

The instructions for completing the activity are as follows.

1. Tell participants that this activity is called Race to the Wall. Do not hint that it is about privilege by calling it Level Playing Field or Privilege Walk.

2. Ask participants to line up next to each other in the center of the space (if inside, equally distant from the opposite walls) and hold hands with those on either side.

3. Begin with simple directions to explain the process, such as the following.

    - Take one step forward if you are right-handed.
    - Take one step back if you grew up in another country.
    - Take one step forward if you graduated from either a two-year or four-year college.
    - Take one step back if you are a single parent.

4. Ask participants to return to their places in the original line. Here are the directions to give once participants are lined up and ready to go.

    - If you read thoroughly about the history of your race in K–12 schoolbooks, take one step forward.
    - If you have *never* had difficulty renting or purchasing housing because of your race, take one step forward.
    - If you have never had difficulty with your neighbors because of your or your family's race, take one step forward.
    - If you have ever been made to feel self-conscious because of physical characteristics associated with your race, take one step back.
    - If you are often asked to present extra identification when using credit cards, take one step back.
    - If you do *not* have to teach your children to be aware of people who may dislike or harm them because of their race, take one step forward.
    - If you have *never* been harassed or treated with disrespect by police, clerks in stores, or just people on the street because of your race, take one step forward.

- If you were discouraged, directly or indirectly, from pursuing activities, careers, or schools of your choice by educators because of your race, take one step back.
- If you have experienced rejection or disregard from teachers, potential employers, coworkers, and so on because your name in some way identifies your race or ethnicity, take one step back.
- If you were raised in a community where most police and politicians were of your racial group, take one step forward.
- If you have ever had clerks or security guards follow you around in a store because of your race, take one step back.
- If you have *never* been asked to speak for all the members of your racial group, take one step forward.
- If you went to K–12 schools where the majority of your teachers were of the same race as you, take one step forward.
- If you have experienced being the only person or just one of two people of your race in a situation, take one step back.
- If you have to worry about racial prejudice against yourself or your family as a routine matter, take one step back.
- If you rarely encounter people of your race who are health care providers, car salespeople, social workers, and so on, take one step back.
- If you rarely have to think about race as part of your normal, everyday routine, take one step forward.
- If you feel physically, emotionally, and even financially threatened by the existence of White nationalist groups in the United States because of your race, take one step back.

When you have completed the list of directions, ask those at the front of the group to turn around so all participants are facing each other. It will be obvious there is a racial or ethnic distribution across the space. Ask participants to take three deep breaths and notice any feelings and thoughts that arise in that moment. Then ask them to move to a discussion area. At this point, you have two options for the discussion groups: (1) all participants meet as one group or (2) BIPOC participants meet in one group and White participants meet in another group. If you (or the participants) decide on this second option, the groups should come back together to share key points.

Discussion questions can include the following, but it is likely that only a few questions will be needed to prompt a serious dialogue.

- How did it feel to drop hands with your friends at whatever point you needed to do that?
- How did it feel to be in your position at the end of the activity?
- Was there anything that surprised you when you viewed everyone's positions at the end of the activity?
- Did you find yourself adjusting the size of your steps, forward or back? If so, why?
- How did any of these experiences impact your own life trajectory, if they did?
- What did you learn, or what are you thinking differently about, from this activity?
- If the participants are of differing ages, what generational differences (if any) did you notice in their final positions?

As you conclude your discussion, remind participants that none of these questions are about their individual effort or how smart they are; rather, the questions are about societal practices that impact racial groups differently. Also, remind them that change is possible and questions that might have been appropriate in the past (such as racial representation in the media) are less appropriate now.

Modeling Antibias Leadership Behavior: A Scenario

Following is a detailed scenario describing a preK–3 principal's interactions with two parents. We suggest that you read through the scenario first and then go back through it again, keeping in mind the reflection questions that follow the scenario.

> *One afternoon, around dismissal time at a preK–3 school in a medium-sized, racially and ethnically diverse city, the principal, Elena Jackson, was shepherding students into their bus lines. She heard two women arguing vehemently. She recognized the tall, blond White woman as a parent at the school for several years. The other woman was new this year. Elena guessed she was Latina, maybe from one of the many new families who had recently moved to the city.*

Elena sensed a subtle negative stereotype ("Is she already on welfare?") creeping into her mind about this "newcomer." With years of self-reflection and professional development, as well as close working relationships with colleagues and families from backgrounds different from her own, she could recognize the unconscious bias that still, frustratingly, arose unbidden in her mind. Determined not to let that impact her interactions, she greeted the two parents, introducing herself and asking both for their names.

As Elena requested them to come into her office, a nearby teacher walked their children, second grader Rory and first grader Isabella, to the after-school program in the cafeteria. Elena led the two women to comfortable matching blue chairs she had set up in her office. She knew that asking parents to sit formally across a desk from her didn't nurture positive relationships. Ms. Martinez, Isabella's parent, was on the verge of tears. Rory's mother, Ms. Avery, sat with her arms crossed, staring straight ahead, rigid body language revealing her anger.

Taking several deep, calming breaths, Elena reminded herself to listen carefully before judging to learn the facts of what had caused this rupture. She set a simple ground rule, asking each parent to listen to the other and not interrupt. She then looked directly at Ms. Martinez and encouraged her to speak.

Ms. Martinez described how Isabella had been coming home crying after school every day for weeks but wouldn't tell her why. That morning, Isabella told her mother that she didn't want to ride the bus anymore because Rory always made fun of her: her clothes, her curly black hair, or the different way she speaks English. He told her she was a "wetback" and didn't belong in this country. "Isabella said she told the bus driver, but he did nothing. I left work early to get her from school and saw Rory talking to her, and I got worried, so I said to him he should leave Isabella alone or I would call his mother and maybe the police."

Elena gently responded, "I am so sorry to hear that Isabella feels she has been treated so hurtfully. Tomorrow, one of our counselors, Mrs. Delgado—who also speaks Spanish—will talk with her. When children are feeling hurt in such a situation, we want to give them extra care."

She then turned toward Ms. Avery. "Please tell me what you know about this situation."

Ms. Avery seemed about to explode. "You tell this woman that if she ever threatens my son again, she will pay for it! I don't care what Rory said to her precious Isabella; she had no right to speak to him that way. When I came to pick him up, he told me what she had just said to him. I confronted her about threatening my son and scaring him. He was almost in tears and said he was just teasing Isabella and she took it too seriously, not in fun at all."

Given how upset each of them was at that moment, Elena considered whether this was the best time to continue this discussion with both parents together. "Ms. Martinez, I would like to speak with Rory's mom alone for a few minutes. Could you stop in to see me in the morning when you bring Isabella to school?" Ms. Martinez replied that she would, and as she left the office, she thanked the principal for her help.

Turning to Ms. Avery, Elena said, "Is this the first time you and Ms. Martinez have met each other?"

"No, we used to live a few houses away, but we moved across town because too many of those people moved into our neighborhood where we had lived for years. They all talk to each other in Spanish, don't even try to learn English. Understand, I know there are good and bad in every race, and I certainly don't see color, but that doesn't mean I have to be friends with them!"

Elena sensed her own anger rising at these explicitly racist, xenophobic views. She replied, somewhat intensely, wanting to clearly express her viewpoint, "We can't force you to be friends, but here we are absolutely committed to being a welcoming school community, welcoming and supportive to those who are new as well as those who have lived here a long time. When problems happen among children, we try to help them understand each other better. Same is true for parents."

It was obvious to Elena that Ms. Avery's explicit and implicit biases had infected young Rory. "First, I want to be clear that Rory's words to Isabella are verbal, bias-related bullying, not harmless teasing. We have a districtwide antibullying discipline policy that identifies steps to be taken. We don't want to ignore this situation, but because he is only in second grade, I won't insist on disciplinary consequences. I will, however, speak with him directly about his hurtful words toward Isabella. I will also share with his teacher, Ms. Silverstein, what he has been saying to Isabella."

Elena then added, a bit more gently, "Ms. Silverstein mentioned to me last week that Rory loves animals and is very gentle with the classroom guinea pig. I believe we can help him learn from this situation."

Carefully considering her next words, checking on her anger, and taking a few calming breaths, Elena added, "I can understand how Ms. Martinez speaking *that way with Rory would upset you as well. What I see is that each of you acted from the desire to protect your own child."*

Ms. Avery was surprised at the intensity of this White principal's defense of these Brown people changing their community, but also relieved that she seemed to care about Rory, despite what he had said to Isabella. "Well, I guess I can see that Isabella might have been upset by what Rory said to her, but still her mother had no right to frighten him that way."

Sensing an opening, Elena asked, "Would you be willing to talk with Ms. Martinez, with me there, and hear her side, if she is also willing to hear your side? I can ask her when I speak with her tomorrow."

Ms. Avery looked down at her hands, thinking about the question. "If she is willing to talk with me, then I guess I am also willing. I guess I trust that you can be fair." She stood up and hesitatingly offered her hand to Elena. "I have to go now. Let me know when we can meet again."

After Rory's mother left, Elena calmed her rapid breathing as she considered her next steps. Her school climate team was meeting in a few days. With its diverse members, the team had previously discussed how the staff could work together to help their students develop more empathy toward others and recognize when their words or actions might cause harm. Their social-emotional learning curriculum included many books about diverse children's experiences and cultures. She knew this was one way to help children develop empathy across differences, a term she had learned at a recent early childhood conference. She also believed that offering White children "windows" into the experiences of children of color could support them in developing that empathy.

Also, Elena would ask Ms. Martinez if she was willing to speak with Ms. Avery, whose deep-seated biases could potentially cause even more hurt. There was no simple answer here, but Elena hoped at least to reduce the tension and encourage Ms. Avery to develop some empathy toward this newcomer family.

Consider the following questions.

- How would you, as an early childhood leader, respond to the conflict between Ms. Martinez and Ms. Avery? To Isabella and Rory?
- Review both the implicit bias reduction framework (pages 134, 167–168) and the comparison between the implicit bias reduction framework and the school climate framework (figure 9.2, page 135). What elements in the chart in figure 9.2 can you identify to show how

Elena Jackson responded to the racially and culturally biased parental conflict in this scenario?

- Choose two or three of those elements and write about (or discuss with a partner or small group) how the principal's response may exemplify these examples.
- Is Elena Jackson a restorative leader? If so, in what ways? Does she interact in ways that demonstrate the five core beliefs of restorative leadership (page 142)?
- What, if anything, would you change about your response to the first question in light of your reflections here?

APPENDIX B

Discussion and Challenge Questions for Each Chapter

Note that in the questions, we refer to your school or center. If you are in a university program or are engaged in another activity where you are not currently affiliated with a school or center, please answer the questions by referring to prior experiences or considering the needs at an actual (or imagined) school or center.

Chapter 1 Discussion Questions

Instructions: Use these questions to deepen your self-reflection about the topics presented in chapter 1.

- Examine the seven recommendations for transformative leadership on page 27, and rate yourself on a scale of 1 to 5 for each of them (5 being high).

- What are your current strengths as an antiracist leader?

- What is your current knowledge level of legal and policy concerns related to antiracism? Are there areas where you need to update your knowledge?

Chapter 1 Challenge Questions

Instructions: Examine your school or the education community you are leading or are preparing to lead, and use these questions to challenge yourself to move beyond your present comfort zone.

- Where do you expect to encounter the greatest resistance?

- What unique circumstances do you anticipate?

- What might you achieve? Is there one most pressing need?

Chapter 2 Discussion Questions

Instructions: Use these questions to deepen your self-reflection about the topics presented in chapter 2.

- Focus for a moment on the past five to ten years. What do you recall of the injustices for BIPOC people that have occurred? How did your community react to the injustices?

- Look back over your career as an educational leader, as an educator, and as a student. What do you recall in terms of historical approaches to addressing racism and equity? Was a multicultural, antibias, or antiracist approach dominant? How effective was it?

Chapter 2 Challenge Questions

Instructions: Use these questions to challenge yourself to move beyond your present comfort zone.

- What, if any, books by White authors about racism or antiracism have you read? In your view, how do those books compare to such books by BIPOC authors?

- If you are White or identify as White, have you considered your White privilege when considering your own identity? What conclusions have you reached?

Chapter 3 Discussion Questions

Instructions: Use these questions to deepen your self-reflection about the topics presented in chapter 3.

- Consider how you have handled cultural competence and antiracism using the visualization of the continuum in figure 3.1 (page 46). Where does most of your leadership fall?

- With what you have read so far in this book, can you support an antiracist approach to education? If not, what are your reservations?

- Reread NAEYC's (2019) statement on equity on page 55. What do you agree with? Are there components that your school or center might want to consider to improve your approach to equity?

Reference

National Association for the Education of Young Children. (2019). *Advancing equity in early childhood education position statement.* Accessed at www.naeyc.org/resources/position-statements/equity on January 21, 2024.

Chapter 3 Challenge Questions

Instructions: Use these questions to challenge yourself to move beyond your present comfort zone.

- Examine equity, inclusion, and justice for people of color in your community. Do you see examples of a mindful, heart centered approach?

- Which groups of people in your school or community are most in need of support from a heart centered, mindful lens? Is there anything more you or your colleagues could be doing to be supportive?

Chapters 4 and 5 Discussion Questions

Instructions: Use these questions to deepen your self-reflection about the topics presented in chapters 4 and 5. (Note: Since chapters 4 and 5 both focus on Heart Centered Learning, we have combined the questions for these two chapters.)

- Are you implementing mindfulness or Heart Centered Learning in your school or center?

- If so, how are you doing it? How could it be improved?

- If not, what could you do to strengthen a heart centered approach to addressing racism and cultural awareness?

Chapters 4 and 5 Challenge Questions

Instructions: Use these questions to challenge yourself to move beyond your present comfort zone.

- Do you have a mindfulness or meditation practice? If so, describe it. If not, how might you consider implementing one?

- If you see value to the five Cs approach, how might you implement that in your school or educational setting?

Chapter 6 Discussion Questions

Instructions: Use these questions to deepen your self-reflection about the topics presented in chapter 6.

- Look at the first three parts of HEART+: hope, (self-)education, and acknowledgment. How invested are you in these? How much have you practiced reflecting and acting based on them?

- Review figure 6.3 (page 86) and reflect on the ideas for action it presents. What is most relevant to your current situation or your plans for the future?

- NAEYC presents four goals for antiracist actions (page 89). Reflect on them and, if you have an opportunity, dialogue with others about these goals.

Chapter 6 Challenge Questions

Instructions: Use these questions to challenge yourself to move beyond your present comfort zone. If you have opportunities, dialogue with others to heighten the value of these exercises.

- Consider keeping a journal of your own self-education around racism. How do you think this might help you and your community?

- On page 91, we suggest three situations that can contribute to increasing your own self-awareness around antiracism. Review these and consider how you might further educate yourself.

- On pages 94–95, we ask you to consider a dialogue with staff about four concerns for acknowledging racism. You are asked to consider how you might be contributing to the problem, where you are making assumptions, what forces in your system may be contributing to inequities you see, and how current practices might be contributing to inequity. Schedule a time to discuss this with staff at your school or center. What insights do you have?

Chapter 7 Discussion Questions

Instructions: Use these questions to deepen your self-reflection about the topics presented in chapter 7.

- How well are you doing?

- How well is your community doing?

- What could you do to improve?

Chapter 7 Challenge Questions

Instructions: Use these questions to challenge yourself to move beyond your present comfort zone.

- Consider microaggressions and bullying. Dialogue with those in your school community about how to implement heart centered practices to reduce one or both of these.

- Now that you have reflected on HEART+, how can teachers at your school or center integrate more about equity and antiracism in their instruction of young children?

Chapter 8 Discussion Questions

Instructions: Use these questions to deepen your self-reflection about the topics presented in chapter 8.

- Reflect on your own experiences as a young child. Did you experience racism or some other form of bias or stereotyping? If so, when did you become aware of it, and how did you feel? If not, do you recall any incident when children you knew faced discrimination? How was the situation handled?

- Reflect for a moment on your school or center. Consider implicit and explicit bias and your school's or center's rules and expectations. Are revisions needed?

- Consider the essential role of adults as protective factors in the lives of young children. In light of implicit and explicit bias, is there more that you could be doing as a school leader?

Chapter 8 Challenge Questions

Instructions: Use these questions to challenge yourself to move beyond your present comfort zone. If you have opportunities, dialogue with others to heighten the value of these exercises.

- What do you know about students' racial, cultural, and social identities? How are these supported in your school or center?

- Do any students at your school or center experience a sense of shame related to their racial or cultural identity? How does this appear and what might you do?

- In figure 8.1 (page 129), we present alternative ways of addressing bias based on recommendations from Sarah Sparks (2020). Review these and consider how you might use these in conducting professional development activities with your staff.

- Look again at the suggested books to read in the HEART+ Takeaways for chapter 8 (page 130). Select one of them for a book study with your staff. Which one did you choose and why?
    - *Blindspot: Hidden Biases of Good People* by Mahzarin R. Banaji and Anthony G. Greenwald (2013)
    - *Restorative Leadership: Skills and Processes That Can Support Leaders Model Restorative Day-to-Day Conversations, Meetings, Conflicts, Complaints and Disciplinary Issues* by Belinda Hopkins (2021)
    - *Bolstering Student Resilience: Creating a Classroom With Consistency, Connection, and Compassion* by Jason E. Harlacher and Sara A. Whitcomb (2022)
    - *Implicit Bias in Schools: A Practitioner's Guide* by Gina Gullo, Kelly Capatosto, and Cheryl Staats (2019)

References

Banaji, M. R., & Greenwald, A. G. (2013). *Blindspot: Hidden biases of good people.* New York: Delacorte Press.

Gullo, G., Capatosto, K., & Staats, C. (2019). *Implicit bias in schools: A practitioner's guide.* New York: Routledge.

Harlacher, J. E., & Whitcomb, S. A. (2022). *Bolstering student resilience: Creating a classroom with consistency, connection, and compassion.* Bloomington, IN: Marzano Resources.

Hopkins, B. (2021). *Restorative leadership: Skills and processes that can support leaders model restorative day-to-day conversations, meetings, conflicts, complaints and disciplinary issues.* Mortimer, Berkshire, England: National Centre for Restorative Justice in Youth Settings. Accessed at www.euforumrj.org/sites/default/files/2023-01/Restorative-leadership-06.pdf on May 9, 2024.

Sparks, S. D. (2020, November 17). Training bias out of teachers: Research shows little promise so far. *Education Week.* Accessed at www.edweek.org/leadership/training-bias-out-of-teachers-research-shows-little-promise-so-far/2020/11 on January 18, 2024.

Chapter 9 Discussion Questions

Instructions: Use these questions to deepen your self-reflection about the topics presented in chapter 9.

- How do your school policies and protocols support a compassionate school culture? If your school is not using restorative practices, how do you think this approach might go in your community?

- What are your discipline policies, and what are your recent statistics regarding expulsions and suspensions? Does your school or center need to modify its approach to discipline?

- What sorts of professional learning or development opportunities related to antiracism have you implemented at your school or center?

Chapter 9 Challenge Questions

Instructions: Use these questions to challenge yourself to move beyond your present comfort zone.

- Are there any ways in which you, as a school leader, may be unconsciously furthering racial, ethnic, or other disparities in discipline? Are you willing to be honest with yourself through self-reflection and make changes in your approach, such as learning to implement restorative practices?

- How satisfied are you with your school culture and environment? Is something missing?

Chapter 10 Discussion Questions

Instructions: Use these questions to deepen your self-reflection about the topics presented in chapter 10.

- Find an opportunity to vision with a group about a way to improve justice and equity in your school, center, or community. What insights do you have?

- Practice the mindfulness courage meditation (see page 156). How did it go?

- Work with others to develop an action plan, including three goals. Summarize your goals here.

Chapter 10 Challenge Questions

Instructions: Use these questions to challenge yourself to move beyond your present comfort zone.

- If members of your school community have experienced significant trauma related to racism, how will you involve them in ways that lead to a sense of well-being?

- How do you help bolster the courage of your staff and community as you tackle difficult issues?

Chapter 11 Discussion Questions

Instructions: Use these questions to deepen your self-reflection about the topics presented in chapter 11.

- Develop a professional development plan aligned with the tiered system of equity supports (see figure 11.1, page 174). What are the main points your plan will cover?

- What are some ideas for relational coaching for your school or center? How useful might relational coaching be for staff members who you feel need Tier 3 support in the tiered system of equity supports?

Chapter 11 Challenge Questions

Instructions: Use these questions to challenge yourself to move beyond your present comfort zone. As you think about HEART+—hope, self-education, acknowledgment, resolution, and teaching, all in your local context—consider your daily activities; your interactions with staff, students, and families; and what you hear from them.

- Are staff, students, and families feeling loved, supported, and valued? Have you found ways to talk about what you see and hear when racism appears?

- Are you embedding ideas about antiracism into your leadership and your interactions?

- What types of additional supports are you providing staff who may need more support to address equity?

Chapter 12 Discussion Questions

Instructions: Use these questions to deepen your self-reflection about the topics presented in chapter 12.

- Examine the curriculum used at your school or early learning center. Are you using one of the curricula reviewed in this chapter? If not, what are you using?

- How does your curriculum compare to the curricula we have reviewed?

- Do you see any particular strengths or weaknesses with your curriculum?

Chapter 12 Challenge Questions

Instructions: Use these questions to challenge yourself to move beyond your present comfort zone.

- How aware are you of curriculum options? After reading this chapter, do you see the need to examine more options or learn more about strategies to improve the antiracist approach to using curriculum with your students?

- When it comes to antiracism, are there ways to enhance the implementation of curricula in your school or early childhood center?

Chapter 13 Discussion Questions

Instructions: Use these questions to deepen your self-reflection about the topics presented in chapter 13.

- What is the relationship between the five Cs and early childhood preparation programs in your state? (See the example in this chapter on pages 214–215.)

- How do your state requirements compare to those we highlight for New Jersey, North Carolina, and Washington?

- How is diversity addressed in your state early childhood teacher preparation standards?

- What do you know about the credentialing of staff at your school or center? Have staff participated in courses that address equity and diversity?

Chapter 13 Challenge Questions

Instructions: Use these questions to challenge yourself to move beyond your present comfort zone. If you have opportunities, dialogue with others to heighten the value of these exercises.

- Take the time to compare credentialing at one of your state institutions with recommendations from NAEYC and this book. Where is there alignment and where are there gaps?

- What might you do to address the gaps?

Chapter 14 Discussion Questions

Instructions: Use these questions to deepen your self-reflection about the topics presented in chapter 14.

- How is diversity addressed in your state early childhood teacher preparation standards?

- What are the wages for early childcare workers in your state?

- How could your state improve the cultural competence of early childcare workers?

Chapter 14 Challenge Questions

Instructions: Use these questions to challenge yourself to move beyond your present comfort zone. If you have opportunities, dialogue with others to heighten the value of these exercises.

- Review the T.E.A.C.H. and Child Care WAGE$ initiatives presented on page 230. What might you take away from these programs to improve staffing at your school or center?

- Interview a BIPOC early childhood staff member who has at least five years' experience. Where have they experienced satisfaction and dissatisfaction with their job, including how their wages have improved, if at all, over the past five years?

Chapter 15 Discussion Questions

Instructions: Use these questions to deepen your self-reflection about the topics presented in chapter 15.

- Review the NYC Leadership Academy disposition standards for equity and leadership (page 238). Rate yourself on a scale of 1 to 5 (5 being high) for each of these. What are your strengths? Where could you improve?

- What ideas do you have for addressing resistance to HEART+ and antiracism?

Chapter 15 Challenge Question

Instructions: Use the following question to deepen your understanding of transformative leadership.

- Consider transformative leadership. What actions could you take to bring about greater equity and justice in early childhood education?

References and Resources

Abdelfatah, R., & Arablouei, R. (Hosts). (2020, September 17). James Baldwin's fire [Audio podcast episode]. In *Throughline*. Accessed at www.npr.org/transcripts/912769283 on July 5, 2024.

Adams, A. (2020, December 1). *Healing-centered schools*. Accessed at www.njea.org/healing-centered-schools on July 3, 2024.

Adichie, C. N. (2009, July). *The danger of a single story* [Video file]. TED Conferences. Accessed at www.ted.com/talks/chimamanda_ngozi_adichie_the_danger_of_a_single_story on February 15, 2024.

Administration for Children and Families. (2016, November 7). *Expulsion and suspension policy statement*. Accessed at www.acf.hhs.gov/occ/policy-guidance/expulsion-and-suspension-policy-statement on June 27, 2024.

Aguilar, E. (2018). *Onward: Cultivating emotional resilience in educators*. San Francisco: Jossey-Bass.

Aljabreen, H. (2020). Montessori, Waldorf, and Reggio Emilia: A comparative analysis of alternative models of early childhood education. *International Journal of Early Childhood, 52*(3), 337–353.

Allen, R., Shapland, D. L., Neitzel, J., & Iruka, I. U. (2021). Creating anti-racist early childhood spaces. *Young Children, 76*(2), 49–54.

Alleva, N. (2021, January 4). *Let's talk about race*. Accessed at www.naesp.org/resource/lets-talk-about-race on March 22, 2024.

Al-Shamma, E., Basallaje, A., Bridges, C., Elgart, A., Gee, O., Kamisugi, K., et al. (2021). *Breaking the chains 2: The preschool-to-prison pipeline epidemic*. Oakland, CA: Equal Justice Society. Accessed at https://equaljusticesociety.org/wp-content/uploads/2021/09/Breaking-The-Chains-2-The-Preschool-To-Prison-Pipeline-Epidemic-PDF.pdf on March 22, 2024.

Althoff, L. (2023, July 17). *The long shadows of slavery and Jim Crow: Uncovering the economic impact on Black Americans.* Accessed at www.hoover.org/research/long-shadows-slavery-and-jim-crow-uncovering-economic-impact-black-americans on May 9, 2024.

American Civil Liberties Union. (n.d.). *School-to-prison pipeline* [Infographic]. Accessed at www.aclu.org/issues/juvenile-justice/school-prison-pipeline/school-prison-pipeline-infographic on May 9, 2024.

American Montessori Society. (n.d.a). *Anti-bias, antiracist (ABAR) certificate program.* Accessed at https://learn.amshq.org/abar-certificate-program on January 21, 2024.

American Montessori Society. (n.d.b). *History of Montessori.* Accessed at https://amshq.org/About-Montessori/History-of-Montessori on January 21, 2024.

American Psychological Association. (2020, August 27). *Children notice race several years before adults want to talk about it* [Press release]. Accessed at www.apa.org/news/press/releases/2020/08/children-notice-race on March 22, 2024.

Amodio, D. M., & Cikara, M. (2021). The social neuroscience of prejudice. *Annual Review of Psychology, 72*, 439–469. https://doi.org/10.1146/annurev-psych-010419-050928

ASCD. (2000). How Reggio Emilia encourages inclusion. *Educational Leadership, 58*(1). Accessed at www.ascd.org/el/articles/how-reggio-emilia-encourages-inclusion on January 21, 2024.

Association Montessori Internationale. (2022). *Strategic plan 2023–2028.* Accessed at https://montessori-ami.org/sites/default/files/downloads/news/AMI_strategic_plan_2023.pdf on January 21, 2024.

Astington, J. W., & Edward, M. J. (2010, August). *The development of theory of mind in early childhood.* Accessed at www.child-encyclopedia.com/pdf/expert/social-cognition/according-experts/development-theory-mind-early-childhood on March 22, 2024.

Baldwin, J. (1962, January 14). As much truth as one can bear. *The New York Times.* Accessed at www.nytimes.com/1962/01/14/archives/as-much-truth-as-one-can-bear-to-speak-out-about-the-world-as-it-is.html on January 21, 2024.

Banaji, M. R., & Greenwald, A. G. (2013). *Blindspot: Hidden biases of good people.* New York: Delacorte Press.

Banks, J. A. (2001). Citizenship education and diversity: Implications for teacher education. *Journal of Teacher Education, 52*(1), 5–16. https://doi.org/10.1177/0022487101052001002

Banks, J. A. (2014). Multicultural education and global citizens. In V. Benet-Martínez & Y.-Y. Hong (Eds.), *The Oxford handbook of multicultural identity* (pp. 379–395). New York: Oxford University Press. https://doi.org/10.1093/oxfordhb/9780199796694.013.019

Banks, J. A., & Banks, C. A. M. (Eds.). (2010). *Multicultural education: Issues and perspectives* (7th ed.). Hoboken, NJ: Wiley.

Banks, K., & Maixner, R. A. (2016). Social justice education in an urban charter Montessori school. *Journal of Montessori Research, 2*(2), 1–14. https://doi.org/10.17161/jomr.v2i2.5066

Barack, L. (2021, May 26). *Weaving anti-bias and equity into curricula begins with self-reflection*. Accessed at www.k12dive.com/news/weaving-anti-bias-and-equity-into-curricula-begins-with-self-reflection/600681 on January 21, 2024.

Barch, D., Pagliaccio, D., Belden, A., Harms, M. P., Gaffrey, M., Sylvester, C. M., et al. (2016). Effect of hippocampal and amygdala connectivity on the relationship between preschool poverty and school-age depression. *American Journal of Psychiatry, 173*(6), 625–634. https://doi.org/10.1176/appi.ajp.2015.15081014

Barnett, S., Carolan, M., & Johns, D. (2013, November). *Equity and excellence: African-American children's access to quality preschool*. New Brunswick, NJ: Center on Enhancing Early Learning Outcomes.

Baró, F., Camacho, D. A., Del Pulgar, C. P., Triguero-Mas, M., & Anguelovski, I. (2021). School greening: Right or privilege? Examining urban nature within and around primary schools through an equity lens. *Landscape and Urban Planning, 208*(1), Article 104019. http://dx.doi.org/10.1016/j.landurbplan.2020.104019

Baron, A. S., & Banaji, M. R. (2006). The development of implicit attitudes: Evidence of race evaluations from ages 6 and 10 and adulthood. *Psychological Science, 17*(1), 53–58.

Baxley, T. (2021). *Social justice parenting: How to raise compassionate, anti-racist, justice-minded kids in an unjust world*. New York: HarperCollins.

Beach, H., & Strijack, T. N. (2020). *Reclaiming our students: Why children are more anxious, aggressive, and shut down than ever—and what we can do about it*. Vancouver, British Columbia, Canada: Page Two.

Beachum, F., & Gullo, G. (2020). School leadership: Implicit bias and social justice. In R. Papa (Ed.), *Handbook on promoting social justice in education* (pp. 429–454). Cham, Switzerland: Springer Cham.

Bearss, K., Johnson, C., Handen, B., Smith, T., & Scahill, L. (2013). A pilot study of parent training in young children with autism spectrum disorders and disruptive behavior. *Journal of Autism and Developmental Disorders, 43*(4), 829–840. https://doi.org/10.1007/s10803-012-1624-7

Bedinger, L., & Curtis, S. (2020, October 6). *Restorative practices in early education*. Accessed at https://buildingbrightfutures.org/restorative-practices-in-early-education on January 21, 2024.

Bell, J. (2022). Don't ignore emotions in equity work—embrace them. *The Learning Professional, 43*(6), 30–34.

Belli, B. (2020, December 7). *Kendi: Racism is about power and policy, not people*. Accessed at https://news.yale.edu/2020/12/07/kendi-racism-about-power-and-policy-not-people on January 21, 2024.

Beneke, M. R., & Park, C. C. (2019). Introduction to the special issue: Antibias curriculum and critical praxis to advance social justice in inclusive early childhood education. *Young Exceptional Children, 22*(2), 55–61.

Berger, A. (2011). *Self-regulation: Brain, cognition, and development.* Washington, DC: American Psychological Association.

Bevilacqua, L. (n.d.). *Diversity in core knowledge* [Blog post]. Accessed at www.core knowledge.org/blog/diversity-in-core-knowledge on January 21, 2024.

Bisram, J. (2023, September 14). *Disparities in race, and wealth, impacting how much public school funding certain districts receive.* Accessed at www.cbsnews.com/newyork/news/disparities-in-race-and-wealth-impacting-how-much-public-school-funding-certain-districts-receive on May 15, 2024.

BitterSweet Editors. (2022, May 27). *In support of African American family history research: 27 actions White descendants of enslaver families can take.* Accessed at https://linkedthroughslavery.com/in-support-of-african-american-family-history-research-27-actions-descendants-of-enslaver-families-can-take on March 18, 2024.

Bloom, B. S. (Ed.). (1956). *Taxonomy of educational objectives: The classification of educational goals; Handbook I: Cognitive domain.* New York: McKay.

Bonde, E. H., Fjorback, L. O., Frydenberg, M., & Juul, L. (2022). The effectiveness of mindfulness-based stress reduction for school teachers: A cluster-randomized controlled trial. *European Journal of Public Health, 32*(2), 246–253.

Bonini, L., Rotunno, C., Arcuri, E., & Gallese, V. (2022). Mirror neurons 30 years later: Implications and applications. *Trends in Cognitive Sciences, 26*(9), 767–781. https://doi.org/10.1016/j.tics.2022.06.003

Bouffard, S. (2022). Listening is a powerful tool to disrupt inequity. *The Learning Professional, 43*(6), 5.

Boutte, G. S. (2008). Beyond the illusion of diversity: How early childhood teachers can promote social justice. *The Social Studies, 99*(4), 165–173.

Boykin, A. W. (1992). *Reformulating educational reform: Toward the proactive schooling of African American children.* Arlington, VA: American Institutes for Research. Accessed at https://files.eric.ed.gov/fulltext/ED367725.pdf on March 22, 2024.

Brown, C. S. (2011). Anti-bias education. In D. J. Christie (Ed.), *The encyclopedia of peace psychology* (Vol. 1, pp. 35–38). Malden, MA: Wiley.

Bryan, N. (2017). White teachers' role in sustaining the school-to-prison pipeline: Recommendations for teacher education. *The Urban Review, 49*(2), 326–345. https://doi.org/10.1007/s11256-017-0403-3

Bullock, R. T. (n.d.). *Children's books we use to teach young kids to be anti-racist.* Accessed at www.embracerace.org/resources/we-are-summer-camp-book-list on May 10, 2024.

Buras, K. L. (1999). Questioning core assumptions: A critical reading of and response to E. D. Hirsch's *The Schools We Need and Why We Don't Have Them. Harvard Educational Review, 69*(1), 67–93. Accessed at www1.udel.edu/educ/whitson/897s05/files/Hirsch%20Essay%20Review.pdf on September 30, 2024.

Butler, A., Teasley, C., & Sánchez-Blanco, C. (2019). A decolonial, intersectional approach to disrupting whiteness, neoliberalism, and patriarchy in Western early childhood education and care. In P. P. Trifonas (Ed.), *Handbook of theory and research in cultural studies and education* (pp. 41–58). Cham, Switzerland: Springer Cham.

Byington, T. A. (2023). *Find the joyful leader within: Banishing burnout in early childhood education.* Lewisville, NC: Gryphon House.

Byman, D. L. (2021, April 9). *How hateful rhetoric connects to real-world violence.* Accessed at www.brookings.edu/articles/how-hateful-rhetoric-connects-to-real-world-violence on June 18, 2024.

Cabral, A. (2020). *Allies and advocates: Creating an inclusive and equitable culture.* Hoboken, NJ: Wiley.

Cajete, G. (1994). *Look to the mountain: An ecology of Indigenous education.* Durango, CO: Kivakí Press.

Cajete, G. (Ed.). (2020). *Native minds rising: Exploring transformative Indigenous education.* Vernon, British Columbia, Canada: J Charlton.

California for the Arts. (n.d.). *Home.* Accessed at www.californiansforthearts.org on January 21, 2024.

Camangian, P., & Cariaga, S. (2022). Social and emotional learning is hegemonic miseducation: Students deserve humanization instead. *Race Ethnicity and Education, 25*(7), 901–921.

Canzoneri-Golden, L., & King, J. (2020). *An examination of culturally relevant pedagogy and antibias-antiracist curriculum in a Montessori setting* [Doctoral dissertation, Lynn University]. SPIRAL. https://spiral.lynn.edu/etds/360

Carr, S. (2021, October 26). *The racist and sexist roots of child care in America explain why the system is in shambles.* Accessed at https://hechingerreport.org/the-racist-and-sexist-roots-of-child-care-in-america-explain-why-the-system-is-in-shambles on March 22, 2024.

Carr, S. (2024, March 21). *Curbing private equity's expansion into child care.* Accessed at https://hechingerreport.org/curbing-private-equitys-expansion-into-child-care on March 21, 2024.

Carter, E. R., Onyeador, I. N., & Lewis, N. A., Jr. (2020). Developing and delivering effective anti-bias training: Challenges and recommendations. *Behavioral Science and Policy, 6*(1), 57–70.

Carter, P., Skiba, R., Arredondo, M., & Pollock, M. (2014, November). *You can't fix what you don't look at: Acknowledging race in addressing racial discipline disparities.* Bloomington, IN: Equity Project at Indiana University.

Casas, J. (2017). *Culturize: Every student. Every day. Whatever it takes.* San Diego, CA: Dave Burgess Consulting.

Castagno, A. E. (2014). *Educated in Whiteness: Good intentions and diversity in schools.* Minneapolis, MN: University of Minnesota Press.

Castro, M. (2020, September). *Translanguaging: Teaching at the intersection of language and social justice.* Madison, WI: WIDA. Accessed at https://wida.wisc.edu/sites/default/files/resource/Focus-Bulletin-Translanguaging.pdf on January 21, 2024.

Caven, M. (2020, July 27). *Why we need an anti-racist approach to social and emotional learning* [Blog post]. Accessed at www.edc.org/blog/why-we-need-anti-racist-approach-social-and-emotional-learning on January 21, 2024.

Center for Educational Improvement. (2018). *School-Compassionate Culture Analytical Tool for Educators.* Accessed at https://s-ccate.org on January 21, 2024.

Centers for Disease Control and Prevention. (n.d.). *Early brain development and health.* Accessed at https://archive.cdc.gov/#/details?q=Early%20brain%20development%20and%20health&start=0&rows=10&url=https://www.cdc.gov/ncbddd/childdevelopment/early-brain-development.html on July 3, 2024.

Chang, D. F., Donald, J., Whitney, J., Miao, I. Y., & Sahdra, B. K. (2023). Does mindfulness improve intergroup bias, internalized bias, and anti-bias outcomes? A meta-analysis of the evidence and agenda for future research. *Personality and Social Psychology Bulletin.* https://doi.org/10.31219/osf.io/5wev3

Child Care Aware of America. (2022). *Catalyzing growth: Using data to change child care 2022.* Accessed at www.childcareaware.org/catalyzing-growth-using-data-to-change-child-care-2022 on January 21, 2024.

Child Care Services Association. (2022a). *Child Care WAGE$ overview.* Accessed at www.teachecnationalcenter.org/wp-content/uploads/2022/10/WAGES-overview-2022.pdf on January 21, 2024.

Child Care Services Association. (2022b). *T.E.A.C.H. Early Childhood overview.* Accessed at www.teachecnationalcenter.org/wp-content/uploads/2022/11/TEACH-overview-FactSht-11_16_22.pdf on January 21, 2024.

Chin, M. J., Quinn, D. M., Dhaliwal, T. K., & Lovison, V. S. (2020). Bias in the air: A nationwide exploration of teachers' implicit racial attitudes, aggregate bias, and student outcomes. *Educational Researcher, 49*(8), 566–578.

Chödrön, P. (2019). *Welcoming the unwelcome: Wholehearted living in a brokenhearted world.* Boulder, CO: Shambhala.

Coalition for the Future of Education. (2022, March 30). *"Press the pause button" March 30 letter to the U.S. secretary of education Cardona from the Coalition for the Future of Education* [Executive summary]. Accessed at www.edimprovement.org/coalition-future-education on March 8, 2024.

Coates, T.-N. (2015). *Between the world and me.* New York: Spiegel & Grau.

Coates, T.-N., Cieplak-Mayr von Baldegg, K., Price-Waldman, S., & National Journal. (2015, July 10). Ta-Nehisi Coates, "heir to James Baldwin," reads from his latest book. *The Atlantic.* Accessed at www.theatlantic.com/politics/archive/2015/07/ta-nehisi-coates-heir-to-james-baldwin-reads-from-his-latest-book/432297 on February 13, 2024.

Coffey, M. (2022, July 19). *Still underpaid and unequal: Early childhood educators face low pay and a worsening wage gap.* Accessed at www.americanprogress.org/article/still-underpaid-and-unequal on May 15, 2024.

Cohen, C. P. (1989). United Nations: Convention on the rights of the child. *International Legal Materials, 28*(6), 1448–1476. https://doi.org/10.1017/S0020782900017228

Collado, W., Hollie, S., Isiah, R., Jackson, Y., Muhammad, A., Reeves, D., & Williams, K. C. (2021). *Beyond conversations about race: A guide for discussions with students, teachers, and communities.* Bloomington, IN: Solution Tree Press.

Connecticut Women's Hall of Fame. (n.d.). *Lydia Huntley Sigourney.* Accessed at www.cwhf.org/inductees/lydia-huntley-sigourney on February 22, 2024.

Cooper, K. S., Stanulis, R. N., Brondyk, S. K., Hamilton, E. R., Macaluso, M., & Meier, J. A. (2016). The teacher leadership process: Attempting change within embedded systems. *Journal of Educational Change, 17*(1), 85–113.

Copple, C., & Bredekamp, S. (Eds.). (2009). *Developmentally appropriate practice in early childhood programs serving children from birth through age 8* (3rd ed.). Washington, DC: National Association for the Education of Young Children.

Core Knowledge Foundation. (n.d.). *Curriculum.* Accessed at www.coreknowledge.org/curriculum on January 21, 2024.

Core Knowledge Foundation. (2015). *Curriculum mapping with the Core Knowledge Sequence: Participant workbook.* Charlottesville, VA: Author. Accessed at www.coreknowledge.org/wp-content/uploads/2017/03/CurriculumMapping_CCL_PWB_122015.pdf on January 21, 2024.

Core Knowledge Foundation. (2023). *The Core Knowledge Sequence: Content and skill guidelines for preschool–grade 8.* Charlottesville, VA: Author. Accessed at www.coreknowledge.org/our-approach/core-knowledge-sequence on January 21, 2024.

Costello, B., Wachtel, J., & Wachtel, T. (2019). *The restorative practices handbook: For teachers, disciplinarians and administrators* (2nd ed.). Bethlehem, PA: International Institute for Restorative Practices.

Council for Professional Recognition. (2023, August 18). *Current CDA competency standards.* Accessed at www.cdacouncil.org/wp-content/uploads/2023/08/Current-CDA-Competency-Standards-Cascading-Chart_081823.pdf on July 31, 2024.

Croke, J. (Host). (2021, December 8). Strategies for children with Amy O'Leary [Audio podcast episode]. In *Public hearing.* Accessed at www.actionbydesign.co/public-hearing-episodes/strategies-for-children-with-amy-oleary on August 6, 2024.

Cultural bias. (2018). In *APA dictionary of psychology.* Accessed at https://dictionary.apa.org/cultural-bias on May 15, 2024.

Curby, T. W., Brock, L. L., & Hamre, B. K. (2013). Teachers' emotional support consistency predicts children's achievement gains and social skills. *Early Education and Development, 24*(3), 292–309. https://doi.org/10.1080/10409289.2012.665760

Dahlberg, G. (2012). Pedagogical documentation: A practice for negotiation and democracy. In C. P. Edwards, L. Gandini, & G. Forman (Eds.), *The hundred languages of children: The Reggio Emilia experience in transformation* (3rd ed., pp. 225–232). Westport, CT: Praeger.

Darder, A. (1991). *Culture and power in the classroom: A critical foundation for bicultural education.* New York: Bergin & Garvey.

Darling-Hammond, L., & DePaoli, J. (2020). Why school climate matters and what can be done to improve it. *State Education Standard*, *20*(2), 6–11. Accessed at www.nasbe.org/why-school-climate-matters-and-what-can-be-done-to-improve-it on November 7, 2023.

Darling-Hammond, S. (2023, November 9). Putting restorative practices to work. *Principal Magazine.* Accessed at www.naesp.org/resource/putting-restorative-practices-to-work on July 5, 2024.

Datnow, A., Yoshisato, M., Macdonald, B., Trejos, J., & Kennedy, B. C. (2023). Bridging educational change and social justice: A call to the field. *Educational Researcher*, *52*(1), 29–38.

Dee, T. S. (2005). A teacher like me: Does race, ethnicity, or gender matter? *American Economic Review*, *95*(2), 158–165. https://doi.org/10.1257/000282805774670446

de Guzman, M. R. T., Durden, T. R., Taylor, S. A., Guzman, J. M., & Potthoff, K. L. (2016, February). *Cultural competence: An important skill set for the 21st century.* Lincoln, NE: University of Nebraska–Lincoln Extension. Accessed at https://extensionpublications.unl.edu/assets/html/g1375/build/g1375.htm on January 21, 2024.

Deliso, M. (2023, November 9). *Bias incidents against Muslims, Jews on rise in US amid Middle East war, new data shows.* Accessed at https://abcnews.go.com/US/anti-muslim-anti-jewish-incidents-rise/story?id=104760450 on July 8, 2024.

Derman-Sparks, L. (2016, July/August). Why we practice anti-bias education. *Anti-Bias Education*, 32–35. Accessed at www.antibiasleadersece.com/wp-content/uploads/2016/07/Why-we-do-ABE-PDF.pdf on June 18, 2024.

Derman-Sparks, L., & Edwards, J. O. (2020). *Anti-bias education for young children and ourselves* (2nd ed.). Washington, DC: National Association for the Education of Young Children.

Derman-Sparks, L., & Edwards, J. O. (2021). Teaching about identity, racism, and fairness: Engaging young children in anti-bias education. *American Educator*, *44*(4), 35–40.

Derman-Sparks, L., LeeKeenan, D., & Nimmo, J. (2015). *Leading anti-bias early childhood programs: A guide for change.* New York: Teachers College Press.

Derman-Sparks, L., LeeKeenan, D., & Nimmo, J. (2023). *Leading anti-bias early childhood programs: A guide to change, for change* (2nd ed.). New York: Teachers College Press.

Diamond, J. B. (2008). Focusing on student learning. In M. Pollock (Ed.), *Everyday antiracism: Getting real about race in school* (pp. 254–256). New York: New Press.

Dietrichson, J., Kristiansen, I. L., & Viinholt, B. A. (2020). Universal preschool programs and long-term child outcomes: A systematic review. *Journal of Economic Surveys*, *34*(5), 1007–1043.

Division for Early Childhood & National Association for the Education of Young Children. (2009, April). *Early childhood inclusion: A joint position statement of the Division for Early Childhood (DEC) and the National Association for the Education of Young Children (NAEYC)*. Chapel Hill, NC: Frank Porter Graham Child Development Institute. Accessed at www.decdocs.org/position-statement-inclusion on June 4, 2024.

Dixson, A. D., & Rousseau, C. K. (2005). And we are still not saved: Critical race theory in education ten years later. *Race Ethnicity and Education, 8*(1), 7–27. https://doi.org/10.1080/1361332052000340971

Djonko-Moore, C. M. (2020). Diversity education and early childhood teachers' motivation to remain in teaching: An exploration. *Journal of Early Childhood Teacher Education, 43*(1), 35–53. https://doi.org/10.1080/10901027.2020.1806151

Dore, R. A., Hoffman, K. M., Lillard, A. S., & Trawalter, S. (2014). Children's racial bias in perceptions of others' pain. *British Journal of Developmental Psychology, 32*(2), 218–231.

Doucet, F., & Adair, J. K. (2013). Addressing race and inequity in the classroom. *Young Children, 68*(5), 88–97.

Du, V. (2022, January 31). *The Asian history I never learned in school.* Accessed at https://ny.chalkbeat.org/2022/1/31/22905058/asian-history-schools-chinese-heritage on January 21, 2024.

EAB. (2020, July 9). *How school and district leaders can address systemic racism with their communities* [Blog post]. Accessed at https://eab.com/resources/blog/k-12-education-blog/address-systemic-racism-school-district-leaders on May 9, 2024.

Early Childhood Technical Assistance Center. (n.d.). *State and jurisdictional eligibility definitions.* Accessed at https://ectacenter.org/topics/earlyid/state-info.asp on June 4, 2024.

Early Childhood Technical Assistance Center & National Center for Pyramid Model Innovations. (2023). *Indicators of high-quality inclusion.* Accessed at https://ectacenter.org/~pdfs/topics/inclusion/ece_indicators_of_high_quality_inclusion.pdf on May 17, 2024.

Echo-Hawk, H., & Johnson, M. (2023). Reclaiming the brilliance of Native youth. In C. Mason, M. Patschke, & K. Simpson, *Leading with vitality and hope: Embracing equity, alleviating trauma, and healing school communities* (pp. 55–70). Lanham, MD: Rowman & Littlefield.

Edwards, C. P. (2002). Three approaches from Europe: Waldorf, Montessori, and Reggio Emilia. *Early Childhood Research and Practice, 4*(1), 1–14.

Edwards, C. P., Gandini, L., & Forman, G. (Ed.). (1998). *The hundred languages of children: The Reggio Emilia approach—Advanced reflections* (2nd ed.). Greenwich, CT: Ablex.

Edwards, F., Lee, H., & Esposito, M. (2019). Risk of being killed by police use of force in the United States by age, race–ethnicity, and sex. *Proceedings of the National Academy of Sciences of the United States of America, 116*(34), 16793–16798. https://doi.org/10.1073/pnas.1821204116

Egalite, A. J., & Kisida, B. (2018). The effects of teacher match on students' academic perceptions and attitudes. *Educational Evaluation and Policy Analysis, 40*(1), 59–81. https://doi.org/10.3102/0162373717714056

Egert, F., Dederer, V., & Fukkink, R. G. (2020). The impact of in-service professional development on the quality of teacher-child interactions in early education and care: A meta-analysis. *Educational Research Review, 29*(1), Article 100309. https://doi.org/10.1016/j.edurev.2019.100309

Ekman, P. (2003). *Emotions revealed: Recognizing faces and feelings to improve communication and emotional life*. New York: Holt.

Escayg, K.-A. (2019). "Who's got the power?": A critical examination of the anti-bias curriculum. *International Journal of Child Care and Educational Policy, 13*, Article 6.

Escayg, K.-A. (2020). Anti-racism in U.S. early childhood education: Foundational principles. *Sociology Compass, 14*(4), Article e12764. https://doi.org/10.1111/soc4.12764

Expeditionary Learning Education. (n.d.a). *EL Education's vision, mission, and approach*. Accessed at https://eleducation.org/resources/el-educations-vision-mission-and-approach on January 21, 2024.

Expeditionary Learning Education. (n.d.b). *Learning expeditions videos*. Accessed at https://eleducation.org/resources/collections/learning-expeditions-videos on January 21, 2024.

Expeditionary Learning Education. (n.d.c). *Three dimensions of student achievement*. Accessed at https://eleducation.org/who-we-are/three-dimensions-of-student-achievement on January 21, 2024.

Expeditionary Learning Education. (2013). *ELA G2:M1: Schools and community* [Module]. Accessed at https://curriculum.eleducation.org/curriculum/ela/grade-2/module-1 on January 21, 2024.

Expeditionary Learning Education. (2016). *EL Education*. Accessed at https://files.eleducation.org/web/downloads/ELED-OverviewBrochure-0716-v02-WEB.pdf on January 21, 2024.

Fernández Santín, M., & Feliu Torruella, M. (2017). Reggio Emilia: An essential tool to develop critical thinking in early childhood. *Journal of New Approaches in Educational Research, 6*(1), 50–56.

Fingal, J. (2023, January 17). *10 resources for teaching anti-racism* [Blog post]. Accessed at https://iste.org/blog/10-resources-for-teaching-anti-racism on January 21, 2024.

Firlik, R. (1996). Can we adapt the philosophies and practices of Reggio Emilia, Italy, for use in American schools? *Early Childhood Education Journal, 23*(4), 217–220. https://doi.org/10.1007/bf02353340

First Church Stratford. (n.d.). *Social justice*. Accessed at www.firstchurchstratford.org/social-justice on May 9, 2024.

Fisher, E. S. (2020). Cultural humility as a form of social justice: Promising practices for global school psychology training. *School Psychology International, 41*(1), 53–66. https://doi.org/10.1177/0143034319893097

Forman, G., & Fyfe, B. (2012). Negotiated learning through design, documentation, and discourse. In C. P. Edwards, L. Gandini, & G. Forman (Eds.), *The hundred languages of children: The Reggio Emilia experience in transformation* (3rd ed., pp. 247–272). Westport, CT: Praeger.

Framingham State University. (n.d.). *Detailed course information: EDUC 205—Equity in educational settings* [Course]. Accessed at https://selfservice.framingham.edu/PROD/bwckctlg.p_disp_course_detail?cat_term_in=202290&subj_code_in=EDUC&crse_numb_in=205 on April 12, 2024.

Frank, J. L., Reibel, D., Broderick, P., Cantrell, T., & Metz, S. (2015). The effectiveness of mindfulness-based stress reduction on educator stress and well-being: Results from a pilot study. *Mindfulness, 6*(2), 208–216.

Frederick, R. (2020). Learning from African-centered pedagogical excellence: Implications for recruitment of African-centered teachers. In K. G. Shockley & K. Lomotey (Eds.), *African-centered education: Theory and practice* (pp. 32–44). Gorham, ME: Myers Education Press.

Galloway, M. K., & Ishimaru, A. M. (2020). Leading equity teams: The role of formal leaders in building organizational capacity for equity. *Journal of Education for Students Placed at Risk, 25*(2), 107–125. https://doi.org/10.1080/10824669.2019.1699413

Garcia, A., & Sklar, C. (2022). Preparing pre-K teachers: Policy considerations and strategies. *State Education Standard, 22*(3), 50–54. Accessed at www.nasbe.org/preparing-pre-k-teachers-policy-considerations-and-strategies on March 22, 2024.

Gardner-Neblett, N., Addie, A., Eddie, A. L., Chapman, S. K., Duke, N. K., & Vallotton, C. D. (2023). Bias starts early. Let's start now: Developing an anti-racist, anti-bias book collection for infants and toddlers. *Reading Teacher, 76*(4), 505–510.

Giang, I. T. N., & Park, M. (2022, October). *Dual language learners: Key characteristics and considerations for early childhood programs* [Fact sheet]. Washington, DC: Migration Policy Institute. Accessed at www.migrationpolicy.org/research/dual-language-learner-characteristics on January 21, 2024.

Gilliam, W. S. (2010, June 15). *Pre-kindergartners left behind: Expulsion rates in state pre-kindergarten programs*. Accessed at www.fcd-us.org/prekindergartners-left-behind-expulsion-rates-in-state-prekindergarten-programs on June 27, 2024.

Gilliam, W. S., Maupin, A. N., Reyes, C. R., Accavitti, M., & Shic, F. (2016, September). *Do early educators' implicit biases regarding sex and race relate to behavior expectations and recommendations of preschool expulsions and suspensions?* New Haven, CT: Yale University Child Study Center.

Gilreath, A. (2023, May 12). *Alabama doesn't want early childhood teachers talking about bias. Researchers say they need to*. Accessed at https://hechingerreport.org/alabama-doesnt-want-early-childhood-teachers-talking-about-bias-researchers-say-they-need-to on November 7, 2023.

Ginwright, S. (2018, May 31). *The future of healing: Shifting from trauma informed care to healing centered engagement.* Accessed at https://ginwright.medium.com/the-future-of-healing-shifting-from-trauma-informed-care-to-healing-centered-engagement-634f557ce69c on March 22, 2024.

Giuliano, G. (2020). *Let freedom ring: The exemplary life of John Lewis* [Audiobook]. Buffalo, NY: Author's Republic.

Goff, P. A., Jackson, M. C., Di Leone, B. A. L., Culotta, C. M., & DiTomasso, N. A. (2014). The essence of innocence: Consequences of dehumanizing Black children. *Journal of Personality and Social Psychology, 106*(4), 526–545. https://doi.org/10.1037/a0035663

Goleman, D. (2020). *Emotional intelligence: Why it can matter more than IQ* (25th anniversary ed.). New York: Bantam.

Gonser, S. (2021, March 19). *Addressing race and racism head-on in the classroom.* Accessed at www.edutopia.org/article/addressing-race-and-racism-head-classroom on January 21, 2024.

Greater Good in Action. (n.d.). *Active listening.* Accessed at https://ggia.berkeley.edu/practice/practice_as_pdf/active_listening on May 10, 2024.

Grissom, J. A., Egalite, A. J., & Lindsay, C. A. (2021, February). *How principals affect students and schools: A systematic synthesis of two decades of research.* New York: Wallace Foundation. Accessed at https://cahnfellowsprograms.org/wp-content/uploads/2021/11/How-Principals-Affect-Students-and-Schools.pdf on May 15, 2024.

Gullo, G. (2021). Equity endeavors through the Justice for Bias Framework: Principals addressing implicit bias in schools. In P. Youngs, J. Kim, & M. Mavrogordato (Eds.), *Exploring principal development and teacher outcomes: How principals can strengthen instruction, teacher retention, and student achievement* (pp. 86–100). New York: Routledge.

Gullo, G., & Beachum, F. (2020). Framing implicit bias impact reduction in social justice leadership. *Journal of Educational Leadership and Policy Studies, 3*(3), 1–15.

Gullo, G., Capatosto, K., & Staats, C. (2019). *Implicit bias in schools: A practitioner's guide.* New York: Routledge.

Gutiérrez, N. B. (2021). Walking a tightrope or catapulting from a cannon? *The Learning Professional, 42*(6). Accessed at https://learningforward.org/journal/leading-for-equity/walking-a-tightrope-or-catapulting-from-a-cannon on March 22, 2024.

Hambacher, E., & Ginn, K. (2021). Race-visible teacher education: A review of the literature from 2002 to 2018. *Journal of Teacher Education, 72*(3), 329–341. https://doi.org/10.1177/0022487120948045

Hammond, Z. (2015). *Culturally responsive teaching and the brain: Promoting authentic engagement and rigor among culturally and linguistically diverse students.* Thousand Oaks, CA: Corwin Press.

Hanover Research. (2022, November). *Understanding early childhood education.* Alexandria, VA: AASA.

Hao, W., & Cohen, R. (2020, July). Start strong: Supporting early childhood education through policy. *Education Leaders Report, 4*(1). Alexandria, VA: National Association of State Boards of Education. Accessed at https://files.eric.ed.gov/fulltext/ED609790.pdf on March 8, 2024.

Harlacher, J. E., & Whitcomb, S. A. (2022). *Bolstering student resilience: Creating a classroom with consistency, connection, and compassion.* Bloomington, IN: Marzano Resources.

Harris, A. (2024, February 21). Private equity has its eyes on the child-care industry. *The Atlantic.* Accessed at www.theatlantic.com/ideas/archive/2024/02/private-equity-childcare/677511 on February 21, 2024.

Harte, A. (2022, April 22). *6 strategies for successful diversity, equity, and inclusion training.* Accessed at www.edutopia.org/article/6-strategies-successful-diversity-equity-and-inclusion-training on March 22, 2024.

Haslam, C., Haslam, S. A., Jetten, J., Cruwys, T., & Steffens, N. K. (2021). Life change, social identity, and health. *Annual Review of Psychology, 72,* 635–661.

Hawthorne, B. (2022). *Raising antiracist children: A practical parenting guide.* New York: Simon Element.

Head Start Early Childhood Learning and Knowledge Center. (n.d.). *Alignment with the Head Start Early Learning Outcomes Framework (ELOF).* Accessed at https://eclkc.ohs.acf.hhs.gov/curriculum/consumer-report/criteria/alignment-head-start-early-learning-outcomes-framework-elof on January 21, 2024.

Head Start Early Childhood Learning and Knowledge Center. (2019, December 3). *Emotional and behavioral self-regulation: Know.* Accessed at https://eclkc.ohs.acf.hhs.gov/school-readiness/effective-practice-guides/emotional-behavioral-self-regulation-know on January 21, 2024.

Head Start Early Childhood Learning and Knowledge Center. (2023). *Advancing racial and ethnic equity in Head Start.* Accessed at https://eclkc.ohs.acf.hhs.gov/culture-language/article/advancing-racial-ethnic-equity-head-start on January 21, 2024.

Hendrickson, C. (2022, October 11). *My advocacy journey: The power of early educators to change policy* [Blog post]. Accessed at https://cscce.berkeley.edu/blog/my-advocacy-journey-the-power-of-early-educators-to-change-poli on March 22, 2024.

Henze, R., Lucas, T., & Scott, B. (1998). Dancing with the monster: Teachers discuss racism, power, and White privilege in education. *The Urban Review, 30*(3), 187–210.

Heyward, G. (2022, July 22). *Why it's so hard for schools to teach about slavery.* Accessed at https://capitalbnews.org/slavery-school-curriculum on January 21, 2024.

Higginbotham, G. A. (2020, February 18). *A compelling argument for "true" reparations for the American slave nation and the descendants of American slaves.* Accessed at www.congress.gov/117/meeting/house/111198/documents/HHRG-117-JU10-20210217-SD032.pdf on May 9, 2024.

HighScope. (n.d.a). *Our commitment to equity.* Accessed at https://highscope.org/who-we-are/racial-equity on January 21, 2024.

HighScope. (n.d.b). *Preschool curriculum.* Accessed at https://highscope.org/our-practice/preschool-curriculum on January 21, 2024.

Hobson, K. (2020, April 19). What are Reggio Emilia schools? *The New York Times.* Accessed at www.nytimes.com/2020/04/19/parenting/reggio-emilia-preschool.html on January 21, 2024.

Holcombe, E., Harper, J., Ueda, N., Kezar, A., Dizon, J. P. M., & Vigil, D. (2023). *Capacity building for shared equity leadership: Approaches and considerations for the work.* Washington, DC: American Council on Education.

Holland, J. M. (2012). *Successful emergent literacy Head Start teachers of urban African American boys living in poverty* [Doctoral dissertation, Virginia Commonwealth University]. VCU Scholars Compass. https://scholarscompass.vcu.edu/etd/3147

hooks, b. (1994). *Teaching to transgress: Education as the practice of freedom.* New York: Routledge.

hooks, b. (2000). *Feminist theory: From margin to center.* Cambridge, MA: South End Press.

hooks, b. (2003). *Teaching community: A pedagogy of hope.* New York: Routledge.

Hopkins, B. (2021). *Restorative leadership: Skills and processes that can support leaders model restorative day-to-day conversations, meetings, conflicts, complaints and disciplinary issues.* Mortimer, Berkshire, England: National Centre for Restorative Justice in Youth Settings. Accessed at www.euforumrj.org/sites/default/files/2023-01/Restorative-leadership-06.pdf on May 9, 2024.

Howard-Karp, M. (2024, March 5). *Special education communication with parents: Tools for California schools* [Blog post]. Accessed at https://exceptionallives.org/blog/special-ed-communication-parents-california on June 6, 2024.

Howe, W. A., & Lisi, P. L. (2024). *Becoming a multicultural educator: Developing awareness, gaining skills, and taking action* (4th ed.). Thousand Oaks, CA: SAGE.

Humanium. (n.d.). *Declaration of the Rights of the Child.* Accessed at www.humanium.org/en/declaration-rights-child-2 on January 21, 2024.

Humes, K. R., Jones, N. A., & Ramirez, R. R. (2011, March). *Overview of race and Hispanic origin: 2010.* Suitland, MD: U.S. Census Bureau. Accessed at www.census.gov/content/dam/Census/library/publications/2011/dec/c2010br-02.pdf on January 21, 2024.

Hunt Institute, Educational Alliance, Manny Cantor Center, Century Foundation, & Education Trust. (2022). *Strong foundations: Promoting diverse and inclusive preschool settings* [Issue brief]. Washington, DC: Trust for Learning. Accessed at https://hunt-institute.org/wp-content/uploads/2022/06/Strong-Foundations-Promoting-Diverse-and-Inclusive-Preschool-Settings-2022.pdf on March 19, 2024.

Hurley, K. (2024, July 2). Early education is the most segregated learning space: How researchers Casey Stockstill and Halley Potter hope to change that. *Early Learning Nation.* Accessed at https://earlylearningnation.com/2024/07/early-education-is-the-most-segregated-learning-space on July 8, 2024.

Indian Country Today. (2021, August 13). *2020 census: Native population increased by 86.5 percent.* Accessed at https://ictnews.org/news/2020-census-native-population-increased-by-86-5-percent on May 15, 2024.

Individuals With Disabilities Education Act, 20 U.S.C. § 1400 (2004).

Interaction Institute for Social Change. (2019). *Summary of stages of racial identity development.* Accessed at https://interactioninstitute.org/wp-content/uploads/2019/01/FFRJW-Updated-Pre-Work-1.3.2019.pdf on January 21, 2024.

Iruka, I. U., Blanchard, S., Commons, C. M., Guzman, R., Kasprzak, C. M., Kemp, P., et al. (2023, January). *Advancing racial equity in early intervention and preschool special education* [Fact sheet]. Chapel Hill, NC: Early Childhood Technical Assistance Center. Accessed at https://ectacenter.org/~pdfs/topics/racialequity/factsheet-racialequity-2023.pdf on January 21, 2024.

Iruka, I. U., Curenton, S. M., Sims, J., Harris, K., & Ibekwe-Okafor, N. (2021, May). *Ethnic-racial identity formation in the early years.* Durham, NC: Hunt Institute. Accessed at https://equity-coalition.fpg.unc.edu/wp-content/uploads/IIruka-et-al_Ethnic-Racial-Identity-Collaborative-Research-Summary-2021.pdf on January 21, 2024.

Iruka, I. U., Gardner-Neblett, N., Telfer, N. A., Ibekwe-Okafor, N., Curenton, S. M., Sims, J., et al. (2022). Effects of racism on child development: Advancing antiracist developmental science. *Annual Review of Developmental Psychology, 4,* 109–132.

Ishimaru, A. M., Lott, J., Fajardo, I., & Salvador, J. (2014, January). *Towards equitable parent-school collaboration: Developing common parent engagement indicators* [Working paper]. Seattle, WA: University of Washington College of Education. Accessed at https://education.uw.edu/sites/default/files/research/centers/UW_IndicatorWhitePaper_1.30.14.pdf on November 7, 2023.

Ivey-Colson, K., & Turner, L. (2020, September 8). 10 keys to everyday anti-racism. *Greater Good Magazine.* Accessed at https://greatergood.berkeley.edu/article/item/ten_keys_to_everyday_anti_racism on April 16, 2024.

Jackson, Y. (2011). *The pedagogy of confidence: Inspiring high intellectual performance in urban schools.* New York: Teachers College Press.

Jackson, Y. (2019, August 22). *Equity for all students—especially those who are marginalized* [Webinar slides]. Accessed at https://mhttcnetwork.org/centers/new-england-mhttc/product/c-tlc-equity-all-students-especially-those-who-are-marginalized on January 21, 2024.

Jackson, Y., & McDermott, V. (2012). *Aim high, achieve more: How to transform urban schools through fearless leadership.* Arlington, VA: ASCD.

Jagers, R. J., Rivas-Drake, D., & Borowski, T. (2018, November). *Equity and social and emotional learning: A cultural analysis.* Chicago: Collaborative for Academic, Social, and Emotional Learning. Accessed at https://drc.casel.org/uploads/sites/3/2019/02/Equity-Social-and-Emotional-Learning-A-Cultural-Analysis.pdf on July 5, 2024.

James, C., & Iruka, I. U. (2018, December). *Delivering on the promise of effective early childhood education*. Silver Spring, MD: National Black Child Development Institute. Accessed at https://buildinitiative.org/wp-content/uploads/2021/06/Delivering-on-the-Promise-of-Effective-Early-Childhood-Education.pdf on July 2, 2024.

Jawaid, A., Roszkowski, M., & Mansuy, I. M. (2018). Transgenerational epigenetics of traumatic stress. *Progress in Molecular Biology and Translational Science, 158*, 273–298.

Johnson, L., & Fuller, C. (2014). *Culturally responsive leadership*. New York: Oxford University Press.

Johnston, V. D. (2011). *Heart wings: An account of children learning through heart-centered education*. Wings of Alaya.

Joseph, G. E., & Alvarez, M. (2022, January 12). *Supporting infants' and toddlers' cognitive self-regulation*. Accessed at https://eclkc.ohs.acf.hhs.gov/teaching-practices/teacher-time-series/supporting-infants-toddlers-cognitive-self-regulation on January 21, 2024.

Kabat-Zinn, J. (2013). *Full catastrophe living: Using the wisdom of your body and mind to face stress, pain, and illness* (Rev. ed.). New York: Bantam Books.

Kahn, M. (2020, September 15). "I hope that we are on the cusp of an awakening": Isabel Wilkerson, best-selling author of the new book *Caste*, in conversation with the groundbreaking playwright Lynn Nottage. *Glamour*. Accessed at www.glamour.com/story/isabel-wilkerson-lynn-nottage-caste-interview on July 8, 2024.

Kamenetz, A. (2016, November 30). *What's going on inside the brain of a bilingual child?* Accessed at www.kqed.org/mindshift/47054/whats-going-on-inside-the-brain-of-a-bilingual-child on January 21, 2024.

Kauerz, K., Ballard, R., Soli, M., & Hagerman, S. (2021). *Leading learning communities: A principal's guide to early learning and the early grades (pre-K–3rd grade)*. Alexandria, VA: National Association of Elementary School Principals.

Kaur, R. (2017). *The sun and her flowers*. Kansas City, MO: Andrews McMeel.

Kendi, I. X. (2016). *Stamped from the beginning: The definitive history of racist ideas in America*. New York: Nation.

Kendi, I. X. (2018, January 13). The heartbeat of racism is denial. *The New York Times*. Accessed at www.nytimes.com/2018/01/13/opinion/sunday/heartbeat-of-racism-denial.html on January 21, 2024.

Kendi, I. X. (2019). *How to be an antiracist*. New York: One World.

Kendi, I. X. (2020). *Antiracist baby* (A. Lukashevsky, Illus.). New York: Kokila.

Kendi, I. X. (2022). *How to raise an antiracist*. New York: One World.

Kendi, I. X., & Stone, N. (2023). *How to be a (young) antiracist*. New York: Kokila.

Kennedy, R. F. (1966, June 6). *Day of affirmation address, University of Cape Town, South Africa* [Speech transcript]. Accessed at www.jfklibrary.org/learn/about-jfk/the-kennedy-family/robert-f-kennedy/robert-f-kennedy-speeches/day-of-affirmation-address-university-of-capetown-capetown-south-africa-june-6-1966 on July 5, 2024.

King, R. (2018). *Mindful of race: Transforming racism from the inside out*. Boulder, CO: Sounds True.

Kishimoto, K. (2018). Anti-racist pedagogy: From faculty's self-reflection to organizing within and beyond the classroom. *Race Ethnicity and Education, 21*(4), 540–554. https://doi.org/10.1080/13613324.2016.1248824

Kouzes, J. M., & Posner, B. Z. (2023). *The leadership challenge workbook* (4th ed.). Hoboken, NJ: Wiley.

Krogh, S. L., & Morehouse, P. (2020). *The early childhood curriculum: Inquiry learning through integration* (3rd ed.). New York: Routledge.

Kuh, L. P., LeeKeenan, D., Given, H., & Beneke, M. R. (2016). Moving beyond anti-bias activities: Supporting the development of anti-bias practices. *Young Children, 71*(1), 58–65.

Ladson-Billings, G. (2014). Culturally relevant pedagogy 2.0: A.k.a. the remix. *Harvard Educational Review, 84*(1), 74–84. https://doi.org/10.17763/haer.84.1.p2rj131485484751

Lambert, D. (2024, April 1). *Disrespect, low pay, lack of support keep Black teachers out of the profession*. Accessed at https://edsource.org/2024/disrespect-low-pay-lack-of-support-keep-black-teachers-out-of-the-profession/708506 on May 9, 2024.

Lang-Raad, N. D. (2018). *Everyday instructional coaching: Seven daily drivers to support teacher effectiveness*. Bloomington, IN: Solution Tree Press.

LaRocque, M., Kleiman, I., & Darling, S. M. (2011). Parental involvement: The missing link in school achievement. *Preventing School Failure, 55*(3), 115–122.

LeeKeenan, D., & Allen, B. (2017, July/August). It can be done! Strategies for embedding anti-bias education into daily programming. *Anti-Bias Education*, 52–56. Accessed at www.antibiasleadersece.com/wp-content/uploads/2017/06/ABE-LeeKeenan-Allen.pdf on April 16, 2024.

Lewis, J. [@repjohnlewis]. (2018, June 27). *Do not get lost in a sea of despair. Be hopeful, be optimistic. Our struggle is not the struggle of a day, a week, a month, or a year, it is the struggle of a lifetime. Never, ever be afraid to make some noise and get in good trouble, necessary trouble. #goodtrouble* [Post]. X. Accessed at https://x.com/repjohnlewis/status/1011991303599607808 on April 16, 2024.

Lillard, A. S., Taggart, J., Yonas, D., & Seale, M. N. (2021). *An alternative to "no excuses": Considering Montessori as culturally responsive pedagogy*. Accessed at www.montessoripublic.org/wp-content/uploads/2021/03/Lillard.21.Taggart.Yonas_.Seale_.JNE_.pdf on January 21, 2024.

Lin, Y.-C., & McDoniel, M. (2023, August). *Understanding child care and early education program closures and enrollment during the first year of the COVID-19 pandemic* (OPRE Report No. 2023-237). Washington, DC: Office of Planning, Research, and Evaluation. Accessed at www.acf.hhs.gov/sites/default/files/documents/opre/2023-237%20COVID%20Highlight.pdf on April 12, 2024.

Linden, R. M. (2002). *Working across boundaries: Making collaboration work in government and nonprofit organizations*. San Francisco: Jossey-Bass.

Lloyd, C. M. (2022, June 27). *Addressing historical inequities in early care and education: Strategies to support workforce equity* [Keynote]. National Research Conference on Early Childhood. Accessed at https://vimeo.com/743255336/748161265 on January 21, 2024.

Lloyd, C. M., Carlson, J., Barnett, H., Shaw, S., & Logan, D. (2021, September). *Mary Pauper: A historical exploration of early care and education compensation, policy, and solutions*. Washington, DC: Child Trends. Accessed at https://earlyedcollaborative.org/assets/2022/04/Mary-Pauper-updated-4_4_2022_FINAL.pdf on January 21, 2024.

Lomas, T., Medina, J. C., Ivtzan, I., Rupprecht, S., & Eiroa-Orosa, F. J. (2017). The impact of mindfulness on the wellbeing and performance of educators: A systematic review of the empirical literature. *Teaching and Teacher Education*, *61*, 132–141.

Louie, N., & Pacheco, M. (2021). Love as a necessary corrective: Toward antiracist schools for our children. *Multicultural Perspectives*, *23*(3), 181–187. https://doi.org/10.1080/15210960.2021.1982367

MacCann, C., Jiang, Y., Brown, L. E. R., Double, K. S., Bucich, M., & Minbashian, A. (2020). Emotional intelligence predicts academic performance: A meta-analysis. *Psychological Bulletin*, *146*(2), 150–186.

MacDonald, S. (2016). *Inspiring early childhood leadership: Eight strategies to ignite passion and transform program quality*. Lewisville, NC: Gryphon House.

MacKee, N. (2021, September 18). *Research against racism: Why strength-based approaches are crucial in Indigenous health research*. Accessed at www.croakey.org/research-against-racism-why-strength-based-approaches-are-crucial-in-indigenous-health-research on May 9, 2024.

MacLeod, K., Causton, J. N., Radel, M., & Radel, P. (2017). Rethinking the individualized education plan process: Voices from the other side of the table. *Disability and Society*, *32*(3), 381–400.

Madu, N. M. (2021). Reimagining early childhood classrooms as sites of love: Humanizing Black boys through head rubs and "playin' the dozens." *Occasional Paper Series*, *46*, Article 6. https://doi.org/10.58295/2375-3668.1413

Magee, R. V. (2022, August 24). *The end of othering: Cultivating just, equitable communities—How mindfulness can assist us in upending othering at its roots*. Accessed at www.mindandlife.org/insight/the-end-of-othering-cultivating-just-equitable-communities on January 21, 2024.

Malaguzzi, L. (1993). For an education based on relationships (L. Gandini, Trans.). *Young Children*, *49*(1), 9–12.

Mandela, N. (1994). *Long walk to freedom: The autobiography of Nelson Mandela*. New York: Little, Brown.

Marcus, D., Cobb, E. B., & Shoenberg, R. E. (2000, May). *Lessons learned from FIPSE projects IV*. Washington, DC: Fund for the Improvement of Postsecondary Education. Accessed at https://files.eric.ed.gov/fulltext/ED443300.pdf on January 21, 2024.

Mascareñaz, L. (2022). *Evident equity: A guide for creating systemwide change in schools.* Bloomington, IN: Solution Tree Press.

Maslow, A. H. (1943). A theory of human motivation. *Psychological Review, 50*(4), 370–396.

Mason, C., Asby, D., Wenzel, M., Volk, K., & Staeheli, M. (2021). *Compassionate school practices: Fostering children's mental health and well-being.* Thousand Oaks, CA: Corwin Press.

Mason, C., & Banks, K. L. (n.d.). *Heart beaming: Positive stress relieving exercises for use in the classroom.* Vienna, VA: Center for Educational Improvement. Accessed at www.edimprovement.org/heart-beaming on January 21, 2024.

Mason, C., Donald, J., Khalsa, K. K., Rivers Murphy, M. M., & Brown, V. (2022). *Cultivating happiness, resilience, and well-being through meditation, mindfulness, and movement: A guide for educators.* Thousand Oaks, CA: Corwin Press.

Mason, C., Kohler, J., & Ikler, J. (Hosts). (2023, September 27). Episode 41: How a school leader creates the conditions for healing [Audio podcast episode]. In *Cultivating resilience: A whole community approach for alleviating trauma in schools.* Accessed at www.quetico coaching.com/trauma-in-schools/41-how-a-school-leader-creates-the-conditions-for-healing on June 18, 2024.

Mason, C., Liabenow, P., & Patschke, M. (2020). *Visioning onward: A guide for all schools.* Thousand Oaks, CA: Corwin Press.

Mason, C., Patschke, M., & Simpson, K. (2023). *Leading with vitality and hope: Embracing equity, alleviating trauma, and healing school communities.* Lanham, MD: Rowman & Littlefield.

Mason, C., Rivers Murphy, M. M., & Jackson, Y. (2019). *Mindfulness practices: Cultivating heart centered communities where students focus and flourish.* Bloomington, IN: Solution Tree Press.

Mason, C., Rivers Murphy, M. M., & Jackson, Y. (2020). *Mindful school communities: The five Cs of nurturing Heart Centered Learning.* Bloomington, IN: Solution Tree Press.

Mason, C., Ross, R., Harris, O., & Flanders, J. (2024). *Little learners, big hearts: A teacher's guide to nurturing empathy and equity in early childhood.* Bloomington, IN: Solution Tree Press.

Massachusetts Department of Education. (2003). *Early childhood program standards: For three and four year olds.* Malden, MA: Massachusetts Department of Education Early Learning Services. Accessed at www.necc.mass.edu/wp-content/uploads/education/student-resources/Early-Childhood-Program-Standards_2011.pdf on January 21, 2024.

Massachusetts Department of Elementary and Secondary Education. (2015, June). *Massachusetts standards for preschool and kindergarten: Social and emotional learning, and approaches to play and learning.* Everett, MA: Author. Accessed at www.doe.mass.edu/sfs/earlylearning/resources/sel-apl-standards.docx on January 21, 2024.

Massachusetts Department of Elementary and Secondary Education. (2019). *Guidelines for preschool and kindergarten learning experiences*. Everett, MA: Author. Accessed at www.mass.gov/doc/guidelines-for-preschool-learning-experiences-updated-november-2019/download on January 21, 2024.

Massachusetts Department of Elementary and Secondary Education. (2022a). *Focus indicators for teaching in 2023–2024*. Everett, MA: Author.

Massachusetts Department of Elementary and Secondary Education. (2022b, March). *Social emotional learning resources for grades 1–3*. Everett, MA: Author. Accessed at www.doe.mass.edu/sfs/earlylearning/resources/sel1-3/resources-g1-3.docx on January 21, 2024.

MasterClass. (2021, June 7). *Understanding cultural bias: 3 examples of cultural bias*. Accessed at www.masterclass.com/articles/understanding-cultural-bias on January 21, 2024.

Matias, C. E., & Mackey, J. (2016). Breakin' down Whiteness in antiracist teaching: Introducing critical Whiteness pedagogy. *The Urban Review, 48*(1), 32–50. https://doi.org/10.1007/s11256-015-0344-7

McCaffrey, M. (2017). *Practicing freedom: Effects of personal anti-racist engagement on a Montessori educator's experience* [Master of arts action research project, St. Catherine University]. SOPHIA. https://sophia.stkate.edu/maed/246

McCraty, R., & Childre, D. (2010). Coherence: Bridging personal, social, and global health. *Alternative Therapies in Health and Medicine, 16*(4), 10–24.

McDonald, M., & Zeichner, K. M. (2009). Social justice teacher education. In W. Ayers, T. Quinn, & D. Stovall (Eds.), *Handbook of social justice in education* (pp. 595–610). New York: Routledge.

McIntosh, K., Girvan, E. J., Horner, R. H., & Smolkowski, K. (2014). Education not incarceration: A conceptual model for reducing racial and ethnic disproportionality in school discipline. *Journal of Applied Research on Children, 5*(2), Article 4. Accessed at https://files.eric.ed.gov/fulltext/EJ1188503.pdf on June 27, 2024.

McLean, C., Austin, L. J. E., Whitebook, M., & Olson, K. L. (2021). *Early childhood workforce index 2020*. Berkeley, CA: Center for the Study of Child Care Employment. Accessed at https://cscce.berkeley.edu/workforce-index-2020/report-pdf on January 21, 2024.

Meek, S., Smith, L., Allen, R., Catherine, E., Edyburn, K., Williams, C., et al. (2020). *Start with equity: From the early years to the early grades*. Tempe, AZ: Children's Equity Project. Accessed at https://childandfamilysuccess.asu.edu/sites/default/files/2020-07/CEP-report-071520-FINAL.pdf on June 4, 2024.

Meltzoff, A. N., & Gilliam, W. S. (2024). Young children and implicit racial biases. *Dædalus, 153*(1), 65–83.

Mensah, F. M. (2021). Culturally relevant and culturally responsive: Two theories of practice for science teaching. *Science and Children, 58*(4), 10–13. Accessed at www.nsta.org/science-and-children/science-and-children-marchapril-2021/culturally-relevant-and-culturally on January 21, 2024.

Migration Policy Institute. (n.d.). *Young dual language learners in the United States and by state*. Accessed at www.migrationpolicy.org/programs/data-hub/charts/us-state-profiles-young-dlls on January 21, 2024.

Mikels, J. A., Maglio, S. J., Reed, A. E., & Kaplowitz, L. J. (2011). Should I go with my gut? Investigating the benefits of emotion-focused decision making. *Emotion, 11*(4), 743–753. https://doi.org/10.1037/a0023986

Milli, J. (2022, May 9). *Why investing in child care providers is essential for providers, children, and families*. Washington, DC: Center for Law and Social Policy. Accessed at www.clasp.org/publications/report/brief/why-investing-in-child-care-providers-is-essential-for-providers-children-and-families on May 15, 2024.

Mincemoyer, C. C. (2016). *Interactions matter: What research says and what you can do!* University Park, PA: Penn State Extension. Accessed at http://bkc-od-media.vmhost.psu.edu/documents/HO_InteractionsMatter.pdf on April 16, 2024.

Morales Pinales, T. (2023, December 11). *How reports of hate crimes in the US were already at record highs, in 4 charts*. Accessed at www.cnn.com/2023/10/29/us/hate-crimes-antisemitism-anti-muslim-dg/index.html on May 9, 2024.

Morrissey, T. (2020, February 18). *Addressing the need for affordable, high-quality early childhood care and education for all in the United States*. Washington, DC: Washington Center for Equitable Growth. Accessed at https://equitablegrowth.org/addressing-the-need-for-affordable-high-quality-early-childhood-care-and-education-for-all-in-the-united-states on May 9, 2024.

Movahedazarhouligh, S., Banerjee, R., & Luckner, J. (2023). Leadership development and system building in early childhood education and care: Current issues and recommendations. *Early Years, 43*(4–5), 1045–1059.

Movement Advancement Project. (2023). *LGBTQ youth: School nondiscrimination laws and related policies*. Boulder, CO: Author. Accessed at www.lgbtmap.org/img/maps/citations-schools-nondisc.pdf on January 21, 2024.

Müller, K., & Schwarz, C. (2020, July 24). *From hashtag to hate crime: Twitter and anti-minority sentiment*. Accessed at https://papers.ssrn.com/sol3/papers.cfm?abstract_id=3149103 on June 27, 2024.

Murray, A. J., Aboulela, H., Sajid, A., Emafo, N., & Debs, M. (2023). Montessori education in Africa: Themes and examples across the continent. In A. K. Murray, E.-M. T. Ahlquist, M. K. McKenna, & M. Debs (Eds.), *The Bloomsbury handbook of Montessori education* (pp. 333–342). New York: Bloomsbury.

Nakamura, D. (2024, March 11). Former Louisville officer faces third trial in Breonna Taylor slaying. *The Washington Post*. Accessed at www.washingtonpost.com/national-security/2024/03/11/former-louisville-officer-faces-third-trial-breonna-taylor-slaying on June 27, 2024.

National Association for Regulatory Administration. (2014). *Child care licensing study 2014*. Minneapolis, MN: Author. Accessed at https://nara.memberclicks.net/assets/docs/ChildCareLicensingStudies/2014CCStudy/NARA%202014%20Licensing%20Survey%20Report.pdf on January 21, 2024.

National Association for the Education of Young Children. (n.d.). *NAEYC's statement on developmentally appropriate practice* [Press release]. Accessed at www.naeyc.org/statement-on-dap on January 21, 2024.

National Association for the Education of Young Children. (2019). *Advancing equity in early childhood education position statement*. Accessed at www.naeyc.org/resources/position-statements/equity on January 21, 2024.

National Association for the Education of Young Children. (2020). *Professional Standards and Competencies for Early Childhood Educators*. Washington, DC: Author. Accessed at www.naeyc.org/sites/default/files/globally-shared/downloads/PDFs/resources/position-statements/standards_and_competencies_ps.pdf on January 21, 2024.

National Association for the Education of Young Children. (2021, September). *State survey data: Child care at a time of progress and peril*. Washington, DC: Author. Accessed at www.naeyc.org/sites/default/files/wysiwyg/user-74/statedata_july2021_gf_092321.pdf on January 21, 2024.

National Association for the Education of Young Children & Education Trust. (2019). *Increasing qualifications, centering equity: Experiences and advice from early childhood educators of color*. Washington, DC: NAEYC. Accessed at www.naeyc.org/sites/default/files/globally-shared/downloads/PDFs/our-work/public-policy-advocacy/increasing_qualifications_centering_equity.pdf on January 21, 2024.

National Association for the Education of Young Children & National Association of Early Childhood Specialists in State Departments of Education. (2003). *Early childhood curriculum, assessment, and program evaluation: Building an effective, accountable system in programs for children birth through age 8* [Position statement]. Accessed at www.naeyc.org/sites/default/files/globally-shared/downloads/PDFs/resources/position-statements/pscape.pdf on January 21, 2024.

National Association of Early Childhood Teacher Educators. (n.d.). *NAECTE—Speak out and move to action*. Accessed at https://naecte.org/wp-content/uploads/NAECTE-Speak-Out-Move-to-Action.pdf on January 21, 2024.

National Center on Early Childhood Development, Teaching, and Learning. (2021, December 10). *A culturally responsive approach to implementing a curriculum*. Accessed at https://eclkc.ohs.acf.hhs.gov/video/culturally-responsive-approach-implementing-curriculum on January 21, 2024.

National Council of Teachers of English. (2016). *Equity and early childhood education: Reclaiming the child*. Accessed at https://cdn.ncte.org/nctefiles/equityearlyedbrief.pdf on January 21, 2024.

National Education Association Center for Social Justice. (2020, November). *10 principles for talking about race in school.* Accessed at www.nea.org/professional-excellence/student-engagement/tools-tips/10-principles-talking-about-race-school on January 21, 2024.

National Indian Education Association. (2024). *The National Indian Education Association whole child approach.* Accessed at www.niea.org/whole-child-approach on June 27, 2024.

National Park Service. (2023). *What happened on the Trail of Tears?* Accessed at www.nps.gov/trte/learn/historyculture/what-happened-on-the-trail-of-tears.htm on January 21, 2024.

National Resource Center for Health and Safety in Child Care and Early Education. (n.d.). *Caring for Our Children: National health and safety performance standards—Guidelines for early care and education programs.* Accessed at https://nrckids.org/CFOC on January 21, 2024.

National School Climate Center. (n.d.). *The 14 dimensions of school climate measured by the CSCI.* Accessed at https://schoolclimate.org/wp-content/uploads/2024/01/14-Dimensions.pdf on March 8, 2024.

New Jersey State Department of Education. (2014). *Preschool teaching and learning standards.* Trenton, NJ: Author. Accessed at www.nj.gov/education/earlychildhood/preschool/docs/PreschoolTeachingandLearningStandards.pdf on January 21, 2024.

Nichols, H. (2022). *Finding your blind spots: Eight guiding principles for overcoming implicit bias in teaching.* Bloomington, IN: Solution Tree Press.

No Child Left Behind (NCLB) Act of 2001, Pub. L. No. 107-110, § 115, Stat. 1425 (2002).

North Carolina Early Education Coalition. (n.d.a). *Worthy wages campaign toolkit.* Accessed at https://express.adobe.com/page/6TRPAWEPnM3bY on January 21, 2024.

North Carolina Early Education Coalition. (n.d.b). *Worthy wages for worthy work.* Accessed at https://ncearlyeducationcoalition.org/worthywages on March 19, 2024.

North Carolina Foundations Task Force. (2013). *North Carolina foundations for early learning and development.* Raleigh, NC: Author. Accessed at https://ncchildcare.ncdhhs.gov/Portals/0/documents/pdf/N/NC_Foundations.pdf on January 21, 2024.

Nosek, B. A., Smyth, F. L., Hansen, J. J., Devos, T., Lindner, N. M., Ranganath, K. A., et al. (2007). Pervasiveness and correlates of implicit attitudes and stereotypes. *European Review of Social Psychology, 18*(1), 36–88. https://doi.org/10.1080/10463280701489053

Nunke, K. F. (2019). *Representation of gender and race in the Core Knowledge of Language Arts curriculum* [Honors thesis, Guilford College]. Guilford College Honors Theses. https://ds.guilford.edu/projects/honors-theses/items/show/490

Nuri-Robins, K. J., Lindsey, D. B., Lindsey, R. B., & Terrell, R. D. (2012). *Culturally proficient instruction: A guide for people who teach* (3rd ed.). Thousand Oaks, CA: Corwin Press.

NYC Leadership Academy. (2020). *Equity leadership dispositions.* Accessed at www.leadershipacademy.org/wp-content/uploads/2020/04/Equity-Leadership-Dispositions.pdf on May 15, 2024.

Obama, B. (2005, May 1). *NAACP Fight for Freedom Fund dinner* [Speech transcript]. Accessed at http://obamaspeeches.com/015-NAACP-Fight-for-Freedom-Fund-Dinner-Obama-Speech.htm on February 12, 2024.

Obasi, C. (2020, June 5). Silent racism: Why not speaking up becomes lethal for the collective. *Harper's Bazaar*. Accessed at www.harpersbazaar.com/uk/culture/culture-news/a32769018/silent-racism-george-floyd on January 21, 2024.

Ocampo, K. A., Knight, G. P., & Bernal, M. E. (1997). The development of cognitive abilities and social identities in children: The case of ethnic identity. *International Journal of Behavioral Development, 21*(3), 479–500.

O'Donohue, J. (2008). *To bless the space between us: A book of blessings*. New York: Doubleday.

Office for Civil Rights. (2016). *2013–2014 civil rights data collection: A first look*. Washington, DC: U.S. Department of Education. Accessed at www2.ed.gov/about/offices/list/ocr/docs/2013-14-first-look.pdf on June 27, 2024.

Office of Head Start. (2022, June 23). *Head Start history*. Accessed at www.acf.hhs.gov/ohs/about/history-head-start on January 21, 2024.

Oluo, I. (2018). *So you want to talk about race*. New York: Seal Press.

Ontario Ministry of Education. (2012). *"SB" memos: 2012*. Accessed at https://efis.fma.csc.gov.on.ca/faab/SB_Memos_2012.htm on January 21, 2024.

Owen, R., & Mason, C. (in press). *Becoming a transformative leader from the inside out: The nested leadership model for educators*. Lanham, MD: Rowman & Littlefield.

Ozturgut, O. (2011). Understanding multicultural education. *Current Issues in Education, 14*(2), 1–11.

Pasadena City College. (n.d.). *CHDV 017: Teaching children in a diverse society* [Course]. Accessed at https://ssb-prod.ec.pasadena.edu/PROD/pw_psearch_sched.p_course_popup?vsub=CHDV&vcrse=017&vterm=202130&vcrn=31563 on April 12, 2024.

Paul, M. (2020). *Speak up* (E. Glenn, Illus.). New York: Clarion Books.

PBS NewsHour. (2016, July 25). *Watch First Lady Michelle Obama's full speech at the 2016 Democratic National Convention* [Video file]. Accessed at www.youtube.com/watch?v=4ZNWYqDU948&ab on January 21, 2024.

Penn State Extension. (n.d.). *Antiracism (part 1): Self-awareness and communication* [Course]. Accessed at https://extension.psu.edu/programs/betterkidcare/lessons/antiracism1 on January 21, 2024.

Pérez, M. S. (2020). Dismantling racialized discourses in early childhood education and care: A revolution towards reframing the field. In F. Nxumalo & C. P. Brown (Eds.), *Disrupting and countering deficits in early childhood education* (pp. 20–36). New York: Routledge.

Perlman, S. (1928). *A theory of the labor movement*. New York: Macmillan.

Perry, I. (2022). *South to America: A journey below the Mason-Dixon to understand the soul of a nation*. New York: HarperCollins.

Peterson, E. R., Rubie-Davies, C., Osborne, D., & Sibley, C. (2016). Teachers' explicit expectations and implicit prejudiced attitudes to educational achievement: Relations with student achievement and the ethnic achievement gap. *Learning and Instruction*, *42*, 123–140.

Pianta, R. C., Whittaker, J. E., Vitiello, V., Ruzek, E., Ansari, A., Hofkens, T., et al. (2020). Children's school readiness skills across the pre-K year: Associations with teacher-student interactions, teacher practices, and exposure to academic content. *Journal of Applied Developmental Psychology*, *66*, Article 101084. https://doi.org/10.1016/j.appdev.2019.101084

Polacco, P. (2001). *Mr. Lincoln's way*. New York: Penguin.

Pollock, M. (2004). Race wrestling: Struggling strategically with race in educational practice and research. *American Journal of Education*, *111*(1), 25–67.

Pollock, M. (Ed.). (2008). *Everyday antiracism: Getting real about race in school*. New York: New Press.

Popli, N. (2023, September 15). What to know about the expiration of federal emergency childcare funding. *TIME*. Accessed at https://time.com/6314455/federal-childcare-funding-expiring-what-to-know on May 15, 2024.

Potiker, J. (2019, August 1). *Using mindfulness to overcome shame and guilt*. Accessed at https://mindfulmethodsforlife.com/using-mindfulness-to-overcome-shame-and-guilt on January 21, 2024.

Power to the Profession. (2020, March). *Unifying Framework for the early childhood education profession*. Accessed at https://powertotheprofession.org/wp-content/uploads/2020/03/Power-to-Profession-Framework-03312020-web.pdf on January 21, 2024.

Project Zero & Reggio Children. (2001). *Making learning visible: Children as individual and group learners*. Reggio Emilia, Italy: Reggio Children.

Rajmohan, V., & Mohandas, E. (2007). Mirror neuron system. *Indian Journal of Psychiatry*, *49*(1), 66–69. https://doi.org/10.4103/0019-5545.31522

Rambusch, N. M. (1962). *Learning how to learn: An American approach to Montessori*. Baltimore: Helicon Press.

Rambusch, N. M. (2007). What makes a Montessorian? *Montessori Life: A Publication of the American Montessori Society*, *19*(1), 82–83.

Ramos, R. (2022, October). *Whole child initiative* [Conference presentation]. Fifty-third annual National Indian Education Association conference, Oklahoma City, OK.

Reggio Children. (n.d.). *Reggio Emilia approach*. Accessed at www.reggiochildren.it/en/reggio-emilia-approach on January 21, 2024.

Regional Educational Laboratory Program. (n.d.). *Regional Educational Laboratory Pacific*. Accessed at https://ies.ed.gov/ncee/rel/region/pacific on January 21, 2024.

Reynolds, J., & Kendi, I. X. (2020). *Stamped: Racism, antiracism, and you*. New York: Little, Brown.

Rinaldi, C. (2012). The pedagogy of listening: The listening perspective from Reggio Emilia. In C. P. Edwards, L. Gandini, & G. Forman (Eds.), *The hundred languages of children: The Reggio Emilia experience in transformation* (3rd ed., pp. 233–246). Westport, CT: Praeger.

Rispoli, K. M., Hawley, L. R., & Clinton, M. C. (2018). Family background and parent–school interactions in parent involvement for at-risk preschool children with disabilities. *The Journal of Special Education, 52*(1), 39–49.

Roberts, S. O., & Rizzo, M. T. (2021). The psychology of American racism. *American Psychologist, 76*(3), 475–487. https://doi.org/10.1037/amp0000642

Romero, V. E., Warner, A. N., & Hendrickson, J. (2022). *Race resilience: Achieving equity through self and systems transformation*. Thousand Oaks, CA: Corwin Press.

Rose, J. (2020, January 20). *Martin Luther King Jr. on making America great again.* Accessed at www.aaihs.org/martin-luther-king-jr-on-making-america-great-again on July 5, 2024.

Rosenthal, L., Earnshaw, V. A., Carroll-Scott, A., Henderson, K. E., Peters, S. M., McCaslin, C., et al. (2015). Weight- and race-based bullying: Health associations among urban adolescents. *Journal of Health Psychology, 20*(4), 401–412. https://doi.org/10.1177/1359105313502567

Ross, R. (2013). School climate and equity. In T. Dary & T. Pickeral (Eds.), *School climate practices for implementation and sustainability* (School Climate Practice Brief No. 1, pp. 39–42). New York: National School Climate Center. Accessed at https://safesupportivelearning.ed.gov/sites/default/files/School%20Climate%20Practices%20for%20Implementation%20and%20Sustainability.pdf on January 21, 2024.

Ross, R., Brown, P., & Hamilton Biagas, K. (2020). Creating equitable school climates. *State Education Standard, 20*(2), 17–22.

Rothstein, R. (2017). *The color of law: A forgotten history of how our government segregated America*. New York: W. W. Norton.

Saloojee, A. (2003, January). *Social inclusion, anti-racism and democratic citizenship* (Working Paper). Toronto, Ontario, Canada: Laidlaw Foundation. Accessed at https://laidlawfdn.org/assets/wpsosi_2003_jan_social-inclusion-anti-racism.pdf on January 21, 2024.

Saylor Academy. (2024). *Perceptions*. Accessed at https://learn.saylor.org/mod/book/tool/print/index.php?id=60384 on May 9, 2024.

Schaffner, B. F. (2020). *The acceptance and expression of prejudice during the Trump era*. New York: Cambridge University Press.

Scheurich, J. J. (1993). Toward a White discourse on White racism. *Educational Researcher, 22*(8), 5–10.

Schonleber, N. S. (2011). Hawaiian culture-based education and the Montessori approach: Overlapping teaching practices, values, and worldview. *Journal of American Indian Education, 50*(3), 5–25.

Schroeder-Yu, G. (2008). Documentation: Ideas and applications from the Reggio Emilia approach. *Teaching Artist Journal, 6*(2), 126–134. https://doi.org/10.1080/15411790801910735

Seager, A. (2022, November 17). Students take to streets for walk to celebrate civil rights icon. *Pacifica Tribune*. Accessed at www.pacificatribune.com/news/students-take-to-streets-for-walk-to-celebrate-civil-rights-icon/article_fa4f388e-6545-11ed-94c0-cf45b097e45b.html on January 21, 2024.

Seaver, M. (2023, March 29). 5 mindfulness breathing exercises you can do anywhere, anytime. *Real Simple*. Accessed at www.realsimple.com/health/mind-mood/breathing-exercises on January 18, 2024.

Seppälä, E. (2016). *The happiness track: How to apply the science of happiness to accelerate your success*. New York: HarperOne.

Sharma, M. (2017). *Radical transformational leadership: Strategic action for change agents*. Berkeley, CA: North Atlantic Books.

Shockley, K. G., & Lomotey, K. (Eds.). (2020). *African-centered education: Theory and practice*. Gorham, ME: Myers Education Press.

Shonkoff, J. P., Slopen, N., & Williams, D. R. (2021). Early childhood adversity, toxic stress, and the impacts of racism on the foundations of health. *Annual Review of Public Health, 42*, 115–134.

Simmons, D. (2019). Why we can't afford whitewashed social-emotional learning. *Educational Leadership, 61*(4). Accessed at www.ascd.org/el/articles/why-we-cant-afford-whitewashed-social-emotional-learning on January 18, 2024.

Skinner, A. L., Meltzoff, A. N., & Olson, K. R. (2017). "Catching" social bias: Exposure to biased nonverbal signals creates social biases in preschool children. *Psychological Science, 28*(2), 216–224. https://doi.org/10.1177/0956797616678930

Smart Richman, L., & Leary, M. R. (2009). Reactions to discrimination, stigmatization, ostracism, and other forms of interpersonal rejection: A multimotive model. *Psychological Review, 116*(2), 365–383.

Smidt, S. (2020). *Creating an anti-racist culture in the early years: An essential guide for practitioners*. New York: Routledge.

Sorenson, R. D. (2022). *Equity, equality, and empathy: What principals can do for the well-being of the learning community*. Lanham, MD: Rowman & Littlefield.

Soukakou, E., Dionne, C., & Palikara, O. (2024). *Promoting quality inclusion in early childhood care and education: Inclusive practices for each and every child*. Paris: United Nations Educational, Scientific and Cultural Organization. Accessed at https://wrap.warwick.ac.uk/183898/1/WRAP-unesco-report-2024.pdf on June 4, 2024.

Sparks, S. D. (2020, November 17). Training bias out of teachers: Research shows little promise so far. *Education Week*. Accessed at www.edweek.org/leadership/training-bias-out-of-teachers-research-shows-little-promise-so-far/2020/11 on January 18, 2024.

Srikanth, A. (2020, June 11). Black people 5 times more likely to be arrested than Whites, according to new analysis. *The Hill*. Accessed at https://thehill.com/changing-america/respect/equality/502277-black-people-5-times-more-likely-to-be-arrested-than-whites on January 18, 2024.

Storey, T. (2023, April 21). *Alabama early childhood education secretary resigns after pre-K educator book pulled.* Accessed at www.wtvy.com/2023/04/21/alabama-early-childhood-education-secretary-resigns-after-pre-k-educator-book-pulled on January 21, 2024.

Strategies for Children. (n.d.a). *The 9:30 call.* Accessed at www.strategiesforchildren.org/930Call.html on March 19, 2024.

Strategies for Children. (n.d.b). *About us.* Accessed at www.strategiesforchildren.org/about.html on March 19, 2024.

Success for All Foundation. (n.d.). *Curiosity corner.* Accessed at www.successforall.org/our-approach/schoolwide-programs/curiosity-corner on January 21, 2024.

Sue, D. W. (2015). Therapeutic harm and cultural oppression. *The Counseling Psychologist, 43*(3), 359–369. https://doi.org/10.1177/0011000014565713

Sullivan, J., Wilton, L., & Apfelbaum, E. P. (2021). Adults delay conversations about race because they underestimate children's processing of race. *Journal of Experimental Psychology: General, 150*(2), 395–400. https://doi.org/10.1037/xge0000851

Swayne, M. (2015, June 25). *Head Start program played anti-segregation role in the Deep South.* Accessed at www.psu.edu/news/research/story/head-start-program-played-anti-segregation-role-deep-south on January 21, 2024.

Systemic racism. (n.d.). In *Merriam-Webster's online dictionary.* Accessed at www.merriam-webster.com/dictionary/systemic%20racism on January 21, 2024.

Tatum, B. D. (1999). *Why are all the Black kids sitting together in the cafeteria? And other conversations about race.* New York: Basic Books.

Teachstone. (n.d.a). *Improve interactions with tailored professional development.* Accessed at https://teachstone.com/improve on January 21, 2024.

Teachstone. (n.d.b). *Proving CLASS effectiveness: A research summary.* Accessed at https://info.teachstone.com/hubfs/CLASS%20Research%20Summary.pdf on January 21, 2024.

Theoharis, G. (2009). *The school leaders our children deserve: Seven keys to equity, social justice, and school reform.* New York: Teachers College Press.

Thigpen, L., & Reinking, A. (2021). Unsilencing the silenced Black voice in education courses and professional development: Partnering with educators to create equitable environments. *School-University Partnerships, 14*(4), 47–65.

Thompson, B., Banwo, B. O., & Kuykendall-Walker, R. (2020). The Roots model: African-centered education. In K. G. Shockley & K. Lomotey (Eds.), *African-centered education: Theory and practice* (pp. 45–63). Gorham, ME: Myers Education Press.

Thornton, L., & Brunton, P. (2015). *Understanding the Reggio approach: Early years education in practice* (3rd ed.). New York: Routledge.

Trent, M., Dooley, D. G., Dougé, J., Cavanaugh, R. M., Jr., Lacroix, A. E., Fanburg, J., et al. (2019). The impact of racism on child and adolescent health. *Pediatrics, 144*(2), Article e20191765. https://doi.org/10.1542/peds.2019-1765

Trout, L. (2021). *The toolkit before the toolkit: Centering adaptive and relational elements of restorative practices for implementation success.* Accessed at www.wested.org/resources/adaptive-relational-elements-to-support-restorative-practices on September 30, 2024.

Tschannen-Moran, B., & Tschannen-Moran, M. (2010). *Evocative coaching: Transforming schools one conversation at a time.* San Francisco: Jossey-Bass.

Turner, N. S. (2023). *Simply instructional coaching: Questions asked and answered from the field* (Rev. ed.). Bloomington, IN: Solution Tree Press.

United Nations. (2017, October 18). *Make "we the peoples" reality by transcending differences to overcome increasing conflicts, inequality, secretary-general says in message for United Nations Day* [Press release]. Accessed at http://press.un.org/en/2017/sgsm18754.doc.htm on March 19, 2024.

United Nations Educational, Scientific and Cultural Organization. (2014). *Teaching respect for all: Implementation guide.* Paris: Author. Accessed at https://unesdoc.unesco.org/ark:/48223/pf0000227983 on January 21, 2024.

U.S. Bureau of Labor Statistics. (n.d.). *Occupational employment and wage statistics.* Accessed at www.bls.gov/oes on June 25, 2024.

U.S. Department of Education. (2023). *About OCR.* Accessed at www2.ed.gov/about/offices/list/ocr/aboutocr.html on May 9, 2024.

U.S. Department of Justice. (2023). *2022 FBI hate crimes statistics.* Accessed at www.justice.gov/crs/highlights/2022-hate-crime-statistics on May 9, 2024.

van den Bergh, L., Denessen, E., Hornstra, L., Voeten, M., & Holland, R. W. (2010). The implicit prejudiced attitudes of teachers: Relations to teacher expectations and the ethnic achievement gap. *American Educational Research Journal, 47*(2), 497–527. https://doi.org/10.3102/0002831209353594

Vittrup, B. (2016). Early childhood teachers' approaches to multicultural education and perceived barriers to disseminating anti-bias messages. *Multicultural Education, 23*(3–4), 37–41. Accessed at https://files.eric.ed.gov/fulltext/EJ1119398.pdf on April 16, 2024.

Vygotsky, L. S. (1978). *Mind in society: The development of higher psychological processes.* Cambridge, MA: Harvard University Press.

Walker, A., & Walker, C. (Eds.). (1997). *Britain divided: The growth of social exclusion in the 1980s and 1990s.* London: Child Poverty Action Group.

Wallis, J. (2017). *America's original sin: Racism, White privilege, and the bridge to a new America.* Grand Rapids, MI: Brazos Press.

Wallis, P. (2014). *Understanding restorative justice: How empathy can close the gap created by crime.* Chicago: Policy Press.

Walter, H. L., & Fox, H. B. (2021). Understanding teacher well-being during the COVID-19 pandemic over time: A qualitative longitudinal study. *Journal of Organizational Psychology, 21*(5), 36–50. https://doi.org/10.33423/jop.v21i5.4716

Walter, H. L., Tuckwiller, B. D., Howard, L. C., Spencer, K. H., & Frey, J. R. (2023). A mixed-methods approach to understanding early childhood special educators' well-being. *Early Childhood Research Quarterly, 65*, 374–384.

Warikoo, N., Sinclair, S., Fei, J., & Jacoby-Senghor, D. (2016). Examining racial bias in education: A new approach. *Educational Researcher, 45*(9), 508–514. https://doi.org/10.3102/0013189X16683408

Warner-Richter, M., Paschall, K., Tout, K., & Lowe, C. (2020, September). *Understanding facilitators and barriers to professional development use among the early care and education workforce* (OPRE Research Brief No. 2020-103). Washington, DC: Office of Planning, Research, and Evaluation. Accessed at www.acf.hhs.gov/opre/report/understanding-facilitators-and-barriers-professional-development-use-among-early-care on January 21, 2024.

Washington Post Staff. (2013, August 28). Rep. John Lewis's speech on 50th anniversary of the March on Washington [Transcript]. *The Washington Post*. Accessed at www.washingtonpost.com/politics/transcript-rep-john-lewiss-speech-on-50th-anniversary-of-the-march-on-washington/2013/08/28/fc2d538a-100d-11e3-8cdd-bcdc09410972_story.html on January 21, 2024.

Washington State Department of Children, Youth and Families. (2023, May). *2023–24 0–3 ECEAP performance standards*. Bellevue, WA: Author. Accessed at www.dcyf.wa.gov/sites/default/files/pdf/2023-24-0-3-ECEAP-Performance-Standards.pdf on January 21, 2024.

Weir, K. (2023, May 18). *Raising anti-racist children*. Accessed at www.apa.org/monitor/2021/06/anti-racist-children on May 9, 2024.

What Works Clearinghouse. (2009). *Curiosity corner*. Accessed at https://ies.ed.gov/ncee/wwc/EvidenceSnapshot/126 on January 21, 2024.

Whitaker, M. C. (2023). *Public school equity: Educational leadership for justice*. New York: Routledge.

Wien, C. A. (Ed.). (2008). *Emergent curriculum in the primary classroom: Interpreting the Reggio Emilia approach in schools*. New York: Teachers College Press.

Wilkerson, I. (2010). *The warmth of other suns: The epic story of America's Great Migration*. New York: Random House.

Wilkerson, I. (2020). *Caste: The origins of our discontents*. New York: Random House.

Will, M., & Najarro, I. (2022, April 18). What is culturally responsive teaching? *Education Week*. Accessed at www.edweek.org/teaching-learning/culturally-responsive-teaching-culturally-responsive-pedagogy/2022/04 on April 16, 2024.

Workman, E. (2019). *Earning while learning with early educator apprenticeship programs*. Washington, DC: New America. Accessed at www.newamerica.org/education-policy/reports/earning-while-learning-with-early-educator-apprenticeship-programs on January 21, 2024.

World Education Forum. (2000). *The Dakar framework for action: Education for all—Meeting our collective commitments*. Paris: United Nations Educational, Scientific and Cultural Organization. Accessed at https://unesdoc.unesco.org/ark:/48223/pf0000121147 on July 2, 2024.

Wright, B. L. (2021). Black boys and policing: Rethinking the community helpers curriculum. *The Learning Professional, 42*(3). Accessed at https://learningforward.org/journal/action-for-racial-equity/black-boys-and-policing-rethinking-the-community-helpers-curriculum on January 21, 2024.

Wymer, S. C., Corbin, C. M., & Williford, A. P. (2022). The relation between teacher and child race, teacher perceptions of disruptive behavior, and exclusionary discipline in preschool. *Journal of School Psychology, 90*(2), 33–42. https://doi.org/10.1016/j.jsp.2021.10.003

Yuhas, D. (2013, March 1). Mirror neurons can reflect hatred. *Scientific American*. Accessed at www.scientificamerican.com/article/mirror-neurons-can-relfect-hatred on June 7, 2024.

Zaccaro, A., Piarulli, A., Laurino, M., Garbella, E., Menicucci, D., Neri, B., et al. (2018). How breath-control can change your life: A systematic review on psycho-physiological correlates of slow breathing. *Frontiers in Human Neuroscience, 12*, Article 353. https://doi.org/10.3389/fnhum.2018.00353

Zarate, K., Maggin, D. M., & Passmore, A. (2019). Meta-analysis of mindfulness training on teacher well-being. *Psychology in the Schools, 56*(10), 1700–1715.

Zelazo, P. D., & Lyons, K. E. (2012). The potential benefits of mindfulness training in early childhood: A developmental social cognitive neuroscience perspective. *Child Development Perspectives, 6*(2), 154–160.

Zeng, S., Corr, C. P., O'Grady, C., & Guan, Y. (2019). Adverse childhood experiences and preschool suspension expulsion: A population study. *Child Abuse and Neglect, 97*, Article 104149. https://doi.org/10.1016/j.chiabu.2019.104149

ZERO TO THREE. (n.d.). *Equity statement*. Accessed at www.zerotothree.org/about/equity-statement on September 23, 2024.

Zinn Education Project. (2022, September 14). *How to—and how not to—teach role plays*. Accessed at www.zinnedproject.org/news/how-to-teach-role-plays on January 21, 2024.

Zippia. (2024). *Early childhood teacher demographics and statistics in the U.S.* Accessed at www.zippia.com/early-childhood-teacher-jobs/demographics on January 21, 2024.

Zoller, K. (2015). The philosophy of using communicative intelligence for cross-cultural collaboration. In N. D. Erbe & A. H. Normore (Eds.), *Cross-cultural collaboration and leadership in modern organizations* (pp. 303–320). Hershey, PA: IGI Global.

Index

A

accreditation, 217–220
acknowledgment, 20–21, 50, 52, 85–86, 93–95, 140, 169, 243, 268, 274
   before healing, 36–38
   benefits of antiracism resources, 98
   broken systems?, 95–96
   empathy and the brain, 42–43
   encouraging, 115
   guidance from those speaking aloud hard truths, 38–42
   how it impacts early childhood leadership, 97–100
   how it impacts leadership, 97–100
   pause and reflect, 38
acting on your plan with courage, 152, 158–161
action planning, 5, 10, 143, 238
   heart centered, 149–161
   HEART+ takeaways, 161
   sample plans, 154, 159
   self-reflection questions, 283–284
active disruption, 35–36
active listening, 80, 96, 133, 136
activism, 89
   advocacy and organizing, 234–236
addressing compensation needs, 233
"Addressing Race and Racism Head-On in the Classroom" (Gonser), 98
affordable and accessible higher education, 230
African-Centered Education (Schockley & Lomotey), 241
Aguilar, E., 183–184
Aim High, Achieve More (Jackson & McDermott), 53
Alleva, N., 35
Almaguer, E., 213–214
alternative early childhood curricula, 190–191
   Core Knowledge, 186, 191, 196
   Curiosity Corner, 186, 191, 201
   Expeditionary Learning Education, 186, 199–200
   Head Start, 186, 191–193
   HighScope, 186, 191–194
   Montessori, 186, 194–196
   Reggio Emilia, 186, 197–198
Althoff, L., 48

American Academy of Pediatrics, 14
American Montessori Society, 218
American Psychological Association, 12
American Rescue Plan, 220
Anti-Apartheid Movement, 251
antibias and antiracism training, 205–208
   similarities and differences between culturally relevant pedagogy and antibias and antiracism training, 206
   vs. culturally relevant pedagogy, 206
antibias education, 10, 119–121
   bias and its impact on young children, 121–127
   continuum to antiracism, 46
   defined, 12
   HEART+ takeaways, 128–130 antibias strategies, 129
   in service of hope, 88–89
   lack of consistent standards, 96
   mindfulness, 76–77
   pause and reflect, 121, 126
   reducing implicit bias, 128
   resources, 130
   self-reflection questions, 278–280
antiracism
   addressing with mindfulness, 77–78
   comparing curricula through, 201–204
   heart centered learning and, 73–78
   in teacher education, 210–214
   resources, 98
"Antiracism" course (Pennsylvania State University), 211
antiracist curriculum and staff support, 11, 163
   curricula for young children, 11, 185–208
   equitable professional pathways, 11, 221–236
   equity in early childhood educator standards, 11, 209–220
   leadership to embrace change, 11, 237–242
   professional development and supports, 11, 165–184
antiracist education
   bold steps, 26–27
   clear message, 21–22
   collaborating with families, 24–6

continuum from multiculturalism to, 46
defined, 12
encompasses multiculturalism, cultural competence, and antibias approaches, 48
exercise in hope, 85–89
focus on, 13–15
high-quality early childhood programs, 22–23
lack of consistent standards, 96
leaders supporting leaders, 23–24
leadership in early childhood settings, 21
pause and reflect, 24, 26
reflective assessment, 26
antiracist leadership in early childhood settings, 21
bold steps, 26–27
clear message, 21–22
collaborating with families, 24–6
high-quality early childhood programs, 22–23
leaders supporting leaders, 23–24
pause and reflect, 24, 26
reflective assessment, 26
approaches to professional development, 166–170
decision-making supports, 170–171
scenario, 171–173
Arredondo, M., 36
associate's degree, 227, 230
avoiding advice giving, 137
avoiding judgment, 137

B

bachelor's degree, 228, 230
Baldwin, J., 157, 240
Banaji, M. R., 124, 127, 130, 280
Banks, K. L., 63
Banwo, B. O., 241
Barnett, H., 223
Beachum, F., 167–168, 170
Becoming a Multicultural Educator (Howe & Lisi), 47
Becoming a Transformative Leader (Owen & Mason), 242
Bedinger, L., 141
being aware of your own biases, 27
believe in goodness and incorporate HEART+, 7, 245
belonging, 88, 140–141
Beneke, M. R., 120–122
Bernal, M. E., 146
Better Kid Care (Pennsylvania State University), 211
Between the World and Me (Coates), 39
Beyond Conversations About Race (Collado et al.), 77
beyond tolerance, 212
bias
being mindful of, 76–77
cultural, 12
curriculum evaluation for, 91–92
explicit vs. implicit, 123–126
impact on teacher expectations, 127
impact on young children, 121–123
implicit and explicit, 51–54
implicit, 37
institutional, 238
measuring, 127
observing for, 5

reducing in early childhood education, 128
Biles, S., xx
BIPOC children
ignorance about and dehumanizing actions against, 20
implicit bias affects, 170–173
mission to improve their lives, 145–146
racism in school, 59–60
with disabilities and concerns regarding disparities, 28–32
"Black Boys and Policing" (Wright), 92
Black Lives Matter, 213–214
Black, Indigenous, and people of color (BIPOC), 3
defined, 11–12
history of racism in the U.S., 36–38, 40–41
staff often excluded, 56
wage discrimination, 224–225
Blindspot (Banaji & Greenwald), 124, 130, 280
Bloom, B., 249
The Bloomsbury Handbook of Montessori Education (Murray et al.), 195–196
bold steps, 26–27
Bolstering Student Resilience (Harlacher & Whitcomb), 130, 170–171, 280
Bonazzi, R., 197
book study activity, 255–256
Bouffard, S., 94
Bridges, R., 160–161
broken systems?, 95–96
Brookings Institution, 124
Broward Principals' and Assistant Principles Association, 77
Brown v. Board of Education, 93
Brown, V., 79
building on diversity, 80
building relationships. *See* fostering relationships
bullying, 73, 104–105, 107, 277
guarding against, 27
Buras, K. L., 203
Butler, A., 214–215
Byington, T. A., 69, 239–240

C

Cajete, G., 40–41, 144, 255
calling out vs. calling in, 110–111
Calm website, 79
Camangian, P., 121–122
capacity building, 4–7
Capatosto, K., 126, 280
career pathways, 226–228
Carey, J., xx
Cariaga, S., 121–122
Caring for Our Children (National Resource Center for Health and Safety in Child Care and Early Education), 218
Carlson, J., 223
Carr, S., 223, 233
Carter, P., 36
Casas, J., 80
Caste (Wilkerson), 39–40
celebration of differences approach, 97

celebrations, 160–161
Center for Educational Improvement, 83–84, 144–145, 153, 155, 248
Center on the Developing Child (Harvard University), 216
Century Foundation, 232
Child Care Aware of America, 218
Child Care Services Association, 235
Child Care WAGE$, 230, 292
child development associate credential, 227, 230
Child Trends, 223
childcare certificate, 227
Childre, D., 67
Chiles, J., xx
Chödrön, P., 177, 179
Chugh, D., 69
Civil Rights Act of 1964, 27
Civil Rights Movement, 45–47, 251
civility, 16
Class Observation Tool (NAEYC), 155
Classroom Assessment Scoring System (CLASS) Teaching Through Interactions framework (Teachstone), 112, 155
classroom organization, 112
clear message A, 21–22
Clinton, M. C., 32
coaching. *See* relational coaching for equity
Coalition for the Future of Education, 144–145
Coates, T.-N., 39–40, 255
collaborating
 for resolution, 243
 with families, 24–26
Collaborative for Academic, Social, and Emotional Learning (CASEL), 189
Collado, W., 77
"colorblind" approach, 97
comfort zone, 180
coming to the table activity, 257
Coming to the Table website, 257
communicating high expectations, 238
community college baccalaureates, 232
community, 71, 73, 82, 183, 215, 243
community-building practices, 138–139
comparison of curricula from an antiracist perspective, 201–203
compassion, 71–72, 80, 82, 183, 214, 243, 248–249, 251
compensation, 224–228, 291–292
 low pay for teachers, 95
 median hourly wages by childcare occupation, 224
Competency 1: Child development and how it affects instruction and interactions, 253
Competency 2: Family and community partnerships, 254
Competency 4: Equitable opportunities, 254
complicity, 35–36
comprehensive training, 233
concentric circles for earliest messages, 175–177
confidence, 71, 73, 82, 183, 214, 243
confronting institutional bias, 238
connection to a bigger strategic plan, 167

consciously preparing the ground, 152–156
consciousness, 71–72, 82, 183, 214, 243
continuum from multicultural to antiracist movements, 45–48
 antiracism education encompasses multicultural, cultural competence, and antibias approaches, 48
 coming to the table activity, 257
 HEART+ takeaway, 57
 historical continuum of frameworks, 46
 privilege and bias, 48–54
 self-reflection questions, 270–271
 the way to change, 54–57
 understanding bias activity, 256–257
Cooper, K. S., 2
Corbin, C. M., 60
Core Knowledge, 186, 191, 196, 201–203
Core Knowledge Foundation, 196
Costello, B., 141
costs/fees for credentials/certification, 95–96
courage, 71, 73, 82, 183, 214–215, 243
 acting, 152
 acting on your plan with, 158–161
 meditating for, 156–158
 meditating, 152
COVID-19 pandemic, 2
 BIPOC families had less digital/technology access, 37
 what is required right now?, 147
creating a culture of empathy and equity, 21, 27
Creating an Anti-Racist Culture in the Early Years (Smidt), 82
credentials, 289
crosswalk between school climate and implicit bias reduction frameworks, 135
Cultivating Happiness in Schools, 248
Cultivating Happiness, Resilience, and Well-Being Through Meditation, Mindfulness, and Movement (Mason et al.), 79
Cultivating Resilience podcast, 111–112
cultural bias, 12
cultural competence
 continuum to antiracism, 46
 defined, 12
 in teacher education, 210–214
 lack of, 11
 linguistic diversity and, 226–229
 mindfulness, 75–76
 prioritizing training, 97
 through multiple career pathways, 226
cultural humility
 continuum to antiracism, 46
 defined, 13
cultural proficiency, 12
 defined, 13
cultural racism, 37
culturally competent self-awareness, 254
culturally competent teacher preparation, 224–226
 cultural competence and linguistic diversity, 226–229
 cultural competence through multiple career pathways, 226

early childhood education career pathways, 227–228
culturally relevant pedagogy, 185, 204–205
    vs. antibias and antiracism training, 206
Culturally Responsive Approach to Implementing a Curriculum (NCECDTL), 2055
culturally responsive interventions, 169
culturally responsive practices, 87–88, 132
Culturize (Casas), 80
Curiosity Corner, 186, 191, 201
curricula, 288–290
    alternative, 190–201
    comparison from an antiracist perspective, 201–203
    evaluation for bias, 91–92
    for young children, 11, 185–187
    HEART+ takeaways, 208
    pause and reflect, 190
    self-reflection questions, 287–288
    state standards, 187–190
    supplementation for more inclusive and representative learning experiences, 204–208
curriculum supplementation for more inclusive and representative experiences, 204
    antibias and antiracism training, 205–208
    culturally relevant pedagogy, 204–205
Curtis, S., 141

D

Darling-Hammond, S., 138–139
Datnow, A., 52–53
de Guzman, M. R. T., 212
Dear Good People (Chugh), 69
decision-making
    process, 168
    supports, 168, 170–173
defining objectives and issues, 172
defining the problem, 172
Delivering on the Promise of Effective Early Childhood Education (James & Iruka), 217
Derman-Sparks, L., 12, 25–26, 119–120, 122, 146
developing alternatives, 172
developmentally appropriate pedagogy, 132
Diamond, J. B., 126
differentation and vertical alignment, 166
Dionne, C., 28
disabilities
    BIPOC students and concerns regarding disparities, 28–32
    legal and policy considerations, 27–28
discipline and restorative practices, 138, 168
    staff preparation, 138–139
    with staff, 141–142
    with young children, 140–141
discussion, 179–180
diversifying leadership, 5, 89, 96, 106
    equitable professional pathways, 221–236
diversity, 212
Division for Early Childhood, 28–29
Djonko-Moore, C. M., 211
Donald, J., 79
Dore, R. A., 125
Durden, T. R., 212

E

early childhood career pathways, 227–228
early childhood education standards, 11, 209
    HEART+ takeaways, 220
    standards for teacher and early childcare provider preparation, 215–220
    teacher preparation programs, 210–215
early childhood staff support. *See* equitable professional pathways
Early Childhood Technical Assistance Center, 29–31
Early Learning Nation, 2–3
Early Learning Outcomes Framework (Head Start), 191
Early Learning Program (NAEYC), 218
echo, 109–110
Echo-Hawk, H., 41
educate, 109–110
Education Trust, 225, 229–232
Educational Alliances, 232
Edutopia, 166
Edwards, J. O., 122
Egalite, A. J., 3
Ekman, P., 42–43
emotional support, 112
empathy, 80, 156, 168, 243–244
    and the brain, 42–43
    complexity of, 42
    expressing, 137
    leadership to support, 2–7
encouraging dramatic play, 208
enforcing antiracist policies, 91
engaging in self-study and self-reflection, 210
engaging students and families in learning through meaningful partnerships, 187
Environment Rating Scales (Environmental Rating Scales Institute), 155
Environmental Rating Scales Institute, 155
equitable professional pathways, 11, 221–222
    compensation and culturally competent teacher preparation, 224–229
    HEART+ takeaways, 236
    roots of disrespect for early childhood educators, 222–223
    self-reflection questions, 291–292
    solutions for workforce support at all levels, 229–236
equity
    hiring for, 5
    implicit bias affects, 133–135
    in early childhood educator standards, 11, 209
    in educational settings, 210
    leadership to support, 2–7
    relational coaching for, 182–184
    self-reflection questions, 289–290
    standards for teacher and early childcare provider preparation, 215–220
    teacher preparation programs, 210–215
equity conversations, 5

Equity, Equality, and Empathy (Sorenson), 5
Escayg, K.-A., 51
estimating consequences of decision choices, 172–173
ethnic identity, 122–123
Eurocentric approach, 203
Everyday Antiracism (Pollock), 126
Evident Equity (Mascareñaz), 169
Evocative Coaching (Tschannen-Moran & Tschannen-Moran), 182
Exceptional Lives in California, 32
Expeditionary Learning Education, 186, 199–200
    guiding questions, 200
    three dimensions of student achievement, 199–200
experiences with racism and heart centeredness, 68
explaining the three zones, 179
explicit bias, 51–54, 278
    vs. implicit, 123–126

F

facilitating reflective practices, 112
factors impact a safe, supportive school culture, 132
family-school partnerships, 132, 253
    activity, 254–255
feasible pursuit of higher education, 231–233
Find the Joyful Leader Within (Byington), 69
Finding Your Blind Spots (Nichols), 90
Fingal, 98
five Cs of heart centered learning, 10, 71–73, 183, 214–215, 243, 273, 289
    graphic, 73
    heart centered learning and antiracism, 73–78
    HEART+ takeaways, 82
    scenarios and actions aligned with, 74
    schoolwide approach to heart centered learning, 78–82
    self-reflection questions, 272–274
Flanders, J., 50
    reflections on what matters, 248–249
flight, fight, or freeze mode, 66
Floyd, G., 47, 212
focus groups, 155
focus on action A, 10, 103
    HEART+ takeaways, 117
    local needs, 113–114
    navigating HEART+ in early childhood education, 114–118
    pause and reflect, 114
    resolution, 103–111
    teaching, 111–113
focus on racism and antiracism, 13–15
fostering an equitable school climate, 5
fostering relationships, 134, 168, 249
foundations, 10, 17
    five Cs of heart centered learning, 10, 71–82
    HEART+ of the matter, 10, 83–100
    leadership, 10, 19–34
    historical threads of bias, 10, 35–44
    support for all students, 10, 45–57
    heart centered lens A, 10, 59–70

Fox, H. B., 156
Frederick, R., 241
free speech, 16
funding, 217–220

G

Gaia website, 79
Gallegos, A., 111–112
Galloway, M. K., 5
Ganguly, S., 161
Gardner-Neblett, N., 60
Ginn, K., 214–215
Ginwright, S., 150
glossary, 12–13
Gonser, S., 98
graffiti walls, 116–117
Greater Good Magazine, 4
Greater Good Science Center, 136
Greenfield Community College, 213
Greenwald, A. G., 124, 127, 130, 280
Grissom, J. A., 3
guidance from those speaking hard truths, 38–42
Gullo, G., 126, 130, 134, 167–170, 280
Guterres, A., 252
Gutiérrez, N. B., 90
Guzman, J. M., 212

H

Hambacher, E., 214–215
Hammond, Z., 19–20
Happify website, 79
harassment, 73
    guarding against, 27
Harlacher, J. E., 130, 170–171, 280
Harris, O., 113–117, 239–240
    reflections on what matters, 249–250
Harte, A., 166–167
Harvard University, 155
    Center on the Developing Child, 216
    Graduate School of Education, 199
Haslam, C., 122
Hawley, L. R., 32
Head Start, 27–28, 96, 99, 105, 213
    curriculum, 186, 191–194
    Early Learning Outcomes Framework, 191
Headspace website, 79
"healing-centered" engagement, 150–151
Heart Beaming (Mason & Banks), 63
heart beaming exercise, 63
heart centered action planning, 149–152
    acting on your plan with courage, 158–161
    consciously preparing the ground, 152–156
    meditating for courage, 156–158
    sample action plans, 154, 159
heart centered and everyday lenses, 65
Heart Centered Learning® (HCL), 6–7, 9, 83–85, 134, 151–152
    antiracism and, 73–78
    five Cs of, 10, 71–82
    HEART+ and, 84
    mindfulness addressing antiracism, 77–78

mindfulness with antibias, 76–77
mindfulness with cultural competence, 75–76
mindfulness with multicultural education, 75
schoolwide approach to, 78–82
heart centered lens, 10, 59–60, 71–72, 243
heart centered and everyday lenses, 65
heart centeredness, 61–68
HEART+ takeaways, 70
self-reflection questions, 272–274
tools and actions to address equity, 68–70
heart centered roadmap to equity, 8
heart centeredness, 61–66
experiences with racism and heart centeredness, 68
heart beaming exercise, 63
heart intelligence, 67–68
role of kindness, 66–67
heart intelligence, 67–68
Heart Wings (Johnston), 62
HEART+ framework, 6–7
focus on action, 103–117
in early childhood education, 113–117
incorporating, 245
inventory, 250
self-reflection questions, 276–277
White privilege and, 49–51
HEART+ of the matter, 10, 83–85
acknowledgment, 93–100
HEART+ and heart centered learning, 84
HEART+ takeaways, 100
hope, 85–89
self-education, 89–93
self-reflection questions, 274–275
summary of HEART+, 85
HEART+ takeaways
A stands for acknowledging wrongdoing, 20–21
antibias education, 128–130
curricula, 208
early childhood education standards, 220
equitable professional pathways, 236
five Cs of heart centered learning, 82
focus on action, 117
heart centered lens, 70
HEART+ of the matter, 100
leadership, 34, 242
professional development and supports, 184
school culture and restorative practices
support for all students, 57
visioning and action planning, 161
Hechinger Report, 233
Hendrickson, J., 150–151
Henze, R., 202
hierarchy of needs (Maslow), 249
high expectations, 132
communicating, 238
higher education
affordable and accessible, 230
consortia and collaboratives, 232
feasible pursuit of, 231–233
high-quality early childhood programs, 22–23
restorative practices with young children, 140–141
HighScope, 186, 191–194

hiring for equity, 5
Hirsch, E. D., 186, 203
historical continuum of antiracist frameworks, 46
historical threads of bias, 10, 35–36
acknowledgment before healing, 36–43
book study activity, 255–256
HEART+ takeaways, 43–44
self-reflection questions, 268–269
Holland, J. M., 213
hope, 85–87, 169, 243, 250, 274, 286
antibias in the service of, 88–89
considerations for exploring HEART+, 86
fostering, 114
high potential of, 238–240
into action, 240–242
strengths-based and culturally responsive leadership, 87–88
Hopkins, B., 130, 141–142, 172, 280
Horton, C., 106
How to Be a (Young) Antiracist (Kendi & Stone), 62
How to Raise an Antiracist (Kendi), 89
Howe, W. A., 47
Hunt Institute, 232

I

I Am . . . I Am Not, 256–257
IAT (Harvard University), 155
identifying disparities, 254
identity, 89
"The Impact of Racism on Child and Adolescent Health" (American Academy of Pediatrics), 14
Implicit Association Test (IAT), 127, 129
implicit bias, 37, 94, 278
and explicit, 51–54
maintains inequities, 133–134
reducing in early childhood education, 128
reducing, 167–168, 250–251
resources for discussion, 178
vs. explicit, 123–126
Implicit Bias in Schools (Gullo et al.), 126, 130, 169, 280
inclusive hiring practices, 106
equitable professional pathways, 221–236
inclusivity, 167
Increasing Qualifications, Centering Equity (NAEYC & Education Trust), 225
increasing the research base, 233
indicators of high-quality inclusion, 31
Indigenous people, 240–241. *See also* Black, Indigenous, and people of color
essential background information, 40–42
individual education programs (IEPs), 30
Individuals with Disabilities Education Act (IDEA), 31–32
Part C, 29
Section 619, 30
inequity, 13
information building, 168
Inspiring Early Childhood Leadership (McDonald), 146–147
institutional bias, 238

instructional support, 112
intentional breathing, 80
Interaction Institute for Social Change, 14
intergroup contact, 168–170
interpersonal relationships, 134
interrupt, 109
involving family and community, 87
Iruka, I. U., 217
Ishimaru, A. M., 5
Ivey-Colson, K., 4

J

Jackson, Y., 53, 62–63, 73
James, C., 217
Jawaid, A., 54
Jim Crow laws, 48–49
Johnson, M., 41, 240–241
Johnston, V. D., 62
Journal for Negro Education, 195
justice, 89, 103

K

Kaplowitz, L. J., 67
Kaur, R., 83
Kendi, I. X., 21–22, 47, 62, 89
Kennedy, B. C., 52–53
Kennedy, R. F., 251
Khalsa, K. K., 79
kindness
  brain research, 66
  role of, 66–67
King, M. L. Jr., 107
King, R., 66, 92–93
Knight, G. P., 146
Kouzes, J. M., 69
Kuykendall-Walker, R., 241

L

Ladson-Billings, G., 215
lead, 7, 245
leaders
  equity activities for, 253–264
  self- and community assessment for, 247
  supporting leaders, 23–24
  who facilitate visioning, 146–149
leadership, 10, 16, 19–21
  antiracist leadership in early childhood settings, 21–27
  capacity building, 4–7
  efficacy and, 134
  family involvement, 254–255
  HEART+ takeaways, 34, 242
  high potential of hope, 238–240
  hope into action, 240–242
  how acknowledging racism impacts, 97–100
  importance of supporting empathy and equity, 2–7
  legal and policy considerations, 27–33
  reflective assessment activity, 253–254
  responsibilities and opportunities, 2–4
  self-reflection questions, 266–267, 294–294
  strengths-based and culturally responsive, 87–88

to embrace change, 11, 237–238
The Leadership Challenge Workbook (Kouzes & Posner), 69
Leading Anti-Bias Early Childhood Programs (Derman-Sparks et al.), 119–120
Leading with Vitality and Hope (Mason et al.), 41, 146, 149
learning by proxy, 51
The Learning Professional, 94
Lee, S., xx
LeeKeenan, D., 25, 119–120, 122–123
legal and policy considerations, 27–28
  BIPOC students with disabilities and concerns regarding disparities, 28–32
  pause and reflect, 33
  school, state, and district policies, 32–33
Let Freedom Ring (Lewis), 104
level playing field activity, 257–260
Lewis, J., 104, 160, 244
Liabenow, P., 149
licensing, 217–220
Lin, Y.-C., 219–220
Linden, R. M., 153
Lindsay, C. A., 3
linguistic diversity, 226–229
Lisi, P. L., 47
listen and learn, 6, 245
Little Learners, Big Hearts (Mason et al.), xix, 1, 7, 24–25, 37, 42–43, 49–51, 53–54, 57, 60, 68, 72, 92, 104, 107, 112, 122, 123, 131–133, 138, 141–142, 149, 168, 177, 179, 182, 186, 215, 245–248, 250
Lloyd, C. M., 223
local needs, 83, 85–86, 113–114
Logan, D., 223
Look to the Mountain (Cajete), 40–41
Lucas, T., 202

M

Macdonald, B., 52–53
MacDonald, S., 146–147
Madu, N. M., 133
Maglio, S. J., 67
making racial diversity visible, 207
Malaguzzi, L., 197
Mandela, N., 250
Manny Cantor Center, 232
Mansuy, I. M., 54
Martalock, P., 213
Martin, T., 47
Mary Pauper (Child Trends), 223
Maslow, A., 249
Mason, C., xix, 26, 41, 50, 63, 71–72, 78–80, 111, 146–147, 149, 152, 156, 160, 186, 242
  reflections on what matters, 247–248
Massachusetts Department of Elementary and Secondary Education, 187–190
  Early Childhood Programs Standards, 189
  indicators for antiracist and culturally responsive teaching, 188
master's degree, 228

McCraty, R., 67
McDermott, V., 53
McDoniel, M., 219–220
McElroy, S., 113–117
measurement of bias, 127
median hourly wages by childcare occupation, 224
meditating for courage, 152, 156–158
Meek, S., 28
Meren, M., 33
messiness, 93
microaggressions, 78, 91, 105–107, 277
    against BIPOC staff, 56
    assuming English learners are less capable, 106
    defined, 13
    mispronouncing names, 105–106
Mikels, J. A., 67
Mills, A. A., xix–xx
mindful awareness
    of emotions, 81
    of others, 81
    of sensory input, 81
mindful breathing, 179–180
Mindful of Race (King), 92–93
Mindful School Communities (Mason et al.), 78–80
mindfulness, 78–80, 83–84, 168, 248–249
    courage meditation, 156, 283
    moments, 79
    promising approaches, 80–82
    recommendations, 79–80
    techniques, 169
    with antibias, 76–77
    with cultural competence, 75–76
    with multicultural education, 75
modeling
    antibias leadership behavior, 260–264
    personal beliefs, 238
Montessori curriculum, 186, 194–196, 201–202
    American Montessori Society for Montessori programs, 218
Montessori, M., 194
movement beyond your comfort zone, 177–181, 278–279
Mr. Lincoln's Way (Polacco), 54
multicultural education
    continuum to antiracism, 45–57
    defined, 13
    history, 45–46
    lack of consistent standards, 96
    mindfulness, 75
multitiered system of supports (MTSS) model, 173–181
    model graphic, 174
Murray, A. K., 195–196

N

National Association for Family Child Care, 218
National Association for the Education of Young Children, 28–29, 54–55, 88–89, 96, 155, 189, 216, 218, 225, 229–232, 290
National Association of Early Childhood Teacher Educators (NAECTE), 212
National Association of Elementary School Principals (NAEYP), 26, 253–254
National Association of State Boards of Education, 33
National Black Child Development Institute, 217
National Center for Pyramid Model Innovations, 30–31
National Center on Early Childhood Development, Teaching, and Learning (NCECDTL), 205
National Early Childcare Program, 218
National Indian Education Association, 240–241
National Institute for Early Education Research, 216
National Resource Center for Health and Safety in Child Care and Early Education, 218
National School Climate Center, 134
Native Minds Rising (Cajete), 144
need for action, 104–105
New Jersey Preschool Teaching and Learning Standards (New Jersey State Department of Education), 218–219
New Jersey State Department of Education, 218–219
new paradigm, 244–247
next steps, 179
Nichols, H., 90
Nimmo, J., 25, 119–120
9:30 call, 235
No Child Left Behind Act of 2002, 46
North American Reggio Amelia Alliance, 197
North Carolina Early Education Coalition, 234
North Carolina Foundations for Early Learning and Development (North Carolina Foundations Task Force), 219
North Carolina Foundations Task Force, 219
Nosek, B., 127
Nottage, L., 40
NYC Leadership Academy, 238, 293

O

O'Donohue, J., 238
Obama, B., 7
Ocampo, K. A., 146
Office for Civil Rights (OCR) website, 33
Office of Head Start, 192
Oluo, I., 60
Onward (Aguilar), 183
open discussions, 167
opportunities for reflection, 167
Outward Bound, 199
Owen, R., 242

P

Pacifica Tribune, 160–161
Palikara, O., 28
paraphrase, 137
Park, C. C., 120–121
Pasadena City College, 210–211
Patschke, M. D., 26, 149
pause and reflect
    acknowledgment before healing, 38
    antibias education, 121, 126
    antiracist leadership in early childhood settings, 24, 26

curricula, 190
   focus on action, 113
   legal and policy considerations, 33
   professional development and supports, 173, 184
   school culture and restorative practices, 140
   tools and actions to address equity, 70
   visioning, 144
The Pedagogy of Confidence (Jackson), 62–63
peer aggression, 104–105
   guarding against, 27
Pennsylvania State University, 211
Pérez, M. S., 120
Perry Preschool Project, 193
Perry, I., 38–40, 255
plan and play, 201
pledge against racism and discrimination, 96
Polacco, P., 54
Pollock, M., 36, 126
positive guidance, 132
Posner, B. Z., 69
post-2016 presidential election, 124–125
Potter, H., 2–3
Potthoff, K. L., 212
Power to the Profession, 216–217
practical steps for leaders, 10, 101
   antibias education, 10, 119–130
   focus on action, 10, 103–117
   school culture and restorative practices, 10, 131–142
   visioning and action planning, 10, 143–161
prejudice, 123
"preschool-to-prison pipeline," 138
Principal Magazine, 138–139
Principle 1: We can create a better future for young children, 19–21
Principle 10: It takes a team to plan for and implement an antiracist school culture, 143
Principle 11: Advance antiracism and cultural competence through professional development, coaching, and differentiated supports, 165
Principle 12: Enhance early childhood curricula through culturally relevant pedagogy and intentional efforts to furth antiracist practices, 185
Principle 13: Early education teacher preparation programs must address cultural competence, antibias, and antiracist practices to better support the early childcare and education workforce, 209
Principle 14: Change is necessary to attract and keep the best workforce—better wages, better training, and higher regard for this essential work, 221
Principle 15: Hope + action can lead to transformative change, 237
Principle 2: Racism, oppression, and injustice are deep seated; significant and enduring efforts are necessary, 35
Principle 3: All young children have the right to equitable learning opportunities. It is important to not overlook, negate, or minimize racism, 45
Principle 4: Heart centeredness can further much needed compassion, justice, and equity, 59
Principle 5: Consciousness, compassion, confidence, courage, and community are the underpinnings of equity and inclusion, 71
Principle 6: Hope, education, acknowledgment, resolution, and teaching can provide an antidote to racism, 83
Principle 7: Eradicate racism by speaking up and carrying justice in your heart, 103
Principle 8: Address implicit and explicit bias through conscious awareness of your own beliefs, taking steps to build a sense of safety and connectedness.
Principle 9: Listen deeply, build trust, and foster equity, 131
prioritization, 167
prioritizing social-emotional well-being, 187
private equity, 233–234
privilege and bias, 48–49
   being mindful of, 76–77
   implicit and explicit bias, 51–54
   White privilege and HEART+, 49–51
professional development and supports, 11, 27, 106, 165–166, 233
   approaches, 166–173
   HEART+ takeaways, 184
   pause and reflect, 173, 184
   relational coaching for equity, 182–184
   self-reflection questions, 285–286
   tiered system of equity supports, 173–181
   workshops and conferences, 228
Professional Standards and Competencies for Early Childhood Educators (Power to the Profession), 216–217
promoting culturally responsive, antiracist teaching, 187
promoting equitable recruitment, 233
promoting mixed-delivery systems, 232
providing all students with the supports they need, 187
purposefully building the capacity of others, 238

Q

qualified staff, 230–231
questioning, 109, 137
questions
   about school culture, 151, 155
   chapter 1, 266–267
   chapter 10, 283–284
   chapter 11, 285–286
   chapter 12, 287–288
   chapter 13, 289–290
   chapter 14, 291–292
   chapter 15, 293–294
   chapter 2, 268–269
   chapter 3, 270–271
   chapter 6, 274–275
   chapter 7, 276–277
   chapter 8, 278–280
   chapter 9, 281–282
   chapters 4 and 5, 272–273
   for self-reflection and discussion, 15, 94–95
   on the need for change, 92–93

R

Race Resilience (Romero et al.), 150–151
Race to the Wall, 258–259
race-visible teacher education, 214–215
racial identities, 122–123
    teaching accurate words and information about, 207
racism
    cultural, 37
    defined, 13
    fueled by power and fear, 19–21
    seeing and naming, 27
    segregation, 93–94
    stamping out, 21–22
    systemic, 3, 40–41, 95
    transferred by what is said and not said to children, 51–52
    U.S. history of, 77–78
Radical Transformational Leadership (Sharma), 23
"Reclaiming the Brilliance of Native Youth" (Echo-Hawk & Johnson), 41
recognition programs, 87
reducing bias in early childhood education, 128
Reed, A. E., 67
reflections on what matters, 247
    Flanders, J., 248–249
    Harris, O., 249–250
    Mason, C., 247–248
    Ross, R., 250–251
reflective assessment, 26
    activity, 253, 254
Reggio Emilia, 186, 197–198
    eight core tenets, 197
registered apprenticeship programs, 228, 230
"Reimagining Early Childhood Classrooms as Sites of Love" (Madu), 133
relational coaching for equity, 182–184
religious intolerance, 124
repair practices, 139
resistance, 239
resolution, 83, 85–86, 103–104, 169, 268
    microaggressions, 105–107
    need for action, 104–105
    speaking up, 107–111
    suggestions, 115–116
resources
    for discussing implicit bias, 178
    for equitable opportunities, 254
respect, 16
    for diversity, 134
    lack of for early childhood educators, 222–223
responsibilities and opportunities for leaders, 2–4
Restorative Leadership (Hopkins), 130, 141, 172, 280
The Restorative Practices Handbook (Costello et al.), 141
restorative practices. *See* discipline and restorative practices
revising early learning standards, 233
Reynolds, J., 98
Rispoli, K. M., 32
Rivera, H., xx
Rivers Murphy, M. M., 79, 152, 156, 160
role of kindness, 66–67
Romero, V. E., 151
roots of disrespect for early childhood educators, 222–223
Roszkowski, M., 54
Ruby Bridges Walk to School Day, 160–161
rules and norms, 134
Russ, R., 30, 33, 50, 105, 125, 128, 134, 136, 161, 181, 183, 213
    reflections on what matters, 250–251
    story of a Head Start visit, 139

S

safe and supportive school culture, 131–135
    active listening activity, 136–137
    crosswalk between school climate and implicit bias reduction frameworks, 135
    factors in, 132
    trust-building activities, 135–136
sample action plans, 154, 159
    aligned with the five Cs, 74
Sánchez-Blanco, C., 214
school culture and restorative practices, 10, 131, 281–282
    discipline and restorative practices, 138–142
    HEART+ takeaways, 142
    indicators it is becoming toxic, 146–147
    level playing field activity, 257–260
    modeling antibias leadership behavior, 260–264
    pause and reflect, 140
    safe and supporting culture, 131–137
    self-reflection questions, 281–282
    story of a Head Start visit, 139
    vision for, 149
The School Leaders Our Children Deserve (Theoharis), 239
School Superintendents Association, 33
school, state, and district policies, 32–33
School-Compassionate Culture Analytical Tools for Educators (S-CCATE), 153, 155
schoolwide approach to heart centered learning, 78
    mindfulness, 78–80
    mindfulness awareness examples, 81
    mindfulness recommendations, 79–80
    promising approaches, 80–82
Scott, B., 202
Section 504 of the Rehabilitation Act of 1973
self- and community assessment for leaders, 247
self- and community assessment of equity roadmap components, 246
self-awareness, 90–92, 212, 275
    culturally competent, 254
self-compassion, 75–76
self-education, 85–86, 89–93, 243, 268, 274
    promoting, 114
    sample situations, 91–92
self-reflection, 5, 105, 210, 238
    race-visible, 214–215
self-regulation, 67
Seppälä, E., 75
Sharma, M., 23–24

Shaw, S., 223
Sigourney, L. H., 52
similarities and differences between culturally relevant pedagogy and antibias and antiracism training, 206
Simpson, K., 26
Skiba, R., 36
Smidt, S., 82
Social Emotional Learning Alliance for Massachusetts (SEL4MA), 50
social exclusion, 13
social identities, 210–220
social justice
    framework, 80, 134
    leadership for, 120
    leadership for implicit bias reduction framework, 167
social-emotional learning, 104, 134, 212
solutions for workforce support at all levels, 229–230
    advocacy and organizing, 234–236
    individual level, 230
    private equity, 233–234
    program level, 230–231
    systems level, 231–233
Sorenson, R. D., 5–6, 238–239
Soukakou, E., 28
"soul friends," 62–63, 73
South to America (Perry), 38–39
space between us, 238
Sparks, S. D., 128, 279–280
speaking up, 103, 107–111
    calling out vs. calling in, 110–111
    practice basic strategies, 109–110
    prepare yourself, 108
Staats, C., 126, 280
staff preparation for restorative practices, 138–139
Stamped (Reynolds), 98
standards for teacher and early childcare provider preparation, 215–216
    accreditation, licensing, and funding of centers, 217–220
    Unifying Framework, 216–217
Start With Equity (Meek et al.), 28
start, 6, 245
state standards
    curricula, 187–190
    engaging students and families in learning through meaningful partnerships, 187
    Massachusetts indicators for antiracist and culturally responsive teaching, 188
    prioritizing social-emotional well-being, 187
    promoting culturally responsive, antiracist teaching, 187
    providing all students with the supports they need, 187
stereotypes, 123–124
Stockstill, C., 3
Stone, N., 62
Strategies for Children, 235
strengths-based leadership, 87–88
Success for All Foundation, 201

summarizing areas of agreement, 137
"super" vision, 4
support for all students, 10, 45–48
    HEART+ takeaway, 57
    privilege and bias, 48–54
    the way toward change, 54–57
support for difficult conversations, 112
supporting increased and innovative funding, 232
supports
    decision-making, 171–173
    tiered system, 173–181
sustained communication, 82
Sykes, M., 222
synergy, 23–24
systemic racism
    defined, 95
    in the United States, 40–41
    recognizing, 3

T

T.E.A.C.H. Early Childhood, 235, 292
taking turns, 137
The Talk, 92
targeted interventions for skeptical staff, 181
Tatum, B. D., 48
Taylor, B., 38–39
Taylor, S. A., 212
teachers
    bias, 59–60, 127
    compensation, 95, 224–228
    cultural competence and antiracism in teacher education, 210–214
    preparedness programs, 210
    race-visible teacher education and self-reflection, 214–215
    restorative practices with, 141–142
teacher-student relationships, 134
teaching children in a diverse society, 210–211
Teaching Respect for All (UNESCO), 22–23
teaching, 83, 85–86, 111–112, 170, 268
    integrating antiracism, 116
    narratives of colonization from multiple perspectives, 207
    through a Heart Centered Learning lens, 243
Teachstone, 112, 155
teasing, 104–105
Teasley, C., 214
templates
    for steps to implement a vision, 148
    to implement a vision, 148
"10 Principles for Talking About Race in School" (NEA Center for Social Justice), 98
"10 Resources for Teaching Anti-Racism" (Fingal & Mack), 98
Theoharis, G., 239
Thompson, B., 241
Tier 1 supports: universal, 175–177
Tier 2 supports: group, 175, 177–181
Tier 3 supports: individual, 175, 181
tiered system of equity supports (TSES), 166, 173, 285
    concentric circles for earliest messages, 175–177

example, 174
  movement beyond my comfort zone, 177–181
  targeted interventions for skeptical staff, 181
  Tier 1: universal supports, 175–177
  tier 2: group supports, 175, 177–181
  tier 3: individual supports, 175, 181
Title IX of the Education Amendments of 1972, 27
tools and actions to address equity, 68–70
  pause and reflect, 70
tools that promote excellence and equity, 27
toward a more just and inclusive world, 243–244
  new paradigm, 244–247
  reflections on what matters, 247–251
  self- and community assessment for leaders, 247
  self- and community assessment of equity roadmap components, 246
  well-being for all, 251–252
transgenerational trauma, 54
transparent and disaggregated data, 233
trauma-informed care and services, 132, 284
Trejos, J., 52–53
trust building, 133
  activity, 135–136
Tschannen-Moran, B., 182
Tschannen-Moran, M., 182
Turner, L., 4
two truths and a dream, 135–136

U

U.S. Census Bureau, 40, 217–218
U.S. Department of Justice, 28, 38–39
U.S. history of racism, 36–38
understanding bias activity, 256–257
Unifying Framework for the early childhood professional standards and competencies, 216–217
United Nations Convention on the Rights of the Child, 12, 20
United Nations Educational, Scientific, and Cultural Organization (UNESCO), 22–23, 28
Universal Declaration of Human Rights, 22
universal kindergarten
  lack of government support of, 95
universal preschool
  long- and short-term benefits, 33
using body language, 137

V

vision for an antiracist school culture and climate, 149
Visioning Onward (Mason et al.), 149
visioning, 5, 10, 143–145, 238
  bold leadership, 27
  HEART+ takeaways, 161
  leaders who facilitate, 146–149
  pause and reflect, 144
  self-reflection questions, 283–284
  template to implement a vision, 148
  vision for an antiracist school culture and climate, 149
  we are not trying to change the world—yet, 145–146
vitality, 147
Vygotsky, L., 177

W

Wachtel, J., 141
Wachtel, T., 141
Wallis, J., 103–104
Walter, H. L., 156, 254–255
Warner, A. N., 151
Washington Early Childhood Education and Assistance Program Standards (Washington State Department of Children, Youth, and Families), 219
Washington State Department of Children, Youth, and Families, 219
the way toward change, 54–57
we are not trying to change the world—yet, 145–146
Weikart, D., 193
Welcoming the Unwelcome (Chödrön), 177, 179
well-being for all, 251–252
what is the story of your name?, 135
Whitaker, M. C., 60
Whitcomb, S. A., 130, 170–171, 280
White accountability groups (WAGs), 50
White privilege, 269
  defined, 48–49
  HEART+ and, 49–51
White-centric developmental norms, 165–166
Whole Child Initiative, 241
"Whose Got the Power?" (Escayg), 51
Why Are All the Black Kids Sitting Together in the Cafeteria? (Tatum), 48
Wilkerson, I., 39–40, 255
Williford, A. P., 60
Wisconsin Early Childhood Action Needed (WECAN), 234
word usage, 11–12
World Education Forum, 23
Worthy Wages Campaign, 235
  Toolkit, 235
Wright, B. L., 92
Wymer, S. C., 60

X

xenophobia, 123–124

Y

Yoshisato, M., 52–53

Z

ZERO TO THREE, 55
zone of proximal development, 177

Little Learners, Big Hearts
Christine Mason, Randy Ross, Orinthia Harris, Jillayne Flanders

Discover the transformative power of early conversations on racial equity and cultural awareness with *Little Learners, Big Hearts*. Grounded in heart centered learning, it seamlessly weaves principles of hope, self-education, acknowledgment, resolution, and responsive teaching to create an empowering antiracist foundation.

BKG130

Finding Your Blind Spots
Hedreich Nichols

Author Hedreich Nichols infuses this book with a direct yet conversational style to help you identify biases that adversely affect your practice and learn how to move beyond those biases to ensure a more equitable, inclusive campus culture.

BKG022

Mindful School Communities
Christine Mason, Michele M. Rivers Murphy, Yvette Jackson

Build a thriving school community that creates healthy, resilient, and successful students. A companion to *Mindfulness Practices*, this research-backed guide outlines how to teach self-regulation by fostering the five Cs of social and emotional learning and mindfulness: consciousness, compassion, confidence, courage, and community.

BKF912

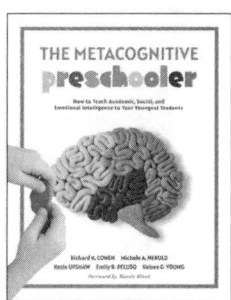

The Metacognitive Preschooler
Richard K. Cohen, Michele A. Herold, Emily R. Peluso, Katie Upshaw, Kelsee G. Young

Preschool teachers and leaders can easily embed a single metacognitive strategy, called structured SELf-questioning, into their existing curricula and routines to overcome academic and behavioral challenges. With clear guidance, all students can learn social-emotional learning competencies that promote success in school and life.

BKG135

Visit SolutionTree.com or call 800.733.6786 to order.

Quality team learning **from authors you trust**

Global PD Teams is the first-ever **online professional development resource designed to support your entire faculty on your learning journey.** This convenient tool offers daily access to videos, mini-courses, eBooks, articles, and more packed with insights and research-backed strategies you can use immediately.